F.V.

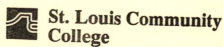

Puerto Rico Past and Present

AN ENCYCLOPEDIA

Ronald Fernandez
Serafín Méndez Méndez
Gail Cueto

GREENWOOD PRESS
Westport, Connecticut • London

Library of Congress Cataloging-in-Publication Data

Fernandez, Ronald.
   Puerto Rico past and present : an encyclopedia / Ronald Fernandez,
Serafín Méndez Méndez, Gail Cueto.
       p. cm.
   Includes bibliographical references and index.
   ISBN 0–313–29822–X (alk. paper)
   1. Puerto Rico—Encyclopedias.   I. Méndez Méndez, Serafín.
II. Cueto, Gail.   III. Title.
F1954.F47   1998
972.95′003—dc21   97–1689

British Library Cataloguing in Publication Data is available.

Library of Congress Catalog Card Number: 97–1689
ISBN: 0–313–29822–X

First published in 1998

Greenwood Press, 88 Post Road West, Westport, CT 06881
An imprint of Greenwood Publishing Group, Inc.

Printed in the United States of America

The paper used in this book complies with the
Permanent Paper Standard issued by the National
Information Standards Organization (Z39.48–1984).

10 9 8 7 6 5 4 3 2 1

To
Karen Beyard

CONTENTS

PREFACE

"What is the exchange rate on Puerto Rican money?" This question was posed to a Puerto Rican professional who was applying, in 1996, for a home mortgage in Connecticut. On the application required to obtain the mortgage, the Puerto Rican applicant had listed certificates of deposit housed in a Puerto Rican bank. The American banker assumed that Puerto Rico was a foreign country and that she needed the exchange rate to compute the resources of her loan applicant accurately.

Even though Puerto Rico has been a part of the United States for the last ninety-eight years, the lack of knowledge displayed by the bank officer is common throughout the United States. In university courses, mainland students still ask, "Can you drive to Puerto Rico?" And in public debates about cutting welfare benefits, Americans who are angry about the consequences of immigration often ask why Puerto Ricans have so many rights. In Florida and Delaware, New York and Maine, schools have rarely conveyed a basic fact: Against their will, Puerto Ricans have been U.S. citizens since 1917.

In the United States there is a conspicuous lack of easily accessible, accurate, relevant and important knowledge about Puerto Rico and its 3.6 million inhabitants. This book seeks to fill that informational void. Thus, *Puerto Rico Past and Present* is a ready reference guide—in the English language—covering over five hundred years of political, economic and cultural development in Puerto Rico. The book offers descriptions ranging from issues like abortion to El Yunque, Puerto Rico's tropical rain forest. There are over 300 separate entries but, since no one-volume work can ever be an exhaustive or definitive account of such a long span of development, the following are the criteria employed in making the selections for *Puerto Rico Past and Present: An Encyclopedia.*

First, Puerto Rico and its 3.7 million inhabitants share a distinctive culture. While that may seem obvious, conventional wisdom in the United States argues that an island like Puerto Rico is still a developing nation. In fact, it is a country whose first settlement was established fully one hundred years before the one in Jamestown, Virginia. Our entries, therefore, reflect a desire to underline the history, achievements and creations of the Puerto Rican people. Given the sharp confines of space, we focused on the nineteenth and, especially, the twentieth centuries. We made every effort to include the poets, novelists, painters, musicians, singers and political leaders, as well as the architectural achievements, at the core of the Puerto Rican culture.

Second, this is a book in English about a Spanish-speaking nation. Since it has been written primarily for a U.S. audience, many of the entries reflect a desire to convey information—about such things as cultural customs or political and economic relationships—that an island audience would already know. The titles of entries appear in English, with Spanish translations in parentheses. In the Spanish language reference works that were surveyed, one rarely finds an entry for *personalismo, dignidad,* enhanced commonwealth, migration, or *los Americanos.* They were included here because they provide the basic cultural, political and economic knowledge required by anyone in the United States who is trying to learn about Puerto Rico and its people. Special efforts were made to include notes that direct readers to sources that will allow them to expand their knowledge quickly about any of the basic concepts and issues discussed. In the vast majority of cases, we have provided English language references for those who wish to investigate a subject in greater detail. However, in a few instances, the most reliable sources were published only in Spanish.

Third, Puerto Rico is a colony, the oldest on earth. The problem is that, while its colonial status is an accepted fact to Puerto Ricans of all political persuasions, this is still a controversial idea to many Americans. Thus, *Puerto Rico Past and Present* includes historical and political entries (e.g., Executive Council, E. Montgomery Reilly, Insular Cases, United Nations) that seek to explain the love/hate relationship that sometimes characterizes contacts between Puerto Rico and the United States. These entries were necessary, not only because this book will be used primarily in U.S. libraries, but also because the United States and Puerto Rico are once again discussing a plebiscite that will determine the ultimate political status of the island. The entries related to political status are intended to help readers understand the extraordinarily complex nature of the ties that bind the United States and Puerto Rico. Happily, for all these entries there are ample sources in the English language. In all cases efforts were made to include easily accessible references, such as the Congressional Record or Congressional Hearing transcripts.

Fourth, this reference work includes a number of entries devoted to individuals or events that have received little attention in Puerto Rican history. Many of these exclusions, frankly, are due to sexism. The book, therefore, includes a separate entry on feminism; some of the entries on the early suffragettes are short because scholars are only now researching the true impact of the suffrage movement on Puerto Rican life. Entries describing Puerto Rican popular culture, via such media as television, radio and tabloid newspapers are also included. The intent is to provide some feel for the flavor of everyday life in Puerto Rico.

Fifth, given the limitations of size, there are virtually no entries that focus on Puerto Ricans in the United States. Many Puerto Ricans living in cities like New York and Chicago have made significant contributions to the political, cultural and economic life of the United States. Indeed, efforts to compile a list immediately produced more than 100 names and concepts! Since this reference guide lacks the space to include so many entries and because no one wanted to risk shortchanging either Puerto Rico or the Puerto Ricans living in the United States, the entries here focus on what happened—and happens—in Puerto Rico.

Sixth, it is our belief that the terms *interesting* and *encyclopedia* are not necessarily mutually exclusive. Thus, each of us tried to add some color to our entries without excluding the facts essential to any reference guide.

Finally, the volume includes a "conceptual map" to the entries included in the book. The aim is to allow readers more easily to place any entry within a historical framework or within a particular artistic, literary or cultural category.

ACKNOWLEDGMENTS

There were many wonderful individuals who provided their guidance, help and assistance throughout this project. We would like to recognize the assistance of many librarians from libraries in Puerto Rico and in the United States. We are grateful to the librarians at Interamerican University in San Germán, at the Luisa Capetillo Room of the University of Puerto Rico in Cayey, at the Centro the Estudios, Recursos y Servicios a la Mujer (CERES), and at the Puerto Rican Collection of the University of Puerto Rico in Río Piedras. Prof. Agnes Mójica, Chancellor of Interamerican University San Germán Campus, facilitated our access to her library and supported the project. Special recognition goes to Joan Packer and Emily Chasse from the reference department at Central Connecticut State University library. They were extremely helpful in providing information and materials.

Most of the photographs from this book come from the photo archives of *El Nuevo Día*. Publisher Antonio L. Ferré gave us permission to use the photo collection of his newspaper. We appreciate his special contribution to this book. The staff from *El Nuevo Día*'s library, in particular José Sánchez, was extremely helpful identifying and locating photographs to illustrate the work. The Museum of the University of Puerto Rico in Río Piedras and at the Ponce Museum of Art also granted us permission to use photos of works from their collection.

Many friends and colleagues volunteered to read specialized entries from the manuscript as well as complete drafts of the book. Dr. Luis Nieves Falcón gave us many useful ideas and suggestions for entries. Special thanks go to Dr. Margarita Ostolaza, Dr. Aristides Cruz, Dr. Raúl Méndez, Attorney Gloria I. del Nido, and Sarah Ramírez. The work of Dr. Ronald Méndez-Clark, from the Latin American and Latino Studies Institute at Fordham University, is greatly appreciated. He reviewed an earlier version of the manuscript and shared many insightful suggestions. Dr. Neysa Rodríguez, from the History Department at Pontifical Catholic University of Puerto Rico, spent many hours reviewing the entries, checking them for historical accuracy, and discussing the work with the authors. Her many useful suggestions and her commitment to preserve the historical integrity of our book is recognized by us.

Members of our families provided great encouragement and assistance during the process of researching and producing this book. Professor Fernandez wishes to thank Brenda Harrison for her support. Professor Cueto recognizes D. Lea Loran for her help and understanding during the last two years. Professor Méndez is grateful to his nephews Fernando Armando Escabí and Fernando José Escabí, and Maria Lizardi for their many excursions to libraries in Puerto Rico securing materials for him. He also appreciates the encourgement of his cousins and friends Sergio Juan Méndez, Luis Benjamín Méndez, Sarita Ruiz, and José "Pepe" González.

We are indebted to all of these individuals and organizations for their assistance and willingness to help. Mil Gracias.

HISTORICAL INTRODUCTION

This introduction is meant to provide a broad overview of Puerto Rico's political and economic affairs. It is intended for those who desire to gain some background for the entries devoted to the island's political, economic and military history.

The modern history of Puerto Rico began in the Vatican. On May 3, 1493, Pope Alexander VI issued a Papal Bull stipulating that the Catholic kings of Spain owned any lands discovered by their royal envoys. Thus, when Christopher Columbus arrived in Puerto Rico on November 19, 1493, the Italian explorer claimed a Caribbean island in the name of Spanish monarchs serving a Roman Catholic deity. Columbus asserted that "this island belongs to the King and Queen of Spain," and, in the process, Cristóbal Colón began a history of European ownership of Puerto Rico that lasted more than 400 years, from 1493 until 1898.

Columbus quickly changed the name of the island from **Boriquen** to San Juan Bautista. He tried to please Queen Isabella by naming the island after her son Juan, while the 30,000 original owners of Puerto Rico—the Taíno indians—tried to make sense of the explorers and their aims. For the Spanish, the island was a colony; it would be governed by officials appointed in Spain, guarded from the English, Dutch and French by the king's soldiers, and developed by the Spanish, for the Spanish.

In 1511 Juan Ponce de León changed the island's name to Puerto Rico, or rich port in English. De León had discovered gold there and, as historian Arturo Morales Carrión emphasized, the explorer never acted out of chance or capriciousness: "It was, on the contrary, a business enterprise that responded, among other motives, to a premeditated and calculated economic plan, that was born of a conjunction of interests between the Spanish Crown and the head of the expedition" (Morales Carrión 1983, 112). Put differently, De León mined the gold because he received a healthy share of the king's profits. Each man sought riches and neither showed special concern for the welfare of the Taíno, a group of copper-colored Indians, who, before they went to battle, painted themselves red (see **Los Taínos**).

One scholar suggests that it was the colorful appearance of the Taíno that led to the persisting stereotype of Indians as "red men." The Taínos believed in the immortality of the Spanish. This belief was based on the fact that the explorers, who brought a variety of new diseases to the new world, survived while the Taíno died. The Spaniards were thought to be immortal until 1511, when a chief named **Urayoán** decided to do a "scientific" experiment. He ordered his followers to hold a Spaniard, Diego Salcedo, under water. The Spaniard drowned and, although the Indians gave him time to revive, he never moved. But the Taíno did. They went to war but were defeated by the Spanish, who then used them as virtual slaves in the mining of gold.

By roughly 1540 the gold was exhausted and the Indian population was devastated; historians estimate that as few as 2,000 Taíno remained out of the original 30,000. In reaction, a few Spaniards increased their number of African slaves—the first two Africans had arrived in 1510—while many more Europeans fled to find riches in Peru or any other Spanish possessions that were ready for quick and easy exploitation. Meanwhile, the Spanish tried to stop the European exodus from Puerto Rico by declaring that emigration was a crime, punishable, in some cases, by the loss of a leg.

By 1550 Puerto Rico entered a period of negligence by the Spanish crown. Forts like the gigantic **El Morro** were built to protect San Juan from attacks by English and other colonial powers but, in terms of social and economic development, Puerto Rico's potential was rarely nurtured. Spain sent money, called **El Situado** or the allowance, but the level of concern was so low that from 1651 to 1662 not a single ship visited Puerto Rico. The crown's indifference produced an official society focused on the military bastion of San Juan; however, owing to several devastating epidemics, San Juan's population increased by only 167 inhabitants between 1647 and 1689. Well into the eighteenth century the island contained only two schools, and the population of 45,000 people (as late as 1765) computed their age by changes in governments, the appearance of hurricanes or, far more rarely, the visit of a Catholic bishop.

Spain's neglect laid the groundwork for 'two" Puerto Rico's, the first centered in San Juan, the second *"en la isla"* (on the island). The surviving Indians, escaped slaves and retired (or escaped) soldiers created *"en el campo"* (in the country) their own version of Puerto Rican culture. Economically, these Puerto Ricans thrived on contraband; for centuries, islanders either disregarded or bypassed San Juan by bartering with French,

English and North American pirates and traders who arrived in such places as **Ponce** and Mayagüez. The Spanish lost both revenues and respect while the islanders produced profits and, a persisting trait of Puerto Rican culture, a deep reverence for place. That is, San Juan belonged to the crown, but Ponce, Coamo and Manatí were nurtured a good distance from—and despite—the crown. They belonged to the Puerto Rican people and were revered because they represented the developing *criollo* (native) culture, not the Spanish import.

In the late eighteenth century, Spain rediscovered its Puerto Rican colony as a result of a devastatingly critical report that the crown received after the visit of its emissary, **Alejandro de O'Reilly**, in 1765. Among other things, O'Reilly stressed that only 5 or 6 percent of the usable land was cultivated and that the most viable economic segment of the society was the "underground" trade in contraband. Based on O'Reilly's report, Spanish officials decided to rebuild Puerto Rico's decaying forts and transform the island's economy by luring new immigrants with promises of huge tracts of land. Equally important, the grants of land could be substantially increased if, along with capital for investment, the new immigrants brought slaves to work the land.

Because of Spanish policies, Puerto Rico entered the nineteenth century swimming against the historical tide. As one European nation after another began to abolish **slavery** and the slave trade, Spain increased its returns from Puerto Rico by underwriting a massive importation of new slaves. In 1765 the number of African slaves was 5,037; the figure in 1802 was 13,333 and the figure in 1846 was 51,265. These slaves typically worked on the huge sugar plantations created by the new immigrants. But, when even the huge influx of slaves failed to provide sufficient labor for the new plantations and farms, Spain mandated a system of forced labor. In 1848 free islanders received a *libreta* (a passbook) that stipulated their obligations to employers requiring workers; the military helped enforce this system and thus contributed to a society that blurred the line between slavery and free labor.

Some of Puerto Rico's most revered nineteenth-century figures, including **Ramón Emeterio Betances**, **Marianna Bracetti Cuevas** and **Eugenio María de Hostos**, passionately challenged the Spanish on issues that ranged from the abolition of slavery to the creation of meaningful rights and opportunities for *criollos*. But, the Spanish had two powerful forces on their side: the army and the new immigrants. With the crown's willing assent, soldiers and *peninsulares* (people from Europe) monopolized the positions of power in every aspect of island life. The result was that, in sharp contrast to the sense of political independence that existed in the United States in 1776, these new immigrants generally supported the reactionary policies that preserved *their* wealth and social standing.

Spain added even more supporters when, after local revolutionaries produced colonial problems in Venezuela, Puerto Rico became a base of operations for Spain's counterrevolutionary efforts. Indeed, when Spain finally lost its Caribbean and South American possessions, the most conservative of Spain's refugees were welcomed in Puerto Rico. By roughly 1860, the island was, from one perspective, a bastion of rich and poor, old and new loyalists who did their best to avoid any of the changes sought by those who produced the American, French and Haitian revolutions.

Resentments continued to simmer. One result was a revolutionary uprising called the **Grito de Lares,** which occurred on September 23, 1868. On this day, a conspiracy of roughly 500 rebels (almost 60 percent of them day workers, small farmers and slaves) proclaimed an independent Puerto Rican nation and then warned the Spaniards living in Puerto Rico that "they had three days to declare themselves in favor of the Republic, to leave for Spain, or to accept the punishment reserved for traitors."

These strong words were never backed by arms or the support of the masses of the Puerto Rican people; therefore, after the Spanish suppressed the revolt, island politics revolved around a series of compromises with Spain. Men like Betances and Hostos still sought complete independence, but the majority argued about the degree of local autonomy they would demand or obtain from Spain. Pragmatism was the order of the day, and it achieved results because, in 1897, Puerto Rico signed an **Autonomic Charter** with the Spanish government that granted Puerto Ricans voting rights in the Spanish parliament. The insular government created by this charter gave islanders the "exclusive power" to frame the island's budget and expenditures and to fix both import and export duties. Most significant of all, "this new constitution could not be amended except by virtue of a law and upon the petition of the insular parliament."

The agreement was a significant achievement for the Puerto Rican *criollo* leadership, including **Luis Muñoz Rivera, José de Diego, José Celso Barbosa** and **Manuel Fernández Juncos.** However, the agreement was effectively annulled before it took effect. As part of their efforts in the Spanish-American War, U.S. soldiers landed at Guánica on July 25, 1898. They quickly defeated the Spanish soldiers, and, as Senator Henry Jackson told the Puerto Rican people in 1974, Puerto Rico then became a permanent part of the United States by "an act of conquest."

General Nelson Miles, who commanded the U.S. forces, like Columbus in 1493 and Ponce de León in 1511, changed the island's name. He spelled Puerto Rico "Porto Rico"; the word *porto* does not exist in Spanish but, for more than thirty years, U.S. and Puerto Rican officials nevertheless misspelled the island's name in everyday discourse and in U.S. government documents.

This caused a small controversy. Much greater sources of disagreement resulted when Puerto Ricans heatedly complained about the alleged gap between what General Miles said and what General Miles did. When he arrived in 1898, the general said, "We have not come to make war upon the people of a country that for centuries has been oppressed but on the contrary to bring you protection . . . to promote your prosperity, and to bestow upon you the immunities and blessings of the liberal institutions of our government" (Wagenheim 1972, 63).

Puerto Ricans believed what the general said. Many revered the U.S. Declaration of Independence and the U.S. Constitution as much as the most loyal American patriot. When the **Treaty of Paris** (August 12, 1898) summarily ceded Puerto Rico to the United States, the islanders were of course concerned; however, when U.S. soldiers maintained a military government for more than a year, the Puerto Ricans publicly complained. In February 1900, prominent Puerto Ricans used the U.S. Constitution as their frame of reference when they petitioned the U.S. Congress for a redress of grievances. Puerto Ricans argued that the freedoms promised by General Miles had never materialized; equally important, after eighteen months of U.S. rule, no less a figure than Secretary of War Elihu Root agreed that the island was in worse economic shape after the U.S. invasion than before. Thus, the pressing question from the Puerto Ricans was, "Have we been invited to come under the sheltering roof, only to starve at the doorstep?" (Congressional Record 1900, 2231).

The starvation was real; it was exacerbated by a severe hurricane in 1899. A more significant issue was the impossible commercial position of island coffee exporters. In 1899 only 15 percent of Puerto Rico's cultivated land was in sugar production. Coffee was king: in 1899, 41 percent of the cultivated land was in coffee production and 56 percent of all farms were involved in some coffee production. Historically, this strong—American advertisers would say robust—coffee was sold in Europe, through Spanish ports and distributors. But, when the Spanish gave Puerto Rico to the United States, they quickly imposed such high tariffs on Puerto Rican coffee that it was no longer competitive. Meanwhile, the U.S. government debated the future of Puerto Rico but never eliminated the high (prewar) tariffs that always made Puerto Rican coffee hard to market in the United States. The result was that, for almost two years, the most important export crop in Puerto Rico rotted on the docks.

Congress's solution came in the form of the **Foraker Act,** passed in April 1900. This act set many important precedents. Puerto Rico became the first unincorporated territory in the history of the United States. When other territories (e.g., Alaska and Hawaii) were annexed to the United States, they received an explicit promise of eventual U.S. statehood. Puerto Rico was the first exception to this rule (see **Insular Cases** and **Jesús Balzac**).

The Foraker Act also made islanders "citizens of Porto Rico," not of the United States. Islanders would pay export and import duties on all items traded, but, as was the rule with the Spanish government, the money was returned (and is still returned) to the island's treasury. Since the Foraker

Act gave Puerto Ricans no voting representation in Congress, keeping revenues from Puerto Rico was taxation without representation. The compromise achieved in the Foraker Act was to tax islanders, return the receipts to the island, and use the funds to help resurrect and transform the economy destroyed by war and nearly two years of military government.

After 1900 sugar quickly become the dominant force in the Puerto Rican economy. Island farmers ruined by the military government sold their lands to U.S. investors and, within fifteen years, coffee, which accounted for 60 percent of export earnings in 1897, accounted for only 19 percent of export earnings in 1914; and sugar, which accounted for 22 percent of export earnings in 1897, accounted for 47 percent of export earnings in 1914. The economy had been transformed but, under the Foraker Act, Puerto Rico could not refine the sugar it produced. That right was retained by U.S. firms so that, from the outset, the growth of the sugar industry was deadended by the laws written in Washington, D.C. Sugar beet producers in the Midwest joined forces with sugar cane producers in Louisiana, and together they kept the competition from Puerto Rico to a minimum. As economist James Deitz summed up the situation, "This meant that Puerto Rican sugar exports depended not only on the U.S. market but also on refining capacity located in the United States, and that the value added in production was created within the U.S. economy and accrued to U.S. companies" (Deitz 1986, 104–5).

Politically, William Willoughby—an architect of the local government created by the Foraker Act—wrote that Puerto Rico was a "dependency partaking of the essential character of a colony" (Willoughby 1905). According to Willoughby, then the treasurer of Porto Rico, the U.S. officials received "such unusual degrees of authority" from the Foraker legislation that "to a large extent (the Executive Council) took the whole control over the manner in which the actual administration of affairs shall be exercised out of the hands of the people of the island itself" (1905, 86) (see also **Executive Council**).

For the first fifteen years of U.S. control, the dominant island political party—the **Union party**—complained about what they believed was an absence of fundamental, democratic rights. They even tried to precipitate a breakdown of the colonial government in 1909 but, when no fundamental changes occurred, the Union party removed statehood—for the first time—from its list of political status options in 1913. In February 1914 the U.S. House of Representatives held hearings on the possibility of giving U.S. citizenship to the Puerto Rican people. As expressed by Secretary of War Lindsay Garrison, the Wilson administration understood the apparent desire of Puerto Ricans for independence. But, "as I [Secretary Garrison] understand the situation . . . there is no suggestion that it [Puerto Rico] should not be connected with the United States for all time, and that we should not in the fullest measure be responsible for it as we are for any other thing that is under our flag" (*A Civil Government* 1914, 31).

Congressman William Jones agreed. He believed that U.S. citizenship should be granted as a way of underlining that "Puerto Rico was a permanent possession of the United States"(49). As citizens, Puerto Rican politicians would cease their "agitation" for independence because they would be forever linked to the United States. In response, Resident Commissioner Luis Muñoz Rivera stressed that "if we cannot be one of your States; if we cannot constitute a country of our own then we will have to be perpetually a colony, a dependency of the United States. Is that the kind of citizenship you offer us? Then, that is the citizenship we refuse"(54).

In March 1914, the Puerto Rican House of Delegates echoed Muñoz's sentiments; the delegates unanimously approved a resolution stating that "we firmly and loyally maintain our opposition to being declared, in defiance of our express wish and without our express consent, citizens of any country whatsoever other than our own beloved soil that God has given us as an inalienable gift and incoercible right" (*Congressional Record* 1914, 6718).

Facing such opposition, Congress tabled the citizenship bill. In 1916 the legislation was brought again to the House and Senate and this time it passed. Muñoz's reply was that "we are the Southerners of the Twentieth century." Congressman Clarence Miller of Minnesota underlined the principal motive of the U.S. Congress for granting U.S. citizenship to the Puerto Rican people: "The agitation for independence in Porto Rico must come to a decided and a permanent end . . . if there is anything that you and I must be agreed upon it is this: That Porto Rico will never go out from under the shadow of the Stars and Stripes" (*Congressional Record* 1916, 7471).

President Woodrow Wilson signed the **Jones Act** on March 2, 1917, which granted **United States citizenship** to Puerto Ricans. He "welcomed the new citizens, not as a stranger but as one entering his father's house." In that hom
e they would now have an elected Senate as well as an elected House of Delegates; but, as the Puerto Ricans received additional powers, so too did the president. He could now veto any legislation passed by the Puerto Rican government, even if it had been passed over the veto of the appointed governor. And, in a little noticed change, the Jones Act added an appointed auditor to the Puerto Rican government. This official, appointed by the U.S. president, often had the final word on expenditures in Puerto Rico.

In response to the Jones Act, the new Puerto Rican legislature allocated $25,000 to conduct a **plebiscite**. Men like José de Diego wanted the Puerto Rican people to express their preference in an open election, but the promised vote never occurred. Instead, the Jones Act ushered in a prolonged period of bitter and often violent conflict between Puerto Rico and the

United States (see **Pedro Albizu Campos** and the **Nationalist Party**). The violence reached such a pitch that in 1936 Albizu Campos was sentenced, with many others, to ten years in jail on a charge of **seditious conspiracy**. Albizu Campos never denied that he wanted to overthrow the U.S. colonial government, and his sentence closed a chapter in Puerto Rican–U.S. relations. While he was in jail, a charismatic figure named **Luis Muñoz Marín** established the **Popular Democratic party** in 1938 and, in the process, initiated the changes that still govern the relationship between the United States and Puerto Rico.

The platform of the Popular Democratic party specifically placed the issue of political status in the background because Muñoz believed that, given the economic devastation wrought by the depression of the 1930s, Puerto Rico had to focus all its energies on economic development. In 1934 Congress passed the Jones-Costigan law, which limited the amount of sugar that Puerto Rico could export to the United States. Thus, the island's biggest industry reached a dead end; even in good years, the sugar had no market. Muñoz struggled to find other ways to produce meaningful economic development.

Meanwhile, the military relationship between Puerto Rico and the United States also changed. Before World War II, Puerto Rico had *potential* military significance for the United States, but that potential was never actualized. In 1940 the U.S. Navy expropriated 70 percent of the land on the Puerto Rican island of **Vieques**; this land was combined with other parcels on the Puerto Rican mainland, and the result was **Roosevelt Roads**, soon the largest naval base in the world. The increased importance of U.S. control of Puerto Rico was emphasized by President Franklin Roosevelt when he declared, in 1943, that the United States was protected by military bases that stretched from Trinidad to Cuba. "And of this island shield Puerto Rico is the center. Its possession or control by any foreign power—or even the remote threat of such possession—would be repugnant to the most elementary principles of national defense" (*Message* 1943, 1).

The president's belief conflicted with the aspirations of many members of the Popular Democratic party. By 1945 it was unquestionably the dominant political force on the island but, instead of postponing the issue of status, many islanders wanted a final resolution of Puerto Rico's political position. Many members of Muñoz's party not only demanded independence but they passed (in February 1946) a bill requiring a plebiscite. The bill was vetoed by Governor Rexford Tugwell, but it was quickly passed over Tugwell's veto by the Puerto Rican legislature. That meant that the buck literally stopped at President Harry Truman's desk. The provisions of the 1917 Jones Act gave him the right to reject summarily any legislation passed by the island's government, and he vetoed the plebiscite because Congress had specifically indicated that it would grant neither statehood nor independence to the Puerto Rican people. (According to Article 4, Section 3 of the U.S. Constitution, Congress reserves the right to make *all* needful rules and regulations for U.S. territories.) From the president's point of view, what was the point of allowing Puerto Ricans to express their preference if Congress had already foreclosed the two dominant options: statehood and independence.

It was at this point—in the late 1940s—that Muñoz declared his preference for a new political status, what is today called the Estado Libre Asociado (**Free Associated State**). He lobbied in Puerto Rico and in Washington for a middle way while the release of Pedro Albizu Campos from prison in 1947 produced a call from the Nationalists for the immediate overthrow of the American colonial government. This confrontation reached its conclusion in October 1950 when the Nationalist party engineered a number of violent actions, all intended to stop the creation of the Free Associated State. But, despite the violence, which included attacks on both President Truman and Governor Muñoz (Muñoz became the first Puerto Rican to be elected governor in 1948), Congress passed the legislation that created the new political status of Free Associated State in 1950, and the Puerto Rican people overwhelmingly approved that status in a 1952 referendum. They also approved a constitution written by their representatives. With some changes, it is the charter that still enforces local political affairs.

The new political status was formally inaugurated on July 25, 1952. It promised change, but Governor Muñoz found that his interpretation of Puerto Rico's new status differed from that of Congress and the representatives of the U.S. State Department. Congress had publicly indicated that the Free Associated State did not create any "fundamental" changes in the relationship between Puerto Rico and the United States. Thus, the first line of the legislation passed in 1950 repeats the 1917 Jones Act: Puerto Rico "belongs" to the United States. Moreover, while Governor Muñoz wanted to use the translation of Free Associated State—Estado Libre Asociado— to describe the new status, the U.S. State Department chose the word commonwealth. According to the State Department, Puerto Rico was not a free state because, according to the U.S. Constitution, only Congress could regulate its territories and possessions.

With all the power and intelligence at his command, Governor Muñoz worked for fifteen years (from 1950 until he stepped down as governor in 1964) to increase the powers of El Estado Libre Asociado. But, Congress continued to cite the U.S. Constitution, and Puerto Rico never received any increased powers from succeeding presidents or from the U.S. Congress.

However, Governor Muñoz did oversee the economic transformation of Puerto Rico (see **Operation Bootstrap** and **Tax Laws and Exemptions** for more specific information). As soon as World War II ended, the Members of the **Popular Democratic party** (*Populares*) engineered the changes that made Puerto Rico dependent not on agriculture, but on manufacturing and services, especially tourism, as the mainstay of the island's economy. From 1947 on, employment in manufacturing substantially increased as outside investors pumped in funds that dramatically enhanced the standard of living of the Puerto Rican people. From infrastructure improvements, such as roads, ports and telephones, to the petrochemical industry that dominated the southwestern part of the island, Puerto Rico became an industrialized society boasting all the conveniences and problems associated with rapid social change. For example, official unemployment was high—12.9 percent of the labor force in 1950 and 11.6 percent in 1968. Despite the abundance of new factories, manufacturing never compensated for all the jobs lost in agriculture, and the problem was exacerbated when analysts noted that, between 1948 and 1960, more than a half million Puerto Ricans had left the island to seek work in the United States. Critics suggested that the *Populares* exported their unemployment problems while advocates of Operation Bootstrap understandably pointed to the dramatically increased standard of living, especially in comparison to other Caribbean nations.

Both sides had a point. The island was transformed by Operation Bootstrap but, because the program depended on federal tax exemptions and other incentives that originated in Congress, Puerto Rico often found that its needs were second to those of Americans who lived on the mainland. For example, U.S. unions continually stipulated that any jobs that went to Puerto Rico could not be jobs taken away from mainland Americans; thus, island planners labeled their approach to industrialization the "fishing net" strategy. They took whatever Congress and the U.S. unions allowed, even if those companies offered no long-term commitment to Puerto Rico and its people. As a Harvard study summarized the situation in 1959, "Gold rush psychology is apparently still a part of the American scene and the possibility of making a killing seems to be much more of an attraction to many businessman than does the rather high probability of a more moderate return" (Barton 1959, 17).

Puerto Rican planners believed they could do better if they had more local autonomy, but that meant more powers from Congress and, despite repeated attempts to achieve what is now called the **enhanced commonwealth,** Congress consistently refused to make any changes. Puerto Rico did hold a plebiscite in 1967 and, when the *Populares* won with 60 percent of the vote, they lobbied Congress and the Nixon and Ford administrations for changes that would give far more autonomy to the island. In Congress, the response came from Senator Henry Jackson in 1974: "Neither independence, developed commonwealth or statehood can be had. Puerto Rico must remain a colony" (*Nixon Project*, 1974).

President Gerald Ford was more sympathetic. The documents at the Ford Presidential Library show that he conducted a serious and laborious analysis of the commonwealth situation. Ultimately, he decided that nothing could be done because the Constitution gave all power in this area to the

U.S. Senate and the U.S. House of Representatives. Thus, shortly before he left office in 1976, President Ford lobbied for statehood as his chosen way to resolve the political status of Puerto Rico.

In Puerto Rico itself the **New Progressive party** (established in 1967) and the Popular Democratic party have now shared power for almost thirty years. The statehooders won in 1968, the *Populares* in 1972; then the statehooders from 1976 to 1984 and the *Populares* from 1984 to 1992; and then the statehooders, under the leadership of **Pedro González Rosselló**, won in 1992 and, once again, in 1996.

But, as former Governor (now Resident Commissioner) Carlos Romero Barceló stresses in his book *Statehood Is for the Poor*, the elections are not necessarily an indication of status sentiment. "The reason for this is that the results of the general elections held every four years hinge on a great many issues, most of which have little or no bearing on the ultimate resolution of Puerto Rico's political status question" (Romero Barcelo 1978, 104).

This is an important insight. In recent years, the problems associated with drugs, urbanization, corruption and crime have had an important bearing on the outcome of the gubernatorial and legislative races. Equally important, no one can say with certainty what the Puerto Rican people actually want as their ultimate political status because the vote of any citizen will change relative to the conditions set by Congress. For example, many analysts suggest that statehood could win if Congress allowed Spanish to remain the official language in the school systems and in government. But, mandate English or indicate that Puerto Rico will lose its separate Olympic status, and the results of any plebiscite would change. Some questions: Will Puerto Ricans on the mainland be permitted to vote in any final plebiscite? What happens to the roughly 14 percent of Puerto Rico that is now either owned or controlled by the U.S. military? Will Puerto Ricans be permitted to hold dual citizenship if the island becomes an independent nation? And will the United States give Puerto Rico the twenty years of economic benefits it gave to the Philippines when that nation became independent of the United States?

In 1991 all three of the island's political parties expressed hope that Congress would provide full details for each of the status options; congressional hearings went on for months, but the House of Representatives offered no specifics so the proposed plebiscite never occurred. In response, Puerto Ricans held their own "referendum" in November 1993; the results were 48.4 percent for commonwealth, 46.2 percent for statehood, and 4.4 percent for independence. However, none of the parties provided accurate definitions of their specific status, and Congress always made it clear that the vote in November 1993 was not in any way binding on Washington.

In early 1997 the deadlock continues. However, in 1995, Congress did end the federal tax exemptions for American businesses operating in Puerto

Rico (see Tax laws and exemptions). The ten-year phaseout of these exemptions could have a significant negative impact on the island's economic development. The incentives were a prime reason for locating manufacturing facilities in Puerto Rico. Equally important, when companies kept their profits in island banks, the interest received on their funds was also tax deductible. By many estimates, U.S. corporations had more than $10 billion in Puerto Rican banks in 1996. Were this money to be removed quickly, it could have a ripple effect across the entire island.

Some island politicians hope for a negative effect. They argue that only a crisis will move the United States to make a final decision—the sooner Congress is forced to focus on Puerto Rico and its problems, the better for all concerned. Other island politicians suggest that this kind of thinking is dangerous. They note that if Puerto Rico were to become a state, it would be entitled to seven or eight congressman. Since that would make Puerto Rico more powerful than at least twenty other states, these states will make it impossible for Puerto Rico to join the union. Thus, Puerto Rico will then enjoy neither the jobs produced by the federal tax benefits nor the statehood promised by those who see an economic crisis as a blessing in disguise.

We make no predictions. The only certainty is that the situation is extraordinarily complicated and that Congress will debate the status of Puerto Rico throughout 1997 (see **Young Bill**). Congressman Donald Young from Alaska introduced legislation in 1996 that gave islanders only two choices: statehood or independence. He argued that since there was no way to enhance the powers of the commonwealth government, it was pointless to include any option that offered no hope of change. The bill made some headway in Congress but, in September 1996, other congressmen attached an amendment requiring that any Puerto Rican state use the English language as the medium of instruction in the Puerto Rican school system. This moved the bill's proponents to remove it from consideration. Congressman Young has nevertheless indicated that he will reintroduce the legislation in 1997, and his colleagues promise once again to add an amendment requiring the use of English in the island's school system.

No one knows what will happen; however, Puerto Ricans of all political persuasions argue that since Congress has claimed and maintained plenary or absolute power over Puerto Rico for the last century, it seems reasonable to ask that Congress also accept primary responsibility for the present political and economic problems of Puerto Rico and its 3.7 million inhabitants.

REFERENCES

Barton, H. C. 1959. *Puerto Rico's Industrial Development Program 1942–1960.* Cambridge: Center For International Affairs, Harvard University Press.

A Civil Government For Porto Rico, Hearings Before the Committee on Insular Affairs, House, 63rd Congress, 2nd Session, February 26, 1914.

Congressional Record. 1900. Senate, 56th Congress, 1st Session.

Congressional Record. 1914. Senate, 63rd Congress, 2nd Session, April 15, 1914.

Congressional Record. 1916. House of Representatives, 64th Congress, 2nd Session, May 5, 1916.

Dietz, James. 1986. *Economic History of Puerto Rico: Institutional Change and Capitalist Development*. Princeton: Princeton University Press.

Message from the President. 1943. 78th Congress, House of Representatives, 1st Session, Document #304.

Morales Carrión, Arturo. 1983. *Puerto Rico: A Political and Cultural History*. New York: Norton.

Nixon Project. Papers of President Richard Nixon. Alexandria, Virginia: White House Central Files, St 51–2.

Romero Barcelo, Carlos. 1978. *Statehood Is For the Poor*. San Juan.

Wagenheim, Kal. 1972. *Puerto Rico: A Profile*. New York: Praeger.

Willoughby, William Frank. 1905. *Territories and dependencies of the United States: Their Government and Administration*. New York: The Century Company.

Willoughby, William Frank. 1907. *American Political Science Review*, I, The Executive Council of Porto Rico.

CHRONOLOGY OF
IMPORTANT EVENTS

September 25, 1493	Christopher Colombus leaves the port of Cádiz, Spain, with seventeen ships and between 1,200 and 1,500 sailors.
November 19, 1493	Colombus arrives on the island of **Boriquen** through the port of Aguada.
July 1508	Juan **Ponce de León** receives permission to visit the island of Boriquen and launches an expedition to colonize it.
December 1508	Ponce de León establishes the first settlement in the Caparra close to the location of Bayamón now. He discovers great gold resources.
January 1512	Juan Fernández de Arévalo is appointed the first Catholic priest on the island.
July 1513	The first royal proclamation (or *cédula*) is issued by Spain, authorizing the introduction of Spanish slaves.
January 1517	The Spanish government authorizes the shipment of 4,000 slaves to Puerto Rico and the other greater **Antilles**.
January 1523	The construction of the first convent is begun.
1528	Pirates and foreign corsairs start to launch attacks on the island of Puerto Rico.

1534	Since the gold mines have been almost emptied, the Spanish government looks toward agriculture as the best possible source of resources on the island. They consider the development of sugar plants.
April 1539	The construction of **El Morro** is authorized by the Spanish government.
1543	French pirates attack the island.
March 1564	Captain Francisco Bahamonde de Lugo becomes the first military governor designated by the Spanish crown for Puerto Rico.
November 1595	Sir Francis Drake attacks Puerto Rico and tries to obtain a treasure of gold and silver under guard at El Morro.
June 1598	George Clifford, the count of Cumberland, attacks the island. He is able to gain hold, and the governor relinquishes power, but eventually Cumberland leaves the island for the Spanish.
1606	The Porta Coeli Chapel is constructed in San Germán.
1625	Puerto Rico is attacked by Dutch forces who cause major destruction to the island.
1630	The Spanish crown starts to build a wall system to surround the city of San Juan and protect it against foreign invaders. Due to this wall, San Juan will become "La Ciudad Amurallada" (the Walled City).
1651	The first convent for religious studies is established in Puerto Rico.
1702	The British launch another unsuccessful attack against Puerto Rico.
1703	Dutch ships attack Puerto Rico again.
1765	Alejandro de O'Reilly arrives on the island. He chronicles the status of the island. He finds 44,883 inhabitants during his census.
April 1797	British troops unsuccessfully attack the island again.
1800	La Puntilla arsenal is built in old San Juan.
1803	The first Puerto Rican bishop, Juan Alejo de Arizmendi, is appointed.
1812	The 1812 Spanish constitution is approved in Cádiz. Puerto Rico is declared a Spanish province.

May 1813	Ramón Power y Giralt is selected to represent Puerto Rico in the Cádiz courts. This gives the first democratic representation to Puerto Ricans before the Spanish government. Power gains major economic and social accomplishments for islanders, but dies in Cádiz from yellow fever.
1814	The 1812 constitution is annulled.
August 10, 1815	Cédula de Gracias (**Warrant of Opportunity**) is decreed.
1825	**Roberto Cofresí**, the pirate, is captured and killed.
1868	**Grito de Lares** occurs.
1870	The Liberal Reformist party is founded.
1871	The Liberal Conservative party is founded.
1873	**Slavery** is abolished in the island.
1876	**El Ateneo Puertorriqueño** is founded.
April 21, 1898	Spanish-American War begins.
July 25, 1898	American troops, under the command of **General Nelson Miles**, invade Puerto Rico.
August 12, 1898	Paris Treaty is signed.
1899	The Labor Socialist party is organized.
	The Republican party of Puerto Rico is organized.
	The Federalist party is founded.
1900	The **Foraker Act** is passed.
1903	**University of Puerto Rico** is established in Río Piedras.
1909	*El Diario de Puerto Rico* is founded. It eventually becomes **El Nuevo Día**.
1912	The Politechnic Institute of Puerto Rico, which will eventually become the **Interamerican University**, is founded in San Germán.
1915	The Socialist party is established under the leadership of **Santiago Iglesias Pantín**.
1917	The **Jones Act** is approved. It grants American citizenship to Puerto Ricans.
1919	**El Mundo**, the newspaper, is founded.

1920	Genara Pagán sues the Joint Board of Elections of San Juan challenging the constitutionality of denying suffrage to women.
1922	The **Nationalist party** is founded.
	The first radio station, WKAQ, is founded.
1924	The **Alliance party** is founded as a result of a union between the **Union party** and the Republican party.
	The **Coalition party** is founded. It unites the Constitutional Historical party and the Republican party.
1928	Hurricane San Felipe storms Puerto Rico.
1930	**Pedro Albizu Campos** becomes president of the Nationalist party.
1932	Hurricane San Ciprián damages the island.
1933	**Luisa Arcelay de la Rosa** is the first woman elected to the legislature.
1934	The **Chardón Plan** comes into effect.
1936	Police Chief E. Francis Riggs is killed by nationalist protesters.
	Albizu Campos is convicted of **seditious conspiracy**.
	General suffrage is granted in Puerto Rico.
1937	The **Ponce Massacre** takes place.
1938	The **Popular Democratic party** is founded.
1942	The economic program known as Fomento is begun.
	Jaime Benítez Rexach is appointed chancellor of the University of Puerto Rico.
1946	**Jesús Piñero** becomes the first Puerto Rican governor.
	The Independence party is founded.
	Felisa Rincón de Gautier is elected mayor of San Juan.
1947	The United States approves the election of the first governor.
1948	Construction of the Catholic University of Ponce, now the Pontifical Catholic University of Puerto Rico, begins.
	Luis Muñoz Marín first Puerto Rican elected as governor of Puerto Rico.
1949	Luis Muñoz Marín establishes the **Community Education Division**.

1950	Law 600, which authorizes Puerto Ricans to draft their own constitution, is passed.
October 30, 1950	The **Nationalist Insurrection of 1950** begins in Puerto Rico.
November 1, 1950	Puerto Ricans attack **Blair House.**
1951	The constitutional convention is convened, generates the constitution and approves it.
1952	The U.S. Congress approves the constitution submitted by Puerto Rico. It is ratified by the people of Puerto Rico. Puerto Rico becomes a commonwealth.
	Graciela Rivera becomes the first Puerto Rican woman to perform at the Metropolitan Opera in New York.
1954	A group of Puerto Ricans attack the U.S. Congress.
	Felisa Rincón de Gautier, the mayor of San Juan, is awarded the title of Mujer de las Americas.
	Commercial television begins in the island.
1955	The Institute of Puerto Rican Culture is founded in San Juan.
1957	The first **Pablo Casals** festival takes place at the University of Puerto Rico.
1959	**Claridad** begins publication.
	The **San Juan Star** begins publication.
1964	Muñoz Marín decides not to run again as governor of Puerto Rico, and Roberto Sánchez Vilella is named the Popular Democratic party successor.
1965	Albizu Campos, leader of the Nationalist party, dies.
	Assistant Attorney General Nilita Vientós de Gastón argued and won the landmark litigation on the language issue in Puerto Rico, confirming Spanish as the official language of the judicial system on the island.
1967	A **plebiscite** to determine the status of Puerto Rico takes place in San Juan. The **commonwealth** is selected.
1968	The New Progressive party wins the elections. **Luis Ferré** is elected governor.
1972	The Popular Democratic party wins the election, and **Rafael Hernández Colón** is elected governor.

1972	Baseball star **Roberto Clemente** dies in a plane crash.
1973	**Luis Aponte Martínez** becomes the first Puerto Rican Catholic cardinal.
	Miriam Naveira is appointed the first woman solicitor general.
1976	The New Progressive party wins the elections, and **Carlos Romero Barcelo** comes into power.
1978	Two pro-independence youngsters are killed by the police in the **Cerro Maravilla** incident.
1979	Puerto Rico is hit by Hurricane David.
	A group of American marines are killed during an operation launched by **Los Macheteros.**
April 30, 1980	Muñoz Marín dies.
1981	Los Macheteros attack a National Guard installation located at Muñiz Air Base in Isla Verde and destroy eight aircraft.
	The first AIDS cases are reported in Puerto Rico.
1984	Hernández Colón is reelected governor of Puerto Rico.
1985	**Miriam Naveira** is appointed to the Puerto Rican Supreme Court. She is the first woman to occupy such a position.
	Seven members of Los Macheteros are arrested in Connecticut.
1990	Antonia Novello is named U.S. Surgeon General.
1992	**Pedro Rosselló González** is elected governor of Puerto Rico for the New Progressive party.
	Victoria Muñoz runs for governor of Puerto Rico as the pro-commonwealth Popular party candidate.
1994	The people of Puerto Rico reaffirm the commonwealth as their status in a plebiscite.
1996	Rosselló González is reelected governor of Puerto Rico.
1997	The U.S. Congress starts a process of public hearings to assess the status of the island.

REFERENCE

Quiñones Calderón, Antonio. *50 Décadas de Historia Puertorriqueña*. San Juan, Puerto Rico: Gobierno Municipal de San Juan, 1992.

A

Abortion The rights of women to have an abortion has been a social, moral, ethical, economic, civil, and political issue that has created social ferment and turmoil in Western societies during the last thirty years. The public controversies around the rights of women to have abortions are as heated in Puerto Rico as they are on the mainland. Puerto Rican society has been polarized with arguments in favor of women's rights to an abortion and those who assume the pro-life stand.

Statistics on the number of abortions performed in Puerto Rico each year vary. Dr. Margarita Ostolaza, a professor at the University of Puerto Rico in Cayey and an expert in sexual politics in Puerto Rico, accepts the estimate that approximately 40,000 abortions are performed in the island each year: one abortion out of every three pregnancies (Ostolaza 1989, 83).

While Puerto Rico is often perceived as a traditional society with strong family values, economic and political changes during the twentieth century and its relationship with the United States, have contributed to a liberalization of the social mores prevalent in the island. As U.S. citizens, Puerto Rican women have been covered by the legal dispositions set by the case of *Roe vs. Wade*, which legalized abortion in the United States. However, their rights to an abortion was tested in the now landmark case of *People of Puerto Rico vs. Pablo Duarte Mendoza*, decided by the Puerto Rican Supreme Court in April 1980. This case is responsible for setting the norms now relevant to abortion in Puerto Rico.

In 1973 Dr. Pablo Duarte Mendoza, a physician licensed to practice medicine in the island, performed an abortion on a sixteen-year-old minor who sought his services to terminate a pregnancy during the first trimester. Duarte was found guilty of performing an illegal abortion under an old section of the 1937 Puerto Rican penal code, which was replaced with a revised version in 1974. He was sentenced to serve between two and four years in prison. His lawyers appealed the sentence to the Puerto Rican Supreme Court which, in April 1980, revoked the sentence of the superior court and fully ascribed to the common law precedents established in the *Roe vs. Wade* and *Doe vs. Bolton* decisions of 1973. The justices emphasized that the ultimate decision on whether to perform an abortion during the first trimester of pregnancy should be made by the physician in charge and that this decision should be made taking into consideration the health of the pregnant patient. Health was understood to mean both the physical and mental health of the woman. This definition certainly expanded the powers of Puerto Rican physicians to perform abortions. The court underscored that any abortion procedure performed in Puerto Rico should be directed at preserving the physical or mental health of the pregnant woman and should not be the object of any penalties under the legal system. The justices made it clear that the age of the patient was not an element to be taken into consideration by the doctor as their clinical judgment supersedes age considerations. Moreover, they stressed that the parents of a pregnant minor who wished to terminate a pregnancy should not have any influence over their daughter's decision.

To a large extent, Puerto Rican abortion regulations are more lenient than those in many American states. While *Roe vs. Wade* determined that abortions during the second and third trimesters of pregnancy could be regulated by local governments in a more stringent way, that is not the case in Puerto Rico; the rights to abortion during the later trimesters are still not regulated at the local level.

In recent years, the Catholic Church and many sectors associated with the American Pro-Life movement have tried to put pressure on the governor and the legislative assembly to pass more rigorous regulations on abortion. Nevertheless, to this day, abortion norms on the island are still dictated by the Duarte case.

SUGGESTED READING

Annette B. Ramírez de Arellano and Conrad Seipp, *Colonialism, Catholicism, and Contraception: A History of Birth Control in Puerto Rico* (Chapel Hill: University of North Carolina Press, 1983); Margarita Ostolaza, *Política sexual en Puerto Rico* (Río Piedras: Editorial Huracán, 1989); Jean P. Peterman, *Telling Their Stories: Puerto Rican Women and Abortion* (Boulder, Colo.: Westview Press, 1996); Proyecto de Estudios de la Mujer, Colegio Universitario de Cayey, Universidad de Puerto Rico, *La realidad del aborto en Puerto Rico: guías para la elaboración de políticas públicas* (Cayey: Proyecto de Estudios para la Mujer, 1993); Puerto Rico Supreme Court, *People vs. Duarte Mendoza* (Hato Rey: Compuclerck, 1990); Lisa Whittle, *Abortion Attitudes of Puerto Rican Women* (Atlanta: Master's Thesis, Emory University, 1989).

African Roots   In areas as diverse as music, graphic arts and literature, African influences have shaped and still shape Puerto Rican culture. Estimates vary but an educated guess is that half of the 10 million slaves brought to the Americas lived and died in the Caribbean. Africans are such a powerful source of Caribbean culture that **José Luis González** argues that Africans are *el primer piso* (the first floor) of Puerto Rican popular culture; this, however, is a controversial argument among scholars of Puerto Rican culture. However it is ultimately resolved, there is conspicuous evidence of significant African influence in elements that extend from language to the Puerto Rican's attitude toward the color of a person's skin. For example, in the 1990 U.S. census, many Puerto Ricans did not know how to respond to the question on race. They left the box blank, not because Puerto Ricans do not see color but because the island's African heritage has helped create a culture that rarely sees things only in terms of black and white. In Puerto Rico, African, Indian and Spanish blood have always mixed; the result is a society that often uses the word *trigueno* (wheat colored) to describe the color of a man in **Ponce** or a woman in Utuado.

In Puerto Rico, the city of **Loíza Aldea** is most commonly associated with the island's African heritage. But the famous *vegigantes* (the papier-mâché masks of horned animal-like figures) of Ponce also have their roots in Africa, and, as many historical and contemporary carvings of the **Three Kings** suggest, African influences have helped transform traditional representations of important Catholic symbols. In one depiction of the Virgen de Los Reyes, the Three Kings are superimposed over the figure of the Virgin Mary; the kings' faces are nicely carved, and, as is traditional in Puerto Rico, at the center is Melchior, the king from Africa, as illustrated on this book's cover.

Proud recognition of African roots is sometimes resisted. The prejudice that divides the world into black and white, into inferior and superior, has also made an appearance in Puerto Rico. Thus, in the Spanish used by islanders, a person can have *pelo malo*, bad or curly hair. One result of prejudice is that the people who are the targets of hate learn to depreciate themselves or their cultural origins. Consequently, the still raging battle over the first, second and third floors of Puerto Rican culture is also a battle about Caribbean versus Western ideas about the meaning and significance of skin color.

SUGGESTED READING

José Luis González, *The Four Storied Country* (New York: Marcus Weiner, 1993); Mark Kurlansky, *A Continent of Islands* (Reading, Pa.: Addison Wesley, 1992); Ramón Romero Rosa, "El Negro Puertorriqueño," in *Sources for the Study of the Puerto Rican Migration*, (New York: Center for Puerto Rican Studies, 1982). See also Lydia Milagros González, *La Tercera Raiz: Presencia African en Puerto Rico* (San Juan: Centro de Estudios de la Realidad Puertorriqueña, 1992).

Agrelot, José Miguel (1927–   ) As a comedian, commentator and media personality, Agrelot has been one of the best-known figures of television and radio in Puerto Rico for the past four decades. His multifaceted work has been central to the development of the genres of stand-up and situation comedy in Puerto Rican media, especially in television. He has developed dozens of characters that have become a daily fixture of Puerto Rican television viewers. Among the most important ones are Don Cholito, Pasión, el Profesor Pulula, and Serafín Sin Fin. Although not always politically correct, his characters satirize and play on the good and the bad that affects contemporary life in Puerto Rican society. He is best known for his character of Don Cholito, a somewhat vocal and sincere commentator of daily events who sees things from the vantage point of a "native" mentality characterized by passion and strong opinions. An important figure in the radio industry, he has hosted the early morning program "Su Alegre Despertar" (Happy Awakenings), for many decades. He is also very active in advertising. Despite the many changes that have affected the media industry in the island, Agrelot has always managed to keep a visible profile partly because of the loyalty of his viewers who appreciate his talents, sincerity and wonderful sense of humor. He has charmed his audiences for years.

SUGGESTED READING

José Miguel Agrelot, *A reir con Agrelot* (Río Piedras, P.R.: Editorial Cultural, 1983).

Aguinaldo This word has two meanings. Generally, it refers to a gift, given to someone during Christmas or another religious festivity. The gift could be money, a toy or a religious object. Affluent individuals have often given *aguinaldos* to poor people from the neighborhood and communities who were important parts of their social groups. The *aguinaldo* traditionally has served as a symbol of gratitude or appreciation. The second meaning of *aguinaldo* refers to a music form presented or interpreted as a gift, or a celebration, during Christmas or some other religious festivity by poor peasants from the countryside. The *aguinaldo* is a poetic, romantic composition that quite often reflects on the nativity and other icons and imagery from Judeo-Christian folklore. Others have a more secular theme that reflects or sings about the mores and traditions of that society as they relate to Christmas. It is sung by a single individual or in duets in a dialogue form; it does not have a chorus. The *aguinaldo* uses typical Puerto Rican instruments, such as the **cuatro**, maracas, the **guiro** and the guitar. Francisco López Cruz identified that aguinaldos have a two-by-four compass, use *décimas* (stanzas of ten verses) as the basis (López Cruz 1967, 184). The verses, in turn, contain six syllables. Because they are not easy to sing, a certain degree of skill or proficiency is necessary to interpret them. There are many variations within the *aguinaldo*. The *aguinaldo* as a form of

musical expression is quickly disappearing in the island as a result of the blending of urban and rural areas. Instead, Puerto Ricans have seen the proliferation of far more popular tunes that are sung during the Christmas holidays—tunes that have a far more secular nature.

SUGGESTED READING

Catherine Downer, *Puerto Rican Music following the Spanish American War* (Boston: University Press of America, 1983); Francisco López-Cruz, *La Música Folklorica de Puerto Rico* (Sharon, Conn.: Troutman Press, 1967); James A. McCoy, *The Bomba and Aguinaldo in Puerto Rico as They Have Evolved from Indigenous, African and European Cultures* (Ann Arbor, Mich.: University Microfilms International); Angel Quintero Rivera, "Ponce, the Danza and the National Question: Notes toward a Sociology of Puerto Rican Music" *Cimarrón* 1 (Winter 1986): 49–65.

AIDS in Puerto Rico   Acquired Immune Deficiency Syndrome (AIDS) poses a grave health threat to the Puerto Rican people. Since the first case of AIDS was reported in Puerto Rico in 1981, there has been a steady increase in the number of diagnosed cases. As of June 1, 1996, 17,917 Puerto Ricans from the island have been diagnosed with the virus. Most of those infected are men—13,891 (77.7 percent)—and 3,673 (22.3 percent) are women. Of those diagnosed, 11,268, or 63 percent, have already died. HIV/AIDS is the leading killer among those between twenty-five and thirty-four years of age; the disease severely affects those between the ages of twenty and twenty-nine (20 percent), thirty to thirty-nine (45 percent) and forty to forty-nine (23 percent). In addition, 346 cases (1.93 percent) have been reported among pediatric populations.

The leading causes of transmissions for men who become infected are intravenous drug use (57 percent) and sex with other men (21 percent). These two categories account for most cases. Women contract it primarily through heterosexual intercourse (55 percent) and through intravenous drug use (39 percent). Although the disease has affected all segments of society, low-income Puerto Ricans seem to be more at risk. Several factors account for the wide spread of the disease in the island. First is drug use. Second, in a nation where culturally established gender roles such as **machismo** still dominate, men who have sex with other men tend to perceive themselves as deviant; therefore, they hide their sexual preferences and engage in homosexual sex without protection. A recent study showed that as many as 20 percent of men in the general population could potentially engage in such behavior. These men, in turn, could expose their female partners.

Traditionally, Puerto Rican culture socializes women to be passive and submissive. Moreover, men still hold economic control of personal relationships. This combination produces a situation in which some women place themselves at risk because they are traditional or because they use sex to gain economic power. A further factor that has affected the wide spread of the epidemic is the role of the government. Influenced by the traditional mores of the culture and the power of the Catholic Church, the government has never taken an aggressive stand against the epidemic. For example, there are few broad educational and public health initiatives to promote safe sexual practices and the use of condoms. Needle exchange programs, which have been proven to be effective in combating the epidemic in Europe and the United States, are rare on the island. The Catholic Church, led by its powerful cardinal, has hindered prevention services by condemning homosexuality and sexual contact outside marriage and by labeling educational efforts as immoral. Throughout the epidemic's existence, the Church has been a staunch opponent to the distribution of condoms in schools and public places and has been able to control government efforts in this area. It has required a great deal of activism by such organizations as Fundación SIDA to bring awareness of the problem to the government and the general public. Finally, it seems that there has been widespread corruption in the funding and establishment of some HIV/AIDS prevention and treatment services on the island.

SUGGESTED READING

Ineke Cunningham, Carlos G. Ramos Bellido and Reinaldo Ortiz Colón, *El SIDA en Puerto Rico: Acercamientos Multidisciplinarios* (Río Piedras: Instituto de Estudios del Caribe, Universidad de Puerto Rico, 1991); Department of Health, "Acquired Immunodeficiency Syndrome: Surveillance Report" (San Juan, P.R.: Office for AIDS Affairs, May 31, 1996); Markku Loytonen and Sonia I. Arbona, "Forecasting the AIDS epidemic in Puerto Rico" *Social Science and Medicine* 42, no. 7 (1996): 997.

Albizu Campos, Pedro (1891–1965)   The leader of the island's **Nationalist party**, as a revolutionary, he advocated the legal or illegal, violent or nonviolent overthrow of U.S. colonial authority. Albizu Campos and **Luis Muñoz Marín** are the two most significant political figures in twentieth-century Puerto Rican history. Albizu was born in **Ponce** on September 12, 1891, and died in San Juan on April 21, 1965. He received his early education in Ponce; in 1912, he won a scholarship to attend the University of Vermont. Within a year, his brilliance dictated a move to Harvard, where he received his first degree in 1916 and his law degree in 1921.

Since Albizu's skin was dark, one myth that still retains currency in Puerto Rico is that he became a revolutionary because he experienced racial discrimination at Harvard or discrimination during his military service in 1917 and 1918. The argument is that Albizu turned his hatred of those who treated him badly against the United States. However, Albizu was a twenty-one-year-old man when he left for the United States. To experience prejudice firsthand he needed only to visit the Spanish and American sugar

Pedro Albizu Campos. (*El Nuevo Día*.)

centrals near his home in Ponce. Equally important, "Pete," his nickname at Harvard, was a very popular student. He served as president of the Cosmopolitan Club; he wrote a prowar, pro-America essay for the *Harvard Crimson* in 1917; his political colleagues indicate that he never spoke harshly about his military service; and, as late as 1921, he voluntarily returned questionnaires to Harvard that let his fellow students know what "Pete" was doing in Ponce.

After his return to Puerto Rico, Albizu Campos practiced law but was becoming a revolutionary. He joined the centrist **Union party**, not the Nationalist party, in 1923, and his early political essays are filled with peaceful ideas for change. As late as April 1924, he asked for a joint resolution of the Puerto Rican legislature to *solicit* from the U.S. Congress permission for Puerto Ricans to hold a constitutional convention. He first sought change within the system but, when the Union party removed independence as one of its political alternatives, he resigned from the party, joined the Nationalists, and began the trek that would lead to more than thirty years of revolutionary violence against U.S. authority. By 1927 he had drawn this fixed conclusion: "Puerto Rico must create a grave crisis for the colonial administration before it will attend to Puerto Rican demands" (Albizu, 1975, 1: 52). Albizu argued that, beginning in 1899, Puerto Ricans had asked for political change and had resisted cultural change. They even asked not to be made U.S. citizens against their will. Albizu argued that, since U.S. officials refused to respond after twenty-nine years of Puerto Ricans working within the system, a revolution was both necessary and justified. As a lawyer, Albizu argued that the **Autonomic Constitution** signed with the Spanish in 1897 made U.S. authority illegal from the day **General Nelson Miles** invaded; and, as a person, Albizu believed "that the only transcendental obligation that any man or woman born in a colony had, was to redeem the nation from its colonial status" (Albizu, 1975, 2: 108). His most well-known phrase is still *la patria es valor y sacrificio* (the nation is valor and sacrifice).

Albizu was an open revolutionary. For example, when he suggested that someone retaliate in kind for the police murder of two Nationalists in 1935, he said this in front of thousands of people. As a result, U.S. Chief of Police Elisha Riggs was assassinated in San Juan in February 1936. Albizu was subsequently convicted of **seditious conspiracy** and sent to prison in Atlanta, Georgia, for ten years. After his prison sentence ended, Albizu returned to Puerto Rico in 1947. He was more committed to revolution than ever; he told a huge crowd in Guánica (on July 25, 1949) that "there are men and women born in 1898. Blessed are those born under United States slavery because they have the right to grasp a dagger and put it through the heart of the Yanquis" (Acosta 1993, 76).

Albizu directed the revolution that occurred in Puerto Rico in October 1950 (see **Nationalist Insurrection of 1950**). His subsequent arrest and pardon (in 1953) highlights the ambiguity manifested by many Puerto Ricans whenever Albizu is discussed. To use violence was wrong, but to keep Albizu in jail was to incarcerate a patriot who wanted to free his country from its colonial status. During his imprisonment, Albizu claimed he was tortured by radiation. Several doctors confirmed that he had burns, but the source of those burns has never been definitively resolved. In recent years, the U.S. government has admitted to performing a number of experiments on humans using radiation; although many of these experiments were conducted against prisoners, there is no evidence that conclusively demonstrates that Albizu Campos was one of those tortured in this manner.

When Albizu was pardoned in September 1953, he refused to leave prison because his Nationalist colleagues had not received the pardon given to him. Albizu was then expelled from prison. After he ordered the **Nationalist Attack on Congress** in 1954, Albizu was returned to jail and, in 1956, he entered a San Juan hospital where he died as a prisoner in 1965.

Over the last thirty years, Albizu's ideas and life have received extensive and serious scrutiny. The reevaluation has made him a role model for contemporary Puerto Rican revolutionaries and, sometimes, a role model for the island government. For example, in 1989, the commonwealth government sponsored an art exhibition which celebrated both Albizu and the Nationalists who attacked the House of Representatives in 1954. One room contained portraits of the weapons used to shoot congressmen; another, paintings that celebrated Albizu and his revolutionary achievements. A definitive biography of Albizu has yet to be written. Many of his letters and other writings are under the control of family members. To date, scholars have not been permitted to examine many of the documents that would permit a more thorough and objective analysis of Albizu's life, beliefs and revolutionary activities.

SUGGESTED READING

Ivonne Acosta, ed., *La palabra como delito* (San Juan, P.R.: Editorial Cultural, 1993); Pedro Albizu Campos, *Obras escogidas*, vols. 1, 2, 3 (San Juan, P.R.: Editorial Jelofe, 1975, 1981, 1983); Surenda Bhana, *The United States and the Development of the Puerto Rican Status Question* (Lawrence: University of Kansas Press, 1975); Gordon Lewis, *Freedom and Power in the Caribbean* (New York: Harpers, 1962); Alfredo Lopez, ed., *The Puerto Rican Papers: Notes on the Reemergence of a People* (Indianapolis: Bobbs Merrill, 1983); Juan Manuel García Passalacqua, *Puerto Rico: Equality and Freedom at Issue* (New York: Praeger, 1984); Marisa Rosado, *Pedro Albizu Campos: Las llamas de la Aurora* (San Juan, P.R., 1991); Young Lord's Party and Michael Abramson, *Palante, Young Lord's Party* (New York: McGraw Hill, 1971).

Alegría, Ricardo (1921–) A distinguished archeologist, writer and advocate for the preservation of all aspects of Puerto Rican culture, Alegría was born in San Juan. He graduated from the **University of Puerto Rico**

and received his doctorate in archaeology from Harvard University. When he returned to the island, he conducted important excavations in **Loiza Aldea** and Luquillo; his work on the ballfields of **Los Taínos** is a model of academic excellence.

In 1955 Alegría became the director of the Institute of Puerto Rican Culture. He masterminded a program that simultaneously recognized, strengthened and promoted the Indian, African and Spanish influences on Puerto Rican culture. He received the Picasso Gold Medal of the United Nations Educational, Scientific and Cultural Organization for his work on the restoration and preservation of Puerto Rican historical monuments. He was especially active in the restoration of Old San Juan as a unique historical district and in the excavation and creation of the Taíno Indian Ceremonial Center outside **Ponce**. He is the director of the Center of Advanced Studies in Puerto Rico and the Caribbean and the founder of the Center of Archaeological and Ethnological Investigations of the University of Puerto Rico. Alegría has also received the Medal of Isabel La Católica from the Spanish government and, from the Puerto Rican government, the Medal of the Fifth Centenary of the Discovery of America and Puerto Rico.

SUGGESTED READING

Ricardo Alegría, *Ball Courts and Ceremonial Plazas in the Caribbean* (New Haven, Conn.: Yale University Press, 1983); Tribute to Dr. Ricardo Alegría, *Congressional Record*, House of Representatives, April 15, 1996.

Alliance Party (La Alianza)   Formed in the early 1920s, La alianza refers to the fragile political partnership created between the **Union party** and some members of the island's Republican party. With his implacable resistance to any advocacy of independence, Governor **E. Montgomery Reilly** threw the island's parties into turmoil. Historian Truman Clark calls this period "the Kaleidoscope of Puerto Rican Politics, 1923–29" (Clark 1975, 76).

Accepting Reilly's demands, the Union party made the creation of a **Free Associated State** the cornerstone of their political platform in 1922. That moved some Unionists to form the **Nationalist party**. Meanwhile, the Unionists would soon join with the Republicans who favored a very long road to statehood. They called their marriage La alianza. La alianza arose because of the failure of a 1924 congressional effort to achieve a "Civil Government of Porto Rico." For example, when he testified in February 1924, José Tous Soto (the head of the Republican party) told Congress that "if we are not going to be an independent country like Cuba, what is going to be our final destiny? A perpetual colony?" That was an "impossible thought." He added, "We are not now in a position to ask Congress for immediate admission to statehood, but after a quarter century of American rule we are entitled to know what Congress has in store for us." Congress effectively answered more of the same, and La alianza was formed within a month after the congressional hearings ended. It was a stormy marriage of convenience; the weakened Unionists needed new allies, and at least some Republicans saw the Alliance party as a way to end their also-ran status in Puerto Rican politics. The Alliance lasted until the end of the decade.

SUGGESTED READING

Civil Government of Puerto Rico, *Hearings before the Committee on Insular Affairs*, 68th Cong., 1st sess., February 1924; Truman Clark, *Puerto Rico and the United States, 1917–1933* (Pittsburgh: University of Pittsburgh Press, 1975); Arthur Dana, *Puerto Rico's Case: Outcome of American Sovereignty* (New Haven, Conn.: Tuttle, Morehouse and Taylor, 1928).

Alonso, Manuel A. (1823–1889)   Alonso was born in San Juan and raised in Caguas. He was trained as a physician and was a significant personality in the world of arts and letters during the nineteenth century. His book of poetry *El Gíbaro* (1849) is considered to be the first truly Puerto Rican book. It reflects on the feelings, personality and nationality of islanders and presents a collection of customs and traditions that are taken to be representative of the Puerto Rico of his time. In fact, *El Gíbaro* is considered to be the first classic of Puerto Rican literature (Babín 1958, 319). One of the most significant characteristics of *El Gíbaro* is that it is written in what critics and linguists assume to be the popular or colloquial Spanish language used by Puerto Rican **jíbaros** at the time. It has provided a fertile ground for linguists to study the evolution of the language in the island. In 1883 Alonso published a second volume to the book.

Alonso was a contributor to the book *Album puertorriqueño*, published by a group of Puerto Rican students in Spain (1844), and to *Cancionero de Borinquen* (1846). He had a successful career as a physician and was very active in the Liberal Reformist party.

SUGGESTED READING

Maria Teresa Babín, *Panorama de la cultura puertorriqueña* (San Juan: Instituto de Cultura Puertorriqueña, 1958); Modesto Rivera, *Manuel Alonso: Su vida y su obra* (San Juan: Editorial Coquí, 1966); Modesto Rivera, *Concepto y expresión del costumbrismo en Manuel A. Alonso* (San Juan: Instituto de Cultura Puertorriqeña, 1980).

Americanization   This refers to the effort made by U.S. political and educational authorities to turn the Puerto Rican people into what were then called, in the United States, 100 percent Americans. When, in 1898, Puerto

Rico became an American colony, the United States contained many movements dedicated to Americanizing the immigrant. On the mainland, this drive focused on such groups as the Italians and the Russians. But, after the U.S. military invaded Puerto Rico, the mainland's zeal to transform the immigrant quickly spread to the Caribbean.

The principal efforts at Americanization were made in the schools. As early as January 1899, U.S. officials mandated that English was the preferred medium of instruction in the school system. Since few native teachers spoke English, colonial officials replaced them with American teachers who, as the U.S. Commissioner of Education reported in 1901, "were mostly young men who came to Porto Rico with the American Army. None of them knew Spanish and some of them knew little English" (*Report* 1901, 498). By 1907 the commissioner reported to Washington that these teachers "not infrequently made themselves ludicrous." However, the push to Americanize the Puerto Ricans never ceased. Schools were renamed to honor American heroes, and students learned about math by counting and multiplying pears, a fruit they had never seen. As late as 1941 *Fortune* magazine doubted "the efficacy of trying to teach Spanish minded youngsters such subjects as geometry, history, and economics in English on alternate days. The result of mixing the languages indiscriminately is apt to be . . . a general negativism" ("Puerto Rico" 1941, 132). In the 1990s memories of the struggle over Americanization materialize whenever anyone discusses statehood. For many of those raised in the 1930s and 1940s, the recollection of being educated in English creates a marked resistance to further efforts at Americanization—especially if it is achieved at the expense of the Spanish language.

SUGGESTED READING

Aida Negron de Montilla, *Americanization in Puerto Rico and the Public School System, 1900–1930* (Río Piedras, P.R.: Edil, 1970); Roland P. Falkner, "The English Language in Porto Rico," *The Forum* 16, no. 3 (1909): 206–12; John Higham, *Strangers in the Land: Patterns of American Nativism* (New Brunswick, N.J.: Rutgers University Press, 1971); "Puerto Rico," *Fortune* (May 1941): 91–; *Report of the Commissioner of Education for Porto Rico* (Washington, D.C.: U.S. Government Printing Office, 1901).

Americans (Los Americanos)   This expression is used by Puerto Ricans when they speak about gringos or, more specifically, anyone born in the United States who is not a Puerto Rican. The phrase *los americanos* is one of the clearest everyday indications that, despite 500 years of Spanish and U.S. control, Puerto Rico has its own unique culture and its own way of seeing self and world. Thus, in conversation, Puerto Ricans on the island will casually refer to *los americanos*. Sometimes the phrase is taken for granted; in other instances, the speaker is being openly derogatory. *Un americano* is pronounced in a tone of voice that indicates disdain. Whichever way the phrase is used, a speaker is always underlining that, despite also being an American, life is separated into "us and them"—the Puerto Ricans and the rest of the world. Incidentally, this phrase is also frequently used by Puerto Rican immigrants in New York and Chicago, Boston and Miami.

Suggested Reading

Juan Flores, *Divided Borders: Essays on Puerto Rican Identity* (Houston: Arte Público, 1993); Esmeralda Santiago, *When I Was Puerto Rican* (New York: Vintage Books, 1994); Earl Shorris, *Latinos: A Biography of the People* (New York: Avon Books, 1992).

Andreu de Aguilar, Isabel (1887–1948)   A suffragist and writer, Andreu de Aguilar was born in Fajardo. Considered a pioneer of the feminist movement (see **Feminism**) in Puerto Rico, Andreu de Aguilar was a member of the first graduating class of the **University of Puerto Rico**, where she received a degree in teaching. During both undergraduate and graduate studies at both the University of Puerto Rico and Columbia University, she was known for her participation in educational, cultural and civic activities. Her leadership role in the field of education led to her becoming the first female trustee of the University of Puerto Rico. However, her major interests were the feminist and suffragist issues brewing at the time.

Two factions constituted this feminist movement: one group was made up of privileged women; the other contained working-class women who labored in everything from the sugar and tobacco industries to the needlework factories and workshops. Andreu de Aguilar was part of a group of upper-class feminist leaders and founding members of the first feminist-suffragist organization formed in Puerto Rico in 1917, the Puerto Rican Feminine League (Liga femínea de Puerto Rico). Their goal was the passage of voting rights for literate women, and these privileged women closely followed the progress of suffragists in the United States with the belief that the imminent passage of the Nineteenth Amendment, giving American women the right to vote, would automatically be enforced or immediately passed in another form in the Puerto Rican legislature. As part of a delegation of the Feminine League on the Island, Andreu de Aguilar went to the United States in 1919 seeking solidarity with her North American sisters. In the end, after the Nineteenth Amendment passed, Washington officials announced that the amendment was not applicable to Puerto Rico; it took twelve more years of hard work before Puerto Rican women won the right to vote.

From 1917 to 1922, Andreu de Aguilar was a member of the board of directors of the Puerto Rican Feminine League, and she presided over the Association of Women Suffragists (Asociación de Mujeres Sufragistas) from 1925 to 1929. In addition, she was president of the island's League of

Women Voters (Asociación Insular de Mujeres Votantes) from 1929 to 1932.

Her activism included membership on the board of directors of the Carnegie Library and of the University of Puerto Rico. As a result of her deep concern for children, she founded an organization dedicated to children's welfare, Junta de Bienestar de la Niñez.

Her career as a writer led to literary achievements in poetry and short stories. In 1926 the **Ateneo Puertorriqueño**, an institution on the forefront of the literary and cultural movement in Puerto Rico at the time, awarded her their prize for distinguished writing in the short story category. She also wrote "Reseña histórica del movimiento feminista en Puerto Rico," *Revista de Puerto Rico* 1, no. 3 (June 1935).

SUGGESTED READING

Willar E. Givens, "Texto . . . ," *Revista de la Asociación de Mujeres Graduadas de la UPR* (July 1942): 45; Tomás Sarramía, *Nuestra gente: Apuntes y datos biográficos de personajes representativos de Puerto Rico* (San Juan: Publicaciones Puertorriqueñas, 1993).

Antilles   This term refers to island groupings in the Caribbean Sea. Geographers separate the Caribbean into the Greater and the Lesser Antilles. Puerto Rico sits at the easternmost tip of the Greater Antilles and, despite its size—35 miles by 100 miles—Puerto Rico is the smallest of the islands in the chain that loosely includes both Cuba and Jamaica, Haiti and the Dominican Republic. However, Puerto Rico's location, right in the middle of the Caribbean and the Greater and Lesser Antilles, has always given it a strategic importance that sets it off from any of its larger or smaller Antillean neighbors. In this sense, Puerto Rico's military significance for world powers blends into the origin of the word Antilles. In Europe, legend taught that, during the Middle Ages, seven Portuguese bishops had fled the advancing Moors and had founded the Seven Cities of Antila or silver in a land across the Atlantic. The Spanish explorers, who brought this legend to the Caribbean, thus named the islands they saw the Greater and Lesser Antilles. It was attempt to fit the New World into the mental map of the Old World. As a result, people now use a Portuguese legend to place Puerto Rico in the center of a group of islands that frequently manifest mixed memories of the inheritance acquired from the Spanish, French, English, American and, in an offhand way, Portuguese colonizers.

SUGGESTED READING

John R. Chávez, "Aztlán, Cibola and Frontier New Spain," in *Aztlán: Essays on the Chicano Homeland*, ed. Rudolfo A. Anaya and Francisco A. Lomeli (Albuquerque: El Norte Publications, 1989); Neil Sealey, *Caribbean World: A Complete Geography* (Cambridge, England: Cambridge University Press, 1995).

Aponte Martínez, Luis (1922–   )   The Roman Catholic cardinal of Puerto Rico, Aponte Martínez is the only Puerto Rican who sits in the Vatican's College of Cardinals. Born in Lajas, Aponte Martínez was the eighth in a family of eighteen children. He received his elementary education in Lajas and attended high school in San Germán. Aponte Martínez entered San Idelfonso Seminary in San Juan in 1940 and then moved on to Saint John Seminary in Boston. Aponte took his vows for the priesthood in 1950. In 1955 he became the secretary of Ponce's bishop James. E. McManus, and in 1963 he became bishop of the diocese of **Ponce**—only the second time that a native Puerto Rican has been appointed to such a position. He was also the director of development of the Catholic University of Puerto Rico and later chancellor of that institution. In 1964 Aponte Martínez became San Juan's archbishop. Appointed cardinal in 1973 by Pope Paul VI, he has participated in the election of Popes John Paul I and John Paul II.

Through his views and his public presence, Cardinal Aponte is a highly visible figure in the daily affairs of the island. As the highest ecclesiastical officer of the Catholic Church, he has tried to assume a leadership role for all Puerto Ricans by trying to act as a spiritual and moral leader. This role has often put him at odds with people who either do not follow his beliefs or disagree with his position. A theological conservative, Aponte Martínez has censured violence and vulgarity on the Puerto Rican media, has been a staunch critic of social policies that favor abortion and the distribution of condoms to youth and has tried to reaffirm the traditional teachings of the Church. The cardinal also speaks out if he believes that political issues or leaders jeopardize the faith of his followers or the Church.

In a period when the Catholic Church in the United States finds it increasingly difficult to attract new priests, Cardinal Aponte has been instrumental in successfully sponsoring the creation of local seminaries that foster the emergence of native priests. He has been greatly responsible for changing the personality of the Church from one that was mostly oriented toward Spain and Europe to one essentially concerned with issues dealing with Puerto Rico.

SUGGESTED READING

Charles Beirne, *The Problem of Americanization in the Catholic Schools of Puerto Rico* (Río Piedras, P.R.: Editorial Universitaria, 1975); *Catholic Archdiocese of San Juan*, resume of Luis Aponte Martínez, San Juan, 1996; Elisa Julián de Nieves, *The Catholic Church in Colonial Puerto Rico (1898–1964)* (Río Piedras, P.R.: Editorial Edil, 1982).

Arana, Alfonso (1927–   )   The painter Alfonso Arana was born in New York City. He is a multifaceted artist. His father was Mexican and his mother was Puerto Rican. Arana's mother belonged to a prominent family of artists and intellectuals from Lares, from whom Arana inherited, if not his talent, his love of art. His artistic formation was influenced dually by his Mexican and Puerto Rican background, and by his French artistic education.

Arana acquired his early education in Puerto Rico. During the forties, he moved to Mexico where he studied with Bardasamo, a famous Spanish painter. From Mexico he went to Paris where he studied at the École des Beaux Arts and the Academie Julian. After returning to Puerto Rico during the early 1950s, he started to teach plastic arts at the **University of Puerto Rico**.

Spanish art critic Juan Antonio Gaya-Nuño points out that Arana's early artistic production went through two developmental stages and artistic transformations. His work has a Mexican period, which consists of realistic oil portraits and pastels. After this, he developed a local or *criollo* period in which his paintings capture elements of local Puerto Rican life and populist folklore (Gaya-Nuño 1984). In the 1970s, Arana moved once again to Paris where his style matured into that which characterizes most of his contemporary production.

Arana's current style is to some extent surreal. It takes realities from this world and transforms them into artificial, impossible, or surreal ones. His art shares elements of the world where the artist has lived but the artist adds surreal elements to it, such as naked figures in a frigid or dormant state, figures dancing valses and heads with exposed skulls and brains. Arana's work from this period is highly praised and acclaimed. It commands great prices in art galleries. His paintings have been exhibited by the Institute of Puerto Rican Culture and by very prestigious galleries in Europe and America. A peculiar biographic fact about this painter is that he uses and signs his art work under the name of Arana, his mother's maiden name, instead of using his father's name, Meléndez. He has recently established the Alfonso Arana Foundation to mentor young artists from Puerto Rico in France.

SUGGESTED READING

Peter Bloch, *Painting and Culture of the Puerto Ricans* (New York: Plus Ultra, 1978); Alejandro Colunga, "Arana" *Latin American Art 5*, no. 4 (1994): 9; Juan Antonio Gaya-Nuño, *La Pintura Puertorriqueña* (Soria, Spain: Centro de Estudios Sorianos, 1994).

Arce de Vázquez, Margot (1904–1990) Margot Arce de Vázquez, who was a writer and teacher, was born in Caguas. Outstanding both as a teacher and a literary critic, Arce de Vázquez, like her colleague **Concha Meléndez**, focused much of her writing on literary criticism and analysis of Latin American literature. In 1926 she was appointed a faculty member of the newly created Department of Hispanic Studies at the **University of Puerto Rico**. Later, she served as chair of the department from 1943 to 1965.

Her book *Impresiones* has been described by **María Teresa Babín Cortés** and others as a key text contributing to culture and the literary knowledge in the island. The book is a collection of essays that depict contemporary life in Puerto Rico. Not an overt politician, she nevertheless succeeds in documenting the political strife of the times as well as affirming, as she viewed it, the elements of nature and culture that distinguish and strengthen the Puerto Rican character.

Her book on the Spanish poet Gracilaso de la Vega (1930) is considered a classic scholarly work in the area of Spanish renaissance literature. Also significant is her 675-page volume on the literary work of **José de Diego**, one of Puerto Rico's most outstanding literary and political figures. Sponsored by the Puerto Rican Institute of Culture, this work represents the most exhaustive of its kind. Her book included the study of his life, writings and political views. In her analysis of de Diego and his work, she suggests that his literary talents have been overshadowed by the overwhelming interest in his involvement as a political thinker and leader of his times. Arce de Vázquez's great body of work is still used by scholars and students of Latin American literature.

Other accomplishments include becoming one of the founders of the Puerto Rican Academy of Spanish and being honored with the title of professor emeritus upon her retirement from the University of Puerto Rico in 1970. In addition, her works *Garcilaso de la Vega* (1931) and *Gabriela Mistral* (1958) received the Institute of Puerto Rican Literature Award.

SUGGESTED READING

Margot Arce de Vázquez, *Impresiones: Notas Puertorriqueñas*, (San Juan, P.R.: Editorial Yaurel, 1950); Margot Arce de Vázquez, *La obra literaria de José de Diego* (San Juan, P.R.: Instituto de Cultura Puertorriqueña, 1967); Margot Arce de Vázquez, "La niña de Guatemala," *Revista de Estudios Hispánicos* 1, 3–4 (1971); Margot Arce de Vázquez, "Los soles truncos: Comedia trágica de René Marqués," *Sin Nombre* 10, 3 (1979); Luis de Arrigoitia, *La ejemplaridad en Margot Arce de Vázquez* (San Juan, P.R.: Fundación Felisa Rincón de Gautier, 1992); Francisco Cabrera Manrique, *Historia de la literatura puertorriqueña* (Río Piedras, P.R.: Editorial Cultural, 1969); Dora I. Russell, "Mujeres ilustres de Puerto Rico," *El Mundo*, October 22, 1962, 18.

Arcelay de la Rosa, María Luisa (1893–1981)   A very successful industrialist and politician, Arcelay de la Rosa was the first woman in Puerto Rico to be elected to the legislature and the first female legislator in Latin America. She represented her native city, Mayagüez, from 1933 until 1940.

Her middle-class upbringing gave her the uncommon (for women of the time) opportunity to get a degree from the **University of Puerto Rico** in 1907. For five years, she practiced her profession as an English teacher; meanwhile, she began to hone her business skills by maintaining the accounts for a number of local businesses. At the age of twenty-two, she had saved enough money to start her own business, a factory dedicated to embroidery and other fine needlework. This investment came at a time when the island's needlework industry underwent significant growth. In the 1920s hundreds of American businessmen relocated their factories from the mainland to Puerto Rico, where they found a cheap labor force and collaboration of the government to manufacture garments that would later be exported to the United States. The needlework industry, which would become the business that employed the most women, also paid the lowest salaries. Arcelay de la Rosa was among the first and few women who at the time had the experience and capital needed for such a venture. She became not only a factory owner but a spokesperson and leader in the needlework industry.

Many island women find Arcelay de la Rosa a controversial figure. She was a woman of intelligence, ambition, vision and political astuteness; in this sense, she was a pioneer, immersing herself in business and political ventures that were almost exclusively dominated by males. However, because she showed little support for women in the labor movement—wages at her factory were no better than those paid by Americans—critics suggest that she lacked the empathy or compassion required to help produce serious social change for the masses of Puerto Rican women. For example, critics note that it was during her tenure in the legislature that the bill for universal voting rights was presented and approved. However, it was through the leadership of Bolívar Pagán, not Arcelay, that voting rights for all women were enacted. Moreover, even though her success at the ballot box was due to the great number of women who voted for her (in 1932 only literate women were allowed to vote), she actively lobbied against a minimum salary for female workers since this would threaten the economic stability of her own factories.

Arcelay de la Rosa is nevertheless a significant figure to many Puerto Ricans. She helped create one of the most important industries in Puerto Rico, and she employed thousands of women in the southwestern region that was the headquarters for the needlework industry.

SUGGESTED READING

Encyclopedia grandes mujeres de Puerto Rico (Hato Rey, P.R.: Ramallo Brothers Printing, 1975); Yamila Azize, *La mujer en la lucha* (Río Piedras, P.R.: Editorial Cultural, 1985).

Arriví, Francisco (1915–   ) Francisco Arriví, a playwright, poet and essay writer, has been one of the pillars of Puerto Rico's traditional **theater**. He was born in San Juan where he attended his elementary, junior and high schools. He graduated from the **University of Puerto Rico** in Río Piedras where he gained an undergraduate degree in education. He also attended Columbia University, where he completed graduate courses in theatrical direction and radio and theater scripting.

Arriví was the founder of *Tinglado Puertorriqueño,* one of the most active and prestigious theatrical production groups in the island. Among his plays are *Alumbramiento* (1945), *María soledad* (1947), *Club de Solteros* (1953), *Bolero y plenas* (1956), *Vejigantes* (1958) and *Sirena* (1959). His theatrical production explored contemporary themes of importance for Puerto Rican society and culture, creating a truly Puerto Rican theater. He also brought popular folklore to the stage and dared to explore race and racism. He worked for the Department of Education of the Commonwealth of Puerto Rico where he was a leader in the development of the School of the Air. Arriví directed the government radio station (WIPR) and the theater program at the Institute of Puerto Rican Culture, which sponsored many theater festivals in the island.

In addition to his work in theater, Arriví has been highly productive as a poet and as an essay writer. Among his poetry books are *Isla y nada* (1958), *Ciclo de lo ausente* (1962), and *Escultor de la sombra* (1965). He has authored essay books such as *Areyto mayor* (1966) and *Conciencia puertorriqueña del teatro contemporáneo* (1967).

SUGGESTED READING

Francisco Arriví, Conciencia puertorriqueña del teatro contemporaneo, 1937–1956 (San Juan: Instituto de Cultura Puertorriqueña, 1967); Matias Montes Huidoro, *Persona: Vida y Máscara en el Tearo Puertorriqueño* (San Juan: Centro de Estudios Avanzados de Puerto Rico y el Caribe, 1984); Rosalina Perales, *50 años de teatro puertorriqueño* (Mexico: Escenología A.C., 1996); Jordan Phillips, *Contemporary Puerto Rican Drama* (Madrid: Playor, 1973).

Arroyo de Colón, María (1908–1992) An educator and politician, originally from Comerío, Arroyo de Colón received her undergraduate degree in teaching from the **University of Puerto Rico** in 1937. From that time until 1956, she practiced her profession and occupied a number of different positions in the educational field. In addition to her experience as an elementary schoolteacher, Arroyo de Colón became a principal and then district assistant superintendent of schools. During these years, she also found time to fulfill the requirements for two master's degrees, one in Spanish (University of Puerto Rico, 1946) and another in education at New York University's School of Administration and Supervision, in 1952. Her distinguished career in the education field earned her the presidency of the Puerto Rico Association of Teachers in 1956.

In her thirteen-year tenure as president of the association, she worked to improve services and benefits for teachers particularly in retirement and health benefits as well as working conditions. One of her most important contributions during this time was the establishment of a retirement system for teachers. Arroyo de Colón was also a writer; as director of the association's publication *El Sol*, she had the opportunity to publish a number of educational and literary essays, among the most outstanding, a 1963 biography of a Puerto Rican poet titled *Vida y obra de Virgilio Dávila* (see **Virgilio Dávila**).

In 1968 she was elected to the senate. As a senator she continued to work for legislation to improve the educational system and the quality of and conditions for teachers who worked in it. As a legislator, she presided over the Commission on Instruction and Culture and also served on commissions that had oversight of commerce and industry as well as urban development. She was a member of the committee that produced the comprehensive study of Puerto Rico's educational system that eventually led to reforms and improvements in educational policies and programs.

SUGGESTED READING

Enciclopedia grandes mujeres de Puerto Rico (Hato Rey: Ramalle Brothers, 1975); Charles E. Miner, "Ofrecen homenaje a la compañera María Arroyo," *Revista de la Asociación de Maestros* (April 1956); Juan José Osuna, *A History of Education in Puerto Rico* (Río Piedras: University of Puerto Rico, 1949).

Ateneo Puertorriqueño, El   Founded in 1876, El Ateneo is an organization dedicated to the preservation and stimulation of Puerto Rican culture. In conversation, the word is generally pronounced in a tone that indicates both respect and admiration because El Ateneo has successfully played the same role in Puerto Rico for more than 120 years. It celebrates and preserves Puerto Rican culture by supporting and showcasting the significant work of anyone devoted to the creation of poetry, science, novels or controversial political thought. Indeed, when advocates of independence found few forums to display and discuss their work in the 1960s and 1970s, El Ateneo often provided an arena for the free discussion of ideas.

El Ateneo is an independent organization with no formal ties to government, business or religious organizations. It uses its donated funds to host exhibitions of island art, presentations of new books, performance of ballet, singing recitals, meetings of civic groups and conferences about any topics that could be of interest to the Puerto Rican people.

El Ateneo is housed in a building, located on the outskirts of Old San Juan, that is architecturally significant. The two-storied, white stucco exterior is accentuated by a series of Victorian supports—all painted black. At the entrance are six pillars decorated with the painted tiles that were, in the late nineteenth century, a hallmark of the best island architecture. Older homes in **Ponce**, for example, contain tiles on the stairways and doorways; but the display at El Ateneo, however, is deliberately pronounced. The exterior seems Moorish—like a palace in Algeria or Morocco—and, inside, the tiles continue as a design that acts as a wall frieze. The ceilings are high, fine wood is everywhere, and, scattered about the building, are mementos of illustrious Puerto Ricans. For example, one of the salons used for book presentations contains an exquisite library table once owned by **José de Diego.**

El Ateneo, which houses one of the best rare book collections in Puerto Rico, also publishes documents. See, for example, a pamphlet written by the Ateneo's director, Eduardo Morales Coll, entitled *Puerto Rico: A Boiling Pot* (El Ateneo, 1990).

Autonomic Charter   This charter, a landmark document in Puerto Rican political history, marks a significant grant of local power from Spain to her Puerto Rican colony. The charter, authorized by Spain on November 25, 1897, covered both Puerto Rico and Cuba. For the Spanish, was a concession to its Caribbean colonies; it represented a last ditch attempt to avoid U.S. intervention in the Cuban War for Independence. However, for Puerto Rico, the agreement represented a significant achievement for a politically divided island. Once the agreement went into effect, the elected representatives of Puerto Rico would become voting members of the Spanish Cortes; the island would have an elected House of Representatives and its Administrative Council would include eight elected and seven appointed (by the governor general) members. Finally, Article Ten of the Autonomic Charter made a very specific point: "Once approved by the Spanish Cortes, the Autonomic Charter could only be modified by legal means, and at the request of the Puerto Rican legislature."

This final clause has had significant repercussions for the last 100 years. When the United States conquered Puerto Rico and took control via negotiations with the Spanish government (see the **Treaty of Paris**), the United States disregarded the Autonomic Constitution in general and Article Ten in particular. Thus, from 1898 to the present, islanders who oppose U.S. colonial authority have always pointed to Article Ten as justification for even violent confrontations with U.S. authority. The argument made by, among others, the Nationalist leader **Pedro Albizu Campos** is that since the Puerto Rican legislature neither consented to, nor petitioned for, U.S. control, mainland officials have been violating international law since July 25, 1898, when U.S. soldiers invaded the island.

Critics of Albizu point out that the agreement never formally went into effect because the consequences of the Spanish-American War stopped its implementation. Thus, since the constitution was never a living reality, the United States broke no laws.

SUGGESTED READING

Ricardo E. Alegría, ed., *Temas de la historia de Puerto Rico* (San Juan: Center for Advanced Studies of Puerto Rico and the Carribean, 1988); Edward J. Berbusse, *The United States in Puerto Rico* (Chapel Hill: University of North Carolina Press, 1966); William D. Boyce, *United States Colonies and Dependencies* (New York: Rand McNally, 1914); Henry K. Caroll, *Report on the Island of Puerto Rico*

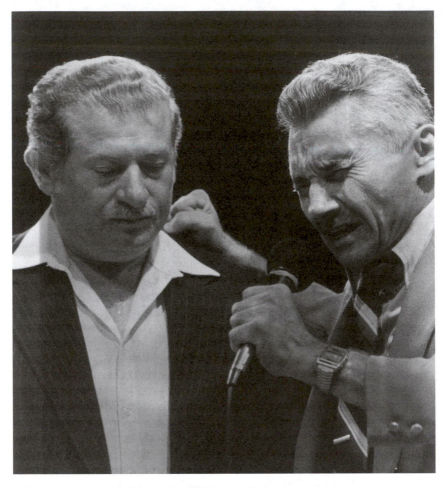

José "Yiye" Avila (*right*), 1981. (*El Nuevo Día.*)

(Washington, D.C.: U.S. Government Printing Office, 1899); Harold Lidin, *History of the Puerto Rican Independence Movement* (Hato Rey, P.R.: n.p., 1981); Kal Wagenheim, *Puerto Rico: A Profile* (New York: Praeger, 1974).

Avila, José Joaquín (1932–)   Evangelical leader and preacher, born in Camuy and known as Yiye, Avila is the most visible leader of the Pentecostal and evangelical religious movements on the island. A former athlete (weight lifter) and high school teacher, Avila has been involved in a very public ministry for the last thirty years. Using his ministry *Cristo Viene* (Christ is coming) as a tool for evangelism and the spread of the Gospel, Yiye preaches a strong rhetoric of fire and brimstone in which he exhorts his audiences to repent, accept the Christian message and convert. He is perhaps the best-known contemporary religious leader in Puerto Rico due to the pervasiveness of his message through the religious media. His message is broadcast every day to thousands of listeners through his *Cadena Cristo Viene* (Christ Is Coming Network) of radio and cable television stations. Using the religious crusades as a conversion tool, he takes his message of faith and healing to thousands of people in Puerto Rico, the United States, and Latin America every year. Avila, a man of strong views and opinions, often voices his beliefs on contemporary issues such as political events which are undoubtedly informed by his religious beliefs. He is highly respected by his followers, and perhaps feared, by many politicians and public figures possibly because he has a huge legion of followers whom he can mobilize easily. Like the Catholic cardinal, he has been a staunch critic of commercial television programming (he calls television sets Satan's boxes) and what he perceives as a general moral decadence in Puerto Rican society owing to a lack of religious values. He is a humble man with extraordinary charisma and rhetorical prowess.

SUGGESTED READING

Arthur James, *Progress and Promise in Puerto Rico* (New York: Board of National Missions of the Presbyterian Church in the U.S.A., n.d.); Emilio Pantojas Garcia, "La iglesia protestante y la americanización de Puerto Rico," *Ciencias Revista Sociales* 18 (June 1974): 99–121; Daniel R. Miller, *Coming of Age: Protestantism in Contemporary Latin America* (Lanham, Md.: University Press of America, 1994).

B

Babín Cortés, María Teresa (1910–1989)   Babín Cortés achieved prominence as a writer, educator, literary critic, biographer, poet and essayist. She completed her primary and secondary schooling in the southern towns of Puerto Rico: Yauco and **Ponce**. She completed her baccalaureate (1931) and master's (1939) degrees at the **University of Puerto Rico**. In 1954 Babín earned a doctoral degree from Columbia University in New York City. Her doctoral dissertation, *El mundo poético de Federico García Lorca* (The poetic world of Federico García Lorca), won the top award of the Institute of Puerto Rican Literature and was the first of her many books about García Lorca (*Federico García Lorca and his Work*, 1939; *García Lorca: His Life and Work*, 1955; *The Magic Prose of García Lorca*, 1962; and *Lorquiano Studies*, 1962). These books deservedly made her a major authority among critics in this field.

Her writings, which have been published in leading Latin American newspapers and journals, include literary, educational and political essays; however, Babín Cortés always made Puerto Rico, its culture and literature, an important theme of her literary work. Thus, in addition to her textbook *Introducción a la cultura hispánica* (Introduction to Hispanic culture, 1949), Babín's works include her more literary essays, "Fantasía Boricua" (Boricua fantasy, 1956) and "Panorama de la cultura puertorriqueña" (Panorama of Puerto Rican culture, 1958); her theatrical fables, *La hora colmada* (1960) and *La gesta de Puerto Rico* (The Puerto Rican feat, 1967); and her poetry collections, *Las voces de tu voz* (The voices of your voice, 1962) and *La barca varada* (The stranded boat, 1982). Among her other works are *The Puerto Rican's Spirit* (1970) and *Borinquen: An Anthology of Puerto Rican Literature*, coedited with Stan Steiner in 1974.

María Teresa Babín Cortés at Columbia University. (*El Nuevo Día*.)

She complemented her work as a writer by becoming one of the most prominent Puerto Rican educators. Although Babín taught at a number of major universities in the United States, it was Lehman College in New York City that provided her with an opportunity to apply her scholarship and expertise on Puerto Rico. She was a professor of Hispanic literature at the Graduate Center of CUNY and a professor of Puerto Rican studies at Lehman College beginning in the early 1960s. Babín was also the first director of Lehman College's Department of Puerto Rican Studies.

In recognition of her many literary and academic achievements, María Babín Cortés received an honorary doctoral degree from her alma mater, the University of Puerto Rico, in 1984.

SUGGESTED READING

María Teresa Babín, *The Culture of Puerto Rico* (New York: Aspira, Inc., 1960); María Teresa Babín, *The Puerto Ricans' Spirit: Their History, Life, and Culture* (New York: Collier Books; 1971); María Teresa Babín, *Borinquen: An Anthology of Puerto Rican Literature* (New York: Knopf, 1974); María Teresa Babín, "The Jibaro: Symbol and Synthesis," *Proceedings of the Comparative Literature Symposium*, Vol. 9, pps. 433–54, (1978); Arturo Morales Carrión, *Puerto Rico, A Political and Cultural History* (New York: W.W. Norton, American Association for State and Local History; 1983); Josefina Rivera, *Diccionario de literatura puertorriqueña* (Rio Piedras: Ediciones de la Torre, UPR, 1955).

Báez, Myrna (1931–) A plastic and graphic artist, painter and printmaker, Báez was born in Santurce and studied at the **University of Puerto Rico** at Río Piedras. Her early studies in painting were conducted under the tutelage of painters Juan Genovés and María Teresa Lomba. Following her desire to become a physician, Báez went to Madrid during the 1950s to study medicine. While she was there, she rediscovered her earlier love of painting. She abandoned her studies in medicine and joined the prestigious Real Academia de Bellas Artes San Fernando in Madrid where she studied for five years. After she returned to Puerto Rico, she joined **Lorenzo Homar**'s Graphic Art Workshops at the Institute of Puerto Rican Culture. During the 1960s she studied at the Pratt Graphic Art Center in New York City.

She has been acclaimed and recognized by art critics throughout the island and Latin America. Báez says she is a feminist and considers herself to be a nationalist painter. As an artist, she has been deeply involved in the political and social struggles of the island. She has said that she "paints with ideas about art from politics and Puerto Ricans" (Pérez-Lizano 1985, 286). Her art is very expressive. She is considered to be one of the leading contemporary Puerto Rican plastic and graphic artists. Art critic Hollister Sturges has said that "Báez's international fame rests primarily on her work as a printmaker" (Sturges 1990, 26). However, she uses many other artistic media, such as woodcut, oil and lithography. She also is a well-known muralist.

Myrna Báez, "Barrio Tokio." (Museo de Arte de Ponce, The Luis A. Ferré Foundation, Inc., Ponce, Puerto Rico.)

Her paintings and prints have received many prizes and honorific mentions both in Puerto Rico and abroad. These include Puerto Rican Athenaeum, for painting (1963, 1967) and for graphics (1970); Pratt Graphic Center, for Graphics, third prize (1975); *Revista sin nombre*, for painting (1974); Friends of UNESCO, University of Puerto Rico (1974); and third prize at the biennial of Cuenca, Ecuador (1987).

Some of her best works are *Palomar* (1960), *Muelle Portuario* (1963), *Barrio Tokio* (1962), *Los Ciclistas* (1967) and *El Mangle* (1977). Báez's paintings and prints have been exhibited in many private as well as public collections, such as the Metropolitan Museum of Art in New York, the Museo Casa de las Américas in Cuba, the Museo del Instituto de Cultura Puertorriqueña and the Ponce Art Museum. She has been a professor of art at many universities and colleges in Puerto Rico.

SUGGESTED READING

Peter Bloch, *Painting and Sculpture of the Puerto Ricans* (New York: Plus Ultra, 1978); Juan Antonio Gaya-Nuño, *La pintura puertorriqueña* (Soria, Spain: Centro de Estudios Sorianos, 1994); Museo de Arte de Ponce, *Colección de arte Latinoamericano* (Ponce: Museo de Arte de Ponce, n.d.); Manuel Pérez Lizano, *Arte Contemporáneo de Puerto Rico 1950–1983* (Bayamón: Universidad Central de Bayamón Ediciones Cruz Ansata, 1985); Beverly Peterson, "I Am a Woman First," *San Juan Star*, January 24, 1964; Myrna Rodríguez, "25 Years of Puerto Rican Painting," *San Juan Star*, April 6, 1986; Hollister Sturges, *New Art from Puerto Rico* (Springfield, Mass.: Springfield Museum of Fine Arts, 1990). Connie Underhill, "20th Century Artist," *San Juan Star*, February 22, 1965.

Baldorioty de Castro, Román (1822–1889) A teacher and also a prominent and influential politician in the latter half of the nineteenth century, Baldorioty was born in Guaynabo and died in **Ponce**. Educated in Spain and France, his vocation was teaching, and his achievements included founding the College of Ponce.

In Madrid, Baldorioty was one of the Puerto Ricans "distinguished by his dissatisfaction with the Spanish colonial government, by his independence aims, and by his Yankee ideas, which moved him in the direction of democracy" (Rosario, Díaz and Martínez 1975, 50–51). Baldorioty favored a form of autonomy based on the Canadian model. Baldorioty so upset the Spanish with his thirst for justice that they compiled a secret file on his activities.

He is best known in Puerto Rico as an able, just and artful conciliator. At the Ponce Assembly, held on March 6, 1887, that founded the Puerto Rican Autonomist party, the delegates harbored views that produced as much dissension as consensus. As elected president of the assembly, Baldorioty managed to create an atmosphere that moved the delegates to accept what were then controversial ideas—uniting with the Cuban Autonomist party to demand that Spain cede substantial political and economic powers to Puerto Rico and its *criollo* inhabitants. For his efforts, the Assembly gave a vote of thanks to Baldorioty for his selfless efforts in pursuit of the autonomist ideal. The Spanish responded by placing the sixty-six-year-old Baldorioty in **El Morro** during *los compontes* (the floggings).

Baldorioty refused to participate in the uprising of 1868, **Grito de Lares**, and some colleagues criticized him for being a reformer instead of a revolutionary.

SUGGESTED READING

Arturo Morales Carrión, *Puerto Rico: A Political and Cultural History* (New York: Norton, 1983); Loida Figueroa, *History of Puerto Rico* (New York: Anaya Books, 1974); Germán Delgado Pasapera, *Puerto Rico: Sus luchas emancipadoras* (San Juan, P.R.: Editorial Cultural, 1984); Rubén del Rosario, Esther Melón de Díaz, and Edgar Martínez Masdeu, *Breve enciclopedia de la cultura puertorriqueña* (San Juan, P.R.: Editorial Cordillera, 1976).

Balzac vs. People of Puerto Rico   Jesús Balzac was a plaintiff in one of the foremost U.S. Supreme Court decisions affecting Puerto Rico. In *Balzac vs. People of Puerto Rico*, the Court determined that, even though Puerto Ricans were U.S. citizens, the U.S. Constitution did not necessarily apply if a Puerto Rican was on the island.

Jesús Balzac edited a newspaper in Puerto Rico. In 1918 he published articles that were called libelous. He was found guilty in a Puerto Rican court but, because he never received the jury trials he demanded, Balzac contended that the court had violated his Sixth Amendment, the U.S. Constitutional right to a jury trial.

The case acquired great significance because it occurred after U.S. citizenship was granted in 1917. Now that Puerto Ricans were American citizens, did the entire Constitution apply on the island? Writing for the majority, Chief Justice of the Supreme Court William Taft argued that "when Porto Ricans [see **Porto Rico**] passed from under the government of Spain, they lost the protection of that government as subjects of the King of Spain, a title by which they had been known for centuries. They had a right to expect, in passing under the dominion of the United States, a status entitling them to the protection of their new sovereign." Balzac had to understand, however, that Puerto Rico remained an unincorporated part of the United States. If Congress wanted to change things in 1917 they would have made their intentions clear; it was, after all, a significant step "to incorporate in the Union these distant ocean communities of a different origin and language from those of our continental people."

Balzac did not have the right to a jury trial because "it is locality that is determinative of the application of the Constitution, in such matters as civil

Pilar Barbosa de Rosario with a bust of her father, José Celso Barbosa, 1990. (Laura Magruder and *El Nuevo Dia.*)

procedure, and not the status of the people who live in it." Decided in 1922, *Balzac vs. People of Puerto Rico*, the last of the **Insular Cases**, underlined that the grant of citizenship did not alter Puerto Rico's fundamental status. The island and its inhabitants remained outside the mainstream of "continental" political life because, as Chief Justice Taft stressed, "Incorporation has always been a step, and an important one, leading to statehood."

SUGGESTED READING

Balzac vs. People of Puerto Rico, 258 U.S. 298 (1922); also Manuel Maldonado-Denis, *Puerto Rico: A Socio-Historic Interpretation* (New York: Vintage, 1972).

Banco Popular   *See* Carrión Pacheco, Rafael.

Bando contra la Raza Africana   *See* Edict against the African Race.

Barbosa de Rosario, Pilar (1897–1997)   Born and raised in San Juan, Barbosa de Rosario distinguished herself as historian and author. She completed her undergraduate studies in education at the **University of Puerto Rico** in 1924 and graduated from Clark University in 1926 with a master's degree in history and international relations.

She began her teaching career in the public school system of the island teaching at the Román Baldorioty de Castro School from 1917 to 1922, and for the next two years at Central High School in Santurce. From there, she went on to teach at the University of Puerto Rico where, during her forty-one-year tenure (1926–1967), her prolific career included research, publications, administration and teaching. Her appointment to the University faculty in 1926 was a historic occasion for she was the first woman designated to a professorial rank and later chairperson of a department in the university's School of Liberal Arts. Three years later, she established the Department of History and Social Sciences and headed a university reform initiative that resulted in the establishment of the History Department, separate from the social sciences and integrated into the Division of Humanities (the Facultad de Humanidades). She served as chair of the History Department from 1929 until 1943. During her tenure as chair, history of Puerto Rico became a required course for graduation for all students, a practice that later was discontinued.

As the heir to her father José Celso Barbosa's personal papers and writings, she organized and compiled these into a series of historic documents that include *Post umbra, problema de razas* (1937), *Orientando al pueblo* (1939, 1987), and *Barbosa, pionero del cooperativismo* (1982). As a historian, she focused her own historiography on researching the origins of the autonomist doctrine in the political discourse of the island, as well as the political writings of her father and his collaborators. Among her publications in this field, she has produced four books that have received the Institute of Puerto Rican Literature Award: *De Baldorioty a Barbosa* (1975, 1986); *La comisión autonomista* (1957), *La política en dos tiempos, "aletofobia"* (1978); *Manuel F. Rossy y Calderón, cuidadano cabal* (1981, 1991), and *Raíces del proceso político puertorriqueño* (1984). These writings approach the autonomist perspective from a different point of view. Her father was the founder of the Republican party and an advocate of statehood for the island. Barbosa de Rosario presents a historiography that examines the other side of the independence issue through the documentation of the ideology and political history of the pro-statehood movement and the Republican party in Puerto Rico.

Through her nineties, she continued to write and publish. A compilation of her father's journalistic writings and another work based on his letters were in progress at the time of her death. The University of Puerto Rico has honored her with the distinction of Professor Emeritus and an honorary doctoral degree in 1992.

SUGGESTED READING

Tío Aurelio, "Semblanza de la Dra. Pilar Barbosa de Rosario," *Revista de la Academia de Artes y Ciencias de Puerto Rico* 1, no. 1 (1986): 118–21; Rosario Barbosa de Pilar, *La obra de José Celso Barbosa* (San Juan: Imprenta, Venezuela, 1937).

Barbosa, José Celso (1857–1921)   Barbosa, a prominent politician and physician who was born in Bayamon and died in San Juan, was educated at the University of Michigan and devoted himself to medicine and government. Under the Spanish, he was an advocate of autonomy and a member of the cabinet that was to take charge under the **Autonomic Constitution**.

When the United States invaded Puerto Rico, Barbosa founded the Republican party, an organization devoted to obtaining statehood for the island. He was a member of the powerful **Executive Council** during the first years of the U.S. administration, and he was elected a senator when the **Jones Act** made the Puerto Rican senate an elective body.

In an essay written in 1907, Barbosa touched on an issue that still divides the Puerto Rican people. Explaining his advocacy of statehood in terms of the number of new rights granted by the Americans—"a greater number than in many independent Latin American nations"—he stressed that he saw no contradiction between being a Puerto Rican and an American. "It is evident," he wrote, "that neither the New Yorker nor the Texan had to sacrifice a whit (*un ápice*) of their local patriotism as a consequence of forming part of the United States" (Barbosa, 1987, p. 73).

SUGGESTED READING

José Celso Barbosa, "Conversación Familiar," *Las ideas anexionistas en Puerto Rico bajo la dominación norteamericana*, ed. Aarón Gamaliel Ramos (San Juan: Huracán, 1987).

Barceló, Antonio R. (1868–1938)   A prominent political figure his entire life, Barceló was born in Fajardo and died in San Juan. He received a law degree from Columbia University, but his passion was politics. His career spanned a series of dramatic events in Puerto Rico's political history. He was, for example, a director of the Autonomist party before the U.S. invasion, he was a founder of the Federal party (later the **Union party**) in 1899, he served in the House of Delegates until 1917, and, with the changes wrought by the Jones Law, he not only became a senator, he chaired the Senate from 1917 to 1930. As a member of the Union party, Barceló favored either independence or some form of associated autonomy. However, after the bitter attacks made against independence by Governor **E. Montgomery Reilly** from 1921 to 1923, Barceló headed the **Alliance party** (La alianza), a political organization that removed independence as an option in order to placate both Governor Reilly and the U.S. Congress. As he told a House Committee in 1924, "the reasonable and logical system would be a regime that would associate us to you, in a permanent and indestructible manner, in the form of an unincorporated State, that would function just as one of your own free States, within the sovereignty symbolized by the flag and by the citizenship that you have already granted us." When La alianza collapsed in 1929, Barceló directed the Liberal party in a manner that generally advocated independence. However, from 1936 to 1938 he and **Luis Muñoz Marín** fought over their stand on the **Tydings Bill**, which offered Puerto Rico independence in four years, and over control of the Liberal party's machinery. Barceló won this internal battle when, like the Unionists a decade earlier, the Liberal party removed independence from its political platform. Muñoz then formed the Popular Democratic party, and, with Barceló's death in 1938, the Liberals soon lost their political and practical influence in Puerto Rican politics.

SUGGESTED READING

Robert W. Anderson, *Party Politics in Puerto Rico* (Stanford, Calif.: Stanford University Press, 1965); Thomas Matthews, *Puerto Rican Politics and the New Deal* (Gainesville: University of Florida Press, 1960).

Bartolomé de las Casas, Fray   Fray Bartolomé was a Spanish priest who, in the 1500s, raised significant moral questions about the Spanish treatment of the Indians and Africans (see **African Roots**). When Christopher Columbus came to the Americas, he bore a letter from Pope Alexander VI: Everything Columbus found on his voyage to the Indies belonged to the Spanish monarchs and to their heirs and successors. In the name of God, only the Spanish could develop the countries, islands and people discovered by the explorers.

Although the idea was to convert the natives, the Spanish, instead, either killed or enslaved them. Soon, conditions were so terrible that some of the Dominican priests accompanying the Spanish began to confront a series of crucial questions and contradictions: with what right and with what form of justice did the Spanish treat these Indians with such cruelty and with horrible servitude? Fray Bartolomé de las Casas was perhaps the most eloquent of the priests who boldly and bitterly criticized the Spanish. In one passage he notes "that we have usurped all the rights and lands of the Indians . . . thus they have the right to make war against us and to scrap us from the face of the earth, and this right will last until the day justice makes an appearance" (Lewis 1983, 50).

In explaining his anger, Bartolomé made an argument that was based on the teachings of Christianity: All the people of the world were men. If one must love one's enemy as one's self, how is it possible to defend the cruelty of the Spanish? When Bartolomé could find no justification, he went to Spain, where he complained to officials and offered this alternative: Since Negro slaves from Africa did not fall under the "we are all men" concept, replace the Indians with African slaves (see **Slavery**). Although for the Africans transported against their will, it was a terrible solution, Bartolomé nevertheless stands out as someone who, from the onset of European colonization, raised some otherwise neglected crucial moral questions. He and his religious colleagues did mitigate the harsh treatment accorded the Indians, and, by the time of his death, Bartolomé argued that, in the eyes of God, *all* people deserved the same treatment. He repented his suggestion of replacing one form of slavery with another. In a period full of cruelty, he stands out as a voice of the Catholic God: This is wrong. We are the sinners.

SUGGESTED READING

Arturo Morales Carrión, *Puerto Rico and the Non-Hispanic Caribbean* (Río Piedras: University of Puerto Rico, 1971); Gordon Lewis, *Main Currents in Caribbean Thought* (Baltimore: Johns Hopkins, 1983); Fernando Picó, *Historia general de Puerto Rico* (San Juan, P.R.: Huracán, 1988).

Baseball   Baseball or *beisbol* is a very popular sport in Puerto Rico. Emilio Huyke, a sports historian, traced the origins of baseball in the island to the children of a Spanish military officer who was stationed in Cuba before coming to Puerto Rico during the Spanish-American War (Huyke 1968, 79). Julio Rúiz Laabe, who studied the early history of the sport in Puerto Rico, provides us with a more detailed account. Its birth goes back to the year 1896 in the area of Puerta de Tierra in San Juan. Amos Iglesias, a Cuban who had migrated to the island, along with Braulio Sánchez, a Puerto Rican, organized the teams *Borinquen* (made up of Puerto Ricans), and *Almendares* (made up mostly of Cubans). The first presentation of the sport was in 1897 on the grounds where the Carnegie Library now stands in San Juan. Their first official debut was in 1898. After the United States took over Puerto Rico that same year, the league was reorganized and new teams began to appear. One of these teams was Company L from the 50th Infantry Division of the American army. By 1909 baseball fields were constructed around the island; the Charles H. Terry field in **Ponce** was one of the first (Rúiz Laabe 1997). World War I boosted the growth and development of the sport in the island. Several new local teams appeared. Islandwide tournaments were held and hosted teams from the island, the Caribbean and the United States (Huyke 1968, 79).

The golden age of baseball in Puerto Rico is marked by the decades of the 1930s and 1940s. The first semiprofessional baseball league was founded in 1938 by Enrique Huyke, a college professor, and Teófilo Maldonado, a journalist. It was made up of seven teams from San Juan, Caguas, Guayama, Ponce, Humacao, and Mayagüez. In 1939, Aguadilla and Santurce joined the league. In 1943, Humacao and Guayama quit playing and began the professional league with Caguas-Guayama as one team, and Aguadilla joined Mayagüez.

The professional league continues to play today. The teams that constitute the league now are the *Senadores* from San Juan, *Cangrejeros* from

Santurce, *Criollos* from Caguas, *Leones* from Ponce, *Indios* from Maya-güez, and *Lobos* from Arecibo. They are associated with the major leagues in the United States and follow most of their rules and regulations since many of their players also play in the United States during their baseball season. The Puerto Rican professional tournament runs from the end of October to the end of February.

In 1954 a Double A, or semiprofessional league, was established. It is divided in four sections of eight teams each. There is a juvenile category for men between fifteen and eighteen years of age, several teen leagues for boys between thirteen and fourteen, and the minor leagues for small boys.

Puerto Rico has produced many important baseball players. Hiram Bithorn, the first Puerto Rican baseball player to play in the American major leagues; **Roberto Clemente**; Francisco "Paquito" Montaner; Francisco "Pancho" Coímbre; Luis Rodríguez Olmo; Luis A. Canena Márquez; Orlando "Peruchín" Cepeda; and Carlos Bernier are some of them.

According to Felix Cardona Quiñones, an official at the Baseball Federation of Puerto Rico, the sport continues to grow in popularity today (Felix Cardona Quiñones 1997). As the oldest established sport, it has a solid legion of fans that follow their teams wherever they play. There are large commercial interests that fuel the professional league; however, profit-making has not distorted its entertainment value as it has happened in the United States.

SUGGESTED READING

Felix Cardona-Quiñones, personal interview (March 28, 1997); Emilio Huyke, *La historia del deporte en Puerto Rico* (Sharon, Conn.: Troutman Press, 1968); Julio Ruiz, personal interview and notes (March 1997); Jaime Varas, *Enciclopedia deportiva Boricua* (Hato Rey: Ramallo Bros. Printing, 1984).

Basketball   Centuries before basketball arrived in the island with its American configuration, there was a traditional Taíno sport that resembled basketball. Today basketball has become the national sport for Puerto Ricans. Emilío Huyke, a noted authority on the history of sports in the island, tracked the origins of basketball to 1902 when it was imported by staffers from the Young Men's Christian Association (YMCA) (Huyke 1968, 59). The Superior Basketball League was created in 1929 and established the National Basketball Championships, which have been played without interruption since then. Fufi Santori, a retired professor of physical education and an important media commentator, has identified many important highlights in the history of the sport since its arrival in the island (Santori 1997).

The decade of the 1950s is considered to be the era of superior basketball in the island. At the time, there was a transition in the sport from an older style of playing to a newer one. Raúl "Tinajón" Feliciano, inducted in the Puerto Rican Basketball Hall of Fame in 1967, was a central agent in this revitalization process. Some of the changes were the introduction of the "jump shot," and more dynamic and aggressive offensive and defensive moves. During that time, many star players and coaches of American basketball went to the island and trained Puerto Rican players and coaches with new techniques. Among these were Tex Winters, John Bach, Lou Rossini, and Red Houseman.

The popularity of the sport in Puerto Rico grew astronomically during the 1970s, due in part to the role of television in broadcasting the sport. Since then, basketball has become the most often viewed sport event in the island. Basketball slang terms such as "Apúntalo!" (score it!) have made their way into the folk language of Puerto Ricans. The sport is a cultural event that provides a platform for social interaction.

One of the most significant aspects of basketball in Puerto Rico is its intensity. The basic championship tournament runs approximately ninety days. It starts in the beginning of May and lasts until the end of July. After that, it moves into the semifinal and the final stages. The eighteen teams that constitute the league now play consecutively almost every day during the season. The Basketball Federation of Puerto Rico rules and regulates basketball. The federation is a hybrid between a public and private corporation. Like the United States, the sport is starting to gain commercial support reflected in the increasing salaries of the players, which can range anywhere between $4,000 and $80,000 per season.

There have been many stars in Puerto Rican basketball throughout the years. Some of them are Raúl Feliciano (Río Piedras), Pachín Vicens (**Ponce**), Raymond Dalmau and Neftalí Rivera (Quebradillas), Teo Crúz (Santurce), Armandito Torres and Piculín Ortiz (San Germán), Mario Morales (Guaynabo), and Rúben Rodríguez (Bayamón). Two of the largest sports coliseums in the island are named after basketball stars: Pachín Vicens and Rúben Rodríguez.

SUGGESTED READING

Emilio Huyke, *La historia del deporte en Puerto Rico* (Sharon, Conn.: Troutman Press, 1968); Fufi Santori, personal interview and notes (March 1997); Raymond Stewart, *El baloncesto en San Germán* (San Germán: First Book Publishing of Puerto Rico, 1994); Jaime Varas, *Enciclopedia deportiva Boricua* (Hato Rey: Ramallo Bros. Printing, 1984).

Belaval, Emilio (1903–1972)   Belaval, a writer and lawyer, was born in Fajardo, a small town in the northeastern corner of the island, the youngest child in a large family. His father was a Spaniard that came to Puerto Rico and his mother was Puerto Rican. Belaval went to elementary school in Fajardo and later graduated from high school in San Juan. He enrolled in the **University of Puerto Rico** in Río Piedras, where he graduated with a law degree in 1927.

Belaval is considered to be one of the premier writers of the **Generation of the Thirties**, particularly for his contributions to the genre of Puerto Rican short story. He started writing short stories for *Puerto Rico Ilustrado* when he was still a youngster. Some of these were to appear later in his *Cuentos de la Universidad* (1935). He was also an essayist and published *Los problemas de la cultura puertorriqueña* (1935) and *Lo que podría ser un teatro puertorriqueño* (1935).

His legacy to the theater and playwriting is considered significant. He was the founder of the Sociedad Teatral Areyto, a leading theatrical group in the island. In addition, he wrote several plays. Among them are *La romanticona* (1926), *La vida* (1953), *La muerte* (1953) and *Hacienda de los cuatro vientos* (1959).

Belaval had a distinguished career as a lawyer. He was a judge in the Bayamón District Court and an associate justice of the Supreme Court of Puerto Rico. He was a member of the Counsel for Higher Learning and a president of **El Ateneo**.

SUGGESTED READING

Flavia Lugo de Marichal, *Belaval y sus "Cuentos para fomentar el turismo"* (San Juan: Editorial El Coquí, 1972); Flavia Lugo de Marichal, *Spanish American Authors: The Twentieth Century*, Angel Flores, ed. (New York: Wilson, 1992); Emilio Belaval, *Cuentos: An Anthology of Puerto Rican Short Stories*, Karl Wagenheim, ed. (San Juan: Instituto de Cultura Puertorriqueña, 1971).

Benítez, Luz Esther (Lucesita) (?–   )   A popular Puerto Rican singer, Lucesita Benítez was the product of *La Nueva Ola* (or new wave) musical movement in Puerto Rico during the 1960s.

She started her singing career in 1964 and became one of the many teen idols whose careers were launched by Alfred D. Herger and Paquito Cordero through their noontime television shows aired by WKAQ-TV and through their recording label Rico-Vox. Dressed in go-go attire, Lucesita sang popular tunes from the "Hit Parade," among them "Acompáñame," "Hablemos del amor" and "Todas las Mañanas." In 1969 she won the First World Festival of Latin American Music with her interpretation of "Genesis." This award gave her career a boost.

During the 1970s, Benítez's style underwent a radical transformation. She became associated with the political pro-independence movement and started to sing protest songs dealing with political and social issues that affected the island. Wearing a signature Afro and assuming a more confrontational and combative artistic style, she distanced herself from the mainstream musical and artistic establishment. Although she was ignored and shunned by the media, she gained a new legion of admirers and followers.

As an artist, she has gone through several artistic transformations that have turned her into one of the most popular and respected performers of

Lucesita Benítez in concert, 1991. (*El Nuevo Día.*)

the island. Benítez's style has evolved further and she now interprets a broad range of music that reflects both the romantic and patriotic elements of Puerto Rican and Latin American music. She is one of the most admired, appreciated and valued performing artists in the island, a sort of Puerto Rican singer laureate.

SUGGESTED READING

Javier Santiago, *Nueva ola portorricensis: la revolución musical que vivió Puerto Rico en la decada del 60* (Santurce: Editorial del patio, 1994).

Benítez Rexach, Jaime (1908–)   A distinguished educator and politician, he is best remembered for his work and legacy to the **University of Puerto Rico** at Río Piedras (1931–1966). From his different positions as a professor in the school of social sciences, chancellor and president of the University of Puerto Rico (1966–1972), he shaped the vision, mission and structure of the university. He contributed to the creation of the university as a center for academic excellence for all Puerto Ricans to prepare them for the many challenges and professions that had opened up as a result of the social, political and economic changes Puerto Rico underwent after the 1940s. He was also instrumental in opening the doors of the university to welcome many illustrious Spanish scholars fleeing from the Franco regime in Spain and later to many Cuban academics fleeing from Fidel Castro's revolution. Among them was Nobel laureate Juan Ramón Jímenez.

Benítez was a close friend and collaborator of **Luis Muñoz Marín**; however, that never stopped the two men from having many differences of opinions and confrontations. He was part of the Constitutional Assembly that drafted the Constitution of Puerto Rico under the commonwealth. After his retirement from the University of Puerto Rico, Benítez became openly involved in party politics with the **Popular Democratic party**. He served as Puerto Rico's **resident commissioner** in Washington, D.C., from 1972 to 1976. Although he is remembered as a leading figure in creating the university as we know it today, he is also remembered for his tight-fisted ruling of the institution and his lack of tolerance for people who disagreed with his political philosophy. Benítez is a distinguished scholar, and his work on Spanish philosopher and writer José Ortega y Gassett is known throughout the Hispanic world.

SUGGESTED READING

Jaime Benítez, *Etica y estilo de la universidad* (Madrid: Aguilar, 1964); Jaime Benítez, *The U.S., Cuba and Latin America: An Occasional Paper on the Free Society* (Río Piedras: University of Puerto Rico Office of Information, 1961).

Benítez Rivera, Celeste (1935–)   A journalist and politician, Celeste Benítez began her career teaching at the **University of Puerto Rico**'s Humacao

Regional College and Arecibo Regional College, and she has been, since 1972, a faculty member of the main campus of the university. Benítez, a native of the San Juan metropolitan area, came from a family who were strong supporters of and activists in **Luis Muñoz Marín**'s 1940s and 1950s campaign for commonwealth status for Puerto Rico and the governorship. Having grown up in a political environment seems to have given her a strong sense of history and its role in a country's governmental system.

One of her first major efforts in the political arena came in 1972 when she organized the largest political gathering in the island's history. Thousands of people gathered on October 8 at the Plaza las Américas, the largest shopping mall on the island at the time, to rally the **Popular Democratic party**'s (PPD) candidate for governor, **Rafael Hernández Colón.** This gathering also saw one of the final addresses made by the former governor and founder of the Commonwealth of Puerto Rico, Luis Muñoz Marín. That same year, she was named secretary of education by Governor Hernández Colón and served in that capacity for two years. She quickly initiated what would be one of the most extensive educational reform initiatives in the history of the Island. Her plan called for a change from the semester system to a system of *quinmestres* (literally, the school year was divided into five periods of forty-five days each); one advantage for students was that, instead of a summer break, they could elect to take their vacation in any one of the forty-five-day periods. The proposed plan for this project presented a rationale that included a more effective evaluation of students; it also included a strategy that provided students with a highly diverse curriculum and smaller classes.

In 1976, while the political party with which she was affiliated lost the governorship, she won her senate seat, receiving the highest number of votes by accumulation. At the same time, she was named alternate whip or speaker of the minority in the Senate. In addition, she was a candidate for mayor of San Juan in 1980 but lost to the incumbent, Hernán Padilla. After her unsuccessful attempt at electoral politics, she temporarily retired from political life. During that time, she returned to her teaching position at the University of Puerto Rico.

Celeste Benítez has also had a successful career in journalism. Throughout the years, she has often made televised appearances as a political commentator, as a columnist for **El Nuevo Día**, and a director of the now defunct newspaper *El Reportero*. Her political columns gained notoriety and criticism, but they were regarded as objective, even when, on a number of occasions, she was critical of her own party and its leaders. This is particularly unusual in Puerto Rico where politics are extremely partisan, and publicly criticizing a member of one's own party is not common. Her journalism has been described by another journalist as follows: "The pro-commonwealth leader exposed the ideas in her columns and television programs with clarity and organization that have gained praise from persons outside her political party. . . . And it's that Benítez gets to the point and can be biting" (Mulero 1995, 10).

Her reappearance in the political arena came as a result of a request made by Miguel Hernández Agosto, then the president of the PPD, for her to become the secretary of the Senate. She served in that capacity until 1990, when Hernández Colón appointed her secretary of education, a post she had originally held in 1972. She served briefly until December 1992, when the PPD lost the elections.

In 1993 she undertook an activity that rivaled the 1972 rally. She spearheaded the PPD's pro-commonwealth campaign within the plebiscite that was held in 1993, and here the commonwealth status was affirmed by the voters. In June 1995, she led one of the most successful televised marathons during which more than $900,000 was raised to help the PPD eradicate the large debt that resulted from the plebiscite efforts. She has been hailed not only as a skilled politician, but also as an outstanding organizer: "Part of her secret is the capacity [she has] to assemble first rate working teams. For the plebiscite, she found a team of young people who gave the PPD a new image" (Mulero 1995, 10).

In 1995, following in the steps of her uncle and hero **Jaime Benítez Rexach**, who had been the **resident commissioner** of Puerto Rico from 1972 to 1976, Celeste Benítez announced her candidacy for that position in the 1996 elections. She lost to **Carlos Romero Barceló** in November 1996; 49.9 percent of the vote went to Romero, and 46 percent of the vote went to Benítez.

SUGGESTED READING

Celeste Benítez, "Perspectiva: Llegó la hora," *El Nuevo Día*, May 25, 1995; Leonor Mulero, "Pruebas de fuego en la vida política de Benítez," *El Nuevo Día*, June 25, 1995, 10; Margarita Ostolaza, *Política sexual* (San Juan, P.R.: Ediciones Huracán 1989); Roberto F. Rexach Benitez and Celeste Benitez, *Puerto Rico, 1964: A People at the Crossroads* (Humacho, P.R.: University of Puerto Rico Press, 1964).

Benítez y Arce de Gautier, Alejandrina (1819–1889)   This poet, born in Mayagüez, was first exposed to poetry by her aunt **María Bibiana Benítez y Constanza**, who raised her from infancy after her mother's death and adopted her. Literature was at the center of most of the activities in the Benítez y Constanza household, particularly the *tertulias*, or gatherings, of the elite for evenings of music, poetry or political discussions.

In 1843 Alejandrina Benítez y Arce de Gautier published her first poems in *Aguinaldo Puertorriqueño*, the first anthology of Puerto Rican poets ever published. In this collection of Puerto Rican verse and prose, Benítez y Arce de Gautier was one of three women whose work was included; also included was the work of her aunt María Bibiana Benítez. Although she was very much influenced by, and reflected, the European Romantic movement of the times, the themes of her work take place on the island. She continued her involvement in other editions of *Aguinaldo Puertorriqueño* and published one of her most famous poems in the 1846 edition. In "La cabaña afortunada," considered her ode to Puerto Rico and one of her best works, she praises the countryside by exposing the Puerto Rican habitat and integrating many of the elements of flora and fauna into the entirety of the work.

Most of her poetry reflects the melancholy so characteristic of the Romantic lyricism of that era. During the period from 1843 to 1846, her poetry displayed an aura of disillusion and pessimism, a lack of conformity with life that was also characteristic of the Romantic lyricists. During the years from 1846 to 1879, considered her second and more developed writing period, she achieved her pinnacle and was recognized as an outstanding poet. It was also a time when her poetry seemed to mature to a higher level of consciousness, and she brought out themes more closely related to historical contexts and patriotism. Poems such as "La patria del genio" and "El cable submarino" are some examples of her work during this period.

In 1851 she married Rodulfo Gautier y de Castro and had four children. Her only son, **José Gautier Benítez**, became one of Puerto Rico's most outstanding poets and thinkers. In 1863 she participated in a poetry contest honoring the Puerto Rican painter **José Campeche** with what came to be an award-winning poem, "La patria del genio" (The native land of the genius).

SUGGESTED READING

Emilio Colón, *Aguinaldo puertorriqueño, colección de producciones originales en prosa y verso* (San Juan, P.R.: Editorial Coguí, 1968); Socorro Giron, *Vida y obra de María Bibiana Benítez y Alejandrina Benítez* (San Juan: Instituto Cultura, 1967); Angela Negrón Muñoz, *Mujeres de Puerto Rico desde el principio de la colonización hasta el proma tercio del siglo xx* (San Juan: Imprenta Venezuela, 1935); Cesáreo Rosa-Nieves, *Plumas estelares en las letras de Puerto Rico*, vol. 1 (San Juan, P.R.: Ediciones de la Torre, 1967);

Benítez y Constanza, María Bibiana (1783–1873) A poet and playwright, Benítez y Constanza was, in the early nineteenth century, one of only a handful of educated Puerto Rican women. It is all the more remarkable, then, that she still stands out as an important contributor to the cultural and intellectual life of Puerto Rico. She was born in Aguadilla to a well-to-do family and grew up in a household surrounded by books and frequent gatherings of the island's intellectual elite. These gatherings, or *tertulias*, would continue throughout her life, furnishing her with one of the best vehicles for her literary and political expression.

Benítez y Constanza's work marks the beginning of the poetic era (1843–1880) known in Puerto Rico as Romanticism. She distinguished herself as a lyric poet whose political ideals and love of country were reflected in her work. Considered the first female poet in Puerto Rico, she was also among the first Puerto Ricans to gain island-wide recognition; her works were printed on some of the first commercial printing presses set up on the island. The publication in 1843 of *Aguinaldo Puertorriqueño*, a Christmas collection of works by poets of the time, marked an important historical landmark: for the first time, the works of three women writers were included, the most outstanding of them all—María Bibiana Benítez.

She was the first of a family of writers and poets. Her nephew, **José Gautier Benítez**, was one of Puerto Rico's most outstanding Romantic poets; during his childhood and adolescence, Gautier was greatly influenced by Bibiana, his great aunt. It was through her and his mother, **Alejandrina Benítez Arce de Gautier**, a poet in her own right, that his mind was opened to the lyrical world.

María Bibiana Benítez y Constanza's work was never limited to poetry. She also distinguished herself as a playwright. Among her more outstanding plays is *La cruz del Morro* (1862), which celebrates the eventual defeat of the Dutch against **El Morro** castle in 1625.

SUGGESTED READING

María Teresa Babín, *Panorama de la cultura puertorriqueña* (New York: Las Americas Publishing, 1958); Socorro Girón, *Vida y obra de María Bibiana y Alejandrina Benítez* (San Juan: Instituto de Culture, 1965); Donald E. Herdeck, *Caribbean Writers: A Bio-Bibliographical-Critical Encyclopedia* (Washington, D.C.: Three Continents Press, 1979); Federico Ribes Tovar, *The Puerto Rican Woman: Her Life and Evolution throughout History* (New York: Plus Ultra Educational Publishers, 1972).

Berriós Martínez, Rubén (1939–　　)　A lawyer and a politician, Berriós has been president of the **Puerto Rican Independence party** for more than twenty-five years, since 1970. Born in Aibonito, he received his B.A. from Georgetown University and a law degree from Yale University; he also studied at Oxford University.

During the Vietnam War, Berriós fought against the **Blood Tax**, the term used to refer to the imposition of the military draft on the people of Puerto Rico. In 1971 he helped lead a "beach-in" on the island of **Vieques**; using the tactic of nonviolent civil disobedience, Berriós and others tried to call attention to the bombing of Vieques and its 10,000 inhabitants. For his efforts, he spent three months in jail. Berriós's party does not advocate the use of violence to end U.S. colonialism. He and his supporters work within the system to change the system. He has also spoken often in the U.S. Congress, trying to explain that "Puerto Rico constitutes a distinct nationality by any definition of the term . . . the primary loyalty of Puerto Ricans is to Puerto Rico" (U.S. Congress 1991, 173–74). Thus, even if the island

were to become a state, Puerto Rico would still be "one of the most ho-
mogeneous nationalities in the New World" (ibid.). It cannot be brought
into the U.S. union without creating a situation similar to the one that
exists in Ireland or the former Yugoslavia.

Berriós who has been a controversial leader of the independence movement, has created significant tensions because of, among other things, the
party's unwillingness to take a more active role in the national movement
to free imprisoned members of the **FALN** and **Los Macheteros**.

SUGGESTED READING

Rubén Burriós Martínez, "Independence for Puerto Rico: The Only Solution," *Foreign Affairs* (April 1976): 561–83; U.S. Congress, Senate, Committee on Energy
and Natural Resources, *Hearings on the Political Status of Puerto Rico*, 102d
Cong., 1st sess. 1, 1991; Norma Tapia, *La crisis del PIP* (Río Piedras, P.R.: Edil,
1980).

Betances, Ramón Emeterio (1827–1898)   One of the foremost political
figures in Puerto Rican history, Betances is a hero to Puerto Ricans of all
political persuasions. Anyone entering the center of Cabo Rojo, where he
was born, sees a commemorative sign that spans almost the entire length
of the public plaza; the sign reads, Cuna (cradle) de Betances. In this manner, the city still proclaims its thanks to Ramón Emeterio Betances.

Educated in France, Betances was a physician, a doctor truly dedicated
not only to the well-being of his patients, but also to the health of the
Puerto Rican nation. Betances was a revolutionary. In a country where
most of his compatriots believed in evolutionary change, Betances argued
that the Spanish would never change the system themselves.

The colonial system was both inherently corrupt and morally destructive
of the rights of free men. Thus, soon after his return to Puerto Rico in
1855, Betances conspired to foment a violent revolution. Harassed and
chased by the Spanish—who threatened to kill him on a number of occasions—Betances lived like a nomad; he moved to Europe, New York City
and the Dominican Republic, always in search of a plan that would forever
free Puerto Rico from colonial domination. A year after the failed insurrection of **Grito de Lares**, Betances's commitment and ideals were still quite
apparent. In his 1869 French translation of an address made by the American abolitionist Wendell Philipps, which commemorated the achievements
of the Haitian revolutionary Toussaint Louverture, Betances ridiculed those
who argue that one race is inherently superior to another—a fallacy as old
as ancient Greece. Instead, Betances linked his own long struggle against
slavery to the struggle against monarchical and colonial domination.
Where, for example, was slavery still practiced? In Spain's Cuba and in
Spain's Puerto Rico. Thus, Gordon Lewis correctly stresses that for Betances "freedom is indivisible." Like the threads in a tightly woven rug,

Ramón Emeterio Betances. (*El Nuevo Día.*)

Betances's efforts to free slaves and his nation were intertwined; he was a true son of the Caribbean.

In the early 1870s, Betances moved to Paris, where he continued his revolutionary activities until the day he died. The terrible significance, to him, of the U.S. military invasion of Puerto Rico was that his never-born nation had forcibly passed from the hands of one imperialist to those of another. He died in Paris in 1898.

SUGGESTED READING

Samuel Betances, "Race and the Search for Identity," in *Borinquen: An Anthology of Puerto Rican Literature*, ed. María Teresa Babín and Stan Steiner (New York: Vintage Books, 1981); Gordon Lewis, *Main Currents in Caribbean Thought* (Baltimore: Johns Hopkins University Press, 1983); Olga Jiménez de Wagenheim, *Puerto Rico's Revolt for Independence: El Grito de Lares* (Boulder, Colo.: Westview Press, 1985).

Blair House   In the fall of 1950, while the White House was being renovated, President Harry Truman lived at Blair House. On November 1, 1950, two armed Puerto Rican nationalists, Griselio Torresola Roura and Oscar Collazo, approached Blair House, and in a shoot-out with the security forces guarding the president's residence, a police officer, as well as Griselio Torresola, was killed. In the United States, reporters wrote that this was an act of insane desperation; to the nationalists, the attack was an integral part of the revolutionary insurrection then occurring in Puerto Rico. Revolutionaries had also attacked **La fortaleza** and had even proclaimed a republic in Jayuya. As Oscar Collazo later told a reporter, no one cared if they ever reached President Truman's quarters. The idea was "to create a scandal that focused the attention of the world on the colonial status of Puerto Rico" (Bruno 1989, 211).

Collazo spent twenty-nine years in jail for his part in the attack on Blair House. Despite repeated offers of a pardon, he refused to leave prison if it meant he had to recognize the legitimacy of U.S. authority over his life. His behavior moved many to call him a fanatic; however, when the Carter administration discussed his release in June 1978, President Carter's aides referred to him as a "Puerto Rican independence fighter"(Fernandez 1994, 198).

SUGGESTED READING

Ronald Fernandez, *Prisoners of Colonialism: The Struggle for Justice in Puerto Rico* (Monroe, Me.: Common Courage Press, 1994); William Hackett, *The Nationalist Party*, Committee on Interior and Insular Affairs, House of Representatives (Washington, D.C.: U.S. Government Printing Office, 1951); Miñi Seijo Bruno, *La insurrección nacionalista en Puerto Rico—1950* (Río Piedras, P. R.: Editorial Edil, 1989).

Blood Tax   This term is used in Puerto Rico to refer to the imposition of the U.S. military draft on Puerto Rican men living on the island. Because Puerto Rico is an unincorporated part of the United States (see **Insular Cases**), the island's citizens are sometimes caught in what critics call a constitutional Catch 22: A Puerto Rican man living on the island cannot vote in a federal election, but he is still eligible for the military draft. Even today this tax generates considerable anger in everyday discussions, especially with the generation that served in the Korean War. In that conflict, Puerto Rico had one casualty for every 600 inhabitants as compared to one casualty for every 1,125 inhabitants in the continental United States. One out of every forty-two casualties in the Korean War was a Puerto Rican. The Blood Tax also was a source of great dissatisfaction during the Vietnam War. It was such a contentious symbol of the consequences of colonialism that many of the individuals who later joined Puerto Rican revolutionary groups received their initiation in island politics by participating in efforts to end the Blood Tax.

SUGGESTED READING

Luis R. Dávila Conón, "The Blood Tax: The Puerto Rican Contribution to the United States War Effort," *Revista del Colegio de Abogados de Puerto Rico* 40 (November 1979): 603–40.

Bomba   *Bomba* is one the traditional dance forms of Puerto Rico. While they are well known to most Puerto Ricans, *bomba* dances are not practiced by the general public. Much of what we know about *bailes de bomba* (bomba dances) is due to the excellent work of ethnomusicologist and historian Francisco López-Cruz. He traces the origins of these dances to African slaves imported to the island from or through the French Antilles during the early nineteenth century. The arrival of this dance form added thus another rich form of cultural expression to the people of Puerto Rico (López Cruz 1967, 49–62).

The term *bomba* groups of many different songs and dances. Traditional *bombas* were danced by the black laborers that worked in the sugar cane establishment in the island. In particular, they were associated with the Afro-Antillean element of the coastal areas such as **Ponce**, Dorado, Salinas, Guayama, Arroyo, Cataño and Loíza. *Bombas* were generally conducted in open spaces in front of the houses or dwellings. They are danced to a rhythm generated by simple instruments such as wooden drums made of discarded barrels and covered by leather skins. The drums gave high and low pitched tones and were accompanied by a rattle-like instrument known as a *maraca*.

An essential part of these dances is a leading cry or voice that is accompanied by the drums. These cries are high pitched and tend to be onomatopoeic as they replicate the structure of the human voice. A chorus of people answers to them. Dancers start to move without touching or coordinating rhythms between themselves but carefully responding to the music. There are many variations of these dances. Some of them are *Kalindá, Lero, Gracima, Cocobalé* and *Yubá. Bomba* dances require substantial improvisation and mastery of both its music and style.

Several contemporary music groups in Puerto Rico have made extraordinary efforts to preserve the essence of traditional *bombas*. They have passed them on to new generations of Puerto Ricans. The Cepeda and the Ayala families of Loíza have made *bomba* dances the centerpiece at the Santiago Apostol festivities. They have showcased this dance form in front of scores of Puerto Ricans through public presentations and television.

There is another musical manifestation of *bomba* that is different from the traditional one. It refers to a series of verses that are recited by dancers during the interpretation of *criollo* dances. It uses the musical platform of the *seis*. These verses tend to be comedic in nature and sometimes have some mischievous or sensual connotation. They are held during the Christmas season and are a source of laughter at these festivities.

SUGGESTED READING

Catherine Dower, *Puerto Rican Music Following the Spanish-American War* (Lanham, Md.: University Press of America, 1983); Peter Bloch, *La-le-lo-lai: Puerto Rican Music and Its Performers* (New York: Plus Ultra Educational Publishers, 1973); Francisco López-Cruz, *La Música Folklorica de Puerto Rico* (Sharon, Conn.: Troutman Press, 1967); Donald Thompson and Annie F. Thompson, *Music and Dance in Puerto Rico from the Age of Columbus to Modern Times* (Metuchen, N.J.: Scarecrow Press, 1991); Gregorio Toro, *Bomba and Plena: The African Roots of Puerto Rican Traditional Music* (Hartford, Conn.: Connecticut Commission for the Arts, 1994); Hector Vega-Drouet, *Historical and Ethnological Survey on Probable African Origins of Puerto Rican Bomba, including a Description of Santiago Apostol Festivities in Loíza Aldea* (Ann Arbor, Mich.: University Microfilms International, 1979).

Boriquen   This word was used by the Taíno Indians (see **Los Taínos**) to refer to Puerto Rico. This is the most common spelling of the word, but books in Puerto Rico and the United States also use Boriquén, Buriquén, Borinquen, Borinquén, and Boricua y Carib. The spelling disagreements are rooted in our lack of precise knowledge about the Taíno language. However, there is no disagreement about the deep, positive meaning the word has for the vast majority of the Puerto Rican people. A comparison in the United States *might* be Jamestown, Valley Forge, or George Washington. Boriquen is sacred. It simultaneously evokes emotional linkages to cultural roots (the Taíno), revolutionary resistance (the national anthem is "La Borinqueña), and the persistence of the Puerto Rican people as a separate and distinct culture. Thus, especially in the United States, a Puerto Rican youngster in Brooklyn, Chicago, or Newark says, "Yo soy boricua." It is a way of affirming ethnicity when it is challenged on the mainland; and, in the Caribbean, it is a way of expressing solidarity with the other islands also subjected to colonial powers. For example, a Dominican comes from Quisqueya (the original Indian name for the island), and when he or she meets a Puerto Rican, neither normally uses the names derived from the European settlers. On the contrary, the sense of solidarity and shared roots arises because one is *boricua*, the other *quisqueyano*.

SUGGESTED READING

María Teresa Babín and Stan Steiner, ed., *Borinquen: An Anthology of Puerto Rican Literature* (New York: Random House, 1974).

Boscana, Lucy (?–   )   One of the most accomplished dramatic actresses from the island of Puerto Rico, Boscana was born in Mayagüez and studied liberal arts at Oberlin College in Ohio. She started her professional dramatic career in Puerto Rico in the 1940s by participating in soap opera productions for Puerto Rican radio. She is remembered for her roles in "María Elena," "El derecho de nacer" and "Peor que las vivoras." Boscana was also a pioneer in La Escuela del Aire, a radio workshop from the Department of Education which produced radio programs for Puerto Rican schools. She was one of the first Puerto Rican women to participate in television soap operas, including "Amorosa" and "Entre monte y cielo." Boscana's career is best remembered for her huge contributions to Puerto Rican **theater**. Her roles in theater have impacted every one who has seen her on stage. She has been a leading actress in Francisco Arriví's *María Soledad* and is best remembered for her role as Doña Gabriela in René Marqués's *La Carreta*, a play that she has interpreted more than 800 times. She is still active in theater and television in Puerto Rico.

SUGGESTED READING

Elsa Fernandez Miralles, "Orquideas para Lucy Boscana," *El Nuevo Día*, January 30, 1983.

Bracetti Cuevas, Marianna (1826–1904)   A Puerto Rican revolutionary and a positive figure to Puerto Ricans of all political persuasions, Bracetti was an active participant and advocate for Puerto Rican independence. She was a member of the Centro Bravo pro-independence group of the Lares Revolutionary Junta. This group, presided over by her brother-in-law Manuel Rojas, was one of many juntas, or councils, that operated in different towns as part of the Puerto Rican Revolutionary Committee's clandestine network.

Three flags flew during the insurrection now known as the **Grito de Lares**; the flag sewn and embroidered by Bracetti survived the attacks. Her flag, now known as the flag of Lares, is also *la bandera* (the flag) that became the official flag of the republic. During the Solemn Te Deum Mass attended by the provisional government celebrating the independence of Puerto Rico, revolutionaries solemnly placed Bracetti's flag at the main altar of Lares' parochial church. During the Lares insurrection, Bracetti Cuevas was detained as an accomplice, but eventually she was released by the Spanish authorities. The active and prominent part she played in the unsuccessful Lares insurrection, particularly her valor, intelligence and patriotism, inspired the pseudonym *Brazo de Oro* (golden arm). It was a name that connoted both respect and affection. To honor and perpetuate the memory of Bracetti Cuevas, **Luis Lloréns Torres**, one of the foremost Puerto Rican poets, paid homage to her in his famous "El Grito de Lares," written in 1914.

SUGGESTED READING

Gayle Hardy, *American Women Civil Rights Activists: Bibliographies of 68 Leaders, 1825–1992* (Jefferson, N.C.: McFarland, 1993); Alfredo Lopez, *The Puerto Rican Papers* (Indianapolis: Bobbs Merrill, 1973); Olga Jiménez de Wagenheim, *Puerto Rico's Revolt for Independence* (Boulder, Colo.: Westview Press, 1985).

Burgos, Julia de (1917–1953) Considered one of the greatest poets of Puerto Rico and America, Julia de Burgos was born in 1917 to a poor family in Carolina. The countryside where she was born and raised was the source of her inspiration at an early age. Through her house ran a small brook, a tributary of the Grand River of Loíza, which she would later immortalize in her work and would be the theme and symbol of her poetic creativity. Her masterful use of nature and her sensual portrayal of the human experience are Burgos's main trademarks.

A teacher by profession, Julia de Burgos has been described as a lyrical poet whose work showed great power and a thorough command of the Spanish language. Her lyrics describe her disdain for conventions and her sense of individual freedom as well as her consciousness of, and empathy for, the oppression faced by women and the poor. Her poetry is known for its eroticism intertwined with her celebration of the Puerto Rican landscape, as well as her depictions of her views on the marginalization of women in both social and literary circles. "Río grande de Loíza" (Grand river of Loíza) is her best-known work.

Militant in her ideal of independence for the island, she was a member of the **Nationalist party**, where she actively participated in demonstrations and dedicated her verses to the imprisoned nationalist leader *Pedro Albizu Campos*.

After the breakup of her marriage to Rubén Rodríguez Beauchamp, she wrote her first poetry collection, "Poemas exactos a mí misma" (Poems to myself). This private collection was shortly followed, at the age of nineteen, by the publication of her first book of poetry, *Poema en veinte surcos* (Poem in twenty furrows), and her award-winning *Canción de la verdad sencilla* (Song of simple truth), in 1939. After receiving this award from the Institute of Puerto Rican Literature, she left for Havana, Cuba, where she began graduate studies in philosophy and literature.

In 1940, by then already recognized as a literary figure in Puerto Rico, she arrived in New York City but found few possibilities for work. That same year, pursuing a romance as well as professional growth, she left for Cuba, where she lived until 1942. She alternately resided in New York City and Havana, and during this time she worked as a journalist while dedicating herself to poetry. It was one of the more gratifying times of her life. She became active in literary circles where she was recognized for her literary talent and where she had the opportunity to meet other writers, such as Pablo Neruda and the Dominican leader Juan Bosch, who like her had political commitments to the progressive political and social movements of that time. It was also a time, when, she was acclaimed "one of the greatest poets of the Antilles" (*Puerto Rican Bibliographies*, 4). In 1942, she returned to New York. It has been said that a combination of elements, a failed relationship in Cuba and the limited prospects for employment in Puerto Rico led her to New York, where she lived for the remainder of her life. Even though she continued to achieve acclaim as a poet, her employment opportunities were scarce. Her jobs included working in a laboratory as a technician and as a factory worker in the garment district. For a short time, however, she was able to work as a reporter for a New York weekly, *Pueblos Hispanos*. The accumulation of unfortunate events in her life, her failed relationships and her isolation from Puerto Rico all contributed to her depression and alcoholism. Her death in New York City, which occurred under tragic circumstances, was considered by many to be a culmination of a tormented existence. During the final years of her life, Julia de Burgos found herself in and out of hospitals in an effort to treat a series of illnesses related to her alcoholism. It was during one of her hospitalizations on Welfare Island that she wrote one of her final poems, which is considered her goodbye to the world, a poem written in English, "Farewell to Welfare Island."

On July 5, 1953, she was found unconscious in the streets of Spanish Harlem and was taken to Harlem Hospital, where she died without ever regaining consciousness. Her remains were transported to Puerto Rico, where today they rest in the Cemetery of Carolina. In 1960 the Second Congress on Puerto Rican Poetry, celebrated in her home town of Carolina, was dedicated to her memory.

SUGGESTED READING

Juan A. Corretjer, "Recordando a Julia de Burgos," *El Mundo*, October 27, 1958, Suplemento sabatino, p. 19; Alfredo Matilla and Iván Silén, ed., *The Puerto Rican Poets* (New York: Bantam, 1972); Juan A. Rodríguez Pagán, *Julia de Burgos: Tres rostros de Nueva York y un largo silencio de piedra* (Humacao, P.R.: Editorial

Oriente, 1987); *Puerto Rican Bibliographies*, "Julia de Burgos (1914–1953)," Evelina Antonetty Puerto Rican Research Collection (New York: Centro de Estudios Puertorriqueños, Hunter College, 1986); Consuelo Lopez Springfield, "I Am the Life, the Strength, the Woman: Feminism in Julia de Burgos' Autobiographical Poetry," *Callaloo* 17, no. 3 (Summer 1994): 701–14; Sherezada Vicioso, "Julia de Burgos: Our Julia," *Callaloo* 17 no. 3 (Summer 1994): 674–83.

C

Cadilla de Martínez, María (1886–1951) A multifaceted woman, who originally came from Arecibo, Cadilla de Martínez was a teacher and university professor by training. She was also an established writer who made outstanding contributions to the fields of history and literature through her poetry and essays. Her doctoral thesis, "La poesía popular en Puerto Rico," is an important historical document that describes the evolution of popular poetry, which permeates all aspects of culture in Puerto Rico. She is admired as one who rescued poetic cultural representations that might otherwise have been lost with time.

Her work's principal focus was Puerto Rican folklore. Over the years, her literary, historic and folklore research on the island's culture uncovered many samples of the varied genres of folklore in Puerto Rico, including *coplas*, **aguinaldos, plenas** and others. She is credited for documenting Puerto Rico's cultural heritage during a time when the Spanish language and culture on the island were relegated to second place because English had been imposed as the official language of instruction.

Cadilla de Martínez was also a strong advocate for women's rights and one of the founders of the feminist/suffragist Puerto Rican Feminine League.

SUGGESTED READING

Yamila Azize, *La mujer en la lucha* (San Juan: Editorial Cultural, 1985); *Centenario Maria Cadilla de Martinez, 1886–1996* (Arecibo, P.R.: Almaca, 1986); Josefina Rivera de Alvarez, *Diccionario de litératura Puertorriqueña* (Rio Piedras: Ediciones de la Torre, UPR, 1955).

Cadilla de Ruibal, Carmen Alicia (1908–1994)   A poet, author and journalist, Carmen Alicia Cadilla was born in Arecibo. As a child, Cadilla was stricken with paralysis, and it is said that this resulted in her becoming more introspective and turning to books. Upon her return from Cuba with a degree in journalism, Cadilla began what was to be a parallel journey—making a living as a journalist and later as the head of the magazine *Alma Látina*—while at the same time steering her literary activities into the writing and publishing of numerous works of poetry. Her more critically acclaimed works include *Antología poética* (1941) and *Mundo sin geografía* (1948). In addition, in 1966, she wrote and illustrated a poetry collection titled *Silencio y Dios*.

Her multifaceted talent has extended into genres other than journalism and poetry. Her children's prose, depicting the traditions and folklore of the island, has been well received and acclaimed, including *Hijos de la raza* (1945) and *Juegos infantiles de Puerto Rico* (1940). In all, her ability as an outstanding writer has been recognized on a number of occasions; the most memorable and prestigious awards were a 1964 award from the Panamerican Literary Contest and an award in 1966 from the Ibero-American Circle of Writers and Poets in New York City.

SUGGESTED READING

María Teresa Babín, *Panorama de la cultura puertorriqueña* (New York: Las Americas Publishing, 1958); Cesáreo Melón and Esther M. Rosa-Nieves, *Biografías puertorriqueñas: Perfil histórico de un pueblo* (Sharon, Conn.: Troutman Press, 1970).

Cájigas, Luis Germán (1934–   )   Cájigas, a native of Quebradillas, is well known as a plastic artist and serigraph painter. Much of the visibility and popularity of contemporary commercial serigraph printing in Puerto Rico is due to the work of this artist during the last four decades. When he was a young man, Cájigas wrote to Doña Inés Mendoza de Muñoz Marín, the former first lady, requesting her assistance in obtaining an education and training in drawing and painting. She arranged for him to be taught and mentored by Felix Bonilla, José Meléndez Contreras, **Lorenzo Homar** and **Rafael Tufiño**, all renowned painters (Gaya-Nuño 1994, 132). He started to work with these artists at the graphic art workshop of the **Community Education Division** of the Department of Education, and later, at Homar's workshop at the Institute of Puerto Rican Culture.

Much of Cájigas's early work concentrated on the production of serigraphs and posters that advertised movies and cultural activities sponsored by the Community Education Division and the Institute of Puerto Rican Culture. He also excelled as a muralist and portrait painter. Cájigas's art explores themes, customs and traditions of Puerto Rican culture, the urban landscape, and life. The vast majority of his work focuses on scenes contextualized within the landscape of Old San Juan, depicting its cobblestone

Luis Germán Cajigas, "La plaza del mercado de San Juan." (Museo de Arte de Ponce, The Luis A. Ferré Foundation, Inc., Ponce, Puerto Rico.)

streets, its colonial architecture and its picturesque surroundings. His serigraphs and paintings are characterized by their vivacious presentations of form and color. Cájigas's most recent production focuses on the marine landscape of *La Parguera*.

Cájigas's paintings and artwork have been awarded many prizes and distinctions given by the Puerto Rican Athenaeum and the Sterling House, and many other organizations. His artwork, which has high commercial value, has been distributed widely in Puerto Rico and the United States.

SUGGESTED READING

Juan Antonio Gaya-Nuño, *La pintura puertorriqueña* (Soria, Spain: Centro de Estudios Sorianos, 1994); El Museo del Barrio, *The Art Heritage of Puerto Rico* (New York: Museo del Barrio, 1973); Museo de Arte de Ponce, *Colección de Arte Latinoamericano* (Ponce: Museo de Arte de Ponce, n.d.).

Calderón, Sila (1942–   )   Born in San Juan, this Puerto Rican politician has had extensive administrative experience in the corporate business sector as well as in government, particularly as a member of the pro-commonwealth **Popular Democratic party** (PPD). From 1973 to 1976, under the leadership of then governor **Rafael Hernández Colón,** Calderón served as special assistant to the governor in charge of economic development. Her B.A. in political science and her M.A. in public administration, combined with her extensive experience as the president of an investment firm on the island, prepared her well for her tenure in government. She returned to the private sector after the 1976 defeat of the PPD by the **New Progressive party** (PNP), which remained in power until the 1984 elections.

In 1984 the newly elected governor, Hernández Colón, once again called on Calderón; this time he offered her the opportunity to be the first woman to hold the position of chief of staff in the governor's administration. In 1986 the position of chief of staff was modified by the legislature and attained cabinet ranking. While she was holding this position, in 1988, the governor appointed her to the position of secretary of state, a position where she served as interim governor and was the constitutional successor to the governor—again, the first time a woman had held this position.

In 1989 she returned to her family's businesses and also voluntarily worked for the recovery of the Cantera Peninsula, a neighborhood that had been devastated by Hurricane Hugo (see **Huracán**). The Cantera Peninsula is also one of the poorest sectors in metropolitan San Juan. Under her leadership, the Corporation for the Development of Cantera was created with the purpose of developing the area socially and economically. Through her administrative skills and political connections, she was able to accelerate the reconstruction of the area.

In 1994 she moved on to another venue and ran for political office. Spending most of that year organizing what would be her campaign for

Sila Calderón, running for mayor of San Juan, 1995. (Tito Guzmán and *El Nuevo Día*.)

mayor of San Juan, on January 1995, she announced her candidacy. Among the first to announce their support for her was the newly formed group Mujeres con Sila, or Women for Sila, an assembly of women from diverse professional sectors of the metropolitan area. With the support of women and many of the residents of Cantera and metropolitan areas, Sila Calderón captured 91 percent of the primary vote, the highest ever recorded in Puerto Rican politics. One of the reviews of the primaries described Calderón's candidacy for mayor in relation to her party's candidate for the governorship: "Sila is running for San Juan, but she is better qualified for the governorship of the country than even Acevedo" (Dávila Colón 1995, 69). Criticizing the political and legal scandals that have rocked the island, she is running on a platform that has as an objective reforming government: "It is necessary to re-establish with great clarity, government's moral purpose and legal responsibility" (Calderón 1995, 69). On November 6, 1996, Sila Calderón became the second woman to occupy the San Juan mayoralty; she won with 50.3 percent of the vote.

SUGGESTED READING

Sila Calderón, "Transparencia, servicio y propósito moral," *El Nuevo Día*, April 1, 1995, 69; Luis Dávila Cólon, "La belleza, la bondad y virtud," *El Nuevo Día*, April 5, 1995, 69.

Campeche, José (1751–1809) José Campeche is one of Puerto Rico's greatest painters. A native of San Juan, he learned the basic principles of drawing and painting from his father, an emancipated slave. He studied at the Colegio de los Dominicos where he received a solid education. After 1775 he received excellent art instruction from Luis Paret Alcázar. Paret, who had been the painter to Prince Luis Antonio de Borbón, had been exiled to the island due to his advanced or revolutionary ideas (Gaya-Nuño 1994, 60–62). Campeche, who already had knowledge of some basic principles of art, received instruction in the uses of color from Paret. In addition, Paret gave him many technical lessons with emphasis on detail and sophistication.

Campeche was a prolific painter. Estimates indicate that he painted more than 500 works; unfortunately, only about 50 remain today. There are two distinct kinds of art in Campeche's legacy: religious art and portraits. According to Rene Taylor, former curator at the Ponce Art Museum, Campeche incorporated in his paintings aesthetic principles from the later baroque period (Taylor n.d.). Many of his portraits, such as *Dama a caballo* and *Doña María Catalina de Urrutia*, focus on members of the elite society living in San Juan. Others portray members of the government. His later work reveals a departure from Paret's influence and a return to a more simplistic style. Among his best-known paintings are *San Sebastian, Descendimiento* and *El Sitio de los Ingleses*.

Campeche is regarded as one of the first great painters of Latin America and undoubtedly the first Puerto Rican master.

SUGGESTED READING

James Gardner, "José Campeche" *Arts Magazine* 63, no. 3 (1988): 89; Juan Antonio Gaya-Nuño, *La pintura puertorriqueña* (Soria, Spain: Centro de Estudios Sorianos, 1994); James Grant Wilson and John Fiske, eds., *Appleton Cyclopaedia of American Biography* (New York: Appleton, 1972); Alejandro Tapia y Rivera,

José Campeche, "Lady on Horseback." (Museo de Arte de Ponce, The Luis A. Ferré Foundation, Inc., Ponce, Puerto Rico.)

Vida del pintor puertorriqueño José Campeche y noticia histórica de Ramón Power (Barcelona: Ediciones Rumbos, 1967); Rene Taylor, "Essay on Campeche" in *Colección de Arte latinoamericano* (Ponce: Museo de Arte de Ponce, n.d.).

Campos Parsi, Hector (1922–) A music composer, critic and essay writer who was born in **Ponce**, Campos Parsi is one of Puerto Rico's most valued and talented composers representing classical and popular music of the second part of this century. Campos Parsi is considered a true man of the renaissance. His eclectic educational and cultural background illustrates this.

He studied at the **University of Puerto Rico** in Río Piedras where he majored in biology. He went to Mexico to study medicine but abandoned these studies to pursue his passion for music. After Mexico, he received a scholarship to study at the New England Conservatory and also attended the Berkshire Music Center in Tanglewood, Massachusetts. During his stay in the United States, he had the opportunity to study with famous music personalities such as Aaron Copland, Serge Koussevitzy and Paul Hindemith. He moved to Paris to receive individualized instruction from Nadia Boulanger who furthered his knowledge of music and composition.

Campos Parsi has authored many significant musical compositions, including *Cuarteto de cuerdas, Cuatro cantos de navidad, Oda a cabo rojo, Tres fantasias para piano, Salmo 121, Romanza, Nueve cantos Antillanos, Petroglifos, Dúo trágico a la memoria de John F. Kennedy, Mercedes* and *Urayoan.* His best-known composition is *Sonatina para piano y violín* for which he received the Maurice Ravel Award in Paris in 1953.

Campos Parsi has been a central figure in cultural circles in the island for more than forty years. He has worked at the University of Puerto Rico where he edited the magazine *La Torre.* For many years, he directed the Music Division of the Institute of Puerto Rican Culture and appeared as the host of a highly praised cultural affairs program broadcast by WIPR, the government's educational television station. One of his latest efforts has been to build a repository and archival collection of Puerto Rican and Latin American music at the University of Puerto Rico in Cayey.

SUGGESTED READING

Fernando H. Caso, *Hector Campos Parsi en la historia de la música puertorriqueña* (San Juan: Instituto de Cultura Puertorriqueña, 1980); José A. Montalvo, *Hector Campos Parsi, His Life and Music: A Biographical Study with an Analysis of Four Selected Works* (Ann Arbor, Mich.: University Microfilms International, 1992).

Canales, Blanca Doña (1906–1996) A member of the **Nationalist party**, a revolutionary and one of the leaders of the **Nationalist Insurrection of 1950**, Canales was born in the barrio of Coabey, in the mountain town of Jayuya, and raised in a home where her parents' library also served as a forum for political discussions that generally included adults and adolescents. Canales reached adulthood at the height of the political controversies caused by Governor **E. Montgomery Reilly**. By eighteen she was already demonstrating a deep reverence for her country and its culture. For example, in 1924, a student group permitted to climb a summit on her parents' property were warned by the farm's manager not to touch the Puerto Rican flag flying on the summit's peak. According to the manager, Blanca Canales "loved the flag more than she loved her own life" (Claridad 1996, 16).

Canales told interviewers that, by 1930, she was "disoriented," a Puerto Rican woman who, while a patriot, also used the governor's wife—Mrs. Theodore Roosevelt, Jr.—as a role model. "We watched what she did and we even wore little white gloves" (Fernandez, 1994, 40). To find a direction, she turned to her mother and **Pedro Albizu Campos**. Her mother had always been an *independentista*, and Albizu provided, at a moment of great political turmoil in Puerto Rico, a way to affirm positively the values learned at home and in Jayuya.

During the insurrection of 1950, the revolutionaries met at Canales's home. They swore to offer life and home for Puerto Rico, and it was Canales who, along with others, cut the phone and radio cables that tied Jayuya to the authorities in San Juan. Then, assuring the crowds gathered in the streets that they had nothing to fear from the Nationalists, Canales raised the Puerto Rican flag over the Hotel Riverside and proclaimed the Republic of Puerto Rico.

Within days, Canales and hundreds of others were arrested by forces loyal to the government. She was tried in 1951 and sentenced to life imprisonment in Puerto Rico. During her trial, lawyers tried to stress Canales's great love for the American flag. Indignant, Canales publicly stated: "Do me the favor of not wrapping me in the American flag in order to defend me. I admire the flag above all the flags in the world; but I prefer the Puerto Rican flag which is my own" (Claridad 1996, 17).

Canales spent sixteen years in jail. She was pardoned in 1967 by Governor Roberto Sánchez Vilella. She remained politically active throughout the rest of her life, and she never lost her sense of commitment to the Nationalist party, to Albizu Campos and to the Catholic religious beliefs that often lent a sacred tone to this political movement. After a long illness, Canales died in San Juan on July 25, 1996.

SUGGESTED READING

Ronald Fernandez, *Prisoners of Colonialism* (Monroe, Me.: Common Courage Press, 1994); Obituary, "Biografía de una patriota," *Claridad*, August 2–8, 1996.

Capetillo, Luisa (1879–1922) Luisa Capetillo was a feminist (see **Feminism**), union activist and author. It was not until the 1970s that historiographers and scholars rediscovered the work of Luisa Capetillo; she was a woman who, long before it was safe or fashionable, defended a woman's right to an education, to participation in the political process and to what we would today call a career.

Capetillo grew up in a period of profound social change. With increasing levels of industrialization, thousands of Puerto Rican women began to join the labor force and to play a more visible role outside of the family. As a labor organizer, Luisa Capetillo was influenced by the activism of other women in the labor movement. She was a leader and activist in the Free Federation of workers where the scope of her activities included union organizer, strike leader, and writer for the *Unión Obrera*, the official union paper.

In comments that underline the norms that dominated Puerto Rico in her time, most writers stress only that Capetillo was the first Puerto Rican woman to wear slacks in public. However, like the use of the term Ms. in the 1960s, her defiance of social conventions was an attempt to challenge people and make them rethink assumptions that were taken for granted. She was arrested in Cuba for wearing a man's suit in public; she openly lived with a man to whom she was not married; and she deliberately bore children out of wedlock.

Her quest for political and economic equality for women led to confrontations with the Catholic religious establishment, which was deemed by her and her followers a very influential component of the system that marginalized women. In her book on women's rights, *Mi opinión sobre las libertades, derechos y deberes de la mujer* (1911), Capetillo asserts her views on women's right to sexual freedom: "Let us emancipate women from the routine and vexing religious calling that expounds as dishonest and shameful, what is a law of nature" (Capetillo 1916, 18).

In this book she also described the inequalities affecting working-class women and the abuses committed against them in the workplace and in the homes of the privileged class. She also condemned domestic violence. One of the enduring themes in all her efforts was the idea that a woman could work outside of the home, take care of the house and still develop as a human being.

Capetillo fought for, but did not live to see, the final success of the suffragist movement. Today, in recognition of her role as a feminist leader, the library of the **University of Puerto Rico**'s Cayey campus has established the Sala Luisa Capetillo, a research library focusing on women and gender, particularly in the Caribbean. There, many of Luisa Capetillo's works, such as *Influencias de las ideas modernas* (1916), can be found.

SUGGESTED READING

Edna Acosta-Belén, *The Puerto Rican Woman: Perspectives on Culture, History, and Society* (New York: Praeger, 1986); Robin Kadison Berson, *Marching to a*

Different Drummer: Unrecognized Heroes of American History (Westport, Conn.: Greenwood Press, 1994); Luisa Capetillo, "Mi opinión sobre las libertades y deberes de la mujer," in *La mujer en Puerto Rico,* ed. Yamila Azize (San Juan, P.R.: Ediciones Huracán, 1987); *Dictionary of Hispanic Biography,* ed. Joseph Tardiff and L. Mpho Mabunda (Detroit, Mich.: Gale Research, 1995).

Carpetas, Las   This term summarizes a highly controversial aspect of contemporary Puerto Rican history: the files maintained by the Puerto Rican police, the U.S. Federal Bureau of Investigation and the Central Intelligence Agency. Each file contained the results of years of surveillance on Puerto Ricans who were allegedly "subversives." When the list became public in the 1980s, islanders sued to obtain copies of their *carpetas.* One revelation was the existence of Puerto Rican double agents, men and women who supposedly were involved in independence activities but who actually were working for the FBI.

Las carpetas can be traced to at least the 1930s. The military headquarters in San Juan sent a "Weekly Summary of Subversive Activities," stamped SECRET, to the United States. Officials received reports of almost anyone who peacefully or violently opposed U.S. colonialism. During the 1950s, **La mordaza** produced another wave of Puerto Ricans spying on Puerto Ricans. The most publicized incidents, however, occurred in the 1960s. Directed by J. Edgar Hoover, the FBI initiated a program called COINTELPRO; it so deliberately sought to sow discord among Puerto Rican independence activists that an investigation ordered by President Jimmy Carter in 1978 produced this conclusion:

Here is a record of a decade of hanky-panky. Conceivably the FBI might be forgiven for keeping a watchful eye on violence prone groups. What is not acceptable is a campaign of disruption of what functioned as a legally constituted party, a campaign that spread to the non-violent prone independence party. What is most damaging is the FBI swashbuckling at the time of the plebiscite (is that self-determination) and even at the time of the 1968 general election.

To many Puerto Ricans, *las carpetas* is a violation of civil rights with a sixty-year history in the colony. In 1989 the Puerto Rican government established a commission which produced a two-volume overview including previously secret documents, of FBI and Puerto Rican government involvement in the subversive lists and their accompaning *carpetas.* Many Puerto Ricans other than the police were shamed when the newspaper *Claridad* published stories, with pictures, of those who had acted as government spies.

SUGGESTED READING

Ivonne Acosta, ed. *La palabra como delito* (San Juan, P.R.: Editorial Cultural, 1993); Estado Libre Asociado de Puerto Rico, Comisión de Derechos Civiles, *Dis-*

crimen y persecución por razones políticas: La práctica gubermental de mantener listas, ficheros, y expedientes de cuidadanos por razón de su ideología política (San Juan, P.R., February 1, 1989), 2 vols., much of it in English.

Carrero, Jaime (1931–   )   Painter, playwright, novelist and poet, Jaime Carrero was born in Mayagüez and received art training at Art Instruction of New York, an undergraduate degree in art from the Instituto Poltécnico de Puerto Rico (now **Interamerican University**) in 1956 and a Master of Fine Arts at the Pratt Institute in New York City in 1957.

The best adjective to describe his pictorial work is *controversial*. His work is filled with social and political commentary that critics have termed irreverent. At times, he has launched attacks against the art establishment on the island. In 1971, for instance, he presented an exposition at the Museum of the Institute of Puerto Rican Culture where he showcased twenty-four works that intended to make fun of and satirize the abstract movement then in full force in Puerto Rican painting circles. Art critics such as Beatrix Ruiz de la Mata were brutal with his work and affixed labels to it that ranged from "a murky palette" to "a retrocession" (Ruiz de la Mata, 1971). As a result, he refused to present his work again in San Juan and decided to undergo a voluntary exile in San Germán.

In 1986 he opened another exposition at the Ponce Museum of Art, which was positively received by art critics. His paintings have a strong tone with severe color and forms that critics often find threatening, intimidating and challenging. Some criticize the strong spirit of independence and revolt presented by his work.

This spirit can be appreciated more easily in his literary work. Carrero has had a fruitful career as a playwright with works such as *Lucky Seven, Noo Jall* and *Cashbox-FM*. His theatrical productions have presented a blatant and poignant criticism of the "underclass" and the false populism sponsored by the political and economic system. Carrero, who is a retired professor from the Art Department at Interamerican University, is a provocative artist who deliberately and successfully confronts his audiences.

SUGGESTED READING

Marimar Benítez, "Jaime Carrero," *San Juan Star*, March 21, 1971; J. A. Collins, "Carrero's 'Cashbox FM' a Theatrical Firebomb," *San Juan Star*, June 22, 1979; Frank Dauster, "Hacia la historia del teatro hispanoamericano,"*Latin American Theater Review*, 6 (2), 1993: 9–16; Beatriz Ruiz de la Mata, "Jaime Carrero," *San Juan Star*, March 21, 1971.

Carrión Pacheco, Rafael (1891–1964)   Carrión was the principal organizer of the Banco Popular, one of the largest and most successful financial institutions in Puerto Rico and the Caribbean. Born in the barrio Machuchal of San Juan on January 3, 1891, he died in San Juan in 1964. In his early years, Carrión labored as a carpenter, a rancher and a farmer; his life changed when, in 1927, he bought part of a bank that was first founded in 1891. Today, Banco Popular is a commercial bank with assets that exceed $12.5 billion; it is the leading institution in the Caribbean for financial services. At last count, it had 133 branches in Puerto Rico; it also has numerous branches in New York, New Jersey, Illinois, Florida and California; and it has just begun a rapid process of expansion in the Caribbean with purchases of banks in Jamaica and the Dominican Republic.

Carrión established not only a bank, but a respected cultural institution, a symbol to many of the care and decency that are such an elemental part of everyday life in Jayuya or Fajardo, San Germán or Ciales, Yauco or San Sebastián. The bank's history of the institution contains numerous pictures of Rafael Carrión Pacheco. Most of the other men wear dark suits, in typical banker style; Carrión invariably sports a white suit, with a black bow tie. He stands out as a banker and as a Puerto Rican carrying on a tradition. Today, in the lobby of the skyscraper that is Banco Popular's San Juan headquarters, the walls contain a large mural in which Carrión, wearing his white suit and black bow tie, sits in the middle next to a sign with great meaning for the bank and its customers: "Banco Popular is a genuinely native institution, dedicated to work exclusively for the social and economic well being of Puerto Rico and inspired by the soundest banking practices. 'El Popular' has dedicated its efforts and will to the development of a banking service for Puerto Rico inside of the strictly commercial norms required by the most progressive community in the world."

Banco Popular is arguably the most successful banking institution in Puerto Rican history; its employees do practice the norms posted on that shining brass sign. Today, the head of the bank is Richard Carrión, representing the third generation in charge of a bank that is an integral part of Puerto Rico's economic development during the twentieth century.

SUGGESTED READING

The bank publishes many documents, in English and Spanish, on its Internet homepage: http://www.bancopopular.com; see also Guillermo A. Baralt, *Tradición de futuro: El primer siglo del Banco Popular de Puerto Rico, 1893–1993* (San Juan, P.R.: Banco Popular de P.R., 1993).

Casals, Pablo (1876–1973) Casals is the most important cellist of the late nineteenth and twentieth centuries. Don Pablo Casals, baptized as Pau, was born in Vendrell, a small Catalonian town. Most people regard Casals as a Spaniard; few know, however, that his mother, Pilar Defiló Casals, was a Puerto Rican from the city of Mayagüez. Casals received his early musical education from his father who was an accomplished musician in his own right. Critics attribute the thorough lessons in *solfeggio* given to him by his

Maestro Pablo Casals practicing the cello at his home in Puerto Rico. (*El Nuevo Día*.)

father as the basis of Casals's solid foundation in music. Casals studied the cello at the Municipal School of Barcelona, at the Barcelona College of Music, at the Madrid Conservatory and in Paris. While studying in Paris he also developed an interest in conducting.

During his noted career, Casals had the chance to conduct some of the most prestigious orchestras in Europe. In 1956, like many other Spanish artists and intellectuals who were running away from the totalitarian regime of Francisco Franco, Casals moved to Puerto Rico where he funded the Music Conservatory, the Puerto Rico Symphonic Orchestra and the Casals Music Festival. This festival is the most important cultural and musical legacy that he left the people of Puerto Rico; it invites to the island and showcases famous classical musicians from around the world. Casals married Marta Casals, one of his former Puerto Rican students, and was the author of multiple musical compositions including the hymn of the United Nations. He died in 1973 and his remains were taken back to Spain after the fall of the Franco regime.

SUGGESTED READING

Robert Baldock, *Pau Casals* (Barcelona: Empories 1993); Margaret Campbell, *The Great Cellists* (North Pomfret, Vt.: Trafalgar Square Publishers, 1989); David Goodnough, *Pablo Casals: Cellist for the World* (Springfield, N.J.: Enslow Publishers, 1997); Frederic Grunfeld, *Pablo Casals* (Alexandria, Va.: Time-Life Books, 1982); Felix A. Guadalupe, *Pablo Casals: A Cellist for History* (Bowling Green: Bowling Green University, 1983).

Casas, Myrna (1934–   )   This dramatist and playwright has been one of the leading female personalities in the **theater** world in Puerto Rico during the second part of the nineteenth century. Casas received her undergraduate education at Vassar College in Poughkeepsie, New York. She later pursued a masters degree at Boston University and obtained a doctoral degree from New York University.

Casas has been a leader in the development of the theater program at the **University of Puerto Rico** at Río Piedras where she started working as a costume assistant during the decade of the fifties. From there she moved on to teach and eventually became director of the drama department at the university.

One of Casas's most important accomplishments in the field of theater in Puerto Rico was being the cofounder of Producciones Cisne in 1963. This theatrical company was one of the most visible and influential theatrical troupes in the island during the decade of the sixties and the seventies. From this company, she has participated in the production of the plays *Las Troyanas*, *Filomena Marturano*, and *Agnus Deis* among others.

Casas has also made great contributions to Puerto Rican theater through her own plays. Among the works she has written are *Absurdos en la so-*

ledad, Eugenia Herrera, Cuarenta años despues, Cristal roto en el tiempo, La Trampa, and *El Improntu de San Juan*. She has also written several unpublished poetry books and short stories. She is still pretty active in the artistic scene in Puerto Rico and has participated in numerous productions recently.

SUGGESTED READING

Myrna Casas, *Teatro de la vanguardia: Contemporary Spanish American Theater* (Lexington, Mass.: D.C. Heath, 1976); Marie J. Panico, "Myrna Casas: Nacional y Trascendente," *Alba de America: Revista Literaria*, 7 (December 12, 1989); Luz María Umpierre, "Introducción al Teatro de Myrna Casas," *Third Woman*, vol. 1, no. 2, (1982).

Castro Alberti, Margarita (1947–)   An opera singer, Castro, born in San Sebastián, received her elementary and high school education in her hometown and then moved to San Juan where she studied humanities at the **University of Puerto Rico** and sang with the university chorus under the directorship of Augusto Rodríguez. She became interested in pursuing a musical career and studied at Julliard in New York City and in Rome.

Castro has a very lyrical soprano voice. She has made many appearances in Puerto Rico and in Latin America where she made her debut at Teatro Colón in Buenos Aires in 1980. She made her first appearances at New York's Metropolitan Opera House in 1982 where she interpreted Amelia from Verdi's *Un ballio in maschera*.

During the 1980s, she moved to Europe where she has been active in interpreting a variety of roles. She is now married to a French musician and intellectual and has a daughter. Castro Alberti still makes appearances in Puerto Rico.

SUGGESTED READING

Stanley Sadie, *New Grove Dictionary of Opera* (London: Macmillian, 1992).

Cédula de Gracias   *See* **Warrant of Opportunity**.

Ceide, Amelia (1908–1987)   This poet and journalist was born in Aguadilla. Although her training was in education and she practiced her teaching profession for many years, she has been fascinated by poetry since she was eleven years old. In 1936 she published her first book of poetry, *Interior*, which won an award in Cuba. The following year, she married Costa Rican journalist and author Baron Maximilian Von Loewenthal and relocated to that country for the next ten years. While in Costa Rica, she worked as a journalist and editor in chief of the first Central American diplomatic journal, *La Raza*. While in Central America, Ceide published three collections of her verses, *Mi cantar de cantares* (1941), *Puertas* (1946), and *Cuando*

Margarita Castro Alberti, one of the leading soprano singers in Puerto Rico, 1981. (*El Nuevo Día.*)

el cielo sonríe (1946). Many of her poems and articles have been translated into several languages.

Her poetry has been described as deeply personal and somewhat analytical, but it was the psychological aspects of her poetry that first caught the attention of critics. At the same time, and much like her contemporaries of that era, her work includes long, colorful descriptions of the island and its beauty. In 1957, when the island celebrated its first Congress of Puerto Rican Poetry, she was one of six women whose work was presented. The poem she chose to present at this congress was "Monograma," a poem that maintains the Romantic flavor of that period through beautiful descriptions and metaphors of the island. In this poem, Puerto Rico is but "an island worn by the sea in its light and encompassing shawl."

Upon her return to Puerto Rico in 1947, she resumed her work as a journalist for the now defunct newspaper *El Imparcial*, where she worked as an editor and department head. During that time she continued writing poetry and also published *Stahl* (1960), a biographical work on Augustin Stahl, a naturalist.

She has been the recipient of a number of international awards from Argentina and the United States as well as numerous recognitions from her native Puerto Rico. In 1973 she was honored as outstanding citizen in her hometown, Aguadilla, and in 1974 she received the Círculo Literario–Luis Lloréns Torres Award recognizing her poetic works.

SUGGESTED READING

Rigoberto Pérez Vélez, *Puertorriqueños ilustres de todos los tiempos* (Ponce, P.R.: Editorial Centro Pedagógieo, 1986); Instituto de Cultura Puertorriqueña, *Crítica y antología de la poesía puertorriqueña: Primer congreso de poesía Puertorriqueña* (San Juan, P.R.: 1958); Francisco Manrique Cabrera, *Historia de la literatura puertorriqueña* (Río Piedras, P.R.: Editorial Cultural, 1966).

Cerro Maravilla   This phrase refers to the political murders that occurred on July 25, 1978, which remain one of the most controversial political events in Puerto Rican history. Cerro Maravilla, one the highest spots in Puerto Rico, is located above the mountain town of Jayuya. On July 25, 1978, Carlos Soto Arrivi, Arnaldo Dario Rosado and Alejandro González Malavé (an undercover police agent) allegedly went to the mountain top to blow up the television tower that is located on top of the steep incline that leads to Maravilla. Soto and Dario were *independentistas*, advocates of force if necessary to obtain an end to U.S. colonialism. What the two *independentistas* never knew was that González had informed his police colleagues of the alleged plan to blow up the tower. When Soto, Dario and González arrived at the tower, a host of police officers "greeted" them. In minutes, Soto and Dario were dead. In stories released the next day, government officials stated that the two radicals had been killed when they violently resisted arrest. In reality, they were brutally murdered by the police, and the eighteen-year controversy centers as much on the cover-up by Puerto Rican and U.S. officials as it does on the murder of the two young men.

A number of Puerto Rican police have gone to jail for perjury in relation to their testimony about Cerro Maravilla. The nation has at times been mesmerized by long hours of television hearings, and to date there are still lingering doubts about the veracity of the testimony of then governor (now resident commissioner) **Carlos Romero Barceló**.

SUGGESTED READING

Anne Nelson, *Murder under Two Flags: The U.S., Puerto Rico and the Cerro Maravilla Cover-up* (New York: Ticknor and Fields, 1986); Manuel Suarez, *Requiem on Cerro Maravilla: The Police Murders in Puerto Rico and the U.S. Government Cover-up* (Maplewood, N.J.: Waterfront Press, 1987).

Chacón, Iris (1950–)   Iris Chacón, a singer and dancer born in Santurce, became one of the most famous and controversial artistic personalities in Puerto Rico during the 1970s. She attended the Antonio S. Pedreira, Eugenio María de Hostos and William D. Boyce schools in the Puerto Nuevo area of Río Piedras. During her early childhood she impressed her teachers, relatives and friends with her merry disposition and dancing abilities. While she was a student at the Puerto Rico Junior College and later at the **University of Puerto Rico** in Río Piedras, she began to develop a serious interest in acting and dancing.

She started in Puerto Rican television by appearing on the noontime show on WKAQ-TV, which hosted a talent section directed by a popular singer named Sylvia de Grasse. From there, she performed small dancing and comedy sketches on many popular TV shows such as "La Taberna India," and tried acting with the national theater company El Cemí, which brought **Abelardo Díaz Alfaro**'s *Estampas de Tello Gracia* to the island's schools.

During the early 1970s, Chacón shifted her career primarily into singing and dancing. She scored a string of musical hits, including "Caramelo y chocolate" and "Si tu boquita fuera." In 1973 she started her own television show, which made her famous throughout Puerto Rico and Latin America. She also continued performing concerts and dancing revues in hotels and concert halls on the island and in the United States.

Iris Chacón became a cultural icon and a myth of extraordinary proportions in Puerto Rico in the 1970s. As the ultimate sex symbol, she appealed to the cultural machismo of the islanders. Like Brazilian dancer Carmen Miranda and like Madonna now, she used her sexuality to appeal to women and men alike. Much of her popularity was built around her provocative dancing while wearing string bikinis. She made suggestive jokes and movements that pushed the boundaries of morally acceptable discourse and imagery in the Puerto Rican media. At the height of Chacón's popularity, the religious leaders of the island vocally protested her act because of her perceived "vulgar and immoral behavior." However, the more they protested, the more attention they generated, and the more popular she became.

In addition to her artistic work, Chacón has been an important contributor to the cultural life of Puerto Rico because she has been a crucial agent in liberalizing sexual mores in media discourse in Puerto Rican culture.

SUGGESTED READING

Milly Cangiano, ¿Quién es realmente Iris Chacón? (first of a series), *El Reportero*, October 3, 1983; Manuel Ramos Otero, "De la colonización a la culonización," *Revista de la Universidad Metropolitana*, 8 (1991); Edgardo Rodríguez Juliá, *Una noche con Irish Chacón* (San Juan: Editorial Antillana, 1986).

Chardón Plan   This economic plan was generated in 1934; with substantial assistance from Washington, D.C., Carlos Chardón, chancellor of the University of Puerto Rico, hoped to resurrect the sugar industry in particular and the Puerto Rican economy in general. On October 10, 1934, Assistant Secretary of the Interior Oscar Chapman made this statement about the first thirty-six years of U.S. control of Puerto Rico:

Economically the island has not fared so well . . . particularly the extension of the sugar industry, while long yielding handsome returns to the stockholders of corporations which increasingly acquired lands on the island, benefited the Puerto Rican people little. . . . Puerto Rico today represents the picture of a country gradually depleted of its natural resources. (Chapman, 1934, 85)

Created during the middle of the Great Depression, the Chardón Plan was an attempt to revitalize the island's economy. It included plans for the encouragement of labor-intensive industries and tax credits to lure investors to the island. But, the heart of the plan authored by Chardón and officials in both Puerto Rico and Washington was its recommendations for the sugar industry. The Chardón Plan recommended that the government buy the most productive land and redistribute it to the small landowners—the *colonos*—who were struggling to survive. Meanwhile, the land owned by the small landowners would be given to the landless sugar workers as a way of helping them become self-sustaining.

Islanders fought about the Chardón Plan for many years, especially the provisions for displacing the role of large corporations in the island's sugar industry. Critics argued that the plan depended on Washington for its actual implementation and, more important, that the sugar industry had already been dead-ended by the country quotas approved by the Roosevelt administration in 1934. By U.S. law, Puerto Rico was forever limited to a quantity of sugar roughly 100,000 tons under the producers' actual capacity. Where, critics argued, was the room for growth? And why would Congress approve land redistribution when corporations had far more influence in Congress than Puerto Rico and its nonvoting **resident commissioner?** Island political leaders lobbied for land redistribution until the early 1940s. Finally, they adopted a strategy designed to industrialize the island; Operation Bootstrap essentially discarded the agricultural issues at the center of the Chardón Plan.

SUGGESTED READING

James Dietz, *Economic History of Puerto Rico* (Princeton, N.J.: Princeton University Press, 1986); Bailey W. Diffie and Justine Whitfield Diffie, *Porto Rico: A Broken Pledge* (New York: Vanguard Press, 1932); Oscar Chapman, "Affairs of U.S. Territories," *Vital Speeches of the Day*, October 10, 1934; Luis Muñoz Marín, "The Sad Case of Puerto Rico," *America Mercury* 16, no. 62, (February 1929): 136–41.

Church of Mita   Considered the first and only truly Puerto Rican church, the Church of Mita was founded in Arecibo in 1940 by Juanita García Peraza, who later became known as Mita. Based on Christian principles, the church came into being after Juanita experienced a series of mystical visions of the Holy Spirit, during which Juanita was given the name Mita and was instructed to establish the church. The church's main tenets are love, liberty and unity; these principles were conveyed to Mita through the Holy Spirit and the Scriptures. Based on the biblical belief that God speaks through prophets, Mita represented the chosen prophet and was the spiritual leader during the thirty years she led the church. Today, that position is held by Aarón who, during Mita's life, served as a church leader and her confidant.

One of the unique aspects of the church is its organization and self-sufficiency. Initially, for the economic survival of the church, Mita, who herself came from a well-to-do family, established a series of businesses that would provide the church with income. Included in these were two restaurants, a cabinet-making shop and a cement block factory, all run by church members skilled in the particular trade. Later she developed the concept of cooperative businesses for members of the church. By investing small amounts of money, her followers would become stockholders and could collect dividends. It began with a retail store selling food and other provisions that eventually became a supermarket encompassing the first floor of one of the church's many real estate properties. This concept of cooperatives later grew to include a hardware, furniture and shoe store as well as a bakery and a bazaar. As a result of this economic approach, the Church of Mita has become perhaps the only church that does not collect money during its services or ever solicit its members for funds.

During the 1960s, the number of followers reached its peak, when the congregation numbered in the thousands, particularly in the Santurce area. On days of worship, the streets resembled a sea of white, the color worn by her followers. Mita's following increased not only throughout Puerto Rico, but also in neighboring islands and in the United States. There were Mita devotées as far away as Colombia. The boost in membership, particularly on the island, also increased the church's access to the political process and the politicians on the island who came to see Mita's thousands of disciples as a potential source of votes and would occasionally have contact with the church's hierarchy.

Her burial on February 24, 1970, will always be remembered as one of the largest funeral gatherings to take place on the island. The wake lasted three days, and thousands of people, from as far away as Philadelphia and Chicago, attended. Buses were rented in order to accommodate the great number of people that wanted to escort the body to its final resting site. Multitudes assembled along the streets and avenues to catch a glimpse of the funeral procession; some schools suspended class so that students could go out and join the funeral procession. Among the people who addressed the mourners were **Rafael Hernández Colón**, then president of the Senate and later governor of Puerto Rico; Juan Cancel Ríos, vice president of the Senate; and representative Pablo Ortíz as well as other former politicians.

Today, the Church of Mita continues to attract followers, however, not in the great numbers it did during Mita's lifetime. Nevertheless, the concept of entrepreneurship as the economic guiding force still drives the church and its supporters.

SUGGESTED READING

Carmín Cruz, *La obra de mita* (Hato Rey, P.R.: Ramallo Brothers, 1990); *Encyclopedia grandes mujeres de Puerto Rico* (Hato Rey, P.R.: Ramallo Brothers, 1975).

Claridad   This newspaper, published in Puerto Rico since 1959, is the official organ of the Puerto Rican Socialist party. Founded by **Juan Mari Bras**, then the leader of the Popular Independence Movement (PIM), *Claridad* quickly grew from an informal bulletin to a serious, professional weekly of about forty pages per issue.

Claridad sustains and nourishes the dissident discourse of all followers of the independence ideal. However, despite its political orientation, *Claridad* consistently maintains a first-class news operation, characterized by excellent investigative journalism, focusing on government corruption, political persecution and environmental and labor issues. Quite often, *Claridad*'s articles have been able to alter the course of public policy in Puerto Rico, particularly as it relates to the federal government of the island. *Claridad*'s recent in-depth analysis of the potential hazardous effects of a proposed radar station in the Lajas Valley was instrumental in mobilizing local politicians and voters to prevent its installation.

Claridad, which currently sells for 50 cents a copy, has a circulation of about 30,000 issues (Braun 1996). Throughout the years, *Claridad* has also published contributions and articles by some of the most respected and talented personalities in the Puerto Rican arts and literature. During the 1970s and early 1980s, a time of political persecution for Puerto Rican *independentistas, Claridad*'s facilities were firebombed and vandalized many times. In an island thoroughly dominated by one or two mainstream publications, many argue that *Claridad* performs an important and essential role as the main dissident newspaper in Puerto Rico.

SUGGESTED READING

Gary Braun, ed. *Gale Directory of Publications and Broadcast Media* (Detroit: Gale Research Company, 1996); Larry Luxner, "Socialist Tool: Puerto Rico's Claridad struggles in a Post-socialist World," *Editor and Publisher*, May 29, 1993; José A. Romeu, *Panorama del periodismo puertorriqueño* (Río Piedras: UPREX, 1985).

Clemente, Roberto (1934–1972)   Roberto Clemente was unquestionably one of the most accomplished athletes and sports figures ever born and raised in Puerto Rico. Born into a poor family in Carolina, he started his career as a baseball player when he was eighteen years old. He started to play with the Brooklyn Dodgers in 1954. His batting and pitching prowess were so impressive that the Dodgers hid him away from scouts when he was batting so that no one would recruit him away from the team. In 1955 he was lured away by the Pittsburgh Pirates. During his career with the Pirates, he managed to accumulate a startling set of statistics. "Rifle Arm" Clemente, both an outstanding right fielder and a master at the bat, was elected to twelve National League All-Star Teams; won four batting titles; participated in two World Series (1966 and 1977); and was selected as the National League's most valuable player in 1966. He was only the eleventh player to reach the 3,000-hits mark. During his professional life, he held a .317 batting average and held a peak average of .414 during the 1971 season.

Clemente was heavily involved with social and humanitarian causes on the island. He sponsored many athletic programs for disadvantaged youth. In 1972 he organized relief efforts for victims of an earthquake that devastated Managua, Nicaragua, and he died in an airplane crash while carrying supplies and medicine to that city. He was inducted in 1972 to the Baseball Hall of Fame.

SUGGESTED READING

"Nobody Does It Better Than Me," *New York Times Magazine*, April 9, 1972, 38–40; "Obituary," *Sports Illustrated*, January 15, 1973, 11; "Roberto Clemente," *New York Times Biographical Edition* (New York: New York Times Biographical Service, 1972).

Coalition Party (La Coalición)   This 1920s political organization joined some members of the statehood Republican party to the labor-based Socialist party. Organized in the same period as the **Alliance party** (La alianza), La coalición was primarily a response to the politics of Governor **E. Montgomery Reilly**. When Reilly, in 1921, effectively outlawed independence as a status alternative, he contributed to the fracture of Puerto Rican politics. The situation was so confusing that Truman Clark called it the "Kaleidoscope of Puerto Rican politics" during the 1920s (Clark 1975, 77).

La coalición was a union of disparate forces, Republicans who refused to play second fiddle to the Unionists, who dominated La alianza, and the Socialists led by **Santiago Iglesias Pantín**. Together, the votes of the two organizations in 1920 almost equaled those of the winning **Union party**. They saw their coalition as a way in which to achieve dominance in the Puerto Rican colonial government. One problem was the labor ideals of Iglesias. Many of the Republicans in the coalition employed, under questionable conditions, the very people Iglesias meant to empower. For example, when he told Congress that "we [the Socialists] believe that it has been providential for us that the American ideals and institutions went to the island" (U.S. Congress 1924, 58), Iglesias echoed the sentiments of many Republicans. But, when he talked (in 1924) about creating a Department of Labor that would forcefully assert the rights of all workers, his coalición colleagues generally opposed the aims that actually fueled Iglesias's politics. To confidants, Iglesias admitted that the coalición was a case of one hand washing the other; he wanted to use the Republicans as much as they wanted to use him. La Coalición lasted through the 1920s.

SUGGESTED READING

Clarence Senior, *Santiago Iglesias: Labor Crusader* (Hato Rey, P.R.: Interamerican University Press, 1972); Truman R. Clark, *Puerto Rico and the United States, 1917–1933* (Pittsburgh: University of Pittsburgh Press, 1975); U.S. Congress, House, *Hearings before the Committee on Insular Affairs*, 68th Cong., 1st sess., 1924.

Coastwise Shipping Laws   These laws require Puerto Rico to ship its imports and exports exclusively on ships built in the United States of America; furthermore, that Puerto Rico use only members of the American merchant marine to work on those ships. Historically, to protect its own shipbuilders, as well as the American merchant marine that labored on those ships, the United States had always barred foreign vessels and crews from participating in the U.S. coastal trade. Equally important, whenever a territory was added to the United States—even Alaska and Hawaii—it was included in the laws that regulated coastal shipping. Critics argued that counting Hawaii as part of the U.S. coastline stretched the definition to its outer limits but, from 1895 on, Hawaii has always been an incorporated part of the

United States. It was not yet a state but it would be; therefore, it was a supposedly integral part of the United States. Puerto Rico was different. It was never considered a part of the United States; it only belonged to the United States. Nevertheless, from the very beginning of U.S. control, Washington included Puerto Rico within the coastwise shipping laws. The result was that, from 1900 to today, the island's trade is still transported on ships built in the United States of America, manned by the American merchant marine. Estimates vary, but it probably costs Puerto Ricans 15 percent or more over world costs to ship their exports and imports.

Over the last century, the coastwise shipping laws have been a major bone of contention between the U.S. and Puerto Rican governments. During the violence that dominated the 1930s, **Pedro Albizu Campos** consistently used the shipping laws as a blatant example of the selfish consequences of U.S. control. And, in the early 1980s, island politicians came to Washington to plead for exemptions that would allow foreign cruise ships to visit the island. Since the law mandates that the ships be built in the United States of America, cruise ships from other countries were restricted in their access to San Juan and **Ponce**. Eventually, the Puerto Ricans prevailed, and the harbor in San Juan is today full of foreign cruise ships. The lobbyists that represent the shipbuilders and the merchant marine have nevertheless succeeded in maintaining the essence of their monopoly on trade and employment. Thus, as in 1900, in 1996 Puerto Rico continues to help underwrite the health of the U.S. merchant marine and the U.S. shipbuilding industry.

SUGGESTED READING

G. R. Jantscher, *Bread upon the Waters: Federal Aid to the Maritime Industries* (Washington, D.C.: Brookings Institution, 1983); U.S. Congress, House, *Hearings before the Subcommittee on the Merchant Marine*, "Extending Coastwise Privileges," 97th Cong. 2d sess., April/May 1982.

Cock Fighting Cock fighting or *peleas de gallos* is a traditional and most distinctive Puerto Rican sport. It has been engaged in on the island for centuries. The sport relies on the cocks' natural instinct to fight. Cocks are bred and nurtured throughout the years by committed owners who feed them special diets, rub them with special oils and other substances, and groom their feathers and sharpen their spurs. Sometimes, artificial spurs, made of bone, plastic or artificial resins, are used. These are implanted on the cocks, which are then matched only against cocks that also wear artificial spurs.

People across all sectors of society ranging from the poorest to the wealthiest participate in the sport. Cock fights can be held in informal settings, such as the backyard of a house. Most often, though, matches are held in special facilities, known as *galleras*, that are constructed for the purpose. The *galleras* house one or more circular rings covered with wood shavings. Fights are set by the owner of the bird in coordination with the owner of the facility who charges a fee to hold the match. The owners of the cocks pair their birds and place bets on them. Ring-side observers also can place bets throughout the fight. In a typical match, someone screams out a dollar figure and the name of the cock they bet on. Someone from the audience will scream ¡*Vale!* or Go!, which seals the bet. The bets are based on an honor system, and individuals always bind themselves to their bets and stand behind them. A ring-side judge monitors the fight and calls the winners.

This sport has been very much maligned by those opposed to the cruel treatment of animals. Although the sport was practiced in Puerto Rico before the Spanish-American War, after the Americans came into power, it was forbidden by Guy Henry, the second military governor, on grounds of cruelty. Nevertheless, Puerto Ricans still practiced the sport clandestinely. It took many years of serious lobbying for another American governor to lift the ban. Today, there are scores of fighting facilities around the island, and these are closely supervised by government officials. There are clear and stringent regulations on the sport set both by the government and by the private associations and organizations that support the sport. Supporters argue that those who are critical of cock fights sometimes miss the point that fighting behavior is instinctive to these animals and that the aggressive or violent dimensions of the sport do not differ much from other sports such as boxing or dog races.

SUGGESTED READING

Emilio Huyke, *Los deportes en Puerto Rico* (Sharon, Conn.: Troutman Press, 1968).

Cocolos   This is a slang term whose use has grown and has been popularized in Puerto Rico since the seventies. While the term always had racial implications, as it negatively referred to black people of African decent with dark features or traits, it now mostly refers to an interesting subculture associated with **salsa** music. The term *cocolos* is now used to refer to those individuals from lower socioeconomic groups who model their looks and behaviors after the role models provided to them by salsa musicians. *Cocolos* is a dynamic term, whose meaning has evolved throughout the years. The contemporary *cocolo* is someone younger who wears colorful oversized clothes, has lots of gold jewelry, styles their hair like that of salsa musicians, plays salsa music with powerful and sophisticated stereo equipment that blasts the sound either from a boombox, from the car, or from a house or an apartment. *Cocolos* care a lot about the looks of their cars. They drive automobiles with lots of modifications such as magnesium wheels, oversized mirrors, neon lighting, customized painting and upholstery, and Puerto Rican flags.

This term has powerful sociological implications since it highlights the cruel cultural and racial struggles that continuously take place on the island and in Puerto Rican society. For example, *cocolos* generally take the blame for all the crime and violence that takes place around the island. They are thought of as individuals of "low culture." Some argue that the term has been used by people in the upper class to marginalize those individuals who are less privileged and who are closer to "popular" forms. In Puerto Rico, individuals with money often use the United States as a positive role model for behavior, dress and proper social norms and they tend to reject or pass negative judgment on those who don't. Since the seventies, as salsa music has grown in popularity and this genre has been more widely accepted by different segments of society, the stereotype of the *cocolo* has also evolved and changed. The term *cocolo* has a counterpart among the upper classes: **rockero**.

SUGGESTED READING

Jorge Duany, "Popular Music in Puerto Rico: Toward and Anthropology of Salsa," in Vernon Boggs, ed., *Salsiology: Afro-Cuban Music and the Evolution of Salsa in New York City* (New York: Excelsior Music Publishing House, 1992).

Coello de Novello, Antonia (1945–   )   A medical doctor, pediatrician and the U.S. surgeon general from 1991 to 1994, Novello is a native of Fajardo. She completed her grade school education in the public school system in Puerto Rico and attended the **University of Puerto Rico** in Río Piedras where she earned her bachelor's degree in science with high honors in 1966. She finished her medical education at the University of Puerto Rico Medical School and completed a residency in pediatrics at the University of Michigan in Ann Arbor. Novello then moved to the Washington, D.C., area where she undertook further training in pediatric nephrology. After a brief career in private practice, she joined the Public Health Service and occupied a variety of roles at the National Institutes of Health and accumulated an impressive research background. In 1990 President George Bush nominated her to one of the most visible health positions in the nation, that to the U.S. surgeon general.

Novello's motto of "good science and good sense," her eloquence, her sense of humor, her love for her Puerto Rican roots and her compassion for patients all made her a highly popular surgeon general among women, Latinos and fellow Puerto Ricans. As a political conservative, she was criticized by American health activists for not taking a more combative and aggressive attitude in the fight against HIV/AIDS. In 1994, when President Bill Clinton came into power, she was forced to leave the position of surgeon general. In 1995 Antonia Coello de Novello was inducted into the National Women's Hall of Fame. She returned to work for the Public Health Service.

Antonia Coello de Novello, Surgeon General of the United States, 1991–1994 (*El Nuevo Día.*)

SUGGESTED READING

Carol Krucoff, "Antonia Novello: A Dream Come True," *Saturday Evening Post* 263 (May/June 1991): 38–41.

Cofresí, Roberto (1791–1825)   Born in the small seaside town of Cabo Rojo in Puerto Rico, Cofresí, a pirate and a bandit, became a popular hero of mythical proportions. According to popular folk legends, Cofresí became a rebel because of the humiliation he felt as a result of the Spanish colonial oppression and rule of the island of Puerto Rico. One of his sisters allegedly was raped by a group of sailors, and he had been further humiliated by a British captain who slapped him in the face. There is no major historical proof to substantiate any of this legend. It is known, however, that Cofresí came from a fairly well-regarded family in the area of Cabo Rojo and San Germán who protected his criminal endeavors.

There is evidence that Cofresí was engaged in criminal activity by 1818 when he supposedly led a band of robbers in the town of Yauco with another criminal named Juan Bey. Cofresí's criminal enterprise was broad. It included burglaries of businesses and wealthy residences, as well as marine piracy. He had organized a group of criminals that he led in a series of crimes from 1818 to 1925. Cofresí is best known for his piracy on the seas. He formed a band of pirates who terrorized ships that traveled across the Caribbean Sea. Among his most noted acts were the plundering of the American ship *John and William Henry* in 1823 and the Spanish ship *San José y las Animas* in 1824.

Cofresí's headquarters were located on the island of Mona in the western part of Puerto Rico. Since American and British ships were the favorite targets of Cofresí, the American government sought assistance from Spanish governor Miguel de la Torre in capturing him. After many intense pursuits throughout the Caribbean, where he was apprehended several times but was repeatedly able to escape, Cofresí was captured near the coast of Guayama. He was handed over to local authorities who placed him in a military prison in San Juan. Despite the fact that Cofresí was injured and unable to hurt anyone, he was killed by a firing squad of Spanish troops at **El Morro** in San Juan. His shady deeds have been the subject of many literary works in Puerto Rico, including *El Pirata Cofresí*, by Cayetano Coll y Toste, and *Cofresí*, by Alejandro Tapia y Rivera.

SUGGESTED READING

Walter A. Cardona Bonet, *El marinero, bandolero, pirata y contrabandista Roberto Cofresí* (Bayamón, P.R.: Exitos Adaliz, 1991); Arturo Morales Carrión, *Puerto Rico and the Non-Hispanic Caribbean* (Río Piedras: University of Puerto Rico Press, 1952); Jan Rogozinski, *A Brief History of the Caribbean* (New York: Meridian Books, 1994).

College of Lawyers (El Colegio de los Abogados) The English translation of El Colegio de los Abogados, founded on June 27, 1840, is the Puerto Rican Bar Association. That translation is accurate, but it misses the positive emotional connotations that arise when most islanders speak about El Colegio. It is as much a cultural institution as a lawyer's lobby, as much a part of Puerto Rican history as **El Ateneo Puertorriqueño** or **La Fortaleza,** because El Colegio has consistently tried to provide assistance that extends far beyond the technical services offered by any attorney.

El Colegio has played an active and important role in the defense of the Spanish language. Each and every year, the president of the association makes an appearance before the Decolonization Committee of the United Nations; they do not advocate a particular status; they do ask the United Nations to help end U.S. colonialism. El Colegio has also taken a part in the controversies that relate to saluting the American and the Puerto Rican flag in the private schools of Puerto Rico. As a friend of the court, the association has tried to make certain that the rights to free expression for all remains an everyday part of the Puerto Rican educational experience. Finally, El Colegio has played a role in trying to make certain that the United States stores no nuclear weapons in or around such facilities as **Roosevelt Roads**; and it has also been active in trying to preserve the environment in localities, for example, in Culebra, where military or business activities threaten the island's ecology. In general, the association's role has been nonpartisan; it acts on behalf of rights or issues that affect all Puerto Ricans, and it is this role as advocate that has, over 150 years, made El Colegio de los Abogados such an esteemed institution in Puerto Rican life.

The headquarters of the association are located in San Juan, and the facilities are often used by public groups for everything from presentations of new books to discussions of contemporary social issues. The association also publishes a valuable journal, *Revista del Colegio de Abogados de Puerto Rico*.

SUGGESTED READING

Carmen Delgado Cintrón, "Las aportaciones del Colegio de Abogados a la sociedad puertorriqueña, 1840–1990," *Revista del Colegio de Abogados de Puerto Rico* 51 (April-September 1990): 167–205.

Colón Rivera, Juana (1871–1967)   Also known as the "Joan of Arc of Comerío," she was a feminist and union leader during her entire life. A tobacco worker who did not know how to read or write, she nevertheless had the ability, through her oratory, to move and stir the crowds of the union rank and file.

Widowed at a young age, she was always proud to say that she had raised her six children without any help. She augmented her income by taking in other people's laundry, a task she had performed from an early age in order to help her family. One of the discussions she would frequently have with her friends and neighbors concerned the low wages they were paid for the amount of work they did. Her main source of income for many years was the money she received for working in a tobacco factory in her hometown of Comerio. The hardest work of all was *despalillar*, or removing the stem from the tobacco leaves; this work was done by her and hundreds of other women, known as *despalilladoras*. These women had to use their teeth to detach the stem from the tobacco leaf and finish the removal by hand; later they sewed groups of leaves together for shipment. The dust and tobacco smell took their toll on the workers' health.

Her leadership role in the labor movement led to many confrontations with the police, and newspaper reports relate numerous riots and a series of arrests that unsuccessfully tried to stop the efforts of Colón Rivera and of other leaders. The labor strikes of 1917 and 1918, against the Puerto Rico Leaf Tobacco Company, were particularly memorable for their violence. Workers, using sticks and stones, were involved in fierce confrontations with strikebreakers and the police. Together with **Luisa Capetillo** and Emilia Hernández, Colón Rivera worked to improve the oppressive and unfair working and social conditions experienced by Puerto Rican women at the time. Because of her diminutive five-foot frame, according to newspaper accounts, she would use high curbs over sewers, milk boxes, or anything else that could elevate her and allow her to see the workers she was addressing, encouraging them not to give up the struggle for a better life, even if it meant giving up their lives.

The townspeople called her "Joan of Arc of Comerío," and they knew her as one who could give curative *sobos* or rubs on childrens' bellies, particularly those suffering from *empaches* or indigestion. In the same way she addressed the workers, she continuously spoke to children, always coaxing them to move forward in their lives, and to help others. Many years later, these same children, now adults, would stop and visit her to offer to assist in whatever she needed. However, hers was an independent spirit until the very end. Even though her family wanted to care for her, she chose to live alone in her own house, taking care of herself and attending to what she considered important to her, her own "meditations on life."

Colón Rivera, like many in the labor movement, affiliated herself with the Puerto Rican Socialist party. Throughout her life, until her death, her socialist leanings did not waiver. As a sign that she would never back down from her political beliefs, she left instructions that her coffin be draped with the Socialist party flag she had saved from the union marches of the early part of this century. There was also the instruction that music be played during the wake. For the burial, a group of *obreras*, or blue-collar women, carried the coffin while singing the Socialist party anthem. More than 1,000 people marched to the burial site taking turns carrying the coffin. Political and labor movement figures from her hometown and the island attended and spoke at this final ceremony. One of the more moving anecdotes shared at her funeral occurred during one of the last opportunities her friends had to show their love and appreciation for her. On New Year's Day, when she was ninety-six years old, a few weeks before her death, a group of friends came by to give her a *serenata* or serenade. Overcome by her emotion, she fell to her knees and wept.

SUGGESTED READING

Bienvenido Ortíz Otero, "Sepultan a Juana de Arco de Arco de Comerío," *El Mundo*, January 24, 1967, 34; *Yo misma fuí mi ruta: La mujer en la historia y cultura de Puerto Rico*, supplementary material for social studies (San Juan: Centro de Investigaciones Sociales de la Universidad de Puerto Rico, Proyecto de Estudios Sociales e Historia: Presencia de la Mujer, 1983).

Commonwealth *See* **Free Associated State.**

Commonwealth Constitution   *See* **Law**.

Community Education Division   This division of the Department of Education was established under the initiative of former governor **Luis Muñoz Marín** in 1949. The Community Education Division, which was a novel social project when it started to operate in 1950, was intended to provide a mechanism to educate, and empower, local underprivileged communities in the rural parts of the island and to improve their quality of life. A pamphlet from the division published in 1967 summarized the early objectives of the project:

1) help families from the communities to have faith in themselves and in their neighbors and to discover ways to express that faith; 2) to assist the neighbors in understanding that they have the right and responsibility to know and participate in all the affairs that affect community welfare and that they could be instrumental in creating a dynamic community sustained by their own efforts; 3) assist neighbors to develop a group discussion through meetings where democratic participation will be assured and where democratic consensus will take the place of voting; 4) assist them to realize that all planning and community action have to be democratic in nature and based on objective and scientific study; 5) assist neighbors to examine old cultural, influence and power patterns they are aware of so that they will be able to enjoy all the constitutional freedoms they enjoy. (Wale 1967, 5–8)

The division operated under a model that trained facilitators to visit rural communities in Puerto Rico. These facilitators assisted with the organization of small community meetings and provided them with films, reading materials, and topics of conversation and discussion that would allow them to develop initiatives to solve the problems that affected their own communities. By 1967, 327 community projects throughout the island had been launched as a result of the initiatives of the Community Education Division. Many of them were successfully completed. Typical projects undertaken were water systems, roads and bridges, schools and community centers.

The Community Education Division, a powerful arm of Muñoz Marín's government, was used to sell the principles of development that were so crucial for his government. It was also a way of creating a sense of participation and empowerment in poor Puerto Rican communities. To some extent, it was a way to colonize and bring prosperity to poor communities while gaining political support. A significant aspect of the Community Education Division was that Muñoz brought together some of the best talents in Puerto Rico to make it work: **Jack Delano, René Marqués, José Luis González,** Isabel Bernal, **Rafael Tufiño, Lorenzo Homar,** and others worked for the division to create the films, pamphlets, posters and other materials that were needed for education. They produced materials filled with both educational and artistic value. The artistic workshop served as a training ground for scores of Puerto Rican artists who acquired many of their basic skills there. The division has been closed since 1975. (*See also* **Education**.)

SUGGESTED READING

Fred Wale, *El significado de desarrollo de la communidad* (San Juan; P.R.: Departamento de Instruccion Publica; reprinted from the *Journal of Community Development*, London University, 1964).

Compontes, Los   *See* **The Lashings**.

Concepción de Gracia, Gilberto (1909–1968)   He was a prominent politician and, for many years, the leader of the **Puerto Rican Independence party** (PIP). Born in Vega Alta, he died in Santurce on March 15, 1968. He was educated at the **University of Puerto Rico** and at George Washington University, where he obtained a Doctor of Law degree.

Concepción devoted his political life to obtaining independence for Puerto Rico. He was a member of **Nationalist party** during the 1930s, and in 1944 he helped organize El Congreso Pro-Independencia. This group held an August 1944 meeting, which was attended by more than 1,800 delegates, many of them prominent members of the then dominant **Popular Democratic party**. American governor Rexford Tugwell reported that "90% of these politicos" supported independence. (Tugwell Papers 1944, 67). However, **Luis Muñoz Marín** did not. Initially, Concepción tried to keep his efforts nonpartisan but, convinced that the Popular Democratic party had chosen another direction, he founded the PIP in 1946. He led the party through its most difficult days; indeed, despite the gag law (**La mordaza**) enacted in 1948, the PIP won 19 percent of the vote in the 1952 gubernatorial elections. Concepción was a senator from 1953 to 1960 and a candidate for governor in 1964.

SUGGESTED READING

Robert W. Anderson, *Party Politics in Puerto Rico* (Stanford, Calif.: Stanford University Press, 1965); Gilberto Concepción de Gracia, "A Revolution of Our People," in *Borinquen: An Anthology of Puerto Rican Literature*, ed. María Teresa Babín and Stan Steiner, (New York: Vintage, 1981); Roberta Ann Johnson, *Puerto Rico: Commonwealth or Colony* (New York: Praeger Special Studies, 1978): "Tugwell Papers," Roosevelt Library, Box 47, August 27, 1944.

Coquí   The coquí is one of the most beloved symbols of Puerto Rican culture. These frogs connote the cheerfulness, the playfulness, the simple joy that is so often an elemental part of the island's everyday life. To date, scientists have classified no fewer than sixteen varieties of the coquí; however, only two of the sixteen actually engage in the coquí's most admired trait: singing. In **Ponce** or **Vieques**, the coquís are like a choir who never stops. The singing continues all evening, and when a person wants sleep, even the most loyal Puerto Rican sometimes wishes that the coquí would also take a rest!

Scientists now believe that the singing is a form of territoriality, a claim on the land and on the females that occupy it. Legend says that coquís are unable to make this territorial chant or cry when they are taken from the island. Incidentally, following the island custom of underlining each locality's uniqueness, the sixteen varieties of coquí each have a second Latin name; thus the coquí from Vieques and Culebra are called *Eleuthrodactylus antillensis*.

SUGGESTED READING

Nancy Morris, *Puerto Rico: Culture, Politics and Identity* (Westport, Conn.: Praeger, 1995); José Antonio Toro-Sugrañes, *Nueva enciclopedia de Puerto Rico* (Hato Rey, P.R.: Lector, 1995).

Corretjer, Juan Antonio (1908–1985)   A native of the town of Ciales, located in the center of the island, Corretjer is considered one of the island's most influential nationalist and patriotic writers of the twentieth century. As a writer, Corretjer used his poetry and essays to channel his love for the island and as a way to express his anguish over his perceived political oppression and repression fostered by the United States government on Puerto Rico and its people.

As a politician, he was a sympathizer of the nationalist movement from his youth. His political struggles on behalf of the island's independence and his participation in the Nationalist party led to a life of incarcerations in U.S. jails. Such repression further solidified his commitment to the liberation of Puerto Rico from what he perceived was a brutal enemy. He was a Marxist who saw socialist ideologies as the best vehicle to bring equality and true freedom to the people of Puerto Rico. His writings are characterized by the boundless love that he felt for the island, and in which he expressed a nostalgic tone reflecting his long periods of exile.

He started his literary career as a journalist. He left a vast legacy of poetry collected in many books published throughout his lifetime. Some of them are *Agueybana* (1932), *Ulises* (1933), *Don Diego en el cariño* (1956), *Genio y figura* (1961), *Construcción del sur* (1972) and *Aguinaldo escarlata* (1974). He also wrote many other books of essays and short stories.

He was a friend and follower of **Pedro Albizu Campos**, the father of Puerto Rican nationalism and the independence movement in Puerto Rico. In fact, they spent time together in prison.

SUGGESTED READING

Wolfgang Binder, "Una literatura de fronteras: Entrevista a Juan Antonio Corretjer con Doña Consuelo," *Imagine: International Chicago Poetry Journal*, 1, no. 2,

(1984): 7–21; Juan Antonio Corretjer, *Obras completas* (San Juan: Instituto de Cultura Puertorriqueña, 1977); Julio Marzán, ed., *Inventing a New Word* (New York: Columbia University Press, 1982); Amilcar Tirado, Nelida Pérez and Angel Aponte, *Juan Antonio Corretjer: 1908–1985* (New York: Centro de Estudios Puertorriqueños at Hunter College, 1986).

Cortijo, Raphael (1928–1982) Cortijo, a percussionist, bandleader and musician, was born in Santurce into a very poor family, but he became one the leading figures in Latin American music during the 1950s, 1960s and 1970s.

He started his musical career during the 1940s singing with a small ensemble at local night clubs, such as the Habana Madrid, with the Sustache sisters. He was responsible for a revival of **bomba** and **plena** rhythms. Cortijo brought recognition, popularity and respect for these genres throughout Latin America and the United States by using his position as a bandleader to develop new musical instrumentation (strong percussion elements and wind instruments such as the trumpet and trombone). Along with **Ismael Rivera**, his leading singer, he created the legendary Cortijo y su combo musical group, which reached its highest levels of success in around 1954. His band was an artistic platform that was used by key musicians who were to become famous in the **salsa** genre, for example, Rafael Ithier (from el gran combo) and Roberto Rohena (Apollo Sound).

Cortijo y su combo were pioneers of the early days of Puerto Rican television in such programs as "La Taberna India." His band broke up in 1961 when Cortijo was arrested at the Isla Verde Airport carrying drugs (for personal use) into the island. He spent time in prison for an offense that was customary for many musicians then and now. After his incarceration, he lived in New York City where he continued recording hits. His recording "Time Machine," blending a wide variety of musical forms, instruments and themes, became one of the early salsa classic recordings. In 1974 people from his early combo reassembled and recorded some of their earlier hits. When he died, the people from his native Santurce and the public housing project of Lloréns Torres took to the streets to mourn him. His funeral procession included thousands of grateful fans.

SUGGESTED READING

Donald Clarke, *Penguin Encyclopedia of Popular Music* (New York: Penguin Books, 1989); Juan Duchesne Winter, "Multitud y tradición en El Entierro de Cortijo de Edgardo Rodríguez Juliá," *Revista Iberoamericana*, 59 (1993): 162–163.

Crime Crime is a social phenomenon prevalent in most industrialized Western societies. Although much has been made of the high incidence of crime in the island, there needs to be a better understanding of the social, political and economic changes that have led to the rise in crime during the past thirty years.

During the twentieth century Puerto Rico experienced at least two tumultuous forms of rapid social change: industrialization and urbanization. San Juan, a "city" of 13,760 people in 1898, is now a very crowded metropolis of more than a half a million inhabitants. Bayamón, boasting a population of 12,778 in 1898, now contains more than 220,000 people. In addition, Puerto Rico's colonial ties to the United States produced a fluid and often contentious exchange of culture, linked to the personal and family turmoil associated with poverty and fifty years of circular migration. The island's strategic position between the southern and northern hemispheres is also a magnet for the biggest drug dealers in the world. Taken together, these conditions help explain the extraordinary rate and impact of crime in Puerto Rico.

For Puerto Ricans, crime is one of the major concerns in everyday life; when voters are asked what the main issue is in any election, poll after poll produces the same answer: crime, followed by drugs; or, drugs, followed by crime. There are very valid reasons behind their concerns.

FBI statistics on crime reported that as of July 31, 1996, Puerto Rico had the highest rate of any American state or territory in the number of homicides and murders reported (Federal Bureau of Investigation July 1996). In 1994 the island reported 27.5 homicides per 100,000, the average in the United States was 9 per 100,000 people. According to criminal justice scholar Dora Nevares-Muñiz, who has conducted one of the most comprehensive studies in the area, crime in Puerto Rico has increased considerably more than the population has increased. In 1992 Puerto Rico had the highest increase in its crime rate in its history. There were 3,600 type-1 crimes (murder, rape, homicide, robbery, aggravated assault, burglary, and car theft) per each 100,000 people. There was a 22 percent increase in the crime rates between 1980 and 1990. A particular area of concern, as presented by Nevarez's work, is the fact that the kinds of crime that take place in the island have turned more violent. Personal violence, such as murder, manslaughter, robbery, rape and assaults, have increased, but crimes such as burglary and car thefts have decreased (Nevares 1996, 14–17).

Islanders joke that one consequence of these statistics is that *they* are the prisoners because the criminals own the streets. After midnight in San Juan many motorists refuse to stop for red lights owing to their fear of being attacked. Even on the eighth or ninth floor of an apartment house, it is not uncommon to see a steel door in front of the door that leads to an apartment. Throughout the island, houses are shrouded in wrought iron fencing.

The causes of crime and violence include everything from poverty to migration; to increases in school truancy; to the breakdown of the family unit; to (as in the United States) a celebration of violence on television, in films and in the newspaper *El Vocero de Puerto Rico*. In recent years, there has been a demand for government intervention to curb the increase of criminal activity on the island. The past two governors, **Rafael Hernández Colón** and **Pedro Rosselló González**, have campaigned to develop plans to halt the increase of criminal activities. Rosselló, for example, launched a highly publicized, and much criticized, campaign to place public housing complexes, where crime was the highest, under the armed custody of the National Guard. He also has stepped up interdiction efforts against drug dealers. Critics of his initiatives cite the Bill of Rights; proponents cite the rights of the average citizen to enjoy peace of mind as he or she walks the streets of Puerto Rico.

The debate continues. But, whatever the role of the National Guard, the local police, the courts and the prison system, virtually all islanders agree that to reduce the threat and negative consequences of crime, it is necessary to make a systematic and simultaneous assault on poverty, overcrowding and the glorification of violence.

SUGGESTED READING

Federal Bureau of Investigation, *Uniform Crime Reports* (Lanham, Md.: Bernan, 1996); Franco Ferracuti, Simon Dinitz and Esperanza Acosta, *Delinquents and Nondelinquents in the Puerto Rico Slum Culture* (Columbus: Ohio State University, 1965); Dora Nevares, *El Crimen en Puerto Rico: Tapando el Cielo con la Mano* (Hato Rey, P.R.: Instituto de Desarrolo del Derecho, 1996); Dora Nevares and Marvin Wolfgang, *Delinquency in Puerto Rico: The 1970 Birth Cohort Study* (Westport, Conn.: Greenwood Press, 1990).

Cuatro   It is the national musical instrument of the Puerto Rican people. The *cuatro*, which has a melodic sound, is a hollow instrument made from native woods such as Ausubo (*Manikara bidentada*), Capá prieto (*Cerdana alliadora*), Maga (*Mantezuma speciosissima*), Güano (*Ochroma pyramidale*), Yagrumo (*Cercopia peltata*), Pana (*breadfruit tree*), Caoba (*mahogany*) and Roble (*oak*). The *cuatro* is very similar to the guitar; however, it is smaller, containing two concave indentations in its center and five pairs of strings.

The *cuatro* is the main instrument used in the production of native music such as ***aguinaldos*** and ***seis***. This instrument is seen as a descendant of a kind of guitar popular in Spain during the middle ages and imported to Puerto Rico by the Spaniards when they came in the sixteenth century (Cardenas 1992). The *cuatro* is a very resonant instrument that provides a powerful sound to accompany the singers of popular music in Puerto Rico.

The process followed to manufacture the *cuatro* is laborious and painstaking since it requires many woodworking skills. The knowledge and skills needed to create a *cuatro* are often passed down by members of a family from one generation to the next. The wood used has to be dried for years. In addition, the design of the different pieces that make up the instrument

A *cuatro*, the national instrument of Puerto Rico. (Ana Marti-nel and *El Nuevo Día*.)

require substantial knowledge of geometry and math since the proportion of these different components affects the quality of the sound that the instrument will produce.

SUGGESTED READING

Catherine Dower, *Puerto Rican Music following the Spanish-American War* (Lanham, Md.: University Press of America, 1983); Rocio Cárdenas, *Música caribeña* (Calí: Colombia Universidad del Valle, 1992).

Culebra   Always considered an integral part of Puerto Rico, the island of Culebra, which is four miles wide and seven miles long, is located roughly seventeen miles off the east coast of the Puerto Rican mainland. It was first colonized in 1880 by a group of Puerto Rican settlers led by Cayetano Escudero. It became a part of the United States when, in Article VIII of the **Treaty of Paris**, Spain specifically included Culebra in the lands ceded as an indemnity for U.S. costs in the Spanish-American War. Today, the island contains approximately 1,000 inhabitants who make a living by fishing, farming and caring for a variety of livestock.

When President Theodore Roosevelt gave the U.S. Navy control of Culebra's public lands in a proclamation dated December 19, 1901, he began a process that eventually turned the island into a war zone. Culebra became an integral part of the Atlantic Fleet Weapons Range, and by 1970 its inhabitants had experienced over 1,000 airplane bombing sorties each month. In addition, thirteen ships engaged in seventy firing exercises each month. The inhabitants pleaded with local and federal governments to put an immediate end to the bombing of Culebra. They wanted the navy to leave, but the admirals refused, and in 1974 the controversy landed on President Gerald Ford's desk. He received reports that the only reason the navy refused to leave was that its officials "exaggerated" the importance of Culebra in U.S. government hearings. President Ford, a man who took a genuine and serious interest in Puerto Rico, ordered that the shelling be stopped in 1975. Today, the island is quiet, but the remnants of so much bombing can be seen in the military debris that still litters the beaches of Culebra.

SUGGESTED READING

Paolo E. Coletta, ed., *United States Navy and Marine Corps Bases, Overseas* (Westport, Conn.: Greenwood Press, 1989); Carmelo Delgado Cintrón, *Culebra y la marina de Estados Unidos* (Río Piedras, P.R.: Edil, 1989).

Los Cupones   *See* **Food Stamps.**

D

Danza A music form that represents the identity, values and pride of Puerto Rican society. The music and lyrics of *danzas* are representative of the nationalistic sentiment of the nineteenth century when Puerto Ricans were concerned with finding and reaffirming their nationality and culture. As a form of cultural and artistic expression, the music and the lyrics of *danzas* reveal the enormous pride that their composers and interpreters felt for the island, its traditions and its people.

Other Latin American countries have variations of *danzas* and Puerto Rican *danzas* were influenced by some of these: it shares elements of the Spanish *contradanza* (counterdance) and of the Venezuelan and Cuban *danzón*. *Danzas* also were influenced by Spanish military marches (Cardenas 1992). However, the social and political origins of Puerto Rican *danzas* make them unique—they were created by working-class musicians but consumed by the aristocracy and the elite at their casinos and exclusive meeting places. Thus, the roots of *danza* are in the musical styles, themes and concerns of the working class; it has elements of the native *seis* in its form.

As a rhythm designed for dancing, the *danza* uses a two by four music compass. *Danzas* generate a very elegant dancing style that to some extent share similarities with valses. *Danzas* require long steps and elegant turns. They have an introduction, or *paseo*, that allows dancing partners to court, ask for the dance and get to the dancing floor. *Danzas* tend to be sensual and romantic. This rhythm was the dancing music of choice during the nineteenth century, and most of the musical production of *danzas* took place between that century and the first three decades of the twentieth century.

Some of the leading composers of *danzas* were Manuel G. Távarez (1843–1883), who composed many *danzas* but is best known by "Margarita" and "Tu ausencia"; and Juan Morel Campos (1857–1896), whose more popular *danzas* are "Felices Días," and "Laura y Georgina." Other famous composers of *danzas* were Angel Mislán (1862–1911), who composed, among others, "Sara," "Tu y yo," and "La bonita"; and José Ignacio Quintón (1881–1952), who authored "Blanco y ázul" and "Tus ojos."

Puerto Rico's national anthem, "La Borinqueña," is based on a romantic *danza*. Felix Astol composed the original music in 1867. In 1868 Lola Rodiríguez de Tió wrote patriotic lyrics to the music during the **Grito de Lares** insurrection. "La Borinqueña" was officially made the national anthem in 1952 but its music was rearranged by Braulio Dueño Colón and new lyrics were composed by Manuel Fernández Juncos.

Although the production of *danzas* in Puerto Rican popular music has basically stopped in recent decades, Puerto Ricans have a genuine appreciation for this rhythm, which they perceive as distinctively theirs. In the last few years, there has been reemergence in the production of *danzas* and the public's appreciation for them. An example of a more contemporary romantic *danza* is Eladio Torres's "Tu vives en mi pensamiento." And modern writer and singer Antonio Cabán Vale composed the *danza* "Verdeluz." This *danza* is a romantic and patriotic ode that sings to the beauty of the island in the utmost poetic fashion. Many Puerto Ricans consider this *danza* to be a second national anthem.

SUGGESTED READING

María Teresa Babín, *Panorama de la cultura puertorriqueña* (San Juan: Instituto de Cultura Puertorriqueña, 1958); Rocio Cárdenas, *Música Caribeña* (Cali, Colombia: Universidad del Valle, 1992); Ernesto Juan Fonfrias, *Apuntes sobre la danza puetorriqueña* (San Juan: Instituto de Cultura Puertorriqueña, 1967); Peter Manuel, "Puerto Rican Music and Cultural Identity: Creative Appropriation of Cuban Sources from Danza to Salsa" *Ethnomusicology* 38, no. 2 (1994); María Luisa Muñoz, *La música en Puerto Rico: panorama histórico-cultural* (Sharon, Conn.: Troutman Press, 1996).

Dávila, Virgilio (1869–1943) Dávila was born in Toa Baja. As a poet, Dávila is considered to be one of the leading exponents of Puerto Rican *Criollismo*. This literary movement is comprised of a group of artists and authors whose work exalts the nature, culture and values of the island. Dávila's poetry focused on the lifestyles, folklore and culture of Puerto Rico. He was one of the first writers within the *criollo* movement who used correct Spanish vocabulary, syntax and grammar in his writings.

Some of Dávila's most important poetry was presented in his book *Pueblito de antes* (1917). The book has a series of sonnets about important figures who characterized the small towns of Puerto Rico during his time. He was able to bring to his readers the essential traits of people like the local doctor, teacher, midwife and priest who constituted the very fabric of the Puerto Rican society at the end of the nineteenth and beginning of the twentieth century. His work is important because Dávila was able to provide simple but insightful commentaries about the character and personality of Puerto Rican people. In addition, he provided realist depictions of the island's landscape and environment. As a teacher, he paid important attention to the role of the school in his society. Literary critic Carlos Orama Padilla, a specialist on Davila's work, underscores his capacity to produce "animated photographs" of types and characters that defined Puerto Rican life. He also discusses Dávila's capacity to produce light but veiled criticisms of the social and political system (Orama Padilla 1963, 137).

One of Dávila's most popular compositions is his poem "La Tierruca." This poem, which was adapted into a song by Braulio Dueño Colón, is still taught to many schoolchildren of the island during their elementary grades. "La Tierruca" compares Puerto Rico to God's paradise by using simple but powerful metaphors. The song has become a hymn presented during major official functions and activities on the island.

Dávila also wrote patriotic poems. He was a teacher and wrote many books, such as *Patria* (1903), *Viviendo y amando* (1912), *Aromas del Terruño* (1916), *Pueblito de antes* (1917) and *Un libro para mis nietos* (1917).

SUGGESTED READING

Virgilio Dávila, *Obras completas* (San Juan: Instituto de Cultura Puertorriqueña, 1964); Carlos Orama Padilla, *Virgilio Dávila, su vida y su obra* (San Juan: Editorial Cordillera, 1964); Philip Ward, *Oxford Companion to Spanish Literature* (Oxford: Clarendon Press, 1978).

De Diego, José (1867–1918)   One of the most prominent politicians of his generation, he was also a defender of the Spanish language and the Puerto Rican culture. Born in Aguadilla, he died in New York City on July 16, 1918. De Diego first studied in Barcelona, but his attachment to writing poetry proved more compelling than the law: "I wrote verses while I was absent from my classes in Roman law." He was also such an ardent and open spokesman against Spanish colonial rule that he was sentenced to spend time in Spanish jails. In 1891 he received his law degree in Havana where he was influenced by the Cuban writer, revolutionary and patriot José Martí.

During the 1890s De Diego struggled for Puerto Rico's autonomy from Spain, and, despite his youth, he was a member of the cabinet selected to implement the **Autonomic Constitution** granted by Spain in 1897. Under American rule, De Diego helped found one of the most powerful political parties, the **Union party**, in Puerto Rican history. At an assembly held in

1904 he argued for an end to U.S. colonialism; the island must be either a legitimate part of the United States or an independent nation. "Puerto Rican nationality will be our motto if our petitions for reform are left unanswered." De Diego also fought against the use of English as the prime medium of instruction in the Puerto Rican school system. As a poet, he understood the close link between language and culture; to erase the former was to threaten the essence of the latter. Thus, using such forums as **El Ateneo Puertorriqueño,** De Diego championed the use of Spanish, with all its jíbaro and Antillean expressions, as the true voice of the Puerto Rican people (Arrigiotta 1985, 49–60).

Along with other leaders, including **Luis Muñoz Rivera,** De Diego led the charge against the imposition of **United States citizenship;** he traveled to Cuba, Spain and the Dominican Republic in search of moral support against the imperialism of the United States; nevertheless, he was committed to working against the colonial system within the colonial system. After Congress passed the **Jones Act** in 1917, he asked the Puerto Rican legislature to hold a **plebiscite** to determine the actual will of the Puerto Rican people.

De Diego was also well known as an attorney. His practice sometimes created tensions. Occasionally, his clients were U.S. sugar companies who, according to other Puerto Rican patriots, were exploiting the Puerto Rican people under the banner of American colonialism.

His written works include *Cantos de Rebeldía* (1916) and *Cantos de Pitirre* (published posthumously in 1975).

SUGGESTED READING

Delma S. Arrigoitia, "José De Diego: A Legislator in Times of Political Transition," (Ph.D. diss., Fordham University, 1985); Iris Zavala and Rafael Rodriguez, eds., *The Intellectual Roots of Independence: An Anthology of Puerto Rican Political Essays* (New York: Monthly Review Press, 1972).

Delano, Jack (1914–1997)   Jack Delano, a photographer, musician, composer, filmmaker and graphic artist, was born in Kiev, Ukraine, as Jacob Ovcharov. He immigrated to the United States with his father in 1923 and attended the Settlement Music School in Philadelphia and the Pennsylvania Academy of Fine Arts.

In a recent Memoir Delano chronicles that as a photographer for the Farm Security Administration, he first visited Puerto Rico in November 1941 to document a special report the governor of the Virgin Islands was generating about the Virgin Islands and Puerto Rico. Accompanied by his wife, Irene, he became enchanted by the beauty of the island as well as the richness of its traditions and the friendliness of the Puerto Rican people, and in 1946 they returned to the island to stay permanently (Delano 1994).

Delano stayed in Puerto Rico after Governor **Luis Muñoz Marín** asked him to assist his administration in putting together an agency that would help the government of Puerto Rico educate its adult people about the basics of the democratic process and about major problems affecting the island. Assisted by his wife, Delano established the Film and Graphic Arts Division of the Parks and Recreation Services Commission in Puerto Rico, which was the foundation for what later became the **Community Education Division** of the Department of Education. He started a professionally organized film division, and his wife directed the graphic arts division.

Delano was responsible for a score of short films produced to educate the Puerto Rican people, among them *Caña*, about the sugar cane industry; *La voz del pueblo* (*The Voice of the People*), about the democratic process; and *Una gota de agua* (*A Drop of Water*), about the importance of drinking water. He later directed a full-length feature titled *Los peloteros* (*The Baseball Players*), which has been nationally and internationally acclaimed. Under his leadership, the division became a center that nurtured some of the best local talent: **Lorenzo Homar, Rafael Tufiño, René Marqués** and **José Luis González.**

In 1957 Delano became one of the people behind the creation of WIPR, the government public television station where, as a leader in the programming area, he brought excellence to the early years of public television on the island. He eventually became a programming director and director of the facilities. He has composed music for the Ballet de San Juan and has participated in the creation of many musical scores for television. He has also written a musical score, titled *Aves*, about tropical birds and three piano preludes based on **Luis Palés Matos**'s poem "Cancion festiva para ser llorada." He has also illustrated children's books.

During the 1940s and 1950s, Delano shot thousands of photographs showing life in Puerto Rico. This collection constitutes one of the most important photographic sources documenting the lifestyles of the island during that period. These photos are part of the collection of the Library of Congress and also part of the Puerto Rican Historical Archives.

SUGGESTED READING

Jack Delano, *Contrast: Forty Years of Change and Continuity in Puerto Rico* (Washington, D.C.: Smithsonian Institute, 1990); Jack Delano, *De San Juan Ponce en el tren (From San Juan to Ponce on the Train)* (Río Piedras: Editorial de la Universidad de Puerto Rico); Jack Delano, *Puerto Rico Mío: Four Decades of Change* (Washington, D.C.: Smithsonian Institute Press, 1990); Jack Delano, *El goce de crear* (Bayamón, P.R.: Taller de Cine la Red, 1994).

Díaz Alfaro, Abelardo (1918–)   Through his writings, Díaz Alfaro recorded typical Puerto Rican folklore and traditions from the first part of the twentieth century. He is considered one the leading exponents of the *criollo* movement (exalting the nature, culture and values of the island) in

Abelardo Díaz Alfaro, circa 1973. (*El Nuevo Día.*)

Puerto Rican literature. He was born in Vega Baja and attended the Instituto Politécnico de Puerto Rico, now known as **Interamerican University**. He also studied social work at the **University of Puerto Rico** in Río Piedras.

Scholar María Teresa Babín labeled Díaz Alfaro's short stories as "masterful" (Babin 1958, 119). His writings legitimized the importance of the native folklore and brought attention and scholarly recognition to its study. His work is realistic in nature and vividly captures the mindset of the people from the mountains. His short stories present the fundamental differences in values and attitudes held by the privileged class and the working class. Without making political statements, Díaz Alfaro presents the ideologies that molded the worldview of the native Puerto Ricans. He focuses, however, on characterizing the values and traits of his people: fatalism, respect, humbleness. Some of his work reveals the stoicism of the *jíbaro* and his sense of dignity.

One of Díaz Alfaro's most significant contribution's to Puerto Rican literature was his book *Terrazo* (1947), a collection of short stories and vignettes which are rooted in his experiences in the countryside. This book includes the short story "El josco" (a bull), considered to be one of his literary masterpieces. Díaz Alfaro tells the story of an independent bull known as el Josco that, for most of its life, has been used as the stud and guardian of the farm. The owner suddenly replaces el Josco with a bull imported from the outside, including the responsibilities of being a stud. El josco is then forced to work under the yoke. Rather than being submitted to the domination of the yoke, el josco decides to jump off the cliff and commit suicide. The short story is seen as a metaphor about the fatalism and dignity of the Puerto Rican character. In 1956 he wrote the short story "Los perros" for the *Asomante* literary magazine, which once again used metaphors based on animals to make a social commentary. He states that his work was influenced by his experiences at his grandmother's farm in Toa Alta (Díaz Alfaro 1971, 54).

Díaz Alfaro was able to influence the masses with his literary work. He was a popular force behind educational radio in the island and worked as a scriptwriter and developed programs such as "Tello Gracia" and "Retablo en el solar." These programs also showcased the *criollismo* and the experiences of *jíbaros* through characters such as Peyo Mercé.

SUGGESTED READING

Abelardo Díaz Alfaro, *Terrazo* (Bilbao, Spain: Editorial Vasco Americana, 1948); Abelardo Díaz Alfaro, *Cuentos de Puerto Rico* (New York: Plus Ultra Educational Publishers, 1967); Abelardo Díaz Alfaro, in René Marqués, ed., *Cuentos puertorriqueños de hoy* (Río Piedras, P.R.: Editorial Cultural, 1971); María Teresa Babín, *Panorama de la cultura puertorriqueña* (San Juan: Instituto de Cultura Puertorriqueña, 1958); Donald E. Herdeck, *Caribbean Writers: A Bio-Biographical Encyclopedia* (Washington, D.C.: Three Continents Press, 1979).

Tenor Justino Díaz perfoming the role of Christopher Columbus in Miami, 1992. (*El Nuevo Día.*)

Díaz, Justino (1940–   )   Justino Díaz, an opera singer, was born in Santurce and raised in Cataño. He studied at the **University of Puerto Rico** in Río Piedras and at the New England Conservatory where he received specialized classes in operatic technique, acting and singing and training from Frederick Jagel.

He started his operatic career formally in 1957 in San Germán in the role of Ben in Gian Carlo Menotti's *The Telephone*. He debuted with the New England Opera Theater in 1961 and first appeared at the Metropolitan Opera House in New York City in 1963 as part of the competition "Auditions of the Air," where he won first place for his interpretation of the role of Giorgio and was given the opportunity to join the cast of the Met. He opened in the role of Monterone that same year. He was one of the artists selected to inaugurate the Metropolitan Opera at the Lincoln Center in 1966 where he played Antony in Samuel Barber's *Antony and Cleopatra*. He also performed at the premiere of the Kennedy Center in Washington, D.C., in 1971. He has performed with the New York City Opera and has appeared at London's Covent Garden.

Díaz's powerful voice is considered one of the best contemporary bass voices in classical music. He has played an assortment of roles, including Colline, Sparafucile, Figaro and Don Giovanni. He has made many recordings and still makes appearances in Puerto Rico.

Emilio Díaz Varcárcel, 1992. (Laura Magruder and *El Nuevo Día*.)

SUGGESTED READING

Theodore Baker, *Baker's Biographic Dictionary of Musicians* (New York: Scribner Books, a division of Macmillan, 1992); *Biography Index* (New York: H. W. Wilson, 1968); Arthur Jacobs, *Penguin Dictionary of Musical Performers: A Biographical Guide to Significant Interpreters of Classical Music* (London: Viking, 1990); Stanley Sadie, *New Grove Dictionary of Opera* (London: Macmillan, 1992).

Díaz Varcárcel, Emilio (1929–)   Born in Trujillo Alto, Díaz Varcárcel is an author whose extensive literary production focuses on contemporary life in Puerto Rican society and culture. Díaz Varcárcel uses the urban setting to generate his characters. He develops types, personalities and situations that reveal the pains and tribulations of life in the city and sometimes its limited rewards.

Díaz Varcárcel has successfully identified and revealed the fears and pathologies created by modern living on island residents. More important, he is a clear communicator who captures the interest and attention of his readers by presenting a clear text without the many intricacies or artificial devices used by other writers. His work reveals his ability to create psychological profiles of the Puerto Rican people. In a manner similar to that of **Ana Lydia Vega,** he gives insights into the cultural fabric of modern Puerto Rican culture. To a large extent, his work expresses his hidden cry for egalitarianism or pluralism, or perhaps a peace of mind, that has (allegedly) been lost to progress, industrialization, colonialism and materialism. Among his most prominent works are *El Asedio* (1958); *Figuraciones en el mes de marzo* (1972); *Mi mamá me ama* (1981); and *Dicen que de noche tú no duermes* (1985). He has also written many documentary scripts and has contributed to numerous literary magazines. He is currently a professor of Spanish at the **University of Puerto Rico.**

SUGGESTED READING

Eduardo C. Bejar, "Beyond the Puerto Rican Monotheme: The Postmodern Novels of Emilio Díaz Varcárcel," *Mid-Hudson Language Studies*, 11 (1988): 65–71; Emilio Díaz Varcárcel, *El Asedio* (Mexico: Arrecifle, 1958); Emilio Díaz Varcárcel, *Figuraciones en el mes de marzo* (Barcelona, Spain: Seix Barral, 1972); Emilio Díaz Varcárcel, *Mi mamá me ama* (Barcelona, Spain: Seix Barral, 1981); Emilio Díaz Varcárcel, *Dicen que de noche tú no duermes* (Rio Piedras, P.R.: Cultural, 1985); John C. Miller, "The Emigrant in New York City: A Consideration of Four Puerto Rican Writers," *Melus* 5 no. 3, (1978): 82–99.

Dignidad This cultural concept has great significance for Puerto Ricans of all political persuasions and all social classes. The obvious translation of this word is dignity but, along with the word *respeto, dignidad* carries far more significance in Puerto Rican culture than it does in American culture. As if by a natural right, each man and woman in Puerto Rican society *has* dignity and *is owed* respect. This assumption is taken for granted in virtually any social encounter; *dignidad* is the silent partner when you buy something at a store, share a beer in a bar or invite someone to a party in your home. Like **personalismo,** *dignidad* and *respeto* are traits with deep roots in 500 years of colonialism. This attitude, underlined by Governor of Puerto Rico Theodore Roosevelt, Jr., also characterized many of the Spanish colonists: "We [Americans] have one besetting sin in common with many other peoples, including the British. We think we are better than other people. Anyone who does things in different fashion from us is either comic or stupid" (Roosevelt 1937, p. 83). Thus, after 500 years of other people's arrogance, islanders watch out for each other because the colonial authorities did (and do) not.

One additional manifestation of *dignidad* and *respeto* is the courtesy that is an everyday feature of Puerto Rican life. Except when they are driving their cars, islanders are kind and pleasant to one another. And to be hosted by a Puerto Rican in his or her home is to experience a sense of caring— a genuine warmth—that is often lacking in other cultures. In the apartment skyscrapers of San Juan it is still commonplace to be escorted to the elevator by one's host, or even to the street.

The opposite side of these traits is a sensitivity to even the mildest form of criticism, coupled with praise that speaks, not to an objective achievement, but to the dignity that must be stroked. According to Gordon Lewis, "The mediocre person, at all occupational levels, is only too easily tempted to convert notice of his mediocrity into an insult to his 'dignity' and to meet criticism, however legitimate, with a show of injured pride" (Lewis 1963, p. 420).

SUGGESTED READING

Anthony Lauria, "Respeto, Relajo and Interpersonal Relations in Puerto Rico," *Anthropological Quarterly* 37, no. 2 (1964); Gordon Lewis, *Puerto Rico: Freedom and Power in the Caribbean* (New York: Harper, 1963); Theodore Roosevelt, Jr., *Colonial Policies of the United States* (Garden City, N.Y.: Doubleday, 1937).

Diplo   *See* **Ortiz del Rivero, Ramón.**

Discrimination   Discrimination and prejudice are social phenomena found in most societies. Puerto Rico is not immune to them. Both as a Spanish and as an American possession, Puerto Rico has been subjected to the hegemonic forces of foreign oppressors since its discovery and early colonization. As a result, Puerto Ricans always have had the presence of a colonial figure who sits tall at the top echelons of society and who has defined the power elite or ruling class. Whether they were the Spanish potentates that came to colonize and exploit the wealth of the island, extinguishing the native **Taínos** and importing slaves (see **Slavery**), or the American governors and military officers who came after them, the upper class has always been made up by or nurtured by these colonial figures. Clear class boundaries, if artificial, have always been in place in the island of Puerto Rico and have lent themselves to discrimination on the basis of class. Those who have ruled and exploited have looked down on those who have done the work and generated the profits.

José Luis González, the noted writer, has argued in his extended essay *"El país de cuatro pisos"* that Puerto Ricans have found it difficult to develop individual and collective national identities as a result of the many transformations suffered by the colony. If his thesis, which seems plausible, is accepted, it is possible to explain the source of many of the prejudices harbored by Puerto Ricans. Take, for instance, racial prejudice. Although people of assorted racial tonalities and ethnicities have managed to live together and interact without much overt racial turmoil or conflict, many people from the upper classes privately reject or mock and refuse to associate through family relationships with people they perceive as being darker or who have African traits (i.e., wide nose, dark skin or kinky hair; see **African Roots**). Many such people prefer to ignore the fact that they themselves may have these elements in their own heritage because of the many assorted ethnic elements that constitute Puerto Rican race and ethnicity. However, they use their privileged position, mostly economically based, to discriminate against others. To a large extent, racial prejudice is based on the artificial distinctions and values determined by the upper class according to what they think is suitable and acceptable. The blatant racism of many Puerto Ricans toward people from the Dominican Republic who have migrated to the island over the past twenty years is a sad reflection of these dynamics (see **Dominicans**).

It is noteworthy, however, that the political and legal system has tried to acknowledge these problems and to build equity and balance into the system to guarantee access to as many "different" people as possible. Some scholars have argued that the system has been far more progressive than that in the United States. For example, long before the Civil Rights movement of the 1960s and the many laws and regulations that emerged from it, Puerto Rico had a legal mechanism to protect its residents from the consequences of discrimination within society and the workplace. By June 1959, there was already a very clear law that protected Puerto Ricans against discrimination or prejudice in the workplace. Law 100 gave people the right to launch civil actions if they had been discriminated against on the basis of age, color, religion or social conditions. Throughout its recent history, the legal system has been increasingly active in protecting people against discrimination. One recent case decided by the supreme court in Puerto Rico merits our attention because of its proactive stance against age discrimination.

In the case of *Odriozola vs. Superior Cosmetic Distribution Corporation*, decided by the supreme court in June 1985, the court reaffirmed the validity of Law 100 and set up guidelines to protect individuals against age discrimination in the workplace. Odriozola, the plaintiff, sued Superior Cosmetics and Germaine Montiel Cosmetiques Corporation and accused them of firing him when he reached the age of sixty after fifteen years of a fairly successful career with the company. The plaintiff claimed that age discrimination was solely responsible for the firing. The Puerto Rican Supreme Court reaffirmed the validity of Law 100 in protecting the rights of employees. The Odriozola case leaves no room for employers to discriminate on the basis of age, race, gender, religion or social condition and not be punished for their actions.

SUGGESTED READING

José Luis González, *The Four Storeyed Country* (New York: Marcus Weiner, 1993); Puerto Rican Supreme Court, June 28, 1985, *Odriozola vs. Superior Cosmetics Distributors Corporation*, 116. D.P.R. 485.

Dominicans (Los Dominicanos) Approximately 75,000 Dominicans have migrated to Puerto Rico in recent years. Migration, always a fact of Caribbean life, is best exemplified now by the television and newspaper stories about the Haitian "boat people." But, on the other side of Hispaniola, large numbers of Dominicans have also emigrated. Many come legally to the United States; others, in voyages that are every bit as dangerous as those experienced by the Haitians, cross the Mona passage and settle in Puerto Rico. Some try to enter the United States posing as Puerto Ricans and American citizens; others settle on the island because opportunities there are much better than those in the Dominican Republic.

Dominicans often perform Puerto Rico's most menial tasks, and a significant amount of tension exists between native Puerto Ricans and Dominican immigrants. In recent years, Dominican ethnic jokes have begun to appear; they are often as controversial as those told about recent immigrants to the United States.

SUGGESTED READING

Jorge Duany, ed. *Los dominicanos en Puerto Rico: Migración en la semi-periferia* (San Juan, P.R.: Ediciones Huracán, 1990); Barry Levine, ed. *The Caribbean Exodus* (New York: Praeger, 1987).

Drugs Not long ago, when residents of Vega Baja were prowling about in a vacant lot, they discovered a number of buried cans and, to their amazement, millions of dollars stashed in the cans. Some of these citizens began to flaunt their new-found wealth, which alerted the authorities (and the criminals, as well) to the discovery of a small fortune in drug money. Critics laughed at the people who had spent the money so conspicuously, but how many of us could resist such a temptation?

Drugs threaten the honesty of citizens and police from Colombia to Mexico; the problem for Puerto Rico is that it has fast become the entry point in the eastern Caribbean for cocaine from South America and from other parts of the world. An August 1995 U.S. government interagency report indicated that Puerto Rico (and the Virgin Islands) accounted for 26 percent of the *documented* attempts to smuggle cocaine into the United States (*Drug Control* 1996, p. 5).

The island's many miles of beaches have always acted as a magnet for those who seek to air-drop their cargo in isolated areas. But, in recent years, drug traffickers have increasingly relied on "go-fast boats, sailing and fishing vessels, and containerized cargo ships" to transport drugs. The dealers are so sophisticated that "they also use cellular phones and global positioning systems to determine drop coordinates prior to departure. The traffickers then relay the coordinates to the boats who will pick up an airdrop" (p. 12). The result is that Puerto Rico has become a hub, not only for American Airlines, but also for the traffickers who send their goods directly from South America or first to an island like Saint Lucia or Saint Vincent and, then, on the high seas to Puerto Rico. Ultimately, the cocaine and other drugs make their way to the Southeast of the United States and from there to the entire nation.

Daily life in Puerto Rico is affected in a variety of negative ways by drugs—for example, increased corruption at all levels of political and social life, increased levels of addiction, increased levels of **AIDS in Puerto Rico** and, in support of drug habits, increased levels of **crime**. As on the U.S. mainland, even the most incorruptible and sophisticated police interdiction systems can stop only so much of the drug trade. As long as there is a demand—among all social classes—for drugs like cocaine, Puerto Rico will be plagued by the problem. However, the terrible irony in recent years is that as interdiction efforts have produced some success in the Bahamas, traffickers have increasingly relied on Puerto Rico as the "best" place to use for the import (from South America and elsewhere) and export (to the United States) of drugs.

SUGGESTED READING

Drug Control: U.S. Interdiction Efforts in the Caribbean Decline (Washington, D.C.: Government Accounting Office, 1996).

E

Edict against the African Race (Bando contra la Raza Africana)   This 1848 proclamation made by the Spanish government attempted to maintain the institution of **slavery** in Puerto Rico. During the first half of the nineteenth century, one European nation after another began to abolish slavery. When the Spanish feared that the abolitionists would succeed in the Caribbean, they issued the Edict against the African Race. This proclamation made no distinction between Africans who were free and those who were slaves, and Article II reaffirmed the superiority before the law of anyone with white skin. Even if an attack on a white person was justified, it was prohibited. A free African "guilty" of striking a white person lost his right hand. In Article III the edict emphasized that if an African threatened a white person with a stick or criticized a white person, he or she would be condemned to five years in prison.

To understand this proclamation, it is necessary to consider some facts. Between 1601 and 1870, millions of African prisoners arrived in the Caribbean. Between 1811 and 1870, however, none were brought to Trinidad, Jamaica, Barbados or Grenada. Meanwhile, over half a million slaves arrived in Cuba and another 55,000 men and women arrived in Puerto Rico. (Recall the efforts of **Alejandro de O'Reilly** or the **Warrant of Opportunity** or the Cédula de Gracias.) Spain tried to resurrect its Caribbean colonies by underwriting the labors of those who established sugar plantations. The Spanish sought to institutionalize one of the most onerous forms of slavery at the very time that the revolutions in the United States, France and Haiti threatened slavery in both ideological and practical senses. Jan Rogoziński notes that what made slavery on tropical plantations unusual was the master's total freedom of control over his or her slaves . . . slaves working on cane estates always suffered the harshest conditions and labored under the most rigorous controls. For example, during the harvest season slaves started at midnight; they worked 20 hours a day, laboring under the whip wielded by an overseer and near the ovens that resembled hell. (Rogoziński 1992, 128)

As early as 1812, these conditions resulted in one of the first slave revolts in Puerto Rican history. Others quickly followed. In 1821 approximately 1,500 slaves conspired—unsuccessfully—against owners in Bayamón, Toa Alta and Río Piedras. Four years later, slaves revolted in **Ponce**. Well into the 1840s, slaves resisted their masters in Guayama, Vega Baja and Guayanilla. The edict was, therefore, a last-ditch attempt to stem the tide of history. It failed. Slavery was finally abolished in Puerto Rico in 1873. But, as recent scholarship reminds us, the abolition occurred for practical as well as idealistic reasons. Slaves were expensive and they had to be fed and clothed throughout the year. From many an owner's perspective, the easiest way to increase profits was to reduce human overhead by freeing the slaves. (See also **Slavery** and **African Roots**.)

SUGGESTED READING

Ricardo Alegria, ed. *Temas de la historia de Puerto Rico* (San Juan, P.R.: Centro de Estudios Avanzados de Puerto Rico and El Caribe, 1988); Guillermo Baralt, *Esclavos rebeldes* (San Juan, P.R.: Huracán, 1982); Lydia Milagros González and Angell G. Quintero Rivera, *La otra cara de la historia*, 2d ed. (Río Piedras, P.R.: Cerep, 1991); Jan Rogoziński, *A Brief History of the Caribbean* (New York: Meridian, 1992); Francisco Scarano, *Sugar and Slavery in Puerto Rico* (Madison: University of Wisconsin Press, 1984).

Education With the arrival of the Spanish colonists, education on the island became the domain of the Catholic Church and its missionaries. At the age of thirteen, all the sons of *caciques* were required to live with the Franciscan missionaries for four years, where they would be taught reading, writing and religion. For most of the sixteenth and seventeenth centuries, education continued to be fundamentally religious and limited to males. During the nineteenth century, education for males between the ages of six and twelve was compulsory. Wealthy families, however, had the option of sending their children to private schools, hiring tutors or sending their children abroad. In addition, schools, both private and public, began to be supervised by the governor of the island.

In 1820 Tadeo de Rivera addressed, for the first time, the issue of methodology and teaching and developed a teaching manual, titled *Method of Instruction*, as a guide for teachers. His outline for material in the curriculum included religion, morality, reading, writing, grammar, arithmetic and civility. In terms of teaching methods, learning was based on memorization of long literary and religious passages in books, and critical thinking was not encouraged. Education was not well organized; there were no centers for training teachers, and their low remuneration was, at best, irregular. For the colonists in power, education, in an island that was lacking so much in terms of infrastructures and economic base, was not a priority.

The results of a 1958 study conducted on the educational system in Puerto Rico, which included data on the year 1898, commissioned by the legislature, gave the following facts: By the end of the nineteenth century, there were 380 schools for males and 138 schools for females, as well as 26 secondary schools, for a total of 554 schools for 44,861 students. Of the total population of over 810,000 inhabitants, over 80 percent were illiterate. Only 16.7 percent of the 268,639 school-aged children attended schools.

With the arrival of the new colonists in 1898, the school system was dramatically altered, and its structure was based on the American educational system. First and foremost was the separation between church and state. Schools were to be nonsectarian and open to all socioeconomic groups and to both genders. Primary education was mandated by law, and the development and implementation of middle and secondary schools followed shortly thereafter. The management of the school system was centralized under the authority of a commissioner appointed by U.S. government authorities, and his responsibilities included the chancellorship of the **University of Puerto Rico** as well as president of the institution's board of trustees. One of the first mandates of the first appointed commissioner of education, Martin Brumbaugh, was to establish English as the language of instruction. The first commission on education under the **Foraker Act** outlined their educational blueprint to the War Department in a report that included the following recommendations:

We believe that the public school system which now prevails in the United States should be provided for Porto Rico [sic] and that the same system of education and the same character of books now regarded most favorably in this country should be given to them. . . . The teachers in these schools should, in great part, be Americans who are familiar with the methods, system, and books of the American Schools, and they should instruct the children in the English Language. . . . That this education should be in English we are clearly of opinion. Porto Rico is now and henceforth to be part of the American possessions and its people are to be American. (Negrón de Montilla 1970, 51)

For most of the twentieth century, the alterations made to the educational system, to make it resemble the American structure, have been kept in place. The changes that have occurred included the elimination of English as the language of instruction in 1949 as well as the appointment of an education commissioner, now known as the secretary of education.

Since 1949 the secretary of education has been appointed by the island's elected governor, and his or her sole responsibility is to oversee the entire public school instructional system known until 1990 as the Department of Public Instruction and now known as the Department of Education.

Throughout the years, numerous reforms have been initiated in the educational system by the political parties in power at a particular time. Enumerating them would require too much space; however, it is important to note that over 95 percent of the population in Puerto Rico are now literate and that, from the 16.7 percent of the eligible population who attended school during the turn of the century, Puerto Rico can now boast an attendance rate of over 95 percent.

Private schools, particularly Catholic and other religious schools, register about 20 percent of the school-aged population. There has been much debate over the quality of instruction in these schools over public education. In many cases, access to private education has been the domain of those who could afford it, and of those who were awarded scholarships to attend. Although the private school system had been accredited throughout the century by the island's Department of Instruction, it was not until 1958 that the legislature authorized the secretary of education to formulate regulations that would guide the accreditation process for these schools.

The development and expansion of postsecondary educational institutions have also seen a dramatic increase in this last century. The first institution of higher education, the University of Puerto Rico (UPR), started in 1903 with a total enrollment of 154 students; today, its eleven campuses (counting the medical school) serve more than 52,000 students. The Río Piedras campus alone provides education to more than 30,000 men and women. Overall, Puerto Rico has sixteen accredited colleges and universities.

Many of the initiatives that have driven the educational system in the United States have had an impact on the island's system as well. During the 1960s, federal funding for schools began to see an increase, which has been attributed to President Lyndon Johnson's War on Poverty initiatives and his Great Society programs. In Puerto Rico, it was not until the 1970s that these changes were seen with the incorporation of Operation Head Start, special education and other new programs. In addition, the traditional teacher-centered mode of instruction began to give way to a more student-centered, collaborative approach to teaching. The increase in federal funding to higher education, such as Pell Grants and low-interest student loans, boosted registration in many of the island's universities and led to the expansion of UPR campuses around the island. Also during the 1970s, the island saw the most rapid expansion of schooling in the private sector in its history. Many private universities were created during this time, and some U.S. universities established campuses on the island. By 1983, 65 percent of postsecondary students were attending private institutions.

In summary, the educational system in Puerto Rico is very much tied to partisan politics. The UPR chancellor, the secretary of education, and many of the other high positions in the educational system are political appointments. In some ways, implementation of reforms and new programs depend on whether a political party remains in office long enough to see them through. Nevertheless, Puerto Rico remains one of the North American countries with the largest population attending postsecondary institutions.

SUGGESTED READING

Edith Algren de Guitérrez, *The Movement against Teaching English in the Schools of Puerto Rico* (Lanham, Md.: University Press of America, 1987); Charles Beirne, *The Problem of "Americanization" in the Catholic Schools of Puerto Rico* (Río Piedras, P.R.: Editorial Universitaria, 1975); Arthur Liebman, *The Politics of Puerto Rican University Students* (Austin: University of Texas Press, 1970); Alfonso López Yustos, *Historia documental de la educación en Puerto Rico* (San Juan, P.R.: Publicaciones Puertorriqueñas, 1992); Aida Negrón de Montilla, *Americanization in Puerto Rico and the Public School System: 1900–1930* (Río Piedras, P.R.: Editorial Edil, 1970); Juan José Osuna, *A History of Education in Puerto Rico* (Río Piedras: University of Puerto Rico, 1949); Consejo Superior de Enseñanza, *Estudio del sistema educativo puertorriqueño* (San Juan: Informe de la División de Investigaciones Pedagógicas del Consejo Superior de Enseñanza a la Comisión de Instrucción de la Cámara de Representantes, 1960); Catherine Walsh, *Pedagogy and the Struggle for Voice: Issues of Language, Power and Schooling for Puerto Ricans* (New York: Bergin and Garvey, 1991).

El Mundo   During the seven decades of its history, *El Mundo* was one of the most powerful and influential newspapers in Puerto Rico. *El Mundo* was founded in 1919 by Spanish publisher Romualdo Real who was also the publisher of the famous cultural magazine *Puerto Rico Ilustrado*. Despite its modest beginnings—the paper consisted of only twelve pages during the early years—*El Mundo* grew to be the newspaper with the largest circulation in the island. The huge success and prestige of this publication were largely attributed to the vision of Angel Ramos (1902–1960) who became its director in 1924 and who later bought it from Real (Romeu 1985).

El Mundo, published in the standard format, was a well-balanced newspaper that covered a wide array of thematic areas of interest to its diverse readers. Many of Puerto Rico's most distinguished journalists and literary figures wrote at some point for this newspaper, including Teófilo Maldonado, Luis Rechani Agrait, Veicente Geigel Polanco, Samuel R. Quiñones and **Manuel Méndez Ballester**. Columnists such as Jorge Javaris, Miguel Santín and Eliseo Combas Guerra, who were inquisitive observers of the political ferment of the island, respected the voices of the politicians as well as those the public. José Coll Vidal, Pablo Vargas Badillo and Alex W. Maldonado were some of the visionary editorial directors who guided *El*

Mundo through the many changes experienced by Puerto Rican society after the decade of the 1940s.

Throughout its long life, *El Mundo* was a fertile ground for Puerto Rican women journalists and literary figures. **Angela Negrón Muñoz, Nilita Vientós Gastón,** Isabel Cintrón and Norma Valle Ferrer were some of the paper's most visible women journalists. In 1982 *El Mundo* appointed Helga Sérrano, a journalist trained at Columbia University, to be assistant director of the newspaper.

For many years, *El Mundo* had well-structured, efficient circulation, news and advertising departments which made the newspaper appealing to readers and profitable for advertisers. During the decade of the 1970s, however, the newspaper began to experience serious labor conflicts from employees who resisted changes to make the circulation department more efficient (e.g., *El Mundo* had a large transport and distribution fleet that was outmoded). Several strikes led to partial closings, and *El Mundo* lost some of its readers to the other major newspaper—*El Nuevo Día*. In addition, its standard format became outdated, and it started to lose favor among readers who preferred the more compact format of *El Nuevo Día* and the **San Juan Star,** which was easier to read and handle. These problems eventually led to an erosion among its readership base. In addition, *El Nuevo Día* launched a fierce advertising war with rates that *El Mundo* found impossible to match or beat. In 1987 the paper closed. It reopened briefly under a new owner who was unable to bring the paper back to its old glory days. The Angel Ramos Foundation has sold all the assets of the paper. It is unlikely that it will emerge again. Readers with a sense of history can still read the paper on microfilm. Its photographic collection is owned now by the University of Puerto Rico Library, which is digitizing its huge photo collection. It provides, especially for the 1930s, one of the best records of Puerto Rican political and cultural life.

SUGGESTED READING

José A. Romeu, *Panorama del periodismo puertorriqueño* (Río Piedras, P.R.: UPREX, 1985).

El Nuevo Día   *El Nuevo Día* is the most important contemporary newspaper on the island of Puerto Rico. This newspaper was founded in **Ponce** in 1909 under the name of *El Diario de Puerto Rico*. It was owned then by Guillermo Cintrón who used to write in the newspaper under the surname of Bombón. In 1911 the name of *El Diario de Puerto Rico* was changed to *El Día*.

This newspaper was published in Ponce for fifty-nine years. Important journalists and writers who contributed to and worked for the newspaper include Eugenio Astol, Felix Matos Bernier, Guillermo Atiles García and Juan Braschi. Nemesio Canales (1878–1923), one of the most important writers and journalistic figures from the island, bought the newspaper in 1914 and wrote the famous column "Paliques," which provided political and social commentary.

During the decade of the 1950s, **Luis Ferré**, a businessman and later governor of Puerto Rico, bought the newspaper. In 1961 the format of the newspaper was changed from standard to tabloid. A decade later, in 1970, the newspaper moved its operations to San Juan and was renamed *El Nuevo Día* under the stewardship of Antonio Luis Ferré, Ferré's son. At that time, *El Nuevo Día* expanded its coverage of the island. The timing of the move from Ponce was critical to the success of this newspaper. At the time, **El Mundo**, then the leading newspaper of the island, had undergone a long strike, and *El Nuevo Día* was able to attract and take away its readers. Since its beginning, the publishers of *El Nuevo Día* have tried to produce a graphically appealing newspaper which carries large photographs, a dynamic design and a lively presentation of the news. Despite the fact that the newspaper is owned by a family linked and associated to the political establishment of the island, the newspaper has tried to maintain an independent editorial policy. During these years, the newspaper has employed excellent journalists and reporters and has published columns by leading writers, politicians and personalities representing a broad range of opinions, beliefs and viewpoints.

El Nuevo Día is regarded as an inclusive newspaper that fosters the preservation of a wide array of ideas. Prominent women, such as politician and scholar **Celeste Benítez Rivera** and university professor Aida Montilla, are frequent columnists. The paper has also employed a variety of very capable women reporters, among them Eva Lizardi, Nilka Estrada Resto, and Yolanda Rosaly.

El Nuevo Día has had a huge commercial success in the island. When it started, it had an approximate circulation of 40,000 issues daily. Gale Research reports that it now has a circulation of approximately 230,000 newspapers daily and 238,000 on Sundays (Brown 1996). According to its own readership studies, *El Nuevo Día* is read by about 1 million individuals every day. Due to its dynamic style and strong hold over the publishing market, this newspaper has been able to command more of 70 percent of the advertising market shared by the three newspapers of the island. As a result, businessmen and entrepreneurs find it difficult, if not impossible, to launch operations that may compete with *El Nuevo Día*.

SUGGESTED READING

Gary Braun, ed., *Gale Directory of Publications and Broadcast Media* (Detroit: Gale Research, 1996); Nemesio Canales, *Paliques* (Ponce, P.R.: Tipografía La Defensa, 1913); El Nuevo Día, *Historical Semblance* (San Juan: Unpublished Document, 1996); José A. Romeu, *Panorama del periodismo puertorriqueño* (Río Piedras, P.R.: UPREX, 1995).

El Vocero de Puerto Rico A tabloid-style newspaper published daily since 1974, *El Vocero*, as it is popularly known, is the highest circulating paper in the island distributing about 259,000 issues every day and about 193,000 on Saturdays. Published by Alfredo Arias and edited by Gaspar Roca, *El Vocero* is known for its sensationalist coverage of daily events and particularly for its gory coverage of crime scenes. It is not uncommon for *El Vocero* to portray dismembered bodies, photographs of accident and murder victims and the like. *El Vocero* has a unique rhetorical style that makes light of the most grotesque events, and it uses blunt headlines in gigantic red ink to attract the attention of the public. It is jokingly said that if you squeeze a copy of *El Vocero* you will get blood. This newspaper has been characterized by a very light editorial content and specialization in coverage of police and crime scenes. *El Vocero* has been very efficient in establishing a network of reporters around police headquarters, courthouses, hospitals and morgues, which allows them to bring timely information to their readers. *El Vocero* is regarded as the newspaper of the working class.

SUGGESTED READING

Gary Braun, *Gale Directory of Publications and Broadcast Media* (New York: Gale Research, 1996); José A. Romeu, *Panorama del periodismo Puertorriqueño* (Rio Piedras, P.R.: UPREX, 1985).

Enhanced Commonwealth This term refers to the almost fifty years of efforts made by the **Popular Democratic Party** to increase the political, economic and military powers granted to Puerto Rico when, between 1950 and 1952, it became the Commonwealth of Puerto Rico. On June 17, 1959, Governor **Luis Muñoz Marín** presented a four-page memo, "The Status of the Commonwealth," to President Dwight David Eisenhower. The governor complained that the U.S. Congress had refused to pass bills that substantially *enhanced* the powers allegedly granted to the Puerto Rican government in 1952. Thus, Muñoz asked that the president support his contention that the commonwealth included "complete self government for Puerto Rico" and that the president support the congressional efforts designed to give Puerto Rico control over issues that ranged from tariffs to local law. After the governor left the White House, the president asked an aide "to examine into the Commonwealth question which seemed to bother him [Muñoz Marín] so much" (Fernandez 1996, 194–195). Apparently the president had no idea what the commonwealth was. But, even if he did, he too would have confronted the U.S. constitutional barrier that has always been a stumbling block to increasing the powers granted to Puerto Rico in 1952.

Article IV, Section 3 of the Constitution says that "Congress shall have power to dispose of and make all needful rules and regulations respecting the territory or other property belonging to the United States." The first sentence of the law which created the commonwealth says that Puerto Rico "belongs" to the United States. Thus, whether it was Governor Muñoz in 1959 or Governor **Rafael Hernández Colón** in 1974 and 1991, Puerto Rican leaders have been unable to enhance the powers granted to the commonwealth because, from Congress's perspective, it would be unconstitutional to give to Puerto Rico powers the U.S. Constitution explicitly reserves for Congress. In the 1990s advocates of both statehood and independence have argued that, given the limitations of Article IV, Section 3 of the U.S. Constitution, commonwealth is not a viable political alternative for the Puerto Rican people. This is a hotly contested issue in contemporary Puerto Rico. (See also **Free Associated State.**)

SUGGESTED READING

Arturo Morales Carrion, *Puerto Rico and the United States: The Quest for a New Encounter* (San Juan, P.R.: Editorial Academica, 1990); Juan Manuel García Passalacqua, *La crisis politica en Puerto Rico*, 2d ed. (Río Piedras, P.R.: Edil, 1983); Rafael Hernández Colón, *New Theses* (San Juan, P.R., 1979); Henry Wells, *The Modernization of Puerto Rico* (Cambridge, Mass.: Harvard University Press, 1969); Ronald Fernandez, *The Disenchanted Island: Puerto Rico and the United States in the Twentieth Century*, 2d ed. (Westport, Conn.: Praeger, 1996).

Estado Libre Asociado   *See* **Free Associated State.**

Estrada, Noel (1918–1979)   Estrada, a composer, was born in Isabela. Although he wrote hundreds of songs during his lifetime, he is best remembered by his song "En mi viejo San Juan" (My Old San Juan). This song, composed in 1942, is a melancholic ode that masterfully captures the feelings of Puerto Ricans who leave the island and forever treasure the precious memories of life in the city. "En mi viejo San Juan" is one of the most recorded Puerto Rican songs of all times and it is now the official city anthem of San Juan. Many writers and critics consider this composition to be as significant as "La Borinqueña," Puerto Rico's national anthem.

Estrada never received formal music training and played musical instruments only by ear (Sarramía 1993, 86). Instead, Estrada attended the **University of Puerto Rico**, where he majored in business, and for most of his life worked as a protocol officer for the State Department in the island. At the time of his death in 1979, the American entertainment weekly *Variety* reported that Estrada had authored around 600 musical compositions during his musical career (*Variety* 1979, 92). Some of his other important compositions are are "Amor del Alma," "Amor del Cafetal," "El amor del Jibarito," "Amargura" and "Mi romantico San Juan." Many of his songs have patriotic undertones and are characterized for his love of the island's beauties and values. He left a valued musical legacy to Puerto Ricans.

SUGGESTED READING

Tomas Sarramía, *Nuestra gente* (San Juan: Publicaciones Puertorriqueñas, 1993); "Noel Estrada," Obituary, *Variety*, December 19, 1979, 92.

Executive Council   This term refers to an essential component of the Puerto Rican political system after that system was reorganized by the U.S. Congress with the passage in 1900 of the **Foraker Act**. Between 1898 and 1900, U.S. policy makers debated about how to govern their new Caribbean possession. Ultimately they used the English system of colonial control as a general model for Puerto Rico's Executive Council. Since this council dominated Puerto Rican life for almost twenty years (from 1900 to 1917), it was accurately called "the center or keystone" of the entire U.S. political apparatus. The Executive Council was composed of eleven members, all appointed by the president of the United States. The unique thing about the council was that six of its members were simultaneously heads of the island's executive departments (e.g., the Department of Education) and members of the upper house of the island's legislature. In the United States, checks and balances operated to control political ambitions. In Puerto Rico, the Executive Council's unusual degree of authority produced this result according to William Willoughby, a member of the Executive Council from 1900 until 1909: "To a large extent the Executive Council took the whole control over the manner in which the actual administration of affairs shall be exercised out of the hands of the people of the island itself" (Willoughby 1905, p. 86). The council granted all franchises, privileges and concessions of a public nature; it determined the salaries of all officials not appointed by the president of the United States; and it also controlled the budget for the conduct of government. Of the council's eleven members, law mandated that at least five be Puerto Rican. In practice, however, the president of the United States appointed Americans to head each of the six executive departments and gave Puerto Ricans less important roles in the island's governance. The admitted absence of Puerto Rican authority produced a crisis in 1909 when the Puerto Rican House of Delegates—the only elected body in the island's central government—contended that they had ultimate authority over the island's annual appropriations. In response, President William Howard Taft told islanders that "Porto Rico [*sic*] has been the favored daughter of the United States." The crisis in 1909 "was only an indication that we have gone somewhat too fast in the extension of political power to them [the Puerto Ricans] for their own good" (Taft, 1909, p. 5). The Executive Council was abolished in 1917, when the **Jones Act** changed the nature of the island's government.

SUGGESTED READING

Theodore Roosevelt, Jr., *Colonial Policies of the United States* (Garden City, N.Y.: Doubleday, 1937); William Howard Taft, "Affairs in Porto Rico," Message from the President, Senate, 61st Congress, Document 40, 1909; U.S. Congress, Senate, *Affairs in Porto Rico*, message from the President of the United States, 61st Cong., Document no. 40, May 10, 1909; William Frank Willoughby, *Territories and Dependencies of the United States* (New York: Century Company, 1905).

F

FALN The FALN, an acronym for Fuerzas Armadas de Liberación Nacional, or the Armed Forces of National Liberation, is a Puerto Rican revolutionary group that assumed responsibility for 120 bombings in the United States between 1974 and 1981. Their principal aim was to gain independence for Puerto Rico; the primary target of their attacks was government or corporate buildings that, in the eyes of the FALN, symbolized the exploitation of the Puerto Rican people. Five people lost their lives as a result of FALN bombings; more than a dozen members of the group were tried for **seditious conspiracy** (treason), but not for the actual bombings, in the early 1980s. They received sentences that averaged seventy years and, in the mid-1990s, there is a widespread movement to free these political prisoners. However, in the eyes of such people as Resident Commissioner **Carlos Romero Barceló**, the members of the FALN are criminals. This disagreement underlines a 100-year-old controversy in Puerto Rico. What are the limits of protest when all island political parties agree that Puerto Rico is a U.S. colony? To many, one of the most remarkable things about the FALN is that they originated in Chicago; many of the members had spent little time on the island. But, in trying to understand the migration and economic condition of Puerto Ricans in the United States, they drew the conclusion that the root cause of the economic and educational problems experienced by Puerto Ricans in the United States was their colonial relationship to the United States.

SUGGESTED READING

Ronald Fernandez, *Prisoners of Colonialism: The Struggle for Justice in Puerto Rico* (Monroe, Me.: Common Courage, 1994); for a different perspective, William Sater,

Puerto Rican Terrorists: A Possible Threat to U.S. Energy Installations (Palo Alto, Calif.: Rand Corporation, 1981).

Family   It is essential to understand the love, admiration, respect and importance that Puerto Ricans give to the family, or *familia*, to understand Puerto Rican society and culture. Puerto Ricans' concern for the family is one of the traits that best describe them. For most Puerto Ricans, life is defined around the family unit, and considerations for the family will always take precedence over the individual or the self.

What constitutes a family for a Puerto Rican? Although Puerto Rican society is patriarchal in nature, and all families are organized in the traditional nuclear form that distinguishes Western societies (a father, a mother, and their children), the family is a fairly fluid construct for most Puerto Ricans. For them, the family unit is open and extended. As long as there are blood ties or affective links among a group of people, no matter how close or removed, these people will always be regarded as family. It is not uncommon for an individual member removed six or seven generations from a particular family of origin to be considered a family member. It is not uncommon either for someone who is associated to another person through a marriage relationship to be recognized and included as a family member. The word *pariente*, or relative, for instance, is used to describe those relationships. Feelings of respect, care, and consideration will always be extended to anyone considered to be, in one way or another, a family member. The extended family is wide. It entails a great degree of social and moral responsibility. Institutions such as *compadrazgo* (someone who christens someone else's child) will often entail acceptance into the family and a commitment to care for that child if the need arises. If a distant relative is in need, there is an expectation that one will help if one has the resources to do so.

Puerto Rican society has been affected by most of the changes that have affected industrial societies (i.e., industrialization, urbanization and modernization). Consequently, the institution of the family in Puerto Rico has suffered the impact of a myriad of social problems such as divorce, drug dependency, crime and so on. For example, according to Dora Nevares, who uses statistics from the 1990 U.S. Census, 44 percent of all marriages end up in divorce (Nevares 1996, 42). In addition, as a social and cultural institution, the Puerto Rican family has been affected by a gradual liberalization of sexual and gender roles in the society that has lent itself to changes. For example, consensual relationships are starting to be seen as a little bit more normative, there is more tolerance for gay relationships, and while sexual activity among adolescents is still condemned, it is tolerated. Although these attitudes are gradually transforming the family into less of a nuclear unit, Puerto Ricans still use affection and personal closeness to strengthen the family.

The importance of the family has led sociologists to identify a cultural pattern known as *familismo*. It acknowledges that the family is one of the most important social institutions and that the family mediates almost all individual and social dynamics. It is not uncommon for an older son, married and independent, to still take into account and ask for family permission when making an important decision such as buying a house or accepting a new job. In the same vein, the mother is always the most important, venerated or respected figure within the family. Women may still not control some important decisions of their lives in Puerto Rican society, but there is nonetheless a great deal of respect around the female figure in the family. This is known as *marianismo*. For most Puerto Ricans, in contrast to Americans, the family is the element that gives them their character and identity. In Puerto Rican society, who your family is, is who you are.

SUGGESTED READING

Joseph P. Fitzpatrick, *Puerto Rican Americans* (Englewood Cliffs, N.J.: Prentice Hall, 1987); Angela Beatriz Ginorio, *A Comparison of Puerto Ricans in New York with Native Puerto Ricans* (Ann Arbor, Mich.: University Microfilms International, 1979); Reuben Hill, J. M. Stycos and Kurt Black, *The Family and Population Control: A Puerto Rican Experiment in Social Change* (Chapel Hill: University of North Carolina Press, 1959); David Landy, *Tropical Childhood* (Chapel Hill: University of North Carolina Press, 1959); Oscar Lewis, *La Vida* (New York: Random House, 1965); Mayra Muñoz Vázquez and Edwin Fernández Bauzó, *El divorcio en la sociedad puertorriqueña* (Río Piedras, P.R.: Editorial Huracán, 1988); Dora Nevares-Muñiz, *El Crineu en Puerto Rico: Tapando El Cielo en la Mario* (Hato Rey, P.R.: Institute para 1996); Esmeralda Santiago, *When I Was Puerto Rican* (New York: Vintage, 1993).

Feminism   This movement has resurfaced in the last twenty years, but feminism on the island goes back to at least the turn of the century; it includes, for example, the suffragettes' struggle for the right to vote and, during the 1920s and 1930s, the attempt made by women in the labor movement to gain better pay and working conditions. Today feminism has been rekindled: the ballot box has not brought an end to discrimination nor have women achieved equality in the workplace. As in most parts of the world, a feminist in Puerto Rico is any person, male or female, who recognizes the worldwide inequality of the sexes.

Recent research conducted by feminist scholars indicates that the woman's role in the indigenous culture before Spanish colonization was one of active participation in all aspects of the lives of **los Taínos**. Before 1493, women along with men held hierarchical positions, including that of *cacicas* or tribal chiefs. This degree of gender equality allowed the participation of both sexes in war activities, ritual ceremonies and premarital sex.

The colonization of Puerto Rico by the Spaniards brought about drastic changes in the lives of native women. In the absence of European women, male colonists appropriated slaves and indigenous women, in many instances forcibly or through barter or sale. In the eyes of the colonists, women and the children they bore were property to be sold or used as slaves. In the midst of this, the European women who arrived on the island also encountered repression. Reproduction of their species was crucial to consolidate the conquest, thus they were assigned the subservient role of wife, procreator and caretaker. Politics and formal education were not accessible to these women for over a century.

The first time the unequal condition of women was criticized occurred in the nineteenth century when the voices of **Eugenio María de Hostos** and **Alejandro Tapia y Rivera**, as well as the voices of educated middle-class women, such as **Alejandrina Benítez y Arce de Gautier, Lola Rodríguez de Tío** and **Ana Roqué de Duprey**, were heard. Their discourse contributed to the growing idea that women should be educated and play a role in the education of their children. Thus, the beginnings of feminism in Puerto Rico focused almost exclusively on a woman's right to be educated. These circumstances, together with the American invasion of 1898 and the development of an industrial base, would set the stage for broadening the feminist perspective. The socioeconomic changes that began to take place deeply affected the lives of the women on the island.

As the tobacco and needlework industries began to expand during the first three decades of the twentieth century, more and more women became part of the labor force. Once in the labor force, they were confronted with receiving lower salaries than their male counterparts and having no representation in the leadership of the labor force, no equal rights under the judicial system and no right to vote. As early as 1904, over 500 working women, mostly from the tobacco factories, organized into nine unions. In 1907 **Luisa Capetillo**, a feminist and union leader, published "Ensayos libertarios," the first of many written commentaries exhorting the improvement of the living and working conditions of the rank and file and demanding recognition of women's rights. Capetillo was joined in this effort by other women in the labor movement such as **Genara Pagán, Juana Colón Rivera** and Tomasa Yupart. These union leaders led demonstrations, rallies and strikes in their demands for women's equality in the workforce. By 1919 they had been successful in pushing forward the enactment of Law 45, which established a minimum salary for women in the workforce. That same year, under the leadership of Genara Pagán and Emilia Hernández, the Primer congreso de mujeres trabajadoras, or First Congress of Working Women, sponsored by the Free Federation of Labor (Federación Libre del Trabajador), was held. They approved, as their main objective, equality in every aspect of life for working men and women, including the right to vote. Even though men and women in the labor movement collaborated in the struggle for better working conditions, a separate feminist agenda was evolving. That agenda would tie the demands for equality in status and pay for women to demands for real equality in all aspects of social life.

In their quest for the right to vote, the women in the labor movement at times collaborated with the "other" sector of organized feminist women, the professional middle-class women and their *Liga femínea*, or Feminine League. These suffragists were interested primarily in obtaining the right for literate women to vote. This issue of literacy kept the two sectors apart. Because the illiteracy rate on the island at that time was high, the Feminine League was viewed by the women in the labor movement as noninclusive and favoring the ruling class. The leadership of the Feminine League included Ana Roqué de Duprey, **Mercedes Solá** and **Isabel Andreu de Aguilar**. Mercedes Solá, who had begun to advocate the union of both factions, was a participant in the 1919 Congress of Working Women. She was instrumental in achieving unity between the women in the labor movement and the professional women; however, this unity was short lived. Not all educated suffragettes wanted to be identified with the women in the labor movement whose union activities had always been related to the Socialist party. Thus, in 1925, Roqué de Duprey and Andreu de Aguilar established the Puerto Rican Association of Suffragist Women and opted for obtaining voting rights for literate women, a goal achieved in 1929. It was not until 1935 that the Puerto Rican legislature passed the bill that granted universal voting rights to all women.

It has been stated by many feminist scholars that the turning point for women occurred when they obtained access to education. Early on, only those women who came from the middle class or a privileged background had educational opportunities. In 1899 Puerto Rico had a population of over 350,000 of which only a few over 5,000 had attended high school; about a fourth of them were women. After the **University of Puerto Rico** was established, there was a slight increase in the number of professionals, both male and female, and the percentage of female teachers increased from 30 percent in 1899 to 75 percent by 1930. There is very little documented history as to what happened to the feminist movement from the 1930s to the 1970s when feminist issues resurfaced in Puerto Rico.

Since its creation in 1986, the University of Puerto Rico's Center for Studies, Resources and Services to Women (CERES) has engaged in research on women's issues including the feminist movements of the earlier part of the century. In trying to explain the gap between the mid-1930s to the 1970s, they theorize that many women, particularly the educated women, including those active in the suffragist and feminist movements, were incorporated into the state apparatus. Many of these women accepted positions with the government. They were concentrated in the areas of education and health focusing primarily in assisting, through government programs, the poverty-stricken sectors. Consequently, the concept of feminism became synonymous with feminine needs, and emphasis was given to the home, children, children's health and education, paralleling the work many of them had begun to do through the various government initiatives. It is also important to note that the advent of the Great Depression of the 1930s had strong repercussions, particularly in the tobacco and needlework industries where most working women were employed. The loss of jobs and income in many ways severed working women's ties to the labor movement and the unions.

In 1973 the legislature enacted Law 57, which created the Commission for Women's Affairs. Its main goal is to eliminate all barriers that interfere with achieving equality in personal, social and economic areas. The commission, whose five members are appointed by the governor, work to provide equity for women through education and advocacy as well as recommendations to the legislature.

Currently, feminism is focused on advancing the cause of women in the workplace and in politics, particularly in view of the fact that they make up almost 38 percent of the workforce. It is interesting to note, also, that of the 446,000 jobs created in the last thirty-three years, over 59 percent have gone to women. The increase of women in the labor force has been greatly assisted by the feminist movement and the changes it generated, not only through consciousness raising, but also in efforts to change labor laws so that women may better balance their roles as mothers and workers, have access to education that will lead to promotions and higher pay and benefit from affirmative action plans.

Since women obtained the right to vote in 1932, by the 1970s fourteen women have been elected to the legislature at various times. There have also been twenty-nine female mayors of various municipalities. However, the reality, according to most feminists on the island, is that women have barely made an impact on the political system. From 1932 to 1988, fourteen elections were held; women won 1,647 seats and men, 12,296. Most recently, however, their presence as candidates has increased, particularly in the most important elected positions. For the first time in the history of the island, all the candidates for mayor of San Juan, the second most powerful elected political office on the island, are women. The gubernatorial candidate for the **Popular Democratic party** in 1992 was **Victoria Muñoz Mendoza**. Women such as **Sila Calderón, Celeste Benítez Rivera** and **Zaida Hernández Torres**, among others, have been mentioned as potential future candidates for the highest political office on the island.

SUGGESTED READING

Yamila Azize, *La mujer en la lucha* (Río Piedras, P.R.: Editorial Cultural, 1985); Gladys M. Jiménez-Muñoz, "Re-thinking the History of Puerto Rican Women's Suffrage," *Centro de Estudios Puertorriqueños Bulletin* (Winter 1994–1995–Spring 1995): 96–106; Nilsa Torres, Margarita Mergal and Alice Colón, *Participación de la mujer en la historia de Puerto Rico (las primeras décadas del siglo veinte)* (Princeton, N.J.: Rutgers University Press, 1986).

Fernández, Gigi (1964–   )   One of Puerto Rico's athletic stars, professional tennis player Gigi Fernández was born in San Juan with the name Beatríz Fernández. On her eighth birthday, her parents gave her a tennis racket, and by the time she was twelve, she had won the women's open title in doubles in Puerto Rico.

The first professional woman athlete in Puerto Rico, she was named Puerto Rican Female Athlete of the Year for 1988. By 1991 she was ranked number one in the world in doubles. Her tennis career includes the distinction of being the first Puerto Rican ever to win two consecutive gold medals, a feat accomplished at the 1992 and 1996 Olympics with her tennis doubles partner Mary Joe Fernández. In 1995 she won her fifth consecutive Roland Garros doubles title and the U.S. Open doubles title; she was a finalist in the Australian Open and Wimbledon doubles and mixed doubles as well as the U.S. Open mixed doubles. In total, she has earned six Grand Slam women's doubles titles. Although she is exceptionally talented in her sport, Fernández acknowledges the support she has received from her family, as well as others who have influenced and mentored her career. She credits Martina Navratilova, with whom she has had the opportunity to play doubles, for guiding her career.

Her success, however, has not been without some controversy. Her decision to play for the United States as part of the Federation Cup team, as well as her decision to play for the U.S. Olympic team (rather than Puerto Rico's) have been difficult choices.

Gigi Fernández's success and earnings enabled her to establish, in 1992, the Gigi Fernández Charitable Foundation, which plays host to the annual Gigi Fernández Invitational Cup held to raise money for various Puerto Rican charities. From 1992 to 1995, it raised over $180,000.

Fernández has continued her doubles winning streak during 1997. Early in the year, with Arantxa Sánchez as her doubles partner, she won the Sydney International Tournament. Later that year, partnered with Natasha Zvereva, she won two grand slam doubles titles: the 1997 French Open and Wimbledom. She continues to gain attention for her charity work in the United States and Puerto Rico, as well as for her expert commentary on ESPN2 at the 1997 Australian Open.

SUGGESTED READING

Scoop Malinowski, online interview in *ESPNET SportsZone*, 1995; Janet Nomura-Morey and Wendy Dunn, *Famous Hispanic Americans* (New York: Cobble Hill Books, 1996); Diane Telgen and Jim Kamp, eds., *Notable Hispanic Women* (Detroit: Gale Research, 1993); *New York Times*, February 1985, 180–81.

Fernández Juncos, Manuel (1846–1928)   One of the key political leaders in late nineteenth and early twentieth century Puerto Rico, as well as a writer who focused on island culture, Fernández Juncos was born in Spain but died in San Juan. After receiving his early education in Spain, he arrived in Puerto Rico in 1857. As a young adult, he became intensely interested in the customs and culture of the Puerto Rican people. He first published his pieces in newspapers, for example, *El Porvenir* (The future), and later expanded his chronicle of island customs and social types in books, including *Costumbres and Tradiciones* (1882). He also founded the periodical *El Bucapié* (The suggestion), which, for many years, contained gently satirical portraits of the social types of the small town and country life.

In addition to his literary life, Fernández Juncos was deeply involved in island politics. He was secretary of the Autonomist party; he worked with (and often against) **Luis Muñoz Rivera** to obtain the 1897 **Autonomic Constitution** that granted the island a substantial degree of local control; and he was slated to serve as secretary of housing in the government that was erased when the United States invaded on July 25, 1898. Fernández Juncos passionately defended the use of the Spanish language. When, after the American invasion, teachers lacked the Spanish texts required by students, Fernández Juncos wrote the books that enabled teachers to continue teaching in their native language. He was also a founder of **El Ateneo Puertorriqueño**.

SUGGESTED READING

Gordon Lewis, *Main Currents in Caribbean Thought* (Baltimore: Johns Hopkins University Press, 1983); Manuel Maldonado-Denis, *Puerto Rico: A Social Historic Interpretation* (New York: Vintage, 1972); Edward S. Wilson, *Political Development of Porto Rico* (Columbus, Ohio: Fred H. Heer, 1905).

Fernández, Ruth (1919–   )   A popular singer, politician and media personality, Ruth Fernández is known as *"el alma de Puerto Rico hecha canción"* (Puerto Rico's soul made into a song). A native of **Ponce**, she has had a long and distinguished career as a popular singer. She is credited for being one of the first black singers to break the skin color barriers still prevalent in Puerto Rican society during the 1930s and 1940s. She brought her music into some of the most respectable entertainment establishments in Puerto Rico, including the Condado Plaza Hotel and the Casino de Puerto Rico. Fernández is a woman of great charisma whose positive attitude and outlook have won the hearts of her audiences. She is best known for her song "Gracias Mundo," in which she thanks the world for its beauty and kindness. Her rendition of "Lamento Borincano" (see **Rafael Hernández**), which has won praises for her throughout her career, defines a bygone time in Puerto Rican history. For instance, the song caused a controversial incident when she sang it in San Juan's Cathedral during the

Ruth Fernández, 1989. (Laura Magruder and *El Nuevo Día*.)

funeral of former governor **Luis Muñoz Marín**. Catholic Cardinal **Luis Aponte Martínez** labeled it a profane, heretical song and chastised her in front of a multitude of people.

Fernández was a senator for the **Popular Democratic party** from 1973 to 1981. She is an advocate of the rights of artists and entertainers in Puerto Rico. She is still very much involved in artistic circles in Puerto Rico and is a spokeperson and fundraiser for La Casa del Artista, which was established to provide retirement facilities for elderly artists.

SUGGESTED READING

Who's Who among American Woman, 12th ed. (Wilmette, Ill.: Marquis Who's Who, 1981); Who's Who in American Politics (Princeton, N.J.: Booker, 1979).

Fernós Isern, Antonio (1895–1974) A Resident Commissioner of Puerto Rico from 1948 to 1964, Fernós Isern was also one of the most powerful politicians of his time. Born in San Lorenzo, he died in San Juan. In his early years, Fernós Isern was a distinguished physician; he held a number of posts in the island's Department of Health and he also taught at the School of Tropical Medicine. However, he is best known as a principal colleague of Governor **Luis Muñoz Marín**; during the formative years of the commonwealth, Fernós Isern was Resident Commissioner of Puerto Rico and an influential figure in any debates that occurred between Washington, D.C., and San Juan. He introduced the bill to create a constitutional government in Puerto Rico on March 13, 1950. He told the U.S. Congress that the people of Puerto Rico "wish to adopt a local constitution and reaffirm their station within this Union." He stressed that, in Congress, Puerto Ricans did not want the right to elect anything more than a "voteless Resident Commissioner." But, because Puerto Rico had, since 1900, a government comparable to that of an incorporated territory, what Fernós Isern wanted was the right "to perfect such a status for Puerto Rico." The island was "developing a new pattern of federation" and, if given time, Fernós promised that Puerto Rico would be "the advanced guard and the exponents of the American way of life in the Caribbean. All we want now is to maintain it and perfect it. We want to show the world that democracy, not only in practice, but also in principle, always follows the flag" (Fernós Isern, 1950).

These aims set the course for the remainder of Fernós's political life. Along with Governor Muñoz Marín, he struggled for a decade to obtain concessions from the U.S. Congress. A climax occurred in 1959 when Fernós coauthored a bill—the Puerto Rico Federal Relations Act—in which the "permanence of the Commonwealth was made more apparent." Under this bill, the island would forever enjoy a variety of new economic (in relation to tariffs and taxation) and political powers; to Fernós "the terms of reference of its [the commonwealth's] existence, of its attributes, of its responsibilities are better stated. Actually this is the most important purpose of the bill" (Senate, 1959, espec. pp. 16–19).

In response to Fernós's tireless efforts, Senator Henry Jackson said this: "Of course the only question I raise is that we do have a body across the street called the Supreme Court and they have indicated that Congress can only do that which the Constitution gives it the power to do" (Senate, 1959, espec. pp. 45–50). Puerto Rico was a territory; under Article 4, Section 3 of the Constitution, Congress made all needful rules and regulations for the territories. The bill failed because it asked for powers that belonged only to Congress. For the next five years (1959–1964), Fernós worked to change, if not the U.S. Constitution, at least Congress's mind. He never succeeded and, along with Governor Muñoz Marín, he retired from public office in 1964.

SUGGESTED READING

Remarks of the Honorable A. Fernós Isern, *Congressional Record*, House of Representatives, 82nd Cong., 1st sess., March 14, 1950; U.S. Congress, Senate, Committee on Interior and Insular Affairs, *Puerto Rico Federal Relations Act*, 86th Cong., 1st sess. (Washington, D.C.: U.S. Government Printing Office, March 1959).

Ferré, Luis (1904–   )   Governor of Puerto Rico from 1968 to 1972, Ferré is also an industrialist, a philanthropist and one of Puerto Rico's most esteemed past or present politicians. Born in **Ponce** in 1904, Luis Ferré, in 1959, founded the Art Museum of Ponce; it is widely known as one of the best art museums in the **Antilles**.

Ferré studied at the Massachusetts Institute of Technology in Cambridge, where he received bachelor's and master's degrees in science. When he returned to the island, he worked successfully in a number of family businesses but, throughout his life, he has always maintained an active interest in politics. He was, for example, a pro-statehood member of the House of Delegates from 1937 to 1953, and he was also a member of the constitutional convention that wrote the document that was subsequently edited in Washington, D.C.

Ferré founded the **New Progressive party** in 1967. When the **Popular Democratic party** split in 1968, Ferré took advantage of the situation to become the first pro-statehood governor of Puerto Rico. During his administration he made numerous efforts to turn his strong support for President Richard Nixon into greater federal support for the people of Puerto Rico. He tried to convince Washington to create an office that would formally establish a place for Puerto Rico in the federal structure. And he was adamant that Puerto Rico should receive a much greater share of federal funds for public assistance. **Food Stamps** arrived as a result of Governor Ferré's lobbying and as a result of the Nixon administration's desire to use such programs to reduce further Puerto Rican immigration to the United States.

After he lost the gubernatorial election in 1972, Ferré maintained his political interests. He served as president of the island's senate from 1977–1981, and in 1996 he remains a figure whose support lends great credibility to any public or political project.

SUGGESTED READING

Jorge Heine, ed., *Time for Decision: The United States and Puerto Rico* (Lanham, Md.: North-South Publishing, 1983); Edgardo Melendez, *Puerto Rico's Statehood Movement* (Westport, Conn.: Greenwood Press, 1988); Aarón Gamaliel Ramos, ed., *La ideas anexionistas en Puerto Rico bajo la dominación norteamericana* (San Juan, P.R.: Huracán, 1987).

Ferré, Rosario (1938–   )   Rosario Ferré is one of the most important contemporary literary figures in the island. Her work, presented in essays, short stories and novels, uses parody as a key element to expose the gender, cultural, social and political inequities pervasive in Puerto Rican society (Lara-Velázquez 1996). Her work is unique because her texts reveal, perhaps better than any other literary work produced by a contemporary woman writer from Puerto Rico, the influence of the American feminist movement on her thinking and interpretations.

Ferré's literary production started in the 1970s and has since blossomed. She was the editor of the literary magazine *Zona de Carga y Descarga* (1970–1972). Among her most significant pieces are *Papeles de Pandora* (1976), *El medio pollito* (1978), *La muñeca menor* (1979), *Fábulas de la garza desangrada* (1982) and *Los cuentos de Juan Bobo* (1981). She translates many of her works to English and has recently published *The House on the Lagoon* (1995), written originally in the English language.

Her writings reveal a critical and cynical view of the patriarchal elements that are so pervasive in Puerto Rican society and culture. Moreover, they reveal the hypocritical schism that exists between classes. Although she was born to the wealth and privilege of a prestigious family from **Ponce**, Ferré has used her work and experiences to reveal the weaknesses of the elite class and to undermine the power and values of those cultural, social and political institutions established by them. Ferré situates many of her characters and plots inside these institutions and makes them implode and explode with sarcasms and criticisms.

SUGGESTED READING

Rosario Ferré, *The House on the Lagoon* (New York: Farrar, Straus and Giroux, 1995); Suzanne S. Hintz, "Rosario Ferré: The Vanguard of Puerto Rican Feminist Literature," *Revista de Estudios Hispánicos* 20 (1993); Socorro Lara-Velázquez, *La parodia como poder subversivo* (Ann Arbor, Mich.: University Microfilms International, 1996); Augustus C. Puleo, "The Intersection of Race, Sex, Gender and Class in a Short Story of Rosario Ferré," *Studies in Short Fiction* 32 (1995).

Ferré, Sor Isolina (1914–   )   A Catholic nun, Sor Isolina Ferré was born in **Ponce** to a wealthy family and has devoted her life to charity and social work through her Catholic apostolate. She was the youngest child in a large family, and shortly after she was born, her mother contracted a tropical disease that incapacitated her for prolonged periods of time. As a result, Isolina was left under the tutelage of her elder brothers and sister and the household staff. As a child, she was impressed by the charity work undertaken by her mother. Pellín, the household driver, an early influence in her life, exposed her to the difficult living conditions experienced by poor people throughout the area.

By her late teens, Sor Isolina had received God's call to devote her life to charity service, and she began to exchange letters with Father Thomas Augustine Judge who encouraged her in her desire to become a nun. Since her father was not amenable to her wishes, she had to wait until she was twenty-one years old to enter the order of the Missionary Servants of the Holy Trinity in Philadelphia, an order founded by Judge. She completed her basic training there and was ordained as a nun in 1937.

After her ordination, Sor Isolina started a life of missionary work that has taken her to Norton, Virginia, where she performed social work with coal miners; to Brooklyn, New York, where for three years she worked throughout the Northeast on a census to assess the Catholic population in the United States; to Wareham, Massachusetts, where she worked near Cape Cod providing social services to recently arrived Portugese immigrants; and to Long Island, New York, where she performed similar duties. In 1946 she went home to Puerto Rico where she worked for almost ten years in the Cabo Rojo area helping the poor.

In 1956 Sor Isolina returned to Brooklyn where she finished a bachelor's degree at Saint Joseph's College for Women and eventually a master's degree in sociology at Fordham University. While in Brooklyn she became the director of the Dr. White Stelleman Center, which provides an array of medical and social services for poor minorities. She became involved in the struggles of the civil rights era and was appointed by John Lindsay, then mayor of New York, to be a member of the War on Poverty Committee. She accumulated vast experience in working with the young and other needy people, which was important for her future work in Puerto Rico.

Sor Isolina was assigned by her order to work in La Playa de Ponce (a settlement near the coast of **Ponce**) in 1968. The slum area was populated by poor and needy people who had fallen victim to the economic transformations taking place on the island during the 1940s, 1950s and 1960s. People without industrial skills had fallen behind the wave of development. They were particularly affected by the closing of Ponce's ports, which had left them with few skills and fewer resources. As soon as she arrived in Ponce, she launched what became one of the most successful community development projects on the island or in Latin America. Her Centro de la

Playa de Ponce comprises a series of community development initiatives focused on training and development, health treatment and services, arts workshops, sports and youth development programs. They have transformed the area into a model of community development and leadership. Sor Isolina's exemplary life of community and charity work has benefited thousands of people wherever she has lived and worked.

SUGGESTED READING

Sor Isolina Ferré, *Isolina* (Río Piedras, P.R.: Editorial Cultural, 1991); *Who's Who among Hispanic Americans* (Detroit: Gale Research, 1994).

Ferrer, José (1912–1992)   One of the most talented Puerto Rican theater and film actors in the United States, José Ferrer was born in Santurce but moved with his parents to the United States when he was four. He studied architecture at Princeton University where he graduated in 1933, but he preferred stage work to a professional career in architecture. His first incursion into the arts was made as a musician. His band, José Ferrer and his Pied Pipers, which he formed while at Princeton, achieved considerable recognition and toured many European capitals and also performed in the United States. In 1932 he played his first leading role in a student production of *It's the Valet*.

He debuted on Broadway in 1935 with a minor role in a production of Damon Runyon's *A Slight Case of Murder*, but in 1936 he played the leading role in Phillip Barry's *Spring Dance* at the Empire Theater. He played many roles on Broadway during the remainder of the 1930s. His roles as Iago in Shakespeare's *Othello* brought him praise and recognition. During the 1940s he acted in or directed other successful plays.

In the late 1940s, Ferrer made a transition into film and television. His stage portrayal of Cyrano in *Cyrano de Bergerac* was adapted for both television and film. In 1950 he was the first person to earn both a Tony and an Oscar. He was also nominated for an Oscar for his performance of the Dauphin in *Joan of Arc*. He played supporting roles in *Lawrence of Arabia, Ship of Fools, Moulin Rouge, The Caine Mutiny* and *A Midsummer Night's Sex Comedy*.

Ferrer stayed active in the theater during the 1950s, 1960s and 1970s as both an actor and a director. He directed the movies *The Twentieth Century* and *Stalag 17*, and critics considered him to be one of the best character actors of his generation. He remained active in the arts until shortly before his death. He always maintained his strong ties with the island of Puerto Rico where his ashes were taken after his death.

SUGGESTED READING

New York Times Biographical Service, *A Compilation of Current Biographies Information of General Interest*, nos. 1, 2 (Ann Arbor, Mich.: University Microfilms

International, 1992); David Thomson, *Biographical Dictionary of Film* (New York: Alfred A. Knopf, 1994).

Figueroa Family   The members of this family are some of the most talented Puerto Rican musicians of this century. The father, Don Jesús Figueroa (1875–1971), was an accomplished musician and composer who founded his own music academy in San Juan. The mother, Doña Carmen Sanabria, was a pianist. Their sons Guillermo (violinist and conductor), Rafael (cellist), Jaime (violinist), Narciso (pianist), and José (violinist) organized the Figueroa Musical Quintet while they were studying music in Paris. They have been critically acclaimed throughout the world. Daughters Leonor, who died at an early age, Angelina and Carmelina were also distinguished pianists. Angelina taught music at the family academy. Carmelina was instrumental in the creation of the Escuela Libre de Música, which she directed from 1960 to 1974, and taught at the Puerto Rican Conservatory. All of the children of the family studied in Europe, specifically at the École Normal de Musique in Paris and the Royal Conservatory in Madrid, where they participated in numerous musical competitions and received many awards and commendations. Individually and collectively, they have played with the most prestigious musical groups in Puerto Rico, including the Casals Festival Orchestra, Arturo Somohano's Orchestra, and the Puerto Rico Symphonic Orchestra. They have also played with orchestras in the United States.

There is a new generation of musicians from this family—Guillermo's children. Guillermo Figueroa and Ivonne Figueroa Hutchinson are accomplished musicians and are actively involved in classical music and musical education in Puerto Rico.

SUGGESTED READING

Biography Index, a cumulative index to biographical materials in books and magazines, vol. 10, September 1973–August 1976 (New York: H. W. Wilson, 1977).

Figueroa Mercado, Loida (1922–1995)   One of the island's best-known historians and educators, Loida Figueroa Mercado was also actively involved in the island's independence movement. She was born in Yauco and received her B.A. from **Interamerican University** in San Germán. She earned her master's degree from Columbia University and her Ph.D. from the University of Madrid in 1963.

Her writings show great range; they include the novel *Arsenales* (1961) and a series of political essays entitled *Tres puntos claves: Lares, idioma, soberania* (Three key points: Lares, language, and sovereignty), but she is best known for her two-volume *History of Puerto Rico* (1972). What distinguishes these volumes are the depth of the scholarship, linked to prose that is not afraid to express an opinion. When she discusses the visit of

Alejandro de O'Reilly in 1765, Figueroa explains that he was "stupified" when he called for a review of the Spanish troops. In fascinating detail, Figueroa achieves a remarkable feat: She makes history live by rooting her scholarship in the humanity and inhumanity of her subjects.

After a long career teaching at the University of Puerto Rico, Figueroa now returned to her alma mater: Interamerican University in San Germán.

SUGGESTED READING

Loida Figueroa Mercado, *History of Puerto Rico* (New York: Anaya Book Company, 1972).

Film   The twentieth century, which saw the introduction of large-scale film industries in the United States and Europe, also saw the development of a small-scale film industry on the island of Puerto Rico. The development of film, as an independent and prosperous industry on the island, has been affected by a series of economic factors which have halted and hindered its expansion.

Most of the research on the early history of film in Puerto Rico has been done by filmmaker and scholar José Artemio Torres. His work highlights many milestones in Puerto Rican filmmaking. The first attempts at local film production on the island go back to 1916 when the Sociedad Industrial de Cine Puerto Rico was established. This society, led by Rafael J. Colorado and Antonio Capella, produced the films *Por la hembra y el gallo, El milagro de la virgen* and *Mafia en Puerto Rico*. In 1917 the Tropical Film Company was established to film the beauty of the Puerto Rican landscape and culture and present them in the United States and Europe. **Luis Lloréns Torres** and Nemesio R. Canales, noted Puerto Rican literary figures, were instrumental in directing and creating the scripts for these films. They produced *Paloma del monte*. The most professional and serious film undertaking of the time was that of Porto Rico Photo Plays, which filmed *Amor tropical* in 1921 and brought U.S. actors into their Puerto Rican productions. World War II, as well as the Great Depression, halted the development of the film industry in Puerto Rico at the time.

Jack Delano, a North American photographer who came to live in Puerto Rico during the 1940s and who joined the **Community Education Division** of the government of Puerto Rico, was one of the most important men in Puerto Rican filmmaking during the 1940s and 1950s. Because of the educational charter of the division, it was crucial to produce educational films and materials. Delano filmed some of the best productions of the time, which were to be used as resources in the education of adults in Puerto Rican communities. Among the films that he produced were *Una gota de agua*. He also participated with other filmmakers in the division, including Amilcar Tirado, Luis Maisonet and Marcos Betancourt, in the production of the films *Una voz en la mañana, Intolerancia, La guardaraya, Ignacio* and *El yugo.*

One of the best films of the times was *Los peloteros,* directed by Jack Delano in 1950 in black and white film. The purpose of the film was to show the importance of community participation and development. Filmed in Comerio, at a cost of $40,000, it showcased Puerto Rican actress Miriam Colón and **Ramón "Diplo" Ortiz Rivera** and many other people from the community. The film explored the themes of honesty, justice and forgiveness.

Many attempts were made during the 1950s, 1960s and 1970s to shoot films in Puerto Rico. Among them were Probo Films, headed by Axel Anderson and Victor Arrillaga, a film cooperative launched by employees from the Community Education Division, and Pakira Films, headed by three Puerto Rican media entrepreneurs headed by Paquito Cordero. Their films, perhaps the most popular ones of the times, showcased the popular comedian Adalberto Rodriguez, known as Machuchal. Other independent producers, such as Anthony Felon, Miguel Angel Alvarez, Efrain López Neris and Arturo Correa made serious efforts to produce films in Puerto Rico at the time, but these films lacked the sophisticated scripts, talent and production values to make them successful. Many of the productions of the 1960s were heavily influenced by cinematic trends in Spain and Mexico, and the films were therefore full of violence and sexual connotation, which devalued them.

In the more recent past, during the 1980s and 1990s, Puerto Rico has seen a few high-quality film productions, including Marcos Surinaga's *La gran fiesta*; **Jacobo Morales**'s *Dios los cría, Nicolás y los demás,* and *Lo que le pasó a Santiago*; and Luis Molina's *Los cuentos de Abelardo* and *La guagua aérea.* All of these films, positively received by the critics, attracted significant audiences throughout the island. Morales's *Lo que le pasó a Santiago* was nominated for an Oscar.

There has been a very healthy production of documentary cinema on the island funded mostly through the Puerto Rican Foundation for the Humanities. The foundation has been crucial in providing young filmmakers with funding to defray the costs of their films. Documentaries such as Luis Molina's *El Tren (Boleto de ida),* Luis Collazo and Marcos Zurinaga's *Nosotros el pueblo de Puerto Rico* and Angelita Rieckenhoff's *Siempre estuvimos aquí* are some of the quality productions that have been funded by the endowment.

A series of recurrent problems have hindered the capacity of Puerto Rican filmmakers to produce quality films on the island. The most difficult problems, the lack of adequate financing and funding, competition from American movies and the lack of appropriate distribution channels, have all weakened efforts to produce quality films in Puerto Rico. The government has created an office, which is part of the Economic Development Office, which is in charge of facilitating the development of a viable movie and film industry on the island. However, its impact has been limited. The Film Development Corporation, which functions with a very limited budget of around $300,000, has been primarily interested in bringing American film productions to the island rather than developing local producers. In recent years, there has been a substantial increase in the number of American movies that are partially shot in Puerto Rico. The government has also tried to create tax incentives and financing mechanisms to facilitate the emergence of local film production on the island.

Without a doubt, some of the best films made in Puerto Rico were created by the Community Education Division or were created by independent producers during the 1980s and 1990s. The future holds hope for the potential growth of the Puerto Rican film industry.

SUGGESTED READING

Salomé Galib Bras, "75 años de cine," *El Nuevo Día*, March 25, 1990; Jack Delano: "Maestro del cine puertorriqueño," *El Reportero,* February 14, 1984; Kino García, "Los pioneros del cine puertorriqueño," *Imagenes* 11, no. 1 (1985); José Artemio Torres, "Ponce, 1912: Comienza la aventura," *El Nuevo Día,* July 14, 1995; José Artemio Torres, *Breve historia del cine puertorriqueño* (San Germán, P.R.: Unpublished document, 1981); Pedro Zervigón, "Futuro incierto de tres cineastas boricuas," *El Nuevo Día,* May 19, 1989.

Five Hundred Acre Law This U.S. law limited the size of Puerto Rican sugar plantations. When Congress passed the legislation establishing the colonial government in 1900, it attached an amendment that produced fifty years of controversy in Puerto Rico. The 500 acre law stipulated that "corporations organized for the purposes of engaging in agriculture should be restricted in their charters to the ownership of not more than five hundred acres of land."

The law had at least two motives. One was to avoid giant plantations that would eliminate small landowners. The other was to limit the competition Puerto Rico would offer to U.S. (especially Hawaiian) producers of sugar. U.S. growers assumed that, if the size of the island's farms were limited, they would never achieve the economies of scale required to be seriously competitive. The law was never enforced until the early 1940s. Until then, plantations containing thousands of acres dominated Puerto Rico's sugar production.

To many island political leaders, the law nevertheless underlined an important fact about the nature of Puerto Rico's economic development under U.S. control: U.S. interests competed with one another. Some wanted more sugar; some wanted the Puerto Rican competition to disappear. The 500 acre law was therefore a compromise. It reflected concern for U.S. interests, but, even if enforced, it never touched a consensus among all U.S. sugar interests. Whether small or large owners, Puerto Ricans could grow and export sugar to the mainland; however, by U.S. law, all processing occurred in the United States. The result was that Puerto Rico lost the opportunity to create the additional jobs (e.g., in sugar-processing factories) required to attain any self-sufficiency.

SUGGESTED READING

Charles H. Allen, *Opportunities in the Colonies and Cuba* (New York: Scribner, 1902); Rexford Guy Tugwell, *The Stricken Land: The Story of Puerto Rico* (New York: Doubleday, 1947).

Flag of Puerto Rico (La bandera de Puerto Rico) *Bandera* is the Spanish word for flag. There is a great similarity between the Puerto Rican and Cuban flags. The Cuban flag dates from 1849; the Puerto Rican flag dates from 1895. In the 1890s Puerto Rican patriots like **Lola Rodríguez de Tío** were working in New York City with Cuban revolutionaries. Their aim was to free both islands from Spanish domination, and one result of their revolutionary collaboration was the Puerto Rican flag. In recent years, supporters of the commonwealth explained the flag's roots and purposes but incorrectly argued that its origins date to the 1950s; the truth is that it was a symbol of the revolutionary aspirations of the Puerto Rican and Cuban peoples.

The flag of Puerto Rico has extraordinary significance for islanders of all political persuasions. In the United States, it is often seen as a decal on the back window of a car or flying from the radio antenna of automobiles in New Jersey and New York. In a Puerto Rican Day parade held in Chicago, the flags were attached to the windshield wipers of cars and the wipers were turned on high. The flags waved back and forth for hours; meanwhile, Puerto Rican members of the Hell's Angels motorcycle club attached flags to their bikes and loudly powered themselves and the flags down Pedro Albizu Campos Boulevard.

SUGGESTED READING

Lola Rodríguez de Tío, "The Song of Borinquen," in *Borinquen: An Anthology of Puerto Rican Literature*, ed. María Teresa Babín and Stan Steiner (New York: Vintage Books, 1983); Carol Shaw, *Flags: A Guide to More Than 200 Flags of the World* (Philadelphia: Running Press, 1994).

Flores, Pedro (1893–1979) This Puerto Rican music composer is considered to be one of the most prominent composers of popular music in Latin America. A native of Naguabo, he was a teacher by training and a self-educated musical composer. He lived in New York City for thirty years; he also lived in Cuba and in Mexico.

Remembered primarily for his passionate romantic ballads, he composed music characterized by an imaginative and nostalgic tone. His songs spoke about the pains of impossible love, broken relationships, love in the Puerto Rican countryside and the longing for love. He also wrote in the Latin American genre known as *guaracha*, a spicy, vivid beat characterized by lively, warm lyrics.

During his stay in New York, Flores organized the Flores Sextet which spread his music throughout Latin America and the Spanish-speaking United States. He was highly productive and prolific. He used to tell people that he wrote a song every single day of his adult life. Some critics indicate that he left more than 1,000 finished compositions. Among his most popular compositions are "Si no eres tú," "Obsesión," "Linda," "Esperanza inútil," "Perdón," "Despedida," "Contigo," "Venganza" and "Ciego de amor."

Flores and **Rafael Hernández** are considered the premier Puerto Rican musical composers of the twentieth century.

SUGGESTED READING

Centro de Investigaciones y Ediciones Musicales de Puerto Rico, *Compositores contemporaneos puertorriqueños* (San Juan, P.R.: Instituto de Cultura Puertorriqueña, 1981).

Food Stamps (Los Cupones)   *Los cupones* is the slang term for U.S. government food stamps in Puerto Rico. Because it is an unincorporated part of the United States, Puerto Rico is sometimes excluded from federal programs. This was the case with food stamps in 1971 when Governor **Luis Ferré** pleaded with his Republican counterpart, President Richard Nixon, to include Puerto Rico in the food stamp program. Theoretically, the program was to be phased in over time but, when the mayor of San Juan, **Carlos Romero Barcelo**, sued the federal government for equal access to food stamps, a federal court ordered, in 1974, that the program be extended to every city, town, and barrio in Puerto Rico.

Access to food stamps is based on income. Since the per capita income in Puerto Rico was only 50 percent as high as the income in the poorest state of the union (Mississippi), 60 percent of the Puerto Rican people qualified for food stamps. Literally overnight the island received over $800 million a year in food stamp assistance. For many years, more than 60 percent of the people received *los cupones*, while the island's government worried about the long-range consequences of so much assistance. One official noted in 1975 that "the food stamp program is the largest factor improving the position of the poor in Puerto Rico in the past thirty years. No other program has penetrated so deep into the poor man's house." In a memo that went to the White House, President Gerald Ford learned that, while some people wagered food stamps at cockfights, others complained "that this is worse than Hiroshima. Because we people of Puerto Rico have no dignity left." But, as the island government responded, "How can you not give it to them?" (Ford Library 1974, 4).

Today, as a result of scandals with the stamps themselves, and the cost of the program to the U.S. Treasury, the island government receives a block grant, which it distributes to the people. However, no matter how the money is delivered, the island's dependence on food stamps remains enormous. For example, in New York State, with a population of 18 million people, 1.5 million receive food stamps; in Puerto Rico, with a population of 3.5 million people, 1.48 million people receive food stamp assistance. The stamps have also helped create what is now an institutionalized, underground economy. To report income is to risk losing eligibility for the stamp funding; thousands of people therefore work "off the books" or barter with others for needed goods and services. Historian **Fernando Picó** writes that "the stamps were a short term solution. [In 1974] very few people thought that they would come to be a permanent and necessary allowance for the majority of Puerto Ricans" (Picó 1988, pp. 288–289). Many islanders also note that the stamps underline a fundamental dilemma in the relationship between the United States and Puerto Rico: Congress cannot reasonably claim absolute power over Puerto Rico without accepting the primary responsibility for the island's economic situation.

SUGGESTED READING

Ronald Fernandez, *The Disenchanted Island: Puerto Rico and the United States in the Twentieth Century*, 2d ed. (Westport, Conn.: Praeger, 1996); Ford Library, Papers of Jim Cannon, Box 27, 1974; Fernando Picó, *Historia general de Puerto Rico* (San Juan, P.R.: Huracán, 1988); Richard Weisskoff, *Factories and Food Stamps: The Puerto Rican Model of Development* (Baltimore: Johns Hopkins University Press, 1985).

Foraker Act   This act passed by the U.S. Congress established the nature of Puerto Rico's government from May 1, 1900, to March 2, 1917. Also known as the First Organic Act of Puerto Rico, this body of U.S. law established the core organizations that governed the colony: the **Executive Council** and the elected (by the Puerto Rican people) House of Delegates. The Foraker Act also made the dollar legal currency in Puerto Rico; it legitimated the office of a governor appointed by the president of the United States; it made the U.S. Supreme Court the ultimate arbiter of the Puerto Rican legal system; it declared that the island's inhabitants were citizens, not of the United States, but of Puerto Rico; and it established a system of tariffs that taxed islanders despite their lack of representation. U.S. officials argued that, along with the imposition of exorbitant tariffs by the Spanish and the Cubans, the U.S. military occupation "had occasioned complete business stagnation and paralysis. Idleness prevailed and soon tens of thousands were in want, and suffering from the necessaries of life." Thus, the tariffs were necessary because, in the absence of an effective system of taxation, they provided the only way to underwrite the island's government. The taxes also emphasized another essential point. As Senator Foraker summed it up for his colleagues shortly before they voted on the legislation, "The radical, basic difference in the whole matter lies at the very beginning—as to whether or not Porto Rico [*sic*] is a part of the United States." By imposing taxation without representation, Foraker had demonstrated Congress's absolute power as well as the politically ambiguous status of Puerto Rico and its inhabitants. As the Foraker Act made it clear, "Porto Rico belongs to the United States, but it is not the United States, nor a part of the United States" (Congressional Record 1900, 4853–4856).

SUGGESTED READING

Congressional Record, Senate, 56th Cong., April 30, 1900, 4850–57; Horace N. Fisher, *Principles of Colonial Government, Adapted to the Present Needs of Cuba, Porto Rico and the Philippines* (Boston: L. C. Page, 1900); Lyman Gould, *The Foraker Law: Roots of the United States Colonial Politics* (San Juan: University of Puerto Rico Press, 1969).

Fortaleza, La   Located in San Juan, La Fortaleza is one of the oldest buildings in Puerto Rico; it has also been the home for the governor of Puerto Rico since the early 1570s. Spain allocated the money in 1530 to build the fort, but, when the money arrived in 1533, soldiers used it to kill the Carib Indians of Dominica. Actual work on the fort began in 1537.

Designed as a barrier against Indians firing traditional weapons, the walls of La Fortaleza were nevertheless seven feet thick. The idea was to house hundreds of people in a structure that actually resembled "just another flat-roofed house." Before it was completed, soldiers complained to the king that "only a blind man would have chosen such a site for a fort." Exposed on all sides and invisible to approaching ships, the fort never served one of its prime functions: acting as a deterrent to British, French and Dutch invaders. Thus, when the town fathers commissioned a new fort at the site of **El Morro**, they were still stuck with the flat-roofed house. Over time, they created a building that is legitimately called El Palacio de Santa Catalina.

In Old San Juan, it is easy to locate the narrow street that leads to La Fortaleza. It is always guarded by obviously armed officers; meanwhile, the huge gates on any of the fort's many sides are also guarded and always closed. The magnificent white structure is surrounded by a fence of elaborate, black wrought iron work. La Fortaleza, which faces the sea, contains two huge towers, one on either end of the building; when guards prowl the walls, the label of "castle" is particularly apt. Historically, La Fortaleza has housed treasury documents and the Chest of the Three Keys (the chest contained the funds provided from the royal coffers in Spain). Today La

Fortaleza is the place to house and impress visiting VIPs; diplomats and U.S. congressmen get to admire and sleep in a building that is an exquisite reminder, not only of colonialism, but also of the Spaniard who was "blind" enough to commission La Fortaleza more than 460 years ago.

SUGGESTED READING

Albert Manucy and Ricardo Torres-Reyes, *Puerto Rico and the Forts of Old San Juan* (Riverside, Calif.: Chatham Press, 1973).

Free Associated State (Estado Libre Asociado) *Estado Libre Asociado* are the Spanish words that indicate the changed political relationship established between Puerto Rico and the United States between 1950 and 1952. The words have been translated into English as commonwealth; the literal Spanish translation of the words—the Free Associated State—was not used because State Department officials wanted to avoid any confusion. U.S. officials told Governor **Luis Muñoz Marín**, in a letter dated September 25, 1952, that they had decided to use the word commonwealth "inasmuch as the word 'state' in ordinary speech in the United States means one of the states of the Union." As in 1900 when the Foraker Act was passed, the State Department did not want anyone to think that Puerto Rico was, or would soon be, a state of the union.

However *el estado libre asociado* is translated, no one in 1952 thought that Puerto Rico was now a state of the union. Instead, the controversy centered on the definition of the new relationship. In private correspondence to the State Department, Governor Muñoz Marín stated that Puerto Rico was no longer a territory of the United States and that the new relationship was a "compact" that could be changed only by the joint agreement of the United States and Puerto Rican governments. In response, the State Department told the governor (in September 1952) that "the flat statement that Puerto Rican laws cannot be repealed or modified by external authority, and that Puerto Rico's status and the terms of its association with the United states cannot be changed without Puerto Rico's full agreement has been modified to indicate that this is Puerto Rico's view" (National Archives 1952, 1).

Congress was more explicit. The House of Representatives committee that approved the 1952 commonwealth constitution said this in a 1952 public report: "It is important that the nature of and general scope of the law be made absolutely clear. The bill under consideration would not change Puerto Rico's fundamental political, social, and economic relationship to the United States." In Congress's eyes, the governor was wrong. If Puerto Rico was a colony in 1948, and nothing fundamental changed with the new laws and the island's constitution, then, in 1952, *el estado libre asociado* remained, fundamentally, a colony of the United States.

SUGGESTED READING

U.S. Congress, House, *Approving the Constitution of the Commonwealth of Puerto Rico*, 82nd Cong., 2d sess., Report 1832, April 30, 1952; for a good summary of Governor Muñoz's stand, see his testimony before the Senate, Hearings before the Committee on Foreign Relations, 85th Cong., 2d sess., March 10, 1958; finally, see Carlos Ramon Zapata-Oliveras, "United States Puerto Rico Relations in the Early Cold War (1945–1953)," Ph.D. diss., University of Pennsylvania, 1986; Jorge Heine, ed., *Time for Decision: The United States and Puerto Rico* (Lanham, Md.: North-South Publishing, 1983); Robert W. Anderson, "Political Parties and the Politics of Status," *Caribbean Studies* 21 (1988): 143; National Archives, Office of Territories, Record Group 126, September 8, 1968, Box 351, Washington, D.C.

Fuerzas Armadas de Liberación Nacional   *See* FALN.

G

García López, Antonio (1943–1995)   Antonio García López, also known as Toño Bicicleta, was a Puerto Rican outlaw who became a popular hero and an icon of mythical proportions on the island. A native of Yauco, a town in the central region, García López was convicted and given a long sentence for killing his wife. During the 1970s, he escaped from the Sabana Hoyos prison in Arecibo and sought refuge in the mountainside region between Lares, Adjuntas, Yauco, San Sebastián and Las Marias.

Many factors contributed to García López's rise in popularity and to the vast folklore generated about him. He sometimes rode around on a beaten-up bicycle, which gave him his nickname. He also became famous for his overwhelming sex appeal and prowess which led him to a colorful but mean and criminal life of rape, sexual intimidation and harassment. Although he was a violent man who carried guns and toted a sharp machete that he never hesitated to use if threatened, Bicicleta was supported by people from the mountainside who sheltered him from the police and gave him food and protection throughout the years.

As described by Fernando Picó in his book *Los gallos peleados* (1983), farmers and peasants from the mountain region in Puerto Rico resent the police brutality and repression that have been used to control their existence. García López, who was perceived as a humble man, persecuted by the police, galvanized these feelings.

During the 1980s, García López killed his mother's husband who, he thought, was furnishing the police with information about his whereabouts. The police then increased their efforts to find him which forced Toño to hide in the forest and live a nomadic and hermitlike life. In 1995 police in Lares received information that Toño had been seen at a certain location, and they were able to surprise García López there while he was collecting coffee beans with his lover. When he refused to surrender and threatened to shoot the police, he was shot and killed. People from the area were furious because they felt that the shooting was unfair and malicious. After García López's death, however, the police learned from his common-law wife, a woman whom he had abducted when she was an adolescent and who had "learned to love him," that García López had lived a far more violent life than was previously thought. The criminal career of García López has been documented in scores of newspaper articles, books and even a film.

SUGGESTED READING

Fernando Picó, *Los gallos peleados* (San Juan: Huracán, 1983).

García Passalacqua, Juan Manuel (1937–   )   One of the most respected contemporary Puerto Rican political analysts and journalists, García Passalacqua was born in Hato Rey. He graduated from the **University of Puerto Rico** in 1957 and received a master's degree in international relations from Tufts University and a law degree from Harvard University. García Passalacqua was an executive assistant to Governor **Luis Muñoz Marín** from 1962 to 1965 and then executive assistant to Governor Roberto Sánchez Vilella from 1965 to 1967.

After his government service, García Passalacqua became—and remains—a writer who specializes in political and cultural commentary. For nearly thirty years he has skillfully combined a writing career with a strong and—his critics would say—overly optimistic struggle to end colonialism in Puerto Rico. García Passalacqua was especially active in trying to achieve change during the administrations of Presidents Carter and Reagan.

SUGGESTED READING

Juan Manuel García Passalacqua, *La crisis politica en Puerto Rico*, 2d ed. (Río Piedras, P.R.: Edil, 1983); Juan Manuel García Passalacqua, *Vengador del silencio* (San Juan, P.R.: Editorial Cultural, 1991); Juan Manuel García Passalacqua, *Hegemón: Otredad y mismidad de la otra cara* (San Juan, P.R.: Editorial Cultural, 1996).

García Ramis, Magalí (1946–   )   Magalí García Ramis is one of the new contemporary writers whose well-crafted prose, presented through the genres of short stories and novels, has given Puerto Rican women a strong and well-deserved voice in the island's literary circles. A native of Santurce, she received a bachelor's degree in history from the **University of Puerto Rico** and a graduate degree in journalism from Columbia University.

García Ramis started her literary career as a journalist. She worked as a newspaper writer for *El Mundo* and *El Imparcial*. In addition, she wrote for the highly acclaimed magazine *Avance* during the 1970s. Her clear and direct narrative style can be traced back to her early work in journalism.

She cites the influence of her family's expectations and upbringing as a major force in her life. Her middle-class background and the traditional values advocated by her family sheltered and protected her from learning about the diversity of the Puerto Rican people and from many social and political problems that affected the island. She says that she only discovered those during her college years at the University of Puerto Rico (García Ramís 1992).

The family is a central theme in the literary production of this talented writer. Her work has focused on the schisms and incongruities that affect family life. García Ramis also has explored the public and hidden dimensions of family members' personal and collective identities, as well as the nature of relationships and their psychological underpinnings. Her work explores feminist ideas and many of her concerns for the equality of women. García Ramis's new book of short stories, *Noches del riel de oro* (1995) reveals a new trend toward the use of fantastic elements in her narrative.

Some of her major works are *La familia de todos nosotros* (1976); *Felices días Tío Sergio* (1986); *La ciudad que me habita* (1993) and *Noches del riel de oro* (1995). She also has written literary essays and criticism. García Ramis teaches public communication at the University of Puerto Rico.

SUGGESTED READING

Carmen C. Esteves, "Literature/Journalism: The Frontier: An Interview with Magalí García Ramis," *Callaloo* 17, no. 3 (1994); Magalí García Ramis, *Felices Días Tío Sergio* (San Juan: Editorial Antillana, 1986); "Magalí García Ramis" in Angel Flores, ed., *Spanish American Writers* (New York: Wilson, 1992); Magalí García Ramis, *Las noches del riel de oro* (Georgia: Darby Printing, 1995); Ivette López, "Minute and Fragant Memories: Happy Days, Uncle Sergio and Magalí García Ramis" in Guerra Cunningham, ed., *Splintering Darkness: Latin American Women Writers in Search of Themselves* (Pittsburgh: Latin American Review, 1990).

Gautier Benítez, José (1851–1880)   Gautier Benítez, who was born in Caguas, into a family of distinguished Puerto Rican poets, is considered to be one of Puerto Rico's most important poets of the nineteenth century. His father died when he was five; as a result, he was raised by his mother, Alejandrina, at the home of his maternal aunt, María Bibiana (see **Alejandrina Benítez y Arce de Gautier** and **María Bibiana Benítez y Constanza**). Both his mother and his aunt were distinguished poets, and their household in San Juan was a center of literary activity. By the age of twelve, he had published his first poem in a bulletin published by the Catholic Church. This event marked the beginning of a rich literary production. In 1870 he went to Madrid to pursue a military career and further studies, but he became so homesick that he resigned from the Spanish army and returned to the island. He started to work for *El Progreso*, a local newspaper, in 1872 using the pseudonym "Gustavo." After a brief stint at farming the land where he had been born, he returned to San Juan and founded *La Revista Puertorriqueña*, a literary journal, with Manuel Elzaburú.

Gautier Benítez, considered to be one of the island's foremost Romantic poets (Girón 1967), is known as the Puerto Rican Becquer, after the noted Spanish Romantic poet Gustavo Adolfo Becquer. His poetry fits all the characteristics of the Romantic genre. His poetry addresses feelings and romantic love. There is a local, or *criollo*, dimension in his poetry when he writes about the native beauties of the island. Noted biographer and Gautier Benítez scholar **Socorro Girón de Segura** has said than no one expresses better than Gautier Benítez the feelings and emotions that characterized Puerto Ricans during that period in the island's history. His prolific literary production was cut short when he died from tuberculosis at an early age.

SUGGESTED READING

Socorro Girón, *José Gautier Benítez: Antología poética* (San Juan: Biblioteca Popular Instituto de Cultura Puertorriqueña, 1967); Alfredo Matilla and Iván Silén, eds., *The Puerto Rican Poets* (New York: Bantam, 1972); Julio Morazan, ed., *Inventing a Word* (New York: Columbia University Press, 1982).

Gay Activism   Gay activism in Puerto Rico "began" in 1974 when the first group of homosexuals and lesbians formally organized under the name Comunidad de Orgullo Gay (COG), or Gay Pride Community. For three years they published a newsletter, *Pa'Fuera*, meaning "out"; the COG articulated the need for change that would address gay concerns about health, education and the legal system. For example, one law, passed with the support of religious and other groups, mandated that engaging in sexual relations with a member of one's own sex would result in a two-year jail sentence.

The COG's response was a lawsuit brought by four gay San Juan residents who argued that the behavior of two consenting adults did not represent a threat to the state. A second lawsuit, filed on behalf of a lesbian couple and a gay couple, argued that the new code violated a number of their constitutional rights. Both cases, and their subsequent appeals, were lost. In fact, perhaps because 1974 was an election year, all political candidates expressed some degree of support for the new legislation.

The COG existed for three years; it advanced issues affecting the gay community into the mainstream political discourse of the island. The group publicly highlighted the stereotypical representations of gays in the visual and print media. Over time, newspapers began to use the word homosexual or gay instead of the pejorative terms formerly used; and public discussion about gay issues took a more serious tone, and such issues were treated with some respect even by their opponents.

The late 1970s and very early 1980s have been described as a somewhat dormant period for gay activism on the island. Explanations range from the burnout of the movement's leaders to the focus on the AIDS crisis. Fundación SIDA, the AIDS foundation in Puerto Rico, worked with AIDS victims and promoted the concept of gays as a community. Soon a group of gays and lesbians began to meet to discuss issues pertaining to the gay community. From these meetings an organization called the Colectivo de Conscientización Gay (CCG) was formed with the objective of going beyond discussion groups to political action and such activities as generating publications and press releases. This group began to publish a monthly newsletter, "El CCG Informa," which was distributed in gay bars and became another vehicle for promoting the concept of community. Also during the 1980s, the activities of gay groups began to include workshops and symposiums in public places, particularly in universities and the Episcopal church, one of the few institutions that supported the gay and lesbian community at that time. In contrast to the past, these meetings were no longer held in secret; they were announced in their newsletters and in any publication willing to publish these announcements. In 1987 a three-day symposium designated the Reality of Homosexuality and Lesbianism in Puerto Rico was held at an Episcopal church. The CCG also established Tele-Info Gay, a hot line or central network people could call for information on resources and activities of the gay community.

By the late 1980s the Lesbian Feminist Collective, an offshoot of the CCG, was established. This group worked through the early 1990s until the Third Latin American and Caribbean Lesbian Feminist Encounter was held in Puerto Rico. This three-day *encuentro*, which took place in Cabo Rojo on August 14, 15 and 16, 1992, brought together over 150 lesbians from all over Latin America to discuss health, art, politics, economics, child bearing, domestic violence and numerous other issues. It is the only time in history that such an event has taken place on the island.

During the 1990s a significant number of gay groups have formed. The Coalición Orgullo Arcoiris, or Gay Pride Coalition, established the yearly gay pride march held yearly every first Sunday in June. The group meets in the Condado section of San Juan and marches to the Muñoz Rivera Park, the largest public park in the metropolitan area. In 1996 the march was shrouded with controversy when administrators from the Parks Department denied the group the necessary permit for their activities and publicly stated that the park was a "family" place, indicating that a gay and lesbian parade would be inappropriate. As soon as the news became public, government officials interceded, and the group was given the necessary permit. Many gays use that incident to demonstrate how far gay activism in the island has come; in years past, they would not have been able to counteract such an obstacle. As a result of the publicity this incident received, the 1996 march was the largest in the short history of gay activism on the island.

On April 2, 1995, gay leaders announced in *El Nuevo Día* that the gay community was prepared to support political candidates that were willing to "express their respect for their sexual orientation." The article provided the names of the candidates they would support as well as those they would not. The gay community calculated that, in San Juan, their numbers were as high as 60,000 or 10 percent of the population. Considering that most candidates win by smaller margins, it seems that in the near future politicians may be more willing to appreciate the interests and concerns of the gay community.

SUGGESTED READING

Frances Negrón-Muntaner, "Echoing Stonewall and Other Dilemmas: The Organizational Beginnings of a Gay and Lesbian Agenda in Puerto Rico, 1972–1977," Part 1, *Centro de Estudios Puertorriqueños Bulletin* 4, no. 1 (Winter 1989–1990): 76–95, and Part 2, in 4, no. 2 (Spring 1992): 88–97; Luis Penchi, "Advierten los 'gays' su poder electoral," *El Nuevo Día*, April 2, 1995, 11; Comunidad de Orgullo Gay, Constitution Preamble (1974, 1).

Generation of the Thirties   During the 1930s, a huge economic depression was a source of major despair for many members of the Puerto Rican society. It was a time when the deep economic, social and political schism engulfed them. The colonial domination and exploitation suffered by Puerto Ricans suddenly surfaced and started to bother and worry laymen and intellectuals alike: Who are we as a nation? What are the traits that define us? What is the essence of Puerto Rican culture? Who rules and governs? Why are we oppressed? How can we free ourselves of this oppression? Why are we so unhappy? Where should we go for guidance, security and support?

The term "generation of the thirties," or *la generación del treinta*, is used to group the work of some of the most gifted Puerto Rican writers of the time. Their literary production is characterized by their exploration of themes representative of the material and spiritual dilemmas faced by Puerto Ricans at that time. One of the members of this literary group was Enrique Laguerre, who re-created the social and economic malaise that affected the people around the sugar cane plantations and in the countryside. His work brought to the surface the inhumanity suffered by the poor peasants, the **jíbaros,** at the hands of land and sugar mill owners.

Writers of this period collected the folk customs and traditions of the Puerto Rican people in an effort to preserve the roots of their nationality, which was threatened by the process of "Americanization" (assimilation

into the U.S. culture) since 1898. At the same time, they underscored the
ideological struggles affecting the island. Authors belonging to this literary
group produced works across all literary genres. Among them are poets
Graciany Miranda Archilla, Luis Hernández Aquino, Carmen Alicia Cad-
illa, **Juan Antonio Corretjer**, Clara Lair, **Francisco Matos Paoli** and **Luis
Palés Matos** (González 1969). Some of the essay writers of the generation
were Antonio S. Pedreira, Tomás Blanco, Carmen Gómez Tejera, Cesáreo
Rosa-Nieves, Lidio Cruz Monclova, Antonia Sáez, Antonio S. Colorado,
Concha Meléndez, Vicente Géigel Polanco, Samuel Quiñones and Adriana
Ramos Mimoso (Robles de Cardona 1969). Short story writers were **Luis
Muñoz Marín**, Evaristo Ribera Chevremont, Tomás Blanco, **Emilio S. Be-
laval**, Washington Lloréns and Julio Marrero Nuñez. Representative nov-
elists were José A, Balseiro, **Enrique A. Laguerre**, José I. De Diego Padró,
Max Ríos y Ríos and **Manuel Méndez Ballester** (Meléndez 1969). Among
the most significant playwrights of this generation were Luis Lloréns Torres, Manuel Méndez Ballester, Fernando Sierra Berdecía, René Marqués,
Francisco Arriví and Antonio Coll Vidal (Arriví 1969).

The literary contributions of the members of this generation will permeate the cultural and literary landscape of Puerto Rico forever. They made
everlasting contributions to preserve the key features of Puerto Rican nationality and culture while exploring the inner conflicts of the island.

SUGGESTED READING

Francisco Arriví, *La generación de treinta: el teatro* (San Juan: Instituto de Cultura
Puertorriqueña, 1960); José Emilio González, *Los poetas puertorriqueños de la
década de 1930* (San Juan: Instituto de Cultura Puertorriqueña, 1969); Concha
Meléndez, *La generación del treinta: Cuento y novela* (San Juan: Instituto de Cul-
tura Puertorriqueña, 1969); Mariana Robles de Cardona, *El ensayo en la genera-
ción del treinta* (San Juan: Instituto de Cultura Puertorriqueña, 1969); Magalí
Roy-Fequiere, *Race, Gender and the "Generación del Treinta": Toward a Deci-
phering of Puerto Rican National Identity Discourse* (Ann Arbor, Mich.: University
Microfilms International, 1994); Blanca G. Silvestrini and María Dolores Luque de
Sánchez, *Historia de Puerto Rico: Trayectoria de un pueblo* (San Juan: Cultural
Puertorriqueña, 1990).

Girón de Segura, Socorro (1919–   )   This writer and educator, originally
from **Ponce**, has produced, among her many works, the most complete
anthology on **José Gautier Benítez**, poet laureate of Puerto Rico. Her detailed research on the life and literary work of Gautier Benítez was published in a series of books: *Espístolas de José Gautier Benítez* (1956); *José
Gautier Benítez; obra completa* (1960); the Puerto Rican Institute of Culture Award–winning *José Gautier Benítez; vida y época; obra inédita*
(1961); and *José Gautier Benítez; facsímiles de su obra* (1964). In 1967 she
published another award-winning book on the lives of Gautier Benítez's

mother, **Alejandrina Benítez y Arce de Gautier**, and great aunt, **María Bibiana Benítez y Constanza**.

Girón de Segura received her degree in secondary education from the **University of Puerto Rico**, where she specialized in French and Spanish. While working as a teacher, she began to publish articles and poetry in what was then Ponce's daily paper, *El Día*. This work earned her the Institute of Puerto Rican Culture's Award for journalism in 1959, a year in which she had also published her first book of poetry, *A la sombra de la ceiba*. Girón de Segura pursued graduate studies and completed a master's degree in 1961 at the University where she wrote another award-winning thesis that later became the book *Gregorio Marannón*. In 1967 she received a law degree from Catholic University in Ponce, and in 1981 she defended her dissertation on the author Julio Camba and received her doctoral degree. For a brief period of time, she was the director of the editorial division of the Department of Instruction, and since 1970 she has been a Spanish professor at the University of Puerto Rico in Ponce.

During her entire professional life, writing and research have been important components of her work, which is characterized by its focus on the literary yield of Puerto Rican writers. In 1987 she began to work on a project to research and recover the work of Puerto Rican journalist Luis Bonafoux. Like much of her previous research, this effort will make public the work of a prolific literary figure who has remained unknown for many years. Her work in recovering the literary heritage of the island continues to bring her much praise and recognition.

SUGGESTED READING

Josefina Rivera de Alvarez, *Diccionario de literatura Puertorriqueña* (San Juan, P.R.: Instituto de Cultura Puertorriqueña, 1974): 686–87; Salvador Soto Arana, *Prontuario literario biográfico puertorriqueño* (1990: 182–83).

Gómez Tejera, Carmen (1890–1973)   This educator and writer dedicated fifty years of her life to the educational system in Puerto Rico. Originally from Aguadilla, Gómez Tejera's professional experience encompassed teaching at all school levels, elementary through university, as well as occupying numerous administrative positions. Her published work focuses on many aspects of the Spanish language and Puerto Rican literature. In collaboration with other colleagues, she published curriculum guides for teachers as well as textbooks and manuals for language arts teachers.

It was in her role as teacher-educator that Tejera has made her mark in Puerto Rico. Starting with her master's thesis about the Puerto Rican novel ("La novela en Puerto Rico," 1929), published in 1947 as a monograph, she began to produce a series of essays, monographs and books on education on the island. Under her leadership, a collaborative of educators developed and published a curriculum series for teaching Spanish. Published by the island's Department of Instruction in 1938, this series became the most complete elementary and secondary Spanish language arts curriculum ever developed at that time. During that same year, Gómez Tejera, in collaboration with Juan Asencio Alvarez-Torre, published an anthology of Puerto Rican poetry for children. The first of its kind, it was a collection of native poetry initially targeted for elementary school children. In 1955 this series was revised, and another anthology, this time for middle and high school students, was published with the same purpose: to familiarize students with some of their literary and cultural heritage. This collection, a publication of the Department of Public Instruction, was widely used for years, and finally, in 1971, Troutman Press released it in book form. Gómez Tejera has stated in most of her publications that students' understanding of Puerto Rico—its literature, history, politics—is what mattered to her and inspired her to publish. She coauthored one of the first and longest used Spanish reading series, *Serie básica de lectura*. This collection of readers and teachers' manuals was developed for the entire system of kindergarten through twelfth grade. For the first time, and in a pedagogically sequenced way, Puerto Rican students were presented with a wide spectrum of reading materials that included material from Puerto Rican literary figures as well as the traditional Spanish writers that were always part of the curriculum.

In 1934 she was instrumental in establishing the journal *Brújula*, the official publication of the Circle of Spanish Teachers of the Department of Instruction. Under her leadership, this magazine has provided a forum for the exchange of ideas and approaches to the teaching of language arts by public school teachers all over the island. It brought Puerto Rico's literature, folklore and language use into the pedagogical language arts discourse of the time. It was instrumental in highlighting Puerto Rican literary works and stimulated teachers to include them in their courses.

She spent most of her professional life working for the school system as a teacher, as director of the Curriculum Division of the Department of Public Instruction, and as a professor at the **University of Puerto Rico**'s School of Education. After her retirement, she continued working as a consultant to the department overseeing the development of Spanish language arts curriculum for the school system. Carmen Gómez Tejera's imprint on Puerto Rico's educational system can be felt to this day. Her legacy was to validate Puerto Rico's cultural heritage within the educational system.

After her retirement as a university professor, she was named Professor Emeritus of the University of Puerto Rico. Another of the many honors bestowed on her was Puerto Rican Woman of the Year in 1967, by the Association of American Women.

SUGGESTED READING

Associación de Graduadas UPR, "Apuntes biográficos de doña Carmen Gómez Tejera," *Educación* 25 (1969): 1–5; Carmen Tejera Gómez, *Poesía puertorriqueña* (Mexico: Editorial Orion, 1957); Carmen Tejera Gómez, *La escuela puertorriqueña* (Sharon, Conn.: Troutman Press, 1970); María Jesusa Manso de Salgado, "Doña Carmen Gómez Tejera: Su vida y su obra educativa," master's thesis, University of Puerto Rico, 1977. Cesáreo Rosa Nieves and Esther Melón, *Biografía puertorriqueñas: Perfil histórico de un pueblo* (Sharon, Conn.: Troutman Press, 1970;

González, José Luis (1926–1996)   José Luis González was one of the most important Puerto Rican writers of this century. Born in the Dominican Republic to a Puerto Rican father and a Dominican mother, he lived in Mexico from 1955 until his death. He called himself a "Puerto Rican, Caribbean and Latin American writer of Hispanic tongue. And many bloods" (Flores 1992, 378).

González received his undergraduate degree in social sciences from the **University of Puerto Rico** and completed graduate studies at the New School of Social Research in New York. Due to his political ideology, which was perceived as leftist and revolutionary, he was unable to teach in Puerto Rico. He moved to Mexico and relinquished his American citizenship by taking a Mexican one. As a result, the American immigration authorities forbade him to enter the island for twenty years. This involuntary exile from the island shaped many of his writings and nourished many of his ideas.

González's legacy is vast. His socialist ideology permeated his early works. He had a brilliant narrative style that was considered groundbreaking. His early work focused on urban themes and brought to the surface the complex, and often painful, social dynamics that impacted life in Puerto Rican society. His collection of short stories *En este lado* (1950), which contains the now famous short story "En el fondo del caño hay un negrito," exemplifies this.

A common thread that runs through most of his writings is the exploration of social and cultural identity as it relates to the colonial influence from the United States, or, as González called it, "an assault of imperialism" (Flores 1992, 270). A significant portion of his literary production reflected on the social dynamics of migration of Puerto Ricans between the island and the United States. His short story *La noche que volvimos a ser gente* (1973) underscores the inner strengths of Puerto Ricans who migrate to New York, suffer the oppression of life in the city, but still retain their love for the island where their roots are grounded. The later portion of González's work explored the notion of Puerto Rican identity. His book *El país de cuatro pisos* (1980) presented the author's analysis of the social and political factors that have affected the development, or lack of development, of a national Puerto Rican identity.

After his death, literary critic Arcadio Díaz Quiñones reflected on the significance of González's literary legacy (Díaz Quiñones 1996, 4–5). He underscored the importance of González's work in fostering and revitalizing intellectual discussions about issues of culture, nationality and ethnicity with a generation of new scholars in the island; as well as his leading role in triggering and sponsoring the debate about Puerto Rican historiography and the need to review commonly held assumptions about Puerto Rican history through revision and reinterpretation of historical sources and events.

SUGGESTED READING

Arcadio Díaz Quiñones, "José Luis González: el gran ausente," *Revista del Domingo, El Nuevo Día*, December 29, 1996; José Luis González, *The Four Storeyed Country* (Maplewood, N.J.: Waterfront Press, 1992); José Luis González, in Angel Flores, ed., *Spanish American Authors: The Twentieth Century* (New York: Wilson); Juan R. Horta-Collado, *Nationalism versus Marxism in Two Puerto Rican Writers* (Ann Arbor, Mich.: University Microfilms International); Nicolasa Mohr, "Puerto Rican Writers in the United States," *The American Review* 15, no. 2 (1987); Hector M. Otero, *José Luis González and National Mass Consciousness in Puerto Rico* (Ann Arbor, Mich.: University Microfilms International, 1987).

González, Velda (1933–)   An actress and a politician, Velda González has been a popular television personality in Puerto Rico for the past thirty years. A consummate character actress, she has played significant roles in Puerto Rican theater and has also appeared in films. However, she is most admired and remembered for her popular television role as La Criada Malcriada, playing a saucy and perky maid who comes to work at a house in the metropolitan area but sees the reality around her from the vantage point of a *jíbara* from the mountainside (see **Jíbaro**).

González has also had a remarkable career as a senator for the **Popular Democratic party** since 1982. She has been a serious and capable legislator who has undertaken a vanguard role in the defense of Puerto Rican arts and culture but who has shown skill and competence in mastering a wide array of public policy issues.

SUGGESTED READING

Who's Who Among Hispanic Americans, 3d ed. 1994–1995. (Detroit: Gale Research, 1994).

Gran Combo de Puerto Rico   This musical group has been one of the most prominent and visible bands on the island of Puerto Rico for the past thirty-five years. El Gran Combo was founded by pianist Rafael Ithier on May 26, 1962, as a spin-off of the Rafael Cortijo y Su Combo group. La Universidad de la Salsa (The University of Salsa), as it is commonly known, has exported Puerto Rican, Caribbean and tropical rhythms such as **salsa** from

Puerto Rico to the rest of the world. During their early years, this group was clearly influenced by Cortijo's sound, but it quickly developed its own style, which is characterized by powerful vocal resources and the use of humor. The band members are also known for their skillful use of percussion.

El Gran Combo has been enriched by the talent of such performers as Andy Montañez, Pellín Rodriguez (deceased), Eddie Pérez and Roberto Rohena. Their repertoire, which is tropical in nature, includes a wide array of rhythms associated with tropical and Afro-Antillean musical traditions. Among their most recognized hits are "Acangara," "Jala jala," "Ojitos chinos," "Meneito me" and "El caballo pelotero."

Although this group has changed significantly throughout the years, because members have left and new musicians have come into the group, it has been able to maintain its popularity as well as its success. It has perpetuated its success for three decades and across generations. El Gran Combo, a regular fixture of Puerto Rican entertainment circles, has appeared in hundreds of television, radio and live music shows since their foundation. They have recorded dozens of records and have been able to maintain a lively sound enjoyed by thousands of fans throughout the island. El Gran Combo has been one of the leading forces in the internationalization of tropical music in Europe, Japan, Latin America and the United States. To a large extent, they built a platform that made possible the later development of salsa music in New York and Latin America and its acceptance by the music industry and the entertainment world. It celebrated thirty-five years of artistic success on August 8, 1995, with a performance at the Luis A. Ferré Center for Performing Arts, which was the only music outlet in Puerto Rico where they had not yet performed.

SUGGESTED READING

Belen Martínez Cabello, "Sigue sonando igual a pesar de sus cambios," *Vea* (San Juan, P.R.) August 4–10, 1996; Javier Santiago, *Nueva ola portorricensis* (San Juan, P.R.: Editorial del Patio, 1994).

Grito de Lares   The translation of these words is the Shout of Lares, which refers to a revolutionary insurrection against Spain that began on September 23, 1868. A Puerto Rican national holiday, it is one of the few historical events that is still celebrated and revered by members of all the island's political parties. The Shout of Lares was also the catalyst for "La Borinqueña," the national anthem of Puerto Rico.

To understand the insurrection, it is necessary to understand the nature of Spanish colonialism. By the mid-1860s no islander could host a meeting, a dance or any social gathering without first gaining permission from the Spanish authorities. Nine P.M. curfews existed throughout the island, and no one could change residence, read banned books or publish anything deemed offensive by the Spanish. The authorities also resisted the abolition of **slavery**, and, instead of opening the island to native inhabitants, the Spanish actively recruited immigrants from Europe. These "real Spanish" received preference over the *criollos* (native Puerto Ricans) in matters that extended from government positions to the availability of credit.

The ideological roots of the revolution were succinctly expressed in a document entitled "Los diez mandamientos de hombres libres" (The ten commandments of free men) written by **Ramón Emeterio Betances**. Demand number one was the abolition of slavery; two, the right to determine taxes; nine, the inviolability of all citizens; and ten, the people's freedom to elect their own public officials.

Along with other revolutionaries, Betances was expelled from the island in 1867. He first went to Santo Domingo and from there to New York City. His aim was to raise the money and men required to support the insurrection planned for September 29, 1868. The revolutionaries had established secret societies throughout the island. In Lares and Camuy, the societies were especially well organized; in other localities, the low level of enthusiasm moved Betances to complain that he had been deserted by liberals who talked of revolution but remained neutral when the call to action finally came.

Camuy received the honor of beginning the revolution. However, *una chota* (a squealer in American slang) informed the Spanish authorities on September 20, 1868, that a conspiracy was afoot. The next day, Colonel Manuel de Iturriaga took his troops to the home of Manuel María González; there the Spanish arrested the leader of the revolutionary forces in the northern part of the island. Initially, the fighters from Camuy planned to rescue González but they instead united with the forces from Lares. At roughly 10 P.M. on the night of September 23, Manuel Rojas (head of the forces in Lares) spoke to about 600 rebels. He reminded them of Spanish tyranny, and he promised that poor workers would have their debts canceled. To shouts of "Death to Spain, long live liberty, long live free Puerto Rico," the rebels entered Lares. They easily took the town but what they could not know was that Betances's ship, *El Telégrafo* had been confiscated by Danish officials in the Virgin Islands. The rebels would receive neither arms nor men from abroad. They were on their own, and the Spanish knew their predicament. The rebels next attacked Pepino (San Sebastián), but the Spanish had reinforced the town with seasoned soldiers; in addition, citizens loyal to Spain had enough time to organize against the rebel assault. Thus, despite repeated attempts to take the town, the rebels were forced to retreat. They returned to Lares to wait for news of other, successful insurrections on the island. No other town echoed the shout from Lares. With aid from Betances impounded in the Virgin Islands, the insurrection soon ended. Rebels fled to the hills, hoping to fight another day, but the Spanish arrested, not only hundreds of rebels, but also many citizens suspected of sympathy for the revolutionary cause. More than eighty Puerto Ricans died in jail because of the abysmal conditions; others, such as **Marianna Bracetti Cuevas** endured the expected punishment meted out to those who opposed Spanish colonialism.

The Shout of Lares is still celebrated wherever Puerto Ricans live. Indeed, in recent years, the celebration at Lares has moved hundreds of young Puerto Ricans to publicly renounce their U.S. citizenship. In an attempt to resurrect the patriotic spirit of Emeterio Betances, the young men and women argue that the Puerto Rican nation "cannot be spiritually free while politically related to an outside society."

SUGGESTED READING

Olga Jiménez de Wagenheim, *Puerto Rico's Revolt for Independence: El Grito de Lares* (Boulder, Colo.: Westview Press, 1985); Gordon K. Lewis, *Main Currents in Caribbean Thought* (Baltimore: Johns Hopkins University Press, 1983); Germán Delgado Pasapera, *Puerto Rico: Sus luchas empancipadoras* (San Juan, P.R.: Editorial Cultural, 1984).

Guánica Central   This term refers to the sugar-refining facility located in Guánica; in the early part of the twentieth century, this was one of the largest *centrals* in the Western Hemisphere. Until World War II, sugar stood at the center of island life. The Guánica Central, owned by the South Porto Rico Sugar Company, a New Jersey corporation, was the largest sugar "factory" in the island, and, as such, it symbolizes some of the human dimensions associated with sugar production in Puerto Rico. As reported by the *New Republic* in 1916, visitors who entered the *central* first noticed "spacious, modern houses." There were flowers, a YMCA, and even tennis and squash courts. Strolling closer to the huge chimney that stood at the *central*'s center, the visitor would spot a church and a series of houses which, "although less attractive, were still bright and clean." Now, near the chimney that could be literally "hot as hell," the houses turned into "one room, barrack like dwellings, ugly and cheap." Here the "street ends and if you are an American you retrace your steps to the first settlement, which is for Americans only" (Ovington 1916, 27–72).

Along with sugar, places like Guánica Central brought a form of institutional prejudice and segregation to Puerto Rico. It was this, among other complaints, that moved labor leaders, such as **Santiago Iglesias Pantín**, to fight against exploitation by the mostly absentee owners of U.S. sugar plantations. At Guánica, "the peon" was paid sixty cents for a twelve-hour day. The *New Republic* reporter called this a "princely wage" because "a few *centrals* work their men for eighteen hours out of the twenty-four" (271). And then, instead of cash, men received a check redeemable only at the company store.

SUGGESTED READING

Joseph Marcus, *Labor Conditions in Porto Rico* (Washington D.C.: U.S. Government Printing Office, 1919); Sidney Mintz, *Worker in the Cane: A Puerto Rican Life History* (New Haven, Conn.: Yale University Press, 1960); Mary White Ovington, "The United States in Porto Rico," *New Republic*, July 15, 1916, 271–73; Victor Rodríguez, *External and Internal Factors in the Organization of Production and Labor in the Sugar Industry of Puerto Rico, 1860–1934* (Irvine: University of California Press, 1987).

Güiro (or güicharo)   The *güiro*, which is used in a wide array of musical rhythms and forms in the island, is a small instrument made out of the fruit of the calabash tree, which is emptied and then dried. After it is dried, numerous cuts or incisions are made into its cortex or skin. When it is rubbed with a metallic fork with multiple prongs, it makes a sharp noise that is used by musicians to create rhythmic figures, which accompany singers and other musicians in the creation of popular music.

It has been thought that this instrument comes to the island from either the Taíno (see **Los Taínos**) or the Caribe musical heritage because it is mentioned in literature as long ago as Christopher Columbus's second trip by the name of *mayohabao* or *guajey*.

SUGGESTED READING

Rocío Cárdenas, *Música caribeña* (Colombia: Universidad del Valle, 1992).

Guitiérrez del Arroyo, Isabel (1907–   )   Originally from Bayamón, Guitiérrez del Arroyo has distinguished herself as an outstanding historian who has documented and chronicled Puerto Rico's past. Her leadership in this area came during the 1940s when Puerto Rico's history had undergone an official reconstruction under Paul Miller, a representative of the U.S. government in Puerto Rico.

At the age of twenty, she received the equivalent of an associate degree in primary education. In 1943, after thirteen years of working as a teacher, she received her undergraduate degree with honors from the **University of Puerto Rico**. That same year, the university established the Department of History, the first of its kind on the island, and she was appointed as a faculty member. Her interest in research led her to pursue graduate studies in Mexico. In 1948 she completed, cum laude, a master's degree in history, and two years later, she received a doctoral degree summa cum laude from Mexico's National Autonomous University.

Although her greatest contribution to Puerto Rico was as a historian, she was also an accomplished musician. As a young girl, she had studied violin and piano in her native Bayamón. Among her music teachers were Pepito Figueroa and Kachiro Figueroa of the famous **Figueroa family**. During the early part of the 1940s, she met and played with various members of the Figueroa family.

Her books and meticulous research have been very significant in authenticating and establishing a coherent interpretation and a basic framework for historiographers to follow. Among the more outstanding contributions to this field are *Prólogo a la historial geográfica, civil y natural de la isla de Puerto Rico de Abbad y Lasierra* (1948, 1959), "El reformismo ilustrado en Puerto Rico" (in *Asomante* 1953), "La biblioteca histórica de Puerto Rico" (in *Asomante*'s one-hundredth anniversary issue, 1954) and many others. There are numerous works of research published in professional journals that have yet to be edited and brought to the public's attention, including analytical works on Puerto Rican nationality and **Pedro Albizu Campos**.

During her entire professional life, Guitiérrez del Arroyo has maintained an index card system that numbers in the thousands. It contains facts and bibliographies in all areas of history that have some relation to the annals of Puerto Rico's culture, politics, economics, spirituality and ideology. Many historians and other professionals on the island have suggested that the University of Puerto Rico edit and publish this important collection. To date, however, it remains the property of the author.

Biographical data on this woman would be incomplete without including the important role she has played as a history professor. In addition to being a faculty member of the first History Department in an institution of higher education on the island, she has been recognized for the outstanding work she has performed in that role over the years. Her discipline and mastery of the research process, as well as her vast knowledge and understanding of history and its significance to a nation, have earned her accolades from many of her students. In 1987 the Technical College of Bayamón inaugurated and designated a special room in the library where the collection of Puerto Rican works is maintained as the Sala Isabel Gutiérrez del Arroyo.

SUGGESTED READING

Carmelo Delgado Cintrón, "Isabel Gutiérrez del Arroyo: Forjadora," *Diálogo* (May 1987): 39; Manuel Alvarado Morales, "Semblanza de la Doctora Isabel Gutiérrez del Arroyo," *Conference Proceedings of the Fundación puertorriqueña de las Humanidades,* San Juan, P.R., 1987.

H

Health A review of the most recent morbidity and mortality statistics reveals that heart disease is the leading cause of death for Puerto Ricans. It accounted for 20.4 percent of all deaths reported in the island during 1994. Cancer, in the form of malignant tumors, was responsible for 15.1 percent of deaths, followed by diabetes (6.6 percent), AIDS (5.4 percent) and brain and vascular disease (5.0 percent). The rate of infant mortality is 13 deaths for each 1,000 live births (Health Department 1997).

For most of its recent history under the Commonwealth, from 1952 until the present, Puerto Rico has had a "dual" health care system (Feliciano de Melecio 1995, 6). The government has operated the largest component of this system. It has traditionally provided health care services to all Puerto Ricans but targets mostly poor and disenfranchised people. The Department of Health has administered and funded a huge health care establishment that divides the island into seven medical regions and operates large tertiary regional hospitals in each one of the regions, smaller area hospitals, and small community health centers with emergency room services in each one of the towns and municipalities. In addition, the government is involved in the operation of large pediatric, industrial, oncology, cardiovascular and psychiatric hospitals. There is also a private health care industry that owns and operates a wide array of medical facilities throughout the island.

After the election of Governor Pedro Rosselló in 1992, he formulated a plan for a major health reform. He argued that it wasn't practical for the government to keep operating a large health services infrastructure. He believed that such services overburdened the fiscal capacity of the government. Since 58 percent of the population falls under the poverty line, the government has been unable to keep up with the demand for health care services. Deterioration and disrepair had affected most medical facilities owned and operated by the government and had been perceived to provide only low quality services to the patients. As a result, the governor initiated a radical plan to sell government-owned health care facilities to private investors. In fact, it has already sold many of them. The proceeds will be used to fund and sudsidize a medical plan for all poor Puerto Ricans.

This plan, known as "La Tarjetita," has already been implemented in most municipalities throughout the island. Needy individuals who qualify for benefits are given a health card that entitles them to enroll with a primary health provider that operates following a managed care model. If patients need specialized medical services, they are referred to specialists within the network. The plan, offered through a private company, provides comprehensive hospitalization benefits as well as prescription services. "La Tarjetita" is generally perceived as a great success among recipients of services and has generated a lot of support for Governor Rosselló and his Health Secretary Carmen Feliciano de Melecio. For the first time, Puerto Ricans of all socio-economic backgrounds can have access to quality services. There have been many public concerns about the huge costs of this initiative for the government and about the fact that public health services have been turned over to private investors who may not invest in them adequately.

SUGGESTED READING

Department of Health of the Commonwealth of Puerto Rico, Office of Vital Statistics, *Vital Statistics for 1994* (San Juan: Department of Health, 1997); U.S. Congress Committee on Education and Labor, *Puerto Rico's Health Care Delivery System, Its Current Health Care Reform Efforts, and Access to Rural Health Care Services in Puerto Rico*, November 15, 1994 (Washington D.C.; Government Printing Office, 1995).

Hernández Araujo, Carmen (1832–1877)   This poet and playwright was one of a group of outstanding female literary figures of the nineteenth century, which included **Lola Rodríguez de Tío, María Bibiana Benítez y Constanza** and **Alejandrina Benítez y Arce de Gautier.** She wrote her first two plays at the age of fourteen; one of them, *Los deudos rivales,* though not published until 1863, nevertheless has been hailed as majestic and grand in its ability to capture the essence of the Romantic literary style of that period. One of those characteristics, the use of foreign and ancient history, was a feature of European Romanticism present in her work; however, the reason for its use was to avoid the strict censure of the colonial government. Hernández Araujo, and many of her contemporaries, situated the scenes in their work in foreign lands, and the plots took place in an earlier historical period. Her other early play, *Amor ideal,* is a three-act play written in verse about a young couple who are madly in love, confronting apparent indications that they are in reality siblings. The play is full of dramatic tension up to the third act, where the discovery of a document stating they are not brother and sister gives the drama a happy ending. Even though some of the elements of this play may be perceived as risqué for that particular time, the play provides humorous relief and is filled with a deep Christian sentiment. Religious activity was part of her upbringing, as was the daily ritual of attending Catholic religious services.

It was during Hernández Araujo's era that theater on the island was beginning to develop, and her plays were among the first published works of this genre. Inasmuch as they were hailed as literary accomplishments, they were not given the exposure and staging that other dramas, written by males, received.

Hernández Araujo never lost the Christian fervor with which she was raised, and elements of this faith are evident in most of her work, particularly in her poetry. Some of the poems inspired by her Catholicism are "A la santa cruz" and "Agonía de Jesús en el huerto," both deeply religious narratives. In 1863 her poem, "Oda tres coronas," a poetic tribute to the painter José Campeche, was praised and received an award from the Sociedad Económica de Amigos del País.

In 1873 she married Germán Araujo, with whom she lived until her death four years later. Hernández Araujo left an unpublished novel, *Flores o virtudes y abrojos y pasiones*, and a religious novel, *The Biblical Catechism*.

SUGGESTED READING

Federico Ribes Tovar, *The Puerto Rican Woman: Her Life and Evolution throughout History* (New York: Plus Ultra Educational Publishers, 1972); Cesáreo Rosa-Nieves, *Plumas estelares en las letras de Puerto Rico* vol. 1 (San Juan, P.R.: Ediciones de la Torre, 1967).

Hernández Colón, Rafael (1936–   )   A governor of Puerto Rico for three terms, he is one of the most influential and respected politicians of his generation. Born in **Ponce** on October 24, 1936, Hernández Colón was educated in the United States, at the Valley Forge Military Academy and then at Johns Hopkins University. He also has a law degree from the **University of Puerto Rico**, and in 1968 he published a classic law text entitled *Procedimiento civil*.

Hernández Colón served as the nation's secretary of justice and the president of its senate, and he was governor from 1972 to 1976 and then again from 1984 to 1992. One of the most conspicuous accomplishments of his second administration was the restoration and beautification of such cities as Ponce and San Germán. Even his critics agree that this legacy of beauty will survive well into the twenty-first century.

As governor, Hernández Colón struggled to achieve an **enhanced commonwealth**. The roadblock was the U.S. Constitution and the U.S. Senators who dominated U.S. policy. For example, in April 1974, Senator Henry Jackson came to Puerto Rico and, after Governor Hernández Colón said that he was "the man with best knowledge about Puerto Rico in Congress," Jackson said this: "Puerto Rico became a part of the United States by an act of conquest . . . neither independence, developed commonwealth or statehood can be had. Puerto Rico must remain a colony."

Some analysts argue that such attitudes moved Hernández Colón to push the nation quietly toward independence during his second and third administrations. While there is no doubt that the governor asserted Puerto Rico's rights—by trying to negotiate independently with countries like Japan, by excluding the U.S. flag and national anthem from public ceremonies, by pushing to make Spanish the official language of the nation—he nevertheless spent years trying to get Congress to approve a three status options **plebiscite** (i.e., independence, commonwealth and statehood) that would be binding on the U.S. Congress. These efforts failed in 1991, and, when islanders also failed to endorse the governor in a vote on the use of Spanish in Puerto Rican society, Hernandez withdrew from contention for the 1992 governorship.

He now lives in Ponce and teaches at the Pontifical Catholic University of Ponce. He is involved in a wide variety of political and educational endeavors. Hernández Colón has been honored on many occasions for his tireless efforts in support of Puerto Rico's Olympic programs.

SUGGESTED READING

Rafael Hernández Colón, "An Open Letter to Fellow Citizens of the United States from the Governor of Puerto Rico," *New York Times*, April 9, 1991, A25; U.S. Congress, Senate, *Political Status of Puerto Rico*, Hearings before the Committee on Energy and Natural Resources, 102d Cong., 1st sess. (Washington D.C.: U.S. Government Printing Office, 1991).

Hernández, Rafael (1892–1965)   Rafael Hernández is considered to be one of the premier composers of popular music on the island during the first part of the twentieth century. His creations brought the music of the island of Puerto Rico to Latin America, Europe and the United States. His work spans many genres of Puerto Rican and Latin American music—from the romantic and melancholic to the national. While songs such as "Venus," "Campanitas de Cristal," and "Ausencia" reflect on romantic love and relationships, "Lamento Borincano" and "Los carreteros" immortalize elements of Puerto Rican society. There is an obvious element of populism in his interpretations which captures an accurate profile of the ethos and pathos of Puerto Ricans on the island and abroad. His "Cuchifritos," for instance, satirizes the cultural differences between Puerto Ricans and many other American and Latin American neighbors while subtly pointing to a fierce Puerto Rican nationalism. His "Buchipluma Na'ma" and "Cachita" present the many sides of the macho (see **Machismo**) and chauvinistic mentality as well as the gender roles and expectations of the culture and society. His music presents examples of many of the cultural elements and traits that define the Puerto Rican ethnicity.

He was also a talented interpreter of his music. He founded his own musical group: Cuarteto Victoria in New York City during the 1940s. He used his ensemble to bring Puerto Rican music to the world. His music has been interpreted in settings as diverse as cozy and romantic dance floors of a local night club to the ballrooms of major entertainment centers worldwide.

SUGGESTED READING

Rafael Hernández, *Hasta siempre* (Río Piedras: Yarav 1981); Luis O. Zayas Micheli, "Puerto Rico en el Lamento Borincano," *Revista Horizontes* 12, no. 22 (1968).

Hernández Torres, Zaida (1953–   )   This politician is a relative newcomer to Puerto Rican public life. A member of the pro-statehood **New Progressive party** (PNP), in 1993 she became the first Puerto Rican woman to preside over the legislature.

She completed her undergraduate work at the **University of Puerto Rico** and continued her graduate studies in law at **Interamerican University**. In addition, she completed a master's degree in law at the Center for Advanced Judicial Studies at the Catholic University of Puerto Rico. With a law degree in hand, she gained prominence as a criminal prosecutor while working as an assistant district attorney during the early 1980s. Even though she has described herself as having politics in her blood from an early age, her official involvement in this area did not begin until she became the legal counsel for the speaker of the House of Representatives on the island, José Granados Acevedo.

In 1984 she ran for and won her first elected office as a member of the House of Representatives. In 1986 she made history by becoming the first woman to be elected vice president of the **New Progressive party** (PNP). During the 1992 campaign, she was reelected to her legislative post by a record 97 percent of the votes and was chosen to preside as speaker of the House of Representatives. Her tenure as speaker has not been without controversy. Clashes with high-ranking members of her own party, including Governor **Pedro Roselló González** and the president of the Senate as well as her colleagues in the legislature, have made headlines in the island's visual and print media. Her manner has been called abrasive, and many people have alluded to her unmarried status. On the other hand, her defenders describe her critics as men who are not used to having a woman calling the shots, adding that, given the continuous criticism and constant surveillance by both colleagues and adversaries as well as the press, no one in the island's political history matches her leadership and decision-making ability.

In 1995 she announced her candidacy for mayor of San Juan. Like most elected officials running for office, she promised to control crime, improve the economy and improve the overall facilities of the city. The two cornerstones of her political platform, however, were to establish San Juan as an autonomous municipality and to create a subsidized health plan for 30,000 low-income residents of the area. The race was a historic event for all of the candidates were women. In November 1996, Hernández lost the

Zaida Hernández Torres, 1994. (Tito Guzmán and *El Nuevo Día*.)

mayoral contest in a close vote, winning 46.5 percent of the votes to **Sila Calderón's** 50.3 percent of the vote.

SUGGESTED READING

Rafael Castro Pereda, "En la balanza," *El Nuevo Día*, August 1, 1996; Ismael Fernández, "Dos candidates en perspectiva," *El Nuevo Día*, April 10, 1996; Mildred Rivera Marrero, "Aspirante a la autonomía municipal," *El Nuevo Día*, August 4, 1996.

Homar, Lorenzo (1913–   )

Homar, Lorenzo (1913–   )   Homar, a plastic and graphic artist, is one of the most visible, talented and best regarded Puerto Rican artists of the twentieth century. His art, as expressed in his graphics, calligraphy, engravings and paintings, has had a central place in Puerto Rican artistic circles for the past forty years. Through his production, Homar has defined and maintained the character of Puerto Rican plastic arts. His extensive production is rich in color, texture, plasticity and form.

Born in Puerta de Tierra, a suburb of San Juan, he went to New York City when he was fifteen years old. There he studied at Pratt Institute and the Brooking Museum. He also worked as a jewelry designer for Cartier for ten years. He studied and worked with Rufino Tamayo, Arthur Osver and Gabor Peterdi. He served in World War II where he toured the Pacific and then returned to Puerto Rico in 1950. Many of his drawings and cartoons are concerned with his war experience. He was one of the founders of the Center for Puerto Rican Arts.

Homar uses graphic and printing techniques, like few other Puerto Rican masters, to enhance different pictorial needs rather than just for the sake of using them. His work reveals a sophisticated eye that has a capacity to observe details and to replicate them with great precision. He is one of the leading interpreters of Puerto Rican realism in graphics and in painting. One of his most important roles has been as a teacher and mentor. Both from his workshop at the **Community Education Division** and at the Institute of Puerto Rican Culture, Homar has guided the early careers of many notable Puerto Rican painters, such as **Luis Germán Cájigas, Myrna Báez** and others. Homar's work is seen as the heart and spirit behind the popularity of the graphic posters and engravings that have become a key element of the Puerto Rican art establishments.

SUGGESTED READING

Peter Bloch, *Painting and Sculpture of the Puerto Ricans* (New York: Plus Ultra, 1978); Juan Antonio Gaya-Nuño, *La pintura puertorriqueña* (Soria, P.R.: Centro de Estudios Sorianos, 1984); Dale Roylance, "The Art of Lorenzo Homar," *Calligraphy Review*, 11 (1994): 34–37.

Hostos, Eugenio María de (1839–1903)

Hostos, Eugenio María de (1839–1903)   A sociologist, an educator, a writer, and a political revolutionary, Hostos was born in Mayagüez and

Lorenzo Homar, "Le-lo-lai," 1952–53. (Museo de la Universidad de Puerto Rico.)

Eugenio María de Hostos. (*El Nuevo Día.*)

died in the Dominican Republic. Hostos was a giant, a rare blend of intellectual excellence married to political activism. He studied in Spain and even directed in Barcelona an organ, *El Progreso*, that supported liberal causes. By 1869 he was in New York City seeking support for the revolution that would make Puerto Rico an independent nation. To achieve that aim, Hostos traveled throughout his life; in a career that spanned thirty-five years, he journeyed to Chile, Argentina, Venezuela, Europe, the Dominican Republic and, finally, in the late 1890s, again to the United States. In New York, Hostos organized the League of Patriots, an organization dedicated to demanding, as a natural right, the independence of Puerto Rico.

Hostos was one of a group of distinguished Puerto Ricans who went to Washington, D.C., before the **Treaty of Paris** was signed to request that the United States allow Puerto Rico to conduct a **plebiscite** so the nation could decide between annexation to the United States and independence. If independence were chosen, Puerto Rico would spend twenty years in a transition to complete sovereignty. After these deliberations, Hostos returned to Puerto Rico but, given the decided unwillingness of both the United States and his Puerto Rican associates to demand independence, Hostos voluntarily exiled himself to the Dominican Republic in 1900.

Hostos was among the first sociologists in Latin America. As Gordon Lewis correctly points out, his *Moral social* sought to furnish a grand theory that would link the European origins of sociology "to the special Antillean conditions it would be obliged to explain." Among Hostos's other works are *La pergrinación de Bayoan* (1863), *Lecciones de derecho constitucional* (1887) and *El caso de Puerto Rico* (1899).

In a letter written in 1873, Hostos explained the noble aims of his work: "I consecrated with my voice, my pen, and the example of a disinterested life, to the cause of the confraternity of all of these peoples, to the defense of all of these disinherited, whether they be Chinese or Quechua Indians in Peru, herdsmen in Chile, or gauchos and Indians in Argentina" (Lewis 1983, 273). With no dissenting voices, Hostos could have added the people of Puerto Rico.

SUGGESTED READING

Gordon Lewis, *Main Currents in Caribbean Thought* (Baltimore: Johns Hopkins University Press, 1983); Manuel Maldonado-Denis, *Puerto Rico: A Socio-Historical Interpretation* (New York: Vintage Books, 1972).

Huracán   The word *huracán* comes from the Taíno (see **Los Taínos**). Juracán was the malevolent god who, accompanied by terrible winds and torrential rains, brought death and destruction in his unpredictable wake. The Taíno made Juracán a god; in Puerto Rico, he turned into a saint. Tradition mandates that, using the Catholic calendar, hurricanes are humanized by giving them the saint's name associated with that day of the year. Thus, one of the most destructive storms in Puerto Rican history, which occurred on August 8, 1899, and killed more than 3,000 people, is still known as San Ciríaco.

This custom of naming has been abandoned since federal tracking stations now monitor the storms as they develop, and federal officials name the storms. Hugo, which occurred on September 18, 1989, ravaged the mainland but reserved special attention for **Vieques**. In La Casa de Frances, the stone mansion that once served as a plantation house, occupants gathered in an interior room. The thick, stone walls kept Hugo at bay, but nothing contained the storm's impact on the island, which was left bald, stripped of the leaves, flowers and fronds that make Vieques such an extraordinarily beautiful place.

Technically, a hurricane is a weather phenomenon of tropical origin that has winds of more than seventy-four miles per hour and moves in a counterclockwise circular motion with an east to west and south to north movement. Hurricanes have a low-pressure center, known as the eye of the storm, where the winds are completely calm. The edges of the eye have some of the most powerful winds engendered by the storm. Most tropical storms that affect the island of Puerto Rico originate in the tropical waters around Cape Verde on the western coast of Africa. The tropical storm season extends from June 1 to November 1 every year. They are direct by-product of summer when the warmth heats the waters and the humidity and winds create the conditions for a tropical storm or a hurricane.

Puerto Rico has been affected by many powerful hurricanes in the last 500 years. Spanish conquerors recorded the devastating effects of hurricanes on the island and at sea. Some of the most powerful ones recorded were San Ciríaco, San Felipe and San Ciprian, which caused widespread devastation. San Ciríaco, for instance, which passed through the island in 1899, reportedly killed 3,369 people on the island and caused millions of dollars in damage to property and agriculture. The island was spared from major storms from the mid-1950s to the late 1980s. The tropical storms that came close or through the island did not cause any major damage. In September 18, 1989, however, the eastern coast of the island was severely damaged by Hurricane Hugo. It killed two people and caused millions in damage to the eastern coast of the island where power and water services were affected for many days.

During the tropical storm season, islanders closely monitor weather bulletins and reports for information on weather conditions and potential problems. The National Weather Service, which has offices in San Juan, issues periodical bulletins and warnings when storms and hurricanes threaten the island. When there is danger of storms passing through the island or close by, the state government issues directives and opens government buildings to shelter islanders from the storms. In addition, the government freezes the prices of basic consumer goods, such as milk, eggs, plywood and batteries, which people may need to prepare themselves for the possible effects of the storm.

Due to the recent economic development of the island, the quality of local construction has improved. The use of wood and zinc in construction has been reduced. Concrete and iron structures are more prevalent now. Thus, the risks of damage and destruction have been considerably reduced. In addition, during the hurricane season, it is not uncommon to see the windows of apartments in San Juan and elsewhere completely shrouded in metal guards that not only keep out the sun, but also keep out the havoc wrought by a *huracán*. One of the risks that still affects Puerto Ricans, however, is flooding. The increase of unsupervised construction without the best planning has maximized the potential for flooding on the island.

One final point: San Ciríaco and San Felipe (September 13, 1928) both had a particularly ruinous impact on the nation's coffee growers. The destruction of the always fragile coffee plants was so great that, either through loss of wealth or loss of appetite for another hurricane, farmers allowed their lands to be used for such crops as sugar and tobacco.

SUGGESTED READING

Edwin Miner Sola, *Historia de los huracanes en Puerto Rico* (San Juan. P.R.: First Book Publishing of Puerto Rico, 1995); Neal Sealey, *Caribbean World: A Complete Geography* (London: Cambridge University Press, 1994); also Josá Antonio Toro-Sugrañes, *Nueva enciclopedia de Puerto Rico* (Hato Rey, P.R.: Lector, 1995).

I

Iglesias Pantín, Santiago (1870–1930)   This labor leader and politician played an important role in the development of the labor movement in Puerto Rico and eventually in Puerto Rican politics. Iglesias, who was born in Spain and immigrated to Cuba, became a labor leader in Cuba where he was incarcerated because of his perceived revolutionary beliefs—he was a socialist. After his release, he moved to Puerto Rico in 1896 where he also became concerned for the working class and eventually began to organize workers against the unfair practices of industry. He founded the first syndicate on the island; the Federación Regional de Trabajadores (Regional Workers Federation) and started a labor newspaper, *Ensayo Obrero*. The Spanish government incarcerated him for his prolabor beliefs, but he was released by the Americans after the 1898 invasion (a gunshot volley had hurt him while he was in prison).

Iglesias's interests received a huge boost from the American colonial authorities who gave him free reign to conduct his labor crusades. He was therefore able to organize the Workers party (Partido Obrero) and the Free Workers Federation (Federación de Trabajadores Libres). Iglesias Pantín acquired a high profile in Puerto Rican politics and eventually organized the Socialist Labor party (Partido Obrero Socialista). He became a senator who represented this party from 1917 to 1932. Iglesias eventually became a **Resident Commissioner** in Washington, D.C., where he represented a coalition of Republicans and Socialists.

He is a highly controversial figure for sympathizers of the pro-independence movement in Puerto Rico because, although he had a socialist orientation and philosophy, he never advocated independence for the island. Instead, he was an advocate of statehood. The nature of his socialist beliefs has also been questioned. He advocated restructuring economic policies within the system rather than making major changes in the capitalist structure. For socialist leaders today, Iglesias Pantín is a sort of pariah for he lacked the Marxist beliefs and ideologies that were to become fashionable later on. Much of this antagonism is due to the fact that Iglesias was basically an enemy of the father of socialism, **Pedro Albizu Campos**, and his annexionist policies were seen as a betrayal of the socialist and independence movements.

SUGGESTED READING

R. Montanez, "La obra sociologica de Santiago Iglesias," *Puerto Rico Illustrado* (December 6, 1939): 34; Clarence Senior, *Santiago Iglesias* (Hato Rey, P.R.: Interamerican University Press, 1972).

Inés, Doña   A high-ranking member of the Taíno Indians (see **Los Taínos**) and a *cacica* or chief herself, she was the mother of Agüeybaná, the principal *cacique* of the Taínos when Christopher Columbus arrived at **Boriquén** (the Indian name for Puerto Rico). The history books do not record her Indian name; Doña Inés was the name given to her by Juan **Ponce de León**. As was the Taíno custom, when establishing a new friendship, they took the name of the new friend; Agüeybaná took the name Juan Ponce, and Ponce de León, in turn, took the *cacique*'s name.

Even though she was quite old when the Spaniards landed on the island, it is said that she exercised great influence over her son and that it was she who advised him against demonstrating any rebelliousness against the colonizers as other *caciques* had done in Cuba and Santo Domingo. At first this advice served him well. Initially, the Taínos were spared the bloody and deadly counterattacks suffered by the other tribes who had not given the Spaniards a "friendly" welcome. In time, though, the eradication of the Taínos and other Caribbean tribes was accomplished by the conquistadors.

That the Spaniards were able to explore the island safely, and remove the gold and other resources they found is due to the diplomacy and hospitality that this *cacica* demonstrated. This decision also marked the beginning of the end for the Taíno society.

SUGGESTED READING

Jalil Sued-Badillo, *La mujer indígena y su sociedad* (San Juan, P.R.: Editorial Cultural, 1989).

Insular Cases   The term Insular Cases is generally given to a series of nine decisions rendered by the U.S. Supreme Court in 1901; however, some scholars include decisions that extend all the way to 1922. In either case, the Insular Cases focus on issues that relate to the U.S. Constitutional status of, primarily, Puerto Rico and the Philippines.

In arguably the most famous case, *Downes vs. Bidwell* in 1901, the S. B. Downes Company wanted to recover $659.35 in taxes paid in San Juan to import oranges to the United States. It sounds trivial, but it actually touches a vital issue in U.S. law. The Constitution contains a uniformity clause: "All duties, imposts, and excises shall be uniform throughout the United States." When Downes paid the taxes in Puerto Rico, it was already under U.S. civilian authority; therefore, Downes claimed he had been taxed unfairly. The Supreme Court disagreed. Indeed, it set the still reigning Constitutional precedent by declaring that Congress had *plenary* or absolute power over all U.S. territories. It had "the right to create such municipal organizations as it may deem best for all the territories of the United States . . . and to deprive such territory of representative government if it is considered just to do so, and to change such local governments at discretion" (Constitutional History 1964, 121). In the case of Puerto Rico, Congress had established a "temporary government"; the island belonged to the United States but was not an incorporated part of the United States. Thus, Downes had to pay his taxes because "neither military occupation nor cession by treaty makes the conquered territory domestic territory in the sense of the revenue laws" (123).

The phrase "conquered territory" set off sparks in a dissent filed by Justice John Marshall Harlan. He said the Constitution applied to "all the peoples and all the territories" of the United States, and he also argued that "the idea that this country may acquire territories anywhere upon the earth, by conquest or treaty, and hold them as mere colonies or provinces— the people inhabiting them to enjoy only such rights as Congress chooses to accord to them—is wholly inconsistent with the spirit and genius as well as with the words of the Constitution" (Rivera Ramos 1996, 251). The debate continues. But this case nevertheless set the precedent for a hundred years of U.S. legislation in Puerto Rico. For example, in 1991, Attorney General Richard Thornburgh unquestionably claimed plenary power over Puerto Rico; and in a bill presented to the House of Representatives on March 6, 1996, Congress stressed its express authority "to provide for the political status of the inhabitants of the territory." As in 1901, Puerto Rico belonged to the United States.

SUGGESTED READING

Documents on the Constitutional History of Puerto Rico, edited by the Office of the Commonwealth of Puerto Rico, 2d ed. (Washington, D.C.: Commonwealth of Puerto Rico, 1964); Robert J. Hunter, "A Historical Survey of the Puerto Rican Status Question," in *Status of Puerto Rico: Selected Background Studies* (Washington, D.C.: U.S. Government Printing Office, 1965); Efrén Rivera Ramos, "The Legal Construction of American Colonialism: The Insular Cases (1901–1922)," *Revista Jurídica Universidad de Puerto Rico 65*, no. 2 (1996): 225–328.

Interamerican University   The largest private university in Puerto Rico, with its School of Law and School of Optometry, Interamerican comprises eleven campuses throughout the island. It provides education to more than 43,000 students, about 25 percent of all Puerto Ricans in higher education and 40 percent of those who attend private schools.

The picturesque 200-acre campus at San Germán was the site of the school's founding. Created by the Reverend J. Will Harris in 1912, Interamerican was an elementary and secondary school that stressed religious values along with educational accomplishments. In 1921 the school offered its first courses at the university level, and its first graduates received degrees in 1927. Today, Interamerican is a comprehensive university which has never lost its religious roots. School bulletins define Interamerican as a nonprofit, private institution "of a Christian and ecumenical nature." The administrators and faculty take this creed to heart. Mainland U.S. students who attend Interamerican in exchange programs are often pleasantly surprised by the amount of kind attention they receive at Interamerican.

The San Germán campus is also home to the Caribbean Studies Association; this scholarly organization is devoted to study of the Caribbean and its peoples. It was the faculty at Interamerican who, more than anyone else, helped preserve the direction and ambitions of the Caribbean Studies Association. Interamerican also has a deservedly well-known program in "Spanish immersion." Many U.S. students have taken advantage of the Spanish language opportunities offered by the university.

SUGGESTED READING

Catálogo de la Universidad Interamericana de Puerto Rico, 1995.

J

Jíbaro This term is used to refer to the indigenous people who inhabited the Puerto Rican countryside during the first part of the twentieth century. These people lived in the mountains or rural areas of the island and worked the land. *Jíbaros* farmed the soil, raised livestock, cut sugar cane and collected coffee beans. The label is more cultural and socioeconomic than ethnic and does not refer to color or race. Rather, it is a cultural composite of personality and behavioral traits that alludes to a particular group of Puerto Ricans. The *jíbaro* is poor but hopeful, kind but witty, humble but proud, hopeful but fatalistic, ignorant of the modern world that surrounds him but daring. *Jíbaros* are at the very center of the popular culture and folklore of the island. Literature and music have immortalized the stereotypical *jíbaro* through their characterizations and depictions. *Jíbaros* and *jíbaras* are generally depicted as wearing wide-brimmed palm hats and impeccably starched white clothes or flowered dresses while toiling in the hot sun with sharp farming utensils and machetes. *Jíbaros* have been characterized as individuals who are kind, giving, loving and hard working who have a great capacity for love and sacrifice. They have a great sense of stoicism and an innate fatalism. Life for them was tough and difficult, but they faced adverse situations and their destiny with insurmountable strength and grace. *Jíbaros* made their way through life with the motto: *"Ay bendito,"* which reflects great compassion and care. In reality, the *jíbaro* has been eliminated by the economic and political modernism that transformed the island of Puerto Rico from an agrarian society to an industrial one. What is left is the memory of those who gave their lives to build the land only to see it disappear through radical change. **Rafael Her-**

nández, the premier national musical composer, immortalized the *jíbaro* in the lyrics of his song, "Lamento Borincano."

SUGGESTED READING

Juan Flores, *Divided Borders: Essays on Puerto Rican Identity* (Houston, Tex.: Arte Público Press, 1993); Juan Ernesto Fonfrias, *El jíbaro en su origen y manifestación humana y costrumbrista* (Río Piedras: Editorial UPR, 1987); Enrique Laguerre, *El jíbaro de Puerto Rico: Símbolo y figura* (San Juan, P.R.: Caribe Grolier, 1968); Sidney Mintz, "Puerto Rico: An Essay in the Definition of a National Culture" in *Selected Background Studies, U.S. Puerto Rican Commission on the Status of Puerto Rico* (Washington, D.C.: U.S. Government Printing Office, 1966); Eduardo Seda, *Social Change and Personality in a Puerto Rican Agrarian Reform Community* (Evanston, Ill.: Northwestern University Press, 1973; reprint, New York : Praeger, 1979).

Jones Act   This 1917 bill gave Puerto Ricans U.S. citizenship. It also made changes that affected the island's legislature, the role of the U.S. president and the control of local officials over expenditures on the island. Sometimes called the Organic Act, this bill was formally signed into law by President Woodrow Wilson on March 2, 1917. It generated so much controversy in Puerto Rico that, six months after its passage, the leader of the **Union party, José de Diego,** called for a **plebiscite** in 1920. His goal was to "determine authentically the aspirations of the people of Puerto Rico." De Diego acted because he understood the mood and intent of the U.S. Congress. The act was passed because of motives that had nothing to do with the will of the Puerto Rican people (e.g., to silence permanently requests for independence). As Congressman Clarence Miller explained to **Luis Muñoz Rivera** when they debated the bill in 1916, "We are going to give them citizenship. Ten years from now they are going to rise up and bless us for doing so. But we are not going to give everyone the right to vote; and they are going to rise up and bless us for doing that too" (Fernandez 1996, 69).

Few Puerto Ricans blessed this bill because, along with imposed U.S. citizenship, the bill concentrated more political and economic power in the hands of U.S. officials. Under the Jones Act, the president of the United States now had the right to veto legislation passed by the Puerto Rican legislature over the veto of the appointed (by the president) governor. The governor himself now had a line item veto over any appropriations coming from the Puerto Rican legislature and could object to any item, or portion thereof. Adding insult to injury, the Jones Act retained the hated provision of the **Olmstead Act.**

The bill did substitute an elected senate for the **Executive Council,** but this grant of greater democracy came with another provision that severely limited local powers. The Jones Act created a new, sometimes forgotten, position—the auditor, who would be the "watchdog of the Treasury." This appointed (by Washington) official had the right and obligation to examine all accounts of the Puerto Rican government. His jurisdiction "shall be exclusive" and his decisions "final."

The final limitation on Puerto Rico's sovereignty (thus de Diego's call for a plebiscite) was the new powers granted to the commissioner of education. After 1917 this U.S. official prepared "all courses of study," and only he had the statutory authority to prepare rules that governed not only the selection of teachers but also the appointment of those teachers by local school boards.

The first lines of the Jones Act are also the first lines of the federal law that today governs the commonwealth government: "the provisions of this Act shall apply to the island of Puerto Rico and to the adjacent islands *belonging* to the United States" (emphasis added). Puerto Rico is a possession of the United States. The Jones Act deliberately reaffirmed that status and, from that perspective, it was, and remains, a historically significant piece of U.S. legislation.

SUGGESTED READING

Delma S. Arrigoitia, "José De Diego: A Legislator in Times of Political Transition (1903–1918)," Ph.D. diss., Fordham University, 1985; Truman Clark, "Educating the Natives in Self Government," *Pacific Historical Review* 42 (May 1973): 220–33; Ronald Fernandez, *The Disenchanted Island: Puerto Rico and the United States in the Twentieth Century*, 2d ed. (Westport, Conn.: Praeger, 1996); Charles Goodsell, *Administration of a Revolution: Executive Reform in Puerto Rico under Governor Tugwell* (Cambridge, Mass.: Harvard University Press, 1965); L. S. Rowe, *The United States and Porto Rico with Special Reference to the Problems Arising out of Our Contact with the Spanish American Civilization* (New York: Longmans Green, 1904); William Willoughby, *Territories and Dependencies of the United States: Their Government and Administration* (New York: Century Company, 1905).

Juliá, Raúl (1940–1994)   This versatile Puerto Rican actor achieved great success and recognition in theater and film. Juliá, a native of Santurce, received a classical liberal arts education early in his life. He attended the Colegio San Ignacio, a Jesuit preparatory school where he was educated with the elite of San Juan aristocracy. From there, he moved to Fordham University and eventually finished his undergraduate degree at the **University of Puerto Rico** in Río Piedras. Although he participated in some theater and film productions in San Juan, he never achieved much recognition on the island during his early years as an actor.

Juliá's career blossomed in New York City where he participated in the productions of the New York Shakespeare Festival and where critics think he had the chance to develop many of his formidable acting skills. He became a protégé of John Papp who gave him the chance to play more visible characters. He eventually moved to Hollywood where he became

Raúl Juliá, 1994. (*El Nuevo Día.*)

the most visible Puerto Rican actor in the film industry. He participated in box office hits such as *Romero, The Addams Family* and *Kiss of the Spider Woman*, among others. He also participated in the television series "Mussolini." One of his last roles in a theater production was in a highly successful American tour of *Man of La Mancha* where he played the part of Don Quixote and shared the limelight with Sheena Easton, as Dulcinea. Juliá, a fine classical actor, had a magnificent presence achieved primarily through the use of his voice. One of his great talents was his vast dramatic range. He always kept in contact with his Puerto Rican roots and was a role model for many aspiring Puerto Ricans on the island and in the States as well. He had a cameo role in the highly popular Puerto Rican film *La gran fiesta*. Juliá died in New York City in 1994 after a brief illness. He was buried in Puerto Rico where he was eulogized and received national honors from both the government and the Puerto Rican people.

SUGGESTED READING

Mel Gussow, "Raúl Juliá, Broadway and Hollywood Actor, Is Dead at 54," *New York Times*, October 25, 1994, B10; Frank Pérez and Ann Weil, *Raúl Juliá* (Austin, Tex.: Raintree Stock-Vaughn, 1996); Rebecca Stefoff, *Raúl Juliá* (New York: Chelsea House, 1994).

L

Laguerre, Enrique (1906–) Born in Moca, a small city in the north-western region of Puerto Rico, Laguerre, a writer and novelist, finished elementary school in his hometown and high school in Aguadilla, since there was no high school in Moca at that time. He studied at the **University of Puerto Rico** in Río Piedras where he received both his undergraduate and master's degrees in education. He received a doctorate from Columbia University in 1951. According to writer Rosario Ferré (1989), his master's thesis on modern Puerto Rican poetry is still one of the most respected works on the subject.

Laguerre is the best-known Puerto Rican novelist of this century. His speciality is the agrarian novel, or a novel about the land. From his roots in a small town, whose principal economic activity was agriculture, and as a child of coffee growers, Laguerre knew rural life as it was actually lived. As a result, he acquired a wealth of life experiences that informed his literary output for many years.

As a novelist, his early literary efforts focused on the search for Puerto Rican identity. Framed within the agrarian setting, Laguerre's characters were on a quest to find themselves. More important, his novels explored the social and political problems that affected these people and how it contextualized, ritualized and determined their lives. As did many other Latin American writers of that period, including **Manuel Zeno Gandía**, Laguerre tried to explore the links between individuals and their natural environments. One of the most significant dimensions of Laguerre's work is his character development, in particular, the way in which he frames them within their environments. Laguerre's narratives have a broad point of view which allows the reader to gain an understanding of the characters.

He tries to explain their mind-sets and the relationship they have with their land. Through his work, he also tries to assess the impact of the political and economic changes experienced by the Puerto Rican people.

Laguerre's classic novel is *La Llamarada*, which was published in 1937. He has published eleven other novels. Among them are *Solar Montoya* (1941), *El 30 de febrero* (1943), *La resaca* (1949), *Los dedos de la mano* (1951) and *La ceiba en el tiesto* (1956). He has also authored many essays and contributed to newspapers and literary journals. He was a university professor for many years at the University of Puerto Rico.

SUGGESTED READING

Leticia Díaz, *Initiation in the Puerto Rican Novel* (Ann Arbor, Mich.: University Microfilms, 1982); Rosario Ferré, "Enrique Laguerre" in Carlos A. Solé, ed., *Latin American Writers* (New York: Scribners, 1989); Estelle Irizarry, "El concepto de la geopiedad en la novelística de Enrique Laguerre," *La Torre* 8, no. 30 (1982); Enrique Laguerre, *Obras completas* (San Juan: Instituto de Cultura Puertorriqueña, 1964).

Lair, Clara   *See* **Negrón Muñoz, Mercedes.**

Lallande, Anita (1949–   )   Anita Lallande was described by the print and news media in 1966 as the major figure of the Tenth Central American and Caribbean Games, a major two-week sports competition of Latin American countries held every four years. It was an unforgettable moment for Lallande and for the sport of swimming in Puerto Rico. At the end of the games, Anita Lallande had won eight gold and two bronze medals in individual swimming events, as well as two gold medals in swimming relays, for a total of twelve medals. She won a medal for every race in which she participated and set a number of new records. With her performance, the Puerto Rican women's swimming team won first place in the games.

At the age of seventeen, Anita had accomplished a feat that no other athlete has been able to match. Her calm demeanor and self-assurance were the topic of the day. Even Cuba's Fidel Castro, whose team had been assured of "sweeping" victories in the sport, publicly complimented her extraordinary performance.

Her extraordinary physical ability, coupled with the remarkable discipline of practicing every day for three hours before school and as many or more after class, contributed to her success. It also made her a role model for young people, particularly those who began to take up the sport of swimming with dreams of succeeding like Anita.

As a person, Anita Lallande has been described as embodying the characteristics that are the most valued in Puerto Rican society—intelligence and talent combined with straightforwardness and humility. Throughout the course of the events—setting new world records, getting standing ovations and receiving her medals—Lallande smiled candidly and thanked the people. The Tenth Central American and Caribbean Games came to be known as "the games of Anita Lallande."

SUGGESTED READING

Emilio Huyke, *La historia de deportes de Puerto Rico* (San Juan, P.R.: Caribe Grolier, 1989).

Language Language is the principal symbol of the Puerto Rican nationality. Long before the Spaniards arrived on the shores of Puerto Rico, there was language—the language of the natives, the Arawaks and the Taínos (see **Los Taínos**). Indeed, even though the Taínos could not resist the disease and exploitation that wiped out their existence, their language and culture were more resilient. This fact is evidenced by the hundreds of indigenous words included in Puerto Rican Spanish and their use in everyday life. The Arawak Indians named Puerto Rico Borinquen (see Borinquen), a term that is still used today. Many municipalities on the island go by their pre-Columbian names; for example, Arecibo, Jayuya, Ceiba, Caguas, Mayagüez, Yauco, Coamo and Yabucoa. The indigenous population slept in *hamacas*, or hammocks, which are still woven and widely used in Puerto Rico. The god the Arawaks feared the most, Juracán (see **Huracán**), represents a force still feared: the hurricane. Taíno words still are found in the names of rivers (Camuy), mountains (El Yunque), foods (*yuca, cazabe*), animals (*iguana, hicotea*), trees (*caoba, yagrumo*) and many other things. These so-called *tainísmos* are part of everyday language, and even though some are used throughout the Caribbean, some are used exclusively in Puerto Rico (e.g., *boricua, tabonuco, cocolía* and *quenepa*).

After the Spaniards had settled on the island, Spanish became the official language of the new colony. Shortly thereafter, the colonists began importing slaves into Puerto Rico. The lexicon of the Spanish of Puerto Rico reflects the coexistence of these cultures. The African influence (see **African Roots**) is evident in the island's vernacular—a party is referred to as a *bembé*, lips are *bembas*, the juice of crushed sugarcane goes by the name of *guarapo*; too much *guarapo* with rum will make your body go *mongo*, or limp. By the middle of the nineteenth century, Africans made up a fifth of the population, and their language, as well as their culture, had begun to influence the island's culture. **Luis Palés Matos**, one of Puerto Rico's poets and its greatest exponent of Afro-Antillian poetry, is renowned for his combination of Spanish and African language words and elements. This gives the language in some of his poems the musical tonality of rhythmic African drumming. His "Majestad negra," or "Black Majesty," is an excellent example of this.

Another group that had a great influence on the island's language was the **jíbaro** population—the farmers who were black, white and mestizo.

From this group we get the creole, or *criollo* elements of the language. **Rubén del Rosario,** one of the leading scholars of Puerto Rican Spanish, has referred to the creole nomenclature as perhaps the most important aspect of the island's vernacular because these words have come to life in an effort to express the Puerto Rican soul or feeling. Most of this vocabulary originated in the heart of the people, particularly the poorer agricultural population. One characteristic of their speech was changing e for i and o for u as in *estrumento* instead of *instrumento* or *sospiro* for *suspiro*. Changes and substitutions in consonants were also characteristic of *jíbaro* Spanish, which can still be heard today, as in the case of changing r for l, as in *puelta* for *puerta*. The characteristics of *jíbaro* speech are too long to list, however, they can be found in the literary works of many Puerto Rican writers. The first example of the creole aspect of the island's language occurred in 1849 when Manuel A. Alonso published *El Gíbaro*, a series of scenes of contemporary country life of the *jíbaros* of that time. In much of the prose, he uses the *jíbaro* language, imitating the characteristic way of speaking of the country people. The scenes in the book include descriptions of the differences between society balls and the *garabato* dances of the *jíbaros* as well as of cock fights and all of the aspects of that sport. It is a literary work that has been described as a painting portrayal of the island's *jíbaro*, language and all. Juan Ramón Jiménez has also written numerous short stories portraying the *jíbaro* life and language.

In 1898 the arrival of the United States as the new colonists on the island signaled the advent of yet another political, cultural and linguistic influence. One of the first acts of the **Executive Council** in 1902 was to pass the Official Languages Act, mandating the use of English "indiscriminately" in all official public activities. Spanish was relegated to a position of simply another subject in the school curriculum. From its inception as a colonial power, the American government's priority was the Americanization of the islanders. The concept of education, as it existed in the States, was imposed on the island, including the compulsory use of English as the language of instruction by teachers who had little, if any, training in or knowledge of English. The new curricula placed a great deal of emphasis on American patriotic exercises, such as pledging allegiance to the flag and singing the American national anthem. It imposed the American school-day schedule of 8:00 A.M. to 4:00 P.M. without differentiating between the needs of rural and urban schoolchildren. Finally, it was overseen by commissioners who spoke no Spanish and received their orders from Washington, D.C. By the mid-1930s, the dropout rate in the rural areas, where there were three times as many children as in the urban areas, was over 72 percent. By then, children were averaging no more than four years of schooling—an important factor to consider in terms of acquiring reading and writing skills in any language.

For fifty years, the controversy over the language issue dominated politics and education on the island. Puerto Ricans spoke out vehemently against this language policy; primary school students staged strikes and refused to attend classes unless they were instructed in Spanish, teachers became unionized and passed numerous resolutions against the imposition of English and politicians introduced numerous bills in the island's legislature protesting this policy only to have them vetoed by the U.S.–appointed governor. In 1949, when **Luis Muñoz Marín** became the first governor elected by the people of Puerto Rico, Spanish was once again declared the language of instruction in the public school system. English as a second language continues to be a required subject throughout the system's primary and secondary schools, as well as in institutions of higher education.

The influence of English has had linguistic and political repercussions on the island. From a linguistic viewpoint, the major concern has been the increasing use of Spanglish, the simultaneous code switching between English and Spanish. It is a phenomenon most clearly reflected in children and adults who have lived in the continental United States as well as on the island. Spanglish has also been associated with bilingualism and identified as an intergral aspect of bilingual discourse. From a social perspective, it is frowned upon by some Puerto Ricans on the island, some North Americans and some educators as a sign of linguistic deficiency, which, in many cases, translates to a cultural deficiency as well. On the island, where it is viewed as detrimental to the vernacular, it is discouraged, particularly in educated and political circles. In the political arena, the discourse is in the vernacular, and a lack of skills in Spanish may very well label the speaker as the supporter of a particular political philosophy.

Throughout most of this century and even today, the debate on language on the island has been an integral part of the political discourse. In some cases, political affiliations are characterized in terms of one's support for the teaching and use of English or Spanish. In 1991 the legislature on the island passed a law that designated Spanish as the official language of Puerto Rico, overturning the 1902 statute that allowed either Spanish or English to be used in government transactions. The debate between the political factions on this issue restated the arguments in much the same fashion as has been done throughout the century. The pro-statehood political faction saw this as an attempt by the Popular party to diminish its ties to the United States, while the pro-commonwealth side, and the authors of the bill, described it as a manifestation of Puerto Ricans' national pride of their language and culture. The second position was also shared by those who supported independence for the island. In 1992, however, the statehood party won the gubernatorial elections and also won majorities in both legislative houses. The first bill presented to the new legislature and passed in 1993 was one repealing the 1991 language law and reinstating the 1902 law that allowed the arbitrary use of either language in government dealings, thus maintaining the language issue in the political arena.

Even though Puerto Rico's final political status may not be resolved for years to come, the question of language seems to be unofficially settled. The vast majority of Puerto Ricans continue to use Spanish as their principal language of communication, both socially and officially. The 1990 census reports that 52 percent of the islanders characterize themselves as speaking only Spanish with no knowledge of English; another 24 percent said that speaking English was very difficult for them. A 1993 newspaper survey carried out by *El Nuevo Día* reported that 95 percent of those polled stated that they preferred Spanish. There seems to be no doubt about Puerto Rico's commitment to Spanish as the vernacular and as the language of instruction in the public school system, with English as an important second language. In the political arena, however, language will continue to be used as a symbolic manifestation of partisanship.

SUGGESTED READING

Amilcar Antonio Barreto, "Nationalism, Linguistic Security, and Language Legislation in Quebec and Puerto Rico" (Ph.D. diss., State University of New York at Buffalo, 1995); Rubén Del Rosario, *La lengua de Puerto Rico*, 10th ed. (Río Piedras, P.R.: Editorial Cultural, 1975); Nilka Estrada Resto, "Abrumadora preferencia por el español en una consulta," *El Nuevo Día*, January 9, 1993, 16; Luis Palés Matos, *Poesía (1915–1956)* (Rio Piedras, P.R.: Editorial Universitaria, 1974); Edwin Melendez and Edgardo Melendez, *Colonial Dilemma: Critical Perspectives on Contermporary Puerto Rico* (Boston: South End, 1993); Nancy Morris, *Puerto Rico: Culture, Politics and Identity* (Westport, Conn.: Praeger, 1995); Catherine Walsh, *Pedagogy and the Struggle for Voice: Issues of Language, Power and Schooling for Puerto Ricans* (New York: Bergin and Garvey, 1991).

Lashings, The (Los Compontes)   The phrase, *los compontes*, refers to six months of political terror experienced by the Puerto Rican people in 1887. Spain had just sent a new governor, Romualdo Palacio González, to take charge of an island deeply divided by political and cultural ideals. One of the most vocal groups was the Unconditionals, a political party committed to Spain at any cost and totally opposed to the changes sought by those seeking autonomy—not independence—from the mother country. When Palacio arrived, the Unconditionals told him that advocates of autonomy really wanted a complete separation from Spain; indeed, if Palacio needed evidence, said the Unconditionals, he needed only look at the effect of the boycotts so successfully orchestrated by the autonomists. Throughout the island, citizens were in fact boycotting Spanish businesses that, for example, refused to hire *criollos* (native Puerto Ricans) or to support efforts to find better markets for local produce.

In August 1887, Palacio took action. He used soldiers to round up supporters of autonomy, and, after the autonomists had been transported to forts like **El Morro**, Palacio extracted confessions by using the most barbaric means. For example, toothpick-sized sticks were inserted between the fingers and then tightened by the turn of a rope; whips left scars on the backs of others. After six months of protest to the Spanish authorities, Puerto Ricans finally managed to have Palacio removed. He sailed from the island in November 1887, leaving visible scars, not only on the bodies of those who were tortured, but on the political landscape of Puerto Rico. The autonomists were so badly divided that it took almost a decade to recover the solidarity required to achieve the **Autonomic Constitution** of 1897.

SUGGESTED READING

Loida Figueroa, *History of Puerto Rico: From the Beginning to 1892* (New York: Anaya, 1974); Adalberto López, ed., *Puerto Ricans: Their History, Culture and Society* (Cambridge: Schenkman, 1980); Germán Delgado Pasapera, *Puerto Rico: Sus luchas emancipadors* (San Juan, P.R.: Editorial Cultural, 1984).

Law   The 1952 Commonwealth Constitution established an independent judiciary branch within the government. The constitution also established the Supreme Court as the highest court of the land. The Supreme Court has seven justices, appointed by the governor with the advice and consent of the legislature that confirms them. The judges are appointed for life. The constitution gives the legislature, following advice from the Supreme Court, the power to establish the multilevel configuration of the court system. The courts are organized around a municipal court, a district court, a superior court, an appeals court and, ultimately, the Supreme Court.

Puerto Rico's legal system has been directly influenced by the colonial status of the island. Puerto Rico was a Spanish colony for four centuries. It has been an American one for almost a hundred years. The Spanish legal system was, and still is, based on a civil code largely derived from the Roman civil code. Such codes, established by legislative enactment, are a series of statutes or dispositions that rule civil behavior in a society. As a Spanish colony, Puerto Rico developed a civil legal code that is basically identical to the one in Spain. With the transfer of sovereignty of the island from Spain to America, Puerto Rico found itself linked to a nation whose legal system is radically different from the Spanish system or the Puerto Rican one. The United States' legal system operates under the principle of common law. Under the common law system, the courts generate rulings based on previous court decisions, societal doctrine and common usage. As a former Spanish colony, and now an American one, the island of Puerto Rico has developed a hybrid legal system that is a blend of civil (or statute) law and common law. Despite the fact that Puerto Rico has both civil and penal codes, the judicial system established by the 1952 constitution (and subsequently modified) is also reliant upon, and somewhat subjugated to, the common law system used by American courts. Family law, contracts and inheritance laws are regulated by civil law. Corporations, criminal matters and criminal procedure are based on American law. It is important to underscore here that, as an American territory, Puerto Rico is also part of the American federal legal system. Issues that fall directly under the jurisdiction of the U.S. Constitution or that involve corporations or citizens of the continental United States are under the jurisdiction of the district Federal Court in San Juan, the First Circuit Court of Appeals in Boston and the United States Supreme Court.

The coexistence of the civil and common law systems has created problems for Puerto Rican courts. In 1979 Puerto Rico's Supreme Court, in the case known as *Justo Valle vs. American International Insurance*, elucidated the conflict between the two systems and established the parameters for the use of both systems within Puerto Rican courts. The plaintiff, Justo Valle, after being involved in a chain-reaction collision, sued American International Insurance. While five cars were waiting at an intersection, a sixth car approached and hit the car at the end of the line. This produced a chain reaction and Valle's car, second in line, was rear-ended by another car. The case was brought to the Supreme Court by American International Insurance, the carrier of Díaz's policy, who asked the court to reverse a decision from Bayamón's district court, which forced the company to pay for Valle's damages.

Supreme Court Justice José Trias Monge wrote the majority opinion, which nullified and revoked the decision of the lower court. He asserted that there was a complete lack of legislation in Puerto Rico covering these dimensions of tort (or damages) law. The court established that Puerto Rican tort law is based on the fundamentals of civil law, not on British or American common law. The judges discussed all the areas in the Spanish and Italian civil law that pointed toward Díaz's lack of responsibility for the accident. In this landmark decision, Justice Trias Monge established that American common law should not be used to decide those problems pertaining to civil law that can be illuminated by civil law decisions in other places. This case established the actual guidelines used in Puerto Rico to differentiate between the two systems and their appropriate usage.

SUGGESTED READING

General Accounting Office, *Puerto Rico: Information for Status Deliberations* (Washington, D.C.: U.S. Government Printing Office, 1990); David M. Hefeld, "How Much of the United States Constitution and Statues Are Applicable to the Commonwealth of Puerto Rico," U.S. Congress, House, Committee on Interior and Insular Affairs (Washington, D.C.: U.S. Government Printing Office, 1986); *Justo Valle vs. American International Insurance*, 1979, in 108 DPR 692, pp. 94–699; *Codigo cívil de Puerto Rico* (San Juan, P.R.: Forum, 1993); Arnold Liebowitz, *Defining Status: A Comprehensive Analysis of U.S. Territorial Relations* (Dordrecht, Netherlands: Nijhoff Publishers, 1989); Leo S. Rowe, *The United States and Porto Rico* (New York: Longmans and Green, 1904); José Trias Monge, *El choque de dos culturas jurídicas en P.R.: El caso de la responsabilidad civil contractual* (Oxford, N.H.: Equity Publishers, 1991).

Lebrón, Lolita (1919–)   Lolita Lebrón is a Puerto Rican revolutionary. In her twenties and thirties she was a member of the **Nationalist party** and she organized and led the Nationalist assault on the House of Representatives on March 1, 1954 (see **Nationalist Attack on Congress**). Dolores Lebrón Soto was born in Lares. Later, one of her biographers noted that her birth date, November 19, was also the day on which Spanish explorers first discovered Puerto Rico. She completed her high school education in Puerto Rico, with many of her classes in English, and she matured at the height of the Great Depression in a poor family. She began to work in the sewing industry but, due to a variety of family issues, moved to New York City in 1940.

Puerto Ricans formed a distinct numerical minority in 1940—only 25,000 Puerto Ricans then lived in the United States. For a sensitive young woman, the sense of culture shock was overwhelming. The Puerto Rico she left not only was in the midst of the depression but was still very much an agricultural nation. The difference between living in mountainous Lares and living in the slums of Brooklyn was startling. While working in the New York garment industry, Lebrón came to empathize with her coworkers, especially with the Puerto Rican youngsters whose lives were even then being lost to the streets. At this time, **Pedro Albizu Campos** had been released from prison and officials demanded that he serve out his exile in New York. For Lebrón, Albizu was a charismatic figure, a Puerto Rican who blamed both the emigration to New York and the poverty at home on the same root cause—U.S. colonialism. Lebrón soon became a Nationalist, a dedicated follower of Albizu and a committed Catholic. Roman Catholicism was an integral part of the Nationalist movement, and the religious fervor that has characterized Lebrón's adulthood is intimately linked to her political beliefs. As with Albizu, it is impossible to separate one from the other.

When Albizu returned to Puerto Rico in 1947, Lebrón remained in New York. She had become such a trusted associate of Albizu that she was assigned the task of doing something spectacular to call attention to the farce (from the Nationalist perspective) of the United Nation's removal, in November 1953, of Puerto Rico from the list of non–self-governing territories.

She therefore commanded a violent attack on the U.S. House of Representatives on March 1, 1954. But, instead of firing her gun at the legislators, she fired at the ceiling. She also unfurled the **flag of Puerto Rico** and shouted, "Free Puerto Rico now." Along with her three Nationalist col-

Lolita Lebrón. (*El Nuevo Día*.)

leagues, she was immediately arrested, prosecuted, found guilty and sent to prison. She spent twenty-five years in prison, longer than any other female political prisoner in the Western Hemisphere. When she was released in 1979, the Carter administration cited humanitarian concerns. In fact, she and the others were released primarily because of bad political press received throughout Latin America. Unheralded at the time was a simultaneous release of political prisoners held in Cuban jails. The one release was made in exchange for the other because, in private, both the United States and Cuba agreed that these individuals were political prisoners, not criminals.

Since her release from prison Lebrón has lived a quiet life in Puerto Rico. She occasionally makes appearances in support of Nationalist political efforts but now devotes her time primarily to her family.

<small>SUGGESTED READING</small>

Ronald Fernandez, *Prisoners of Colonialism* (Monroe, Me.: Common Courage Press, 1994); William Hackett, *The Nationalist Party* (Washington, D.C.: U.S. Government Printing Office, 1950); Federico Ribes Tovar, *Lolita Lebrón: La prisonera* (New York: Plus Ultra, 1974).

Libreta de Jornalero   This passbook had to be carried by Puerto Rican *jornaleros* (day laborers) in the nineteenth century; *la libreta* was essentially a way for landowners to maintain a close record of the workers' debts and employment records while extracting labor from the working class. In the early and mid-eighteenth century, landowners in Puerto Rico desperately sought to increase the labor force. Morally, they had no compunctions about using slaves, but this alternative was rejected because slaves were expensive; they had to be fed throughout the year, and they could unite to produce a revolution like the one that occurred in Haiti. The Spanish government also attempted to increase immigration, experimenting, for example, with schemes to bring in labor from China. When nothing resulted in the desired number of workers, on June 11, 1848, the island government issued the Bando de Jornaleros, literally the day laborers' decree. The intent of this decree was to force people without property to work wherever they were needed and to eliminate a class of people called *agregados* (squatters). Throughout the island, families squatted on unoccupied land, often growing sufficient amounts of food to meet their basic needs. Squatters resisted attempts to move them and/or eliminate the "rights" that tradition gave to those who had long occupied particular parcels of land.

The new law stipulated that, unless they were paying rent or were personal servants, *agregados* must move to the nearest town. There, all men between the ages of sixteen and sixty, who did not own a substantial amount of land, were given a *libreta* (a passbook). This book, which had to be carried at all times, contained the worker's name, the date he had begun work, comments on his behavior and the debts he had contracted with his employer. In addition, the *libreta* contained the worker's obligations and the pay he could expect, as well as the obligations of the employer. Finally, the *libreta* specified that no worker could leave an employer until he had paid off all his incurred debts. This opened the system to widespread abuse. Because many of the workers were illiterate, unscrupulous landowners could falsify debt records or charge enormous amounts for food and other necessities purchased at the company store. The result was a system that resembled slavery but, from the owners' point of view, eliminated the need to buy slaves or maintain them.

The *libreta* system was officially ended in June 1873. It disappeared, not because of its injustices, but because of its failure to provide sufficient labor. Many squatters found ways to classify themselves as renters or personal servants, and, with the availability of so much land, especially in the interior of the island, it was possible to avoid the Spanish officials who tried to enforce this hated decree.

SUGGESTED READING

Laird Bergad, *Coffee and the Growth of Agrarian Capitalism in Nineteenth Century Puerto Rico* (Princeton, N.J.: Princeton University Press, 1983); Juan M. García-Passalacqua, *Puerto Rico: Equality and Freedom at Issue* (New York: Praeger Special Studies, 1984).

Lloréns Torres, Luis (1878–1944)   Lloréns Torres is one of the most important poets of Puerto Rico. He was born in Collores, a picturesque sector of the town of Juana Díaz in the southeastern region of the island. He studied law and literature in Spain.

Scholar María Teresa Babín labels his poetry as one "crafted with absolute and total sincerity" (1958, 384). She compares him to noted Nicaraguan writer Rúben Dario. As a romantic poet, he wrote allegorical poetry about the *jíbaro,* the beauty of the land, the women and the customs and traditions of the Puerto Rican people. One of his most famous poems is "Valle de Collores," in which he describes the heart-wrenching experience of leaving his native countryside and his family to live in the city. Lloréns's poetry is still very popular because it represents the quintessential expression of the love that Puerto Ricans have for their island.

Lloréns's artistic production was vast. He wrote his first book of poetry *Al pie de la Alhambra* (1899) while he was a student in Spain. He also wrote *Sonetos sinfónicos* (1914), *Canción de las antillas* (1929), *Voces de la campana mayor* (1935) and *Alturas de América* (1940). Lloréns was also a dramatist and wrote the play "El grito de Lares" (1916), based on the Lares insurrection of 1868. He was a very active contributor to many literary journals of his time and his journalistic writings have been collected in the book *Artículos de revistas y periódicos* (1971).

Lloréns was an ardent supporter of the independence movement on the island and was involved in politics all of his life. One of the biggest community housing projects in Puerto Rico, located in the outskirts of Santurce, toward Isla Verde, is named after him. Unfortunately, it has been beset by so much crime, drugs and violence that it has symbolically tarnished the name and image of someone who so loved the beauty and the people of the island.

SUGGESTED READING

María Teresa Babín, *Panorama de la cultura puertorriqueña* (San Juan: Instituto de Cultura Puertorriqueña, 1958); Luis Lloréns Torres, *Obras completas* (San Juan, P.R.: Instituto de Cultura Puertorriqueña, 1967); Luis Lloréns Tores, *Artículos de revistas y periódicos* (San Juan: Editorial Cordillera, 1971); Theresa Ortiz, *Luis Lloréns Torres: A Study of His Poetry* (New York: Plus Ultra, 1977).

Lodge, Henry Cabot, Jr. (1902–1985)   Henry Cabot Lodge was the U.S. ambassador to the **United Nations** when Puerto Rico was removed from the list of non–self-governing territories in November 1953. He is included in this volume because he initiated one of the most controversial incidents in the hundred years of U.S. control over Puerto Rico. During the UN debates, Lodge received a good deal of criticism about U.S. colonialism in Puerto Rico. To counter this embarrassing criticism, Lodge received permission to broadcast a suggestion made by President Dwight Eisenhower at a breakfast meeting on November 20, 1953: Offer the Puerto Ricans independence. This was not something the president could actually do; only Congress had that power. But the president's breakfast suggestion had such a positive effect in the United Nations that Lodge had an assistant prepare a "top secret" message for President Eisenhower. The ambassador wanted to have Governor **Luis Muñoz Marín** sell the idea of independence to his party so that the United States could reduce criticism against it in the United Nations.

The stumbling block for Governor Muñoz was the previous eight years of Puerto Rican political history. As a direct result of U.S. refusal to consider either independence or statehood, Governor Muñoz had convinced the Puerto Rican people to endorse overwhelmingly a **commonwealth** as the island's only viable political and economic alternative. Lodge understood Muñoz's predicament, but he nevertheless pressed the governor to advocate independence. While there is no record of a response from Muñoz in the Eisenhower Library, the president handwrote this message on the letter he received from Ambassador Lodge: "Send to the secret files. DDE" (Fernandez 1996, 189).

President Eisenhower understood how contradictory the United States' positions would appear if Lodge's offer of independence ever became public. However, Ambassador Lodge made the same suggestion again in 1956.

He sought to court goodwill among the African nations who were criticizing the United States; he had an assistant prepare an independence resolution that would be *first* passed by the U.S. Congress. Speaker of the House of Representatives Joseph Martin said, "Congress would gladly shed Puerto Rico at any time and to give him a resolution and he would talk it over with some of the boys" (Eisenhower Library 1956, 1). As in 1954, there is no record in the Eisenhower Library of a response from Governor Muñoz Marín. However, Lodge said this to President Eisenhower:

If the offer [i.e., of independence] was accepted many problems would be solved. If the offer was rejected, our Congress would at the very least have taken a step that would be interpreted as anticolonial and do us a great deal of good throughout the world—notably in Afro-Asian countries . . . it is an idea that has real merit and I do not see what we could possibly lose by it. (1)

At the same time that Lodge was offering independence to Puerto Rico, FBI Director J. Edgar Hoover was doing everything in his power to suppress the Puerto Rican independence movement.

SUGGESTED READING

Eisenhower Library, Office Files 147-F, letter dated March 27, 1956; Ronald Fernandez, *The Disenchanted Island: Puerto Rico and the United States in the Twentieth Century*, 2d ed. (Westport, Conn.: Praeger, 1996); Millard Hensen and Henry Wells, eds., *Annals of the American Academy of Political and Social Sciences*, vol. 285 (New York: American Academy of Political and Social Science, 1953); Luis Muñoz Marín, "Puerto Rico and the United States: Their Future Together," *Foreign Affairs* 32 (1954): 341–51.

Loiza Aldea   This small section in the town of Loiza is filled with colorful examples of Puerto Rican folklore and culture. Loiza Aldea is a small settlement at the mouth of the Loiza River where it enters the Atlantic Ocean. The people of Loiza Aldea deserve most of the credit for preserving the strong links between their **African roots** and the Puerto Rican culture. In particular, they have kept alive many of the religious practices and musical traditions that they inherited from their African ancestors. Loiza is well known for the practice of **Santería**—a cult or religion in which people honor or venerate African gods such as Changó and Yemaya. *Santeros*, or people who practice this craft, engage in religious exercises in which they wear impeccable white starched outfits with colorful collars, dance to the beat of African rhythms and offer food and animals to the gods. People from throughout the whole island, who are in need of spiritual healing or spell casting, still travel to Loiza Aldea to obtain the assistance or services of Santería practitioners who supposedly master a variety of sortileges and witchcraft. Another tradition of Loiza Aldea is Los Bailes de Vegigantes, in which people wear colorful and fancy wooden or papier-mâché masks that are supposed to resemble half human/half monster horned creatures that, according to the folklore, once populated the area. A special festivity is Las Fiestas of Santiago Apostol, during which the people of Loiza Aldea dance to a well-preserved African beat known as la **Bomba** and dress in the *vegigante* outfits. People dance to the beat of congas and recite special verses that relate the predicaments of these fanciful creatures. Although Loiza Aldea is very small, its cultural richness makes it a treasure for all Puerto Ricans.

SUGGESTED READING

Ricardo E. Alegría, *La Fiesta de Santiago Apostol en Loiza Aldea* (Madrid: ARO, 1954); Carlos Mendez-Santos, *Por tierras de Loiza Aldea* (Ponce, P.R.: Producciones Ceiba, 1973).

López Suria, Violeta (1926–)   Known primarily as a poet, this San Juan native has also published short stories and essays. A prolific writer, López Suria created her first poetic works at the age of six. In 1946, with the support of some of her professors at the **University of Puerto Rico**, she published her poetry for the first time in the *Magazine of the Association of Teachers of Puerto Rico*. That same year, Olga André, on her literary radio program for NBC in Latin America, heralded López Suria as the best young poet of the year.

During the early 1950s, she worked as a secondary schoolteacher teaching language and Spanish literature. She also continued to write and publish poetry. In 1953 she participated in a poetry reading of her work in the **Ateneo Puertorriqueño**, which was described as a success by the press. That year she also published two books: *Gotas de mayo*, a collection of poems and short stories, and later *Elegía*. She continued to publish on a yearly basis. *Sentimiento de un viaje* (Sentiments of a trip), published in 1955, chronicled her travels through Europe.

In 1954 López Suria initiated a new project—a literary magazine focusing on poetry written by Puerto Ricans and other Latin American writers. Through this effort she also began to engage in writing literary criticism, an activity that she later continued for other literary magazines on the island. By 1957 her work began to gain wider recognition as well as a number of prestigious awards. That year her poem "Unas cuantas estrellas en mi cuarto" won the third prize of the Yaucano Cultural Circle and the following year, Diluvio received an honorable mention from the same group. From 1958 through the early 1960s, she regularly published short stories in *El Mundo*'s Saturday issue. As a result of one of her rare ventures into playwriting, her play *Mamita Pepa* was televised in 1959. She continued to publish on a yearly basis, including the award-winning works of poetry *Hubo unos pinos claros* in 1961 and *La piel pegada al alma*, which won an award from the Institute of Puerto Rican Culture in 1962. In 1965 her work *Las nubes dejan sobras* was given the prestigious award El Premio, Club Cívico de Damas.

SUGGESTED READING

María Arrillaga, *Women's Literature: A Feminist Literary Criticism Model Applied to the Work of Three Puerto Rican Authors* (Ann Arbor, Mich.: Dissertation Abstracts International, 1993); José Emilio González, "Nuevas perspectives sobre la poesía de Violeta López Suria," *La Torre* 73–74 (1971): 107–40; Alfredo Matilla and Iván Silén, eds., *The Puerto Rican Poets* (New York: Bantam, 1972); Josefina Rivera de Alvarez, *Diccionario de literatura puertorriqueña* (San Juan, P.R.: Instituto de Cultura Puertorriquena, 1974).

M

Macheteros, Los This Puerto Rican revolutionary group was most active from 1978 to 1985. *Los macheteros*, which can be translated as cane cutters or machete wielders, rooted their political ideology in a compelling, deep sense of history. By using the machete as a symbol, they hoped to identify with the Puerto Rican masses, exploited (in their eyes) under both Spanish and U.S colonialism. In their $7.1 million robbery of a Wells Fargo Bank in West Hartford, Connecticut, in 1983, *Los macheteros* deliberately chose the birthdate (September 12) of **Pedro Albizu Campos** for the "expropriation"; the code name for *machetero* Victor Gerena, who worked for Wells Fargo and actually took the money, was *Aquila Blanca*, the name used by José Maldonado when, according to tradition, he fought against the U.S. forces who invaded Puerto Rico in 1898.

A principal problem for *Los macheteros* is to free the minds of Puerto Ricans who, after 500 years of colonialism, doubt their own ability to challenge and overthrow the colonial system. For this reason, *Los macheteros* have often been flamboyant; after their January 12, 1981, attack on Muñoz Airport destroyed nine planes worth more than $50 million, members of *Los macheteros* went on television. Dressed like soldiers, they tried to convey a message: The **pitirre** can defeat the eagle because even a giant can be felled by the sharp beak of a united Puerto Rican people. One educated guess is that *Los macheteros* numbered 300 full-time members at its peak. They are impossible to classify precisely. Included in their numbers are the very well educated and those with only a rudimentary formal education. There are nationalists and communists, women and men, the young and the old. What unites them is a desire for the revolution first inspired by **Ramón Emeterio Betances** and Albizu Campos.

Because *Los macheteros* have sometimes killed U.S. agents, they are often labeled "terrorists." This politically charged term has a variety of definitions. *Los macheteros* would argue that the **United Nations** has labeled colonialism a crime against humanity. Thus, to *Los macheteros*, violence is both a necessary and legitimate means to end 500 years of colonialism. To date, the Puerto Rican people have never unambiguously expressed their own feelings about *Los macheteros*. Analysts only receive hints; for example, the not-guilty verdict rendered for *machetero* Filiberto Ojeda Rios in his 1989 trial in the federal court in San Juan.

SUGGESTED READING

Ronald Fernandez, *Los Macheteros: The Wells Fargo Robbery and the Violent Struggle for Puerto Rican Independence* (New York: Prentice Hall, 1987). For the FBI's perspective see U.S. Congress, Senate, Committee on the Judiciary, Subcommittee on Security and Terrorism *FBI Oversight and Authorization* 98th Congr., 1st sess. (Washington, D.C.: U.S. Government Printing Office, 1983).

Machismo   The cultural institution of the superiority of males and the subordination of females, although not unique to Puerto Rico, has nevertheless ingrained itself in Puerto Rican society and has come to take on an identity of its own. The word *machismo* comes from the word *macho*, which is the gender reference for male animals. Although *machismo* permeates all aspects of culture, it is evident in everyday life, where stereotyped concepts of males as aggressive and strong and females as passive and dependent are encouraged in the socialization process, particularly in the home and school. Statements of *machismo* that are accepted as truisms and are heard often in Puerto Rico include "Women belong in the home, men belong to the streets" and "The man is the one who wears the pants in the house."

In her book on Puerto Rican women, Edna Acosta-Belén defines the current view of *machismo* in Puerto Rico:

Machismo still represents a male ideal of sorts and plays an essential role in maintaining sexual restrictions and subordination for women. As a typical manifestation of patriarchal relations it emphasizes sexual freedom, virility, and aggressiveness for men in contrast to women's sexual repression, femininity and passivity. (Acosta-Belén 1986, 16)

Over the years, efforts have been made to promote changes in both schools and society as a whole. In 1979 a book published by Isabel Picó on *machismo* in the educational system brought to light the stereotypes in textbooks and tasks that were assigned to schoolchildren as well as the roles of teachers. The media have also played an important role, at times bolstering the stereotypical roles of subservient women and dominant men in soap operas and comedy shows as well as in the print media. However, some organizations, such as the Commission for the Advancement of Women's Rights, and various scholars have studied the issues and have brought them to the public's attention.

Even though the concept of equality between the sexes has begun to make some headway, *machismo* is still very noticeable in all aspects of life. Continued equitable and simultaneous changes in the judicial, economic, educational and cultural institutions in Puerto Rico will perhaps yield in time to equality over *machismo*. There is a consensus by the majority of the Puerto Rican people and institutions that *machismo* should not be seen as an intrinsic authentic value of the island's culture.

SUGGESTED READING

Edna Acosta-Belén, *The Puerto Rican Woman: Perspectives on Culture, History, and Society* (New York: Praeger, 1986); Isabel Picó, *Machismo y educación en Puerto Rico* (San Juan P. R.: Comisión para el Mejoramiento de los Derechos de la Mujer, 1979).

Maldonado-Denis, Manuel (1934–1992)   A professor, a writer and an award-winning analyst of Puerto Rican politics and Puerto Rican culture, Maldonado-Denis was born in Santurce and died in San Juan. He received his B.A. from the **University of Puerto Rico** and his master's and Ph.D. degrees (in political science) from the University of Chicago. With occasional stops at other universities (e.g., Queens College in New York), Maldonado-Denis taught for his entire career at the University of Puerto Rico in Río Piedras. He remains one of its most distinguished professors and writers. In 1972 Maldonado-Denis received an honorary doctorate from the University of the Atlantic of Barranquilla, Colombia. He received the award because of his historical and political analysis and his devotion to the cause of Puerto Rican and Latin American liberation. Maldonado-Denis wrote essays on the lives of **Ramón Emeterio Betances** and **Eugenio María de Hostos** as well as their significance to the Puerto Rican people, in particular, and to Latin Americans, in general. His analysis of Puerto Rican political history—especially his book *Puerto Rico—A Socio-Historic Interpretation* (1973)—reopened the doors to a balanced interpretation of the Puerto Rican independence movement. In addition, Maldonado wrote extensively for newspapers and magazines in Puerto Rico, Latin America and the United States. He popularized, in the best sense of the word, a reinterpretation of Puerto Rican history from the perspective of liberation, colonialism and imperialism.

SUGGESTED READING

Manuel Maldonaldo-Denis, *Eugenio María de Hostos: Sociólogico y maestro* (Río Piedras: Editorial Antillana, 1981); Manuel Maldonado-Denis, *Puerto Rico: Mito y realidad* (Barcelona: Ediciones Peninsula, 1969); Manuel Maldonado-Denis, *Puerto Rico: A Socio-Historic Interpretation* (New York: Vintage 1973); Manuel Maldonado-Denis, *The Emigration Dialetic: Puerto Rico and the U.S.A.* (New York: International Publishers, 1980).

Mari Bras, Juan (1928–   ) Juan Mari Bras was born in Mayagüez, on December 2, 1928. He studied at the **University of Puerto Rico** but, due to his leadership of student strikes over the issue of independence, he was expelled in 1948. He later received his B.A. from the University of Florida and his law degree from Washington Law School in 1954.

He was a founder of the Movimiento pro Indepencencia (MPI), which later became the Puerto Rican Socialist party. He was also active during the 1960s in organizations that tried to eliminate the **blood tax**, and he was instrumental in creating support for Nationalist revolutionaries, for example, **Lolita Lebrón**, who were at that time incarcerated in various federal prisons. Mari Bras was a special target of the FBI when its counter-intelligence program tried to undermine independence activists working in Puerto Rico (see **Las Carpetas**).

Mari Bras has also been very active at the United Nations. He has repeatedly testified before the Committee on Decolonization and, despite some health problems, he continues to struggle for Puerto Rican independence. In 1995 he traveled to Venezuela, renounced his U.S. citizenship and asked to be regarded as a Puerto Rican. This action caused a certain amount of public commentary, which, of course, was exactly what Juan Mari Bras wanted.

SUGGESTED READING

Raymond Carr, *Puerto Rico: A Colonial Experiment* (New York: New York University Press, 1984); Lester Langley, *The United States and the Caribbean in the Twentieth Century* (Atlanta: University of Georgia Press, 1985); Juan Mari Bras, *El independentismo en Puerto Rico* (Santo Domingo, Dominican Republic: Editorial Cepa, 1984); Carmen Gautier Mayoral and María Del Pilar Arguelles, *Puerto Rico and la ONU* (San Juan, P.R.: Editorial Edil, 1978).

Marqués, René (1919–1979) René Marqués was a prolific writer of short stories, essays, poetry educational books, journalistic pieces and novels. He is nevertheless best remembered for his contributions to theater and drama. He was born in Arecibo to an affluent family of landowners. He was trained as an agronomist at the College of Agriculture and Mechanical Arts in Puerto Rico but later received instruction in literature at Columbia University and in Spain.

René Marqués, 1992. (*El Nuevo Día.*)

Like many of his literary contemporaries, Marqués was preoccupied with the well-being of Puerto Rican society and its political, social and economic future. Thus, some of his work presents the concerns of those writers associated with the **generation of the thirties**. His writings explore the purpose of human life, question what is and what is not and try to find a meaning behind the painful experiences of daily living. He excels at offering a clear vision of the identity struggles of Puerto Ricans on the island and of those women and men who were the "pioneers" in the United States.

Many of these themes were expressed through his examination of Puerto Rico's political and colonial oppression by the United States and by the social and economic malaise that plagued the agrarian sector during and after the Great Depression. Like **Enrique Laguerre**, Rene Marqués's literary thoughts evolved to reflect such concerns as the potential effects of modernization on Puerto Rican society and the collision between the traditional values held by the islanders and those of the outside modern world. His most important plays were *La carreta* (1952) and *Los soles truncos* (1959). In *La carreta*, considered to be a Latin American dramatic masterpiece, Marqués uses comedy to ponder the many existential dilemmas faced by Puerto Ricans. His work reflected on human dignity, **machismo**, the Puerto Rican ethos and the proverbial overarching question of what and where is Puerto Rico as a nation.

Some of his other dramatic plays were *Juan Bobo y la dama de Occidente* (1955) and *Palm Sunday* (1958), in which he explores the ideological underpinnings of the **Ponce Massacre**. He also wrote short stories such as "Otro día nuestro" (1955) and an acclaimed novel, *La vispera del hombre* (1958). He was a supporter of the Puerto Rican independence movement, yet he also wrote an essay, "El puertorriqueño docil," which argues that, as a people, Puerto Ricans are like sheep. Despite the violence of the 1930s and the revolution in 1950, Marqués believed that Puerto Ricans willingly subordinated themselves to the authority and mandates of others. His fatalism recalls the work of **Antonio Pedreira**, one of his literary contemporaries.

SUGGESTED READING

Martin Banham, *Cambridge Guide to World Theater* (New York: Cambridge University Press, 1988); Mark Hawkins-Dady, *International Dictionary of Theater* (Chicago: St. James Press, 1994); Leonard S. Klein, *Encyclopedia of World Literature in the 20th Century* (1993); William Luis, *Dictionary of Literary Biography* (Detroit: Gale Research, 1991); René Marqués, *The Docile Puerto Rican* (Philadelphia: Temple University Press, 1976); René Marqués, *La carreta* (The oxcart), trans. Charles Pilditch (New York: Scribner, 1969); Esther Rodríguez Ramos, "René Marqués, in *Spanish American Authors: The Twentieth Century*, Angel Flores ed. (New York: H.W. Wilson, 1992).

Martorell, Antonio (1939–)   This distinguished artist, known for his graphics, murals and paintings is a man of many interests. He first studied diplomacy and later turned to arts. He trained in Spain with Julio Martín Caro and under the tutelage of **Lorenzo Homar** at the Institute of Puerto Rican Culture Graphic Arts Workshop.

Martorell has produced in a wide array of plastic art media. He has been an illustrator, an engraver, and a set designer for television and theater. In 1968 Martorell founded his own artistic workshop, Taller Alacrán. He also has illustrated many books.

He has lived and worked in Mexico and New York. In Mexico he was actively involved in preparing sets for television and children's programming. He painted the mural of composer **Sylvia Rexach** at the Luis A. Ferré Center for Performing Arts in Santurce. In addition, he directed the pro-

Antonio Martorell, "Visiones de Proteus." (Museo de Arte de Ponce, The Luis A. Ferré Foundation, Inc., Ponce, Puerto Rico.)

duction of the play *Waiting for Godot* at the **University of Puerto Rico** Theater in Río Piedras. His work has been exhibited throughout the world and he has received many important awards and distinctions. His work has subtle political and social connotations.

SUGGESTED READING

Peter Bloch, *Painting and Sculptures of the Puerto Ricans* (New York: Plus Ultra Educational Publishers, 1978); Ponce Art Museum, *Colección de Arte Latino-americano* (Ponce: Museo de Arte de Ponce, n.d.); Ana Ruitort, *Historia Breve del arte puertorriqueño* (Madrid: Editorial Playor, 1994); Nelson Rivera, *Visual Artists and the Puerto Rican Performing Arts, 1950–1990: The Works of Jack and Irene*

Delano, Antonio Martorell, Jaíme Suarez and Oscar Mestey-Villamil (New York: P. Lang, 1991); K. Mitchell Snow, "Antonio Martorell," *Latin American Art* 5, no. 4 (1994): 72; Octavio Zaya, "Antonio Martorell," *Flash Art*, no. 187 (1996).

Matos Paoli, Francisco (1915–   ) Originally from Lares, this poet's first work, prompted by the death of his mother, was published in 1931, "Signario de lágrimas." This was one of two significant events that took place during his adolescence. The other, in 1930, as a member of the **Nationalist party**, occurred when he met and developed a friendship with **Pedro Albizu Campos**, whom he referred to as his "maestro" or teacher and whom he has admired profoundly throughout his life. In 1937 he published his second poetry collection, *Cardo labriego*, a patriotic work focusing on the island, its people, their customs and the denunciation of the political realities of colonialism.

In high school he studied classical literature, both Spanish and non-Spanish, as well as that of the most outstanding Puerto Rican writers. In addition, he graduated with shorthand and typing skills, which helped him earn an income while at the university. After graduating as the valedictorian of his class in Lares, he went to San Juan to attend the **University of Puerto Rico.**

While at the university, he was mentored by **Carmen Alicia Cadilla de Ruibal,** an outstanding poet and an intellectual force of the **generation of the thirties,** a time when Puerto Rico saw a tremendous leap in the development of a native literature by a cadre of writers. Having graduated with honors, and now pursuing a master's degree in literature, Matos Paoli worked with **Francisco Arriví** in the educational radio station of the Department of Instruction. There in the School of the Air, he developed programs that focused on all aspects of poetry. In addition, he began his tenure as a professor at the University of Puerto Rico, where he distinguished himself by discussing a variety of topics, events and personalities on the island.

In 1944 he published *Teoría del olvido* and *Habitante del eco*, which won an award from the Institute of Puerto Rican Literature that same year. Both works, which reflect a very introspective period in his life, contain poetry that is very deep in its philosophical and religious content and can be described as a search for the eternal and absolute.

During the 1940s, Matos Paoli's continued recognition as a poet earned him a scholarship to pursue graduate studies at the Sorbonne in Paris. While living abroad, he wrote the award-winning "Canto a Puerto Rico" (Song to Puerto Rico, 1949), a poem that evoked the island's landscape, which he missed. It is considered by scholars of poetry as one of the most outstanding poems ever written about Puerto Rico.

Upon his return to the island, Matos Paoli worked as a journalist and taught literature at the University of Puerto Rico. In 1949 he was appointed secretary general of the Nationalist party. As the leader and spokesperson of the party, his speeches, particularly those given in Cabo Rojo, San Juan, Guánica and Lares were deemed subversive, and the authorities accused him of being in violation of Law 53 (**La mordaza**), and he was arrested, tried and sentenced to twenty years in prison; this sentence was later reduced to ten years. He was one of 2,000 people arrested during the revolution of 1950.

During his imprisonment, he wrote *Luz de los héroes* (Light of the heroes), a collection of nostalgic poems, dedicated to his wife and two daughters. This collection also contains patriotic poetry, in which the poet combines religious symbolic concepts with the struggle for independence, so that the struggle and sacrifice, as well as its heroes, acquire mystical proportions.

He was released from prison after approximately a year and a half, only to be imprisoned again during the **Nationalist attack on Congress.** This time he was kept in solitary confinement for ten months, until May 26, 1955, when Governor **Luis Muñoz Marín** pardoned him and reinstated all his civil rights. Even though his release from prison was followed by many years of psychiatric treatment, it was during these years that his creative capacity increased, and these years were his most prolific and creative. His feelings about these years were best expressed in the collection *Canto de la locura* (Song of insanity, 1962). This work is considered the most outstanding work in contemporary Puerto Rican lyrical poetry. In it, the poet gathers his mystical-religious experiences and reaffirms his religious faith and patriotism.

Throughout his poetry, Matos Paoli speaks as an instrument of change, as an element of ethical and social consciousness. His work blends such topics as God, country, justice, beauty and love with others that express his profound social and political concerns. However, he has also distinguished himself through prose, particularly in his 1950 speech, "Ante el Yunque de los héroes," commemorating the Lares uprising (see **Grito de Lares**), and in his book *Diario de un poeta.*

Since 1971 he has been the poet laureate in residence of the University of Puerto Rico, and in 1991 the university awarded him a Doctor Honoris Causa degree. He has received numerous awards nationally and internationally, and his works have been translated into English, French, Italian, Swedish and Portuguese.

SUGGESTED READING

María Teresa Babín, "Ocho poetas de Puerto Rico," *Artes y Letras* (August 1958): 2; Arístides Cruz, "Francisco Matos Paoli," paper presented at the University of

the Caribbean while conferring the degree of Doctor Honoris Causa on Matos
Paoli, May 1996; Alfredo Matilla and Iván Silén, eds., *The Puerto Rican Poets*
(New York: Bantam, 1972); Julio Morazan, ed., *Inventing a Word* (New York:
Columbia University Press, 1982).

Meléndez, Concha (1895–1983) A scholar, poet and teacher originally
from Caguas, Meléndez started writing poetry in high school. Unusual for
women at that time, Meléndez worked as a secondary school teacher while
she completed her undergraduate degree. She obtained her B.A. in 1922
and continued at the **University of Puerto Rico** (UPR). In 1927, after she
had completed her graduate degree in Romance languages at Columbia
University, the chancellor of UPR invited Meléndez to become one of the
first faculty members of the newly created Department of Hispanic Studies.

Already a prolific writer and scholar, Meléndez continued publishing
works about Puerto Rican and Latin American literature. Her works on
Puerto Rican literary figures, among the most numerous in the genre of
Puerto Rican literary history, include *Figuración de Puerto Rico y otros
estudios* (1956), *El arte del cuento* (1961) and *Literatura de ficción en
Puerto Rico: Cuento y novela* (1971). In 1979 the *Complete Works of
Concha Meléndez* was published.

During her lifetime her work received numerous honors, including
awards from the Institute of Puerto Rican Literature, the Puerto Rican
Athenaeum, the Commonwealth of Puerto Rico and the Mexican Academy
of Language. In 1971 she was honored as Woman of the Year in Puerto
Rico by the Association of American Women. Her contribution to Puerto
Rico and Latin American literature was universal in scope. She will always
be remembered as a scholar and poet whose work was instrumental in
helping Hispanics around the world celebrate their history and heritage.

SUGGESTED READING

Concha Meléndez, "Puerto Rican Writer Concha Melendez Reading from Her
Work," Recorded for the Archive of Hispanic Literature on Tape (Library of Con-
gress), recorded on June 12, 1979; Diane Telgen and Jim Kamp, eds., *Notable
Hispanic American Women* (Detroit: Gale Research, 1993).

Méndez, Ana G. (1908–1997) Originally from Aguada, this educator and
entrepreneur established one of the largest private university systems on the
island. She was president of the Ana G. Méndez Foundation, which over-
sees the University System Ana G. Méndez, including three universities and
an educational television channel.

Because she married early and had children to raise, Méndez completed
most of her work for her undergraduate degree by attending classes in the
evenings. She received her B.A. in business education in 1940 and completed a graduate degree in business from New York University in 1948.

In 1941 Méndez began to make her first inroads into the field of education as one of the founders of Puerto Rico High School of Commerce, an enterprise that became, in 1952, Puerto Rico Junior College, which is now a four-year postsecondary institution known as the Colegio Universitario del Este. During the 1970s she expanded her involvement in higher education and formed the Ana G. Méndez University System, which also includes Turabo University and Metropolitan University in the San Juan area, as well as the only nongovernmental educational television channel on the island.

From 1952 until 1972, she served as the president of the board of directors of the Puerto Rico Junior College. In 1972, under the umbrella of the newly created Ana G. Méndez University System, its name was changed to the Colegio Universitario del Este and its curriculum was expanded to include liberal arts, business administration and education. Today, this university alone serves over 2,000 students. The system's campuses currently comprise a faculty and student body of over 8,000.

SUGGESTED READING

Enciclopedia grandes mujeres de Puerto Rico (Hato Rey, P.R.: Ramallo Brothers Printers, 1975); Antonia Guindulain, *Ana G. Méndez* (Barcelona, Spain: Vasgos, 1974).

Méndez Ballester, Manuel (1909–) This newspaper columnist and writer was born in Aguadilla. His social and political commentary, published in *El Mundo* and *El Nuevo Día*, were features of the island's popular culture for many years. With wit, imagination and humor, Méndez Ballester used his columns to make light critical analyses and to satirize the most controversial and sometimes painful events in the island's recent history. Méndez Ballester's most significant contribution to literature is his historical novel *Isla Cerrera* (1941) and his play *Tiempo muerto* (1958). He was an active member of the **Popular Democratic party** and served as a representative for that party during the 1960s.

SUGGESTED READING

Manuel Méndez Ballester, *Isla Cerrera* (Madrid, Spain: Nuevas Ediciones Unidas, 1941); Manuel Méndez Ballester, *Tiempo muerto* (Barcelona, Spain: Ediciones Rumbos, 1967); Donald E. Herdeck, *Caribbean Writers: A Bio-Bibliographical-Critical Encyclopedia* (Washington, D.C.: Three Continent Press, 1979); Bonnie Hildebrand Reynolds, "Puertorriqueñidad: The Force Behind the Development of a Puerto Rican Theater" in Arela Rodríguez Laguna, *Images and identities: The Puerto Rican in Two World Contexts* (New Brunswick, N.J.: Transactions, 1987).

Mendoza de Muñoz Marín, María Inés (1910–1990) An essayist and teacher, this former first lady of Puerto Rico was born in Naguabo. Her professional training at the **University of Puerto Rico** focused on education.

She worked as a primary and secondary schoolteacher during the 1930s and 1940s. Even though one of her areas of specialization was English, she was a tireless advocate for the use of the vernacular in the island's school system at a time when teaching in English was mandated. In 1937 this advocacy caused her to be stripped of her teaching licenses, and the authorities refused to renew her contract at Santurce's Central High School where she was employed. It was not until 1964 that María Inés Mendoza was able to have her primary and secondary teaching licenses renewed.

She received the equivalent of an associate degree from the University of Puerto Rico, and in 1931 she completed her B.A. in administration and supervision at Teachers College of Columbia University. Upon her return to Puerto Rico, she began to work in a parochial school in old San Juan and was a member of the **Nationalist party**. News accounts of that era point to her affiliation with the Nationalists as a factor in her losing her teaching license in 1937. Also during the decade of the 1930s, she met and worked on political activities with **Luis Muñoz Marín**, a senator who would later become the founder and first governor of the Commonwealth of Puerto Rico. In 1948 they married and in 1949 he became governor of Puerto Rico, a position he held until 1964. During her years as first lady, her efforts were focused on improving the quality of life for those living in rural areas. At that time running water and plumbing, as well as electricity, were in their infancy in rural areas. She also took an active role in the welfare of children, both in rural and urban settings, and she worked to promote conservation, particularly nature and plant life.

Doña Inés, as she was called for over thirty years, left a literary legacy of articles and writings concerning her observations of nature, geography and the human condition on the island. The long list of newspapers and magazines that published her writings as early as the 1920s includes *El Mundo*, *El Diario de Nueva York*, *La Prensa* and many others. She also wrote about politics, mostly in the form of essays that were published in local newspapers. Her political writings decreased after she became first lady; she then focused on developing the newly established commonwealth status of Puerto Rico. Recently, her book on conservation, *Sabios árboles, mágicos árboles* (1974), which had been out of print for many years, was reissued, and it is being used widely today, particularly in schools, to teach children about ecology and its importance to the island.

To the end of her life, she continued her interest in politics and, in particular, social justice. She was a lifetime supporter of South Africa's Nelson Mandela and the antiapartheid movement. During the 1984 U.S. presidential campaign, she identified with and supported the Reverend Jesse Jackson. That year, when he visited the island, he made a special trip to meet Doña Inés, a gesture of great importance to her.

Her death in 1990 ended the career of a woman who for many years was regarded as a role model for other Puerto Rican women. During her lifetime, she received recognition from countless organizations throughout the world. Among the most notable were the medals she received from the League of Parent and Teacher Associations, the American Federation of Caribbean Women and the Republic of Haiti. She was also honored as Exemplary Puerto Rican Teacher and was honorary president of the Society for the Conservation of Caribbean Resources. Carrying on the political legacy of the Muñoz Mendoza family is one of her four children, her daughter **Victoria Muñoz Mendoza**, who has been very active in the political arena.

SUGGESTED READING

Gianina Delgado Caro, *Inés María Mendoza vida y palabra: Notas para una biografía* (Hato Rey, P.R.: Fundación Luis Muñoz Marín, 1990); Fernando Picó, "La reciedumbre de doña Inés," *Diálogo* (September 1990): 14; Josefina Rivera de Alvarez, *Diccionario de literatura puertorriqueña* (Río Piedras, P.R.: Ediciones la Torre, UPR, 1955); Enrique Rodríguez Santiago, "Hora de recuerdos" *El Nuevo Día*, January 10, 1995, 47.

Migration   Midnight is an appropriate time to witness the human dimensions of migration. Go to Kennedy Airport in New York City, stand by the counters reserved for flights to Puerto Rico and watch the mountain of cardboard boxes that soon appear. Families returning home pile their belongings beside the baggage ramps, while, in San Juan, another mound of boxes holds the belongings of islanders who are making their first (or second or third) trip to the United States. Puerto Ricans have become "the commuter nation," a people who, for more than thirty-five years, have sent more than 1.5 million people a year to the United States, and another 1.5 million back to Puerto Rico.

This phenomenon, later called circular migration, first started in 1900. Sugar growers in Hawaii wanted workers who would compete with those picked up in Japan and Korea; any body would do, so more than 5,300 Puerto Ricans emigrated to Hawaii between 1900 and 1901. Many worked under such abysmal conditions that their situation resembled the **slavery** recently abolished by Puerto Rico. During World War I, thousands of Puerto Ricans arrived in the United States to fill positions necessitated by the war effort. Many stayed, but the numbers were small by contemporary standards. In fact, as late as 1946, only 70,000 Puerto Ricans had come to the United States; and net migration to the mainland totaled only 24,621 people in 1946. The next year, the numbers started to climb; between 1947 and 1960, there was a net migration of Puerto Ricans to the United States of more than 550,000 men and women. As a percent of the entire island population, this number represented 25 percent of the Puerto Rican people. Per capita it is one of the largest mass migrations of the twentieth century.

Why did so many Puerto Ricans suddenly migrate? There are at least three related answers to this question. First is **Operation Bootstrap**. The well-publicized efforts at industrialization never markedly changed the island's always high rate of unemployment; in fact, even the labor-intensive work required for clothing never compensated for the jobs lost in agriculture. People left the land, migrated to the cities, and, when they were unable to find work there they immigrated to the United States. Second was the active recruitment of Puerto Rican workers by U.S. employers. Since islanders worked for low wages, they were used in everything from truck farming in New Jersey to tobacco picking in Connecticut. Finally, there is the role of the Puerto Rican government. Among other things, it requested that the Federal Aviation Administration set low rates for airfares between Puerto Rico and the mainland. The hope was to encourage the departure of people, who, if they remained, would have, among other things, brought to light the weaknesses of Operation Bootstrap.

Migration statistics hide something very important; each number represents a human being, a person who came to U.S. cities when New York or Chicago or Bridgeport saw its middle class flock to the suburbs and its factory jobs flock to the Far East. From the late 1950s to today, unskilled people have a harder time than ever; so, by the early 1960s, the figures began to even out. As many Puerto Ricans came to the United States as returned to the island; the incessant commuting had become an institutionalized part of the Puerto Rican lifestyle. Increase opportunity at home, and the net migration is there; increase opportunities in the United States, and the net migration is there. In the words of **Juan Manuel García Passalacqua**, "Thousands of Puerto Ricans live literally in the air, in transit, between the metropolis and the colony, between one society and another. We are people in transience" (Torre et al. 1994, 103). The negative educational, language and family consequences of so much movement cannot be exaggerated. People suffer but they rarely blame the system. Instead, decisions are personalized—I lost my job, the family in New York needs me, my spouse and I have separated—and the structural and political factors that actually fuel the migration are rarely challenged. For example, during the 1950s, Puerto Rico manufactured a substantial share of the clothing used in the United States. But when Congress, at the insistence of U.S. unions, mandated higher minimum wages in Puerto Rico, islanders lost the jobs to other nations. As a consequence, workers in Puerto Rico were on the move but, since their jobs fled to the Far East, they entered an already crowded U.S. labor market.

In 1996 circular migration is still an institutionalized fact of Puerto Rican national life. It will end only when leaders on the island and the mainland finally resolve the political and economic issues that have created, nourished and perpetuated the existence of this extraordinary phenomenon: Puerto Rico, the "commuter nation."

SUGGESTED READING

Frank Bonilla and Ricardo Campos, "A Wealth of Poor: Puerto Ricans in the New Economic Order" *Daedalus* 110 (Spring 1981): 133–76; Rita M. Maldonado, "Why Puerto Ricans Migrated to the United States," *Monthly Labor Review* 99, no. 9 (Sept. 1976): 7–18; Elena Padilla, *Up from Puerto Rico* (New York: Columbia University Press, 1958); Clara E. Rodríguez, *Puerto Rican: Born in the U.S.A.* (Boston: Unwin Hyman, 1989); Esmeralda Santiago, *When I Was Puerto Rican* (New York: Vintage, 1993); Carlos Antonio Torre, Hugo Rodríguez Vecchini and William Burgos, ed. *The Commuter Nation* (Río Piedras: University of Puerto Rico, 1994).

Miles, General Nelson (1839–1921)   General Miles commanded the U.S. forces that invaded Puerto Rico on July 25, 1898. Like Governor **E. Montgomery Reilly**, Miles retains historical significance in the eyes of many Puerto Ricans. When the general invaded, he made this promise about the island and its political future: "We have not come to make war upon the people of a country that for centuries has been oppressed but on the contrary to bring you protection . . . to promote your prosperity, and to bestow upon you the immunities and blessings of the liberal institutions of our government" (Wagenheim 1972, 63).

Many prominent Puerto Ricans believed what the general said. Indeed, one partial explanation for the minimal resistance encountered by U.S. forces was the belief that the general would keep his word. However, within one year of the invasion, the elected (under Spanish authority) representatives of the Puerto Rican people sent this message to Congress: "The acceptance of the fostering arm of the United States by Puerto Ricans was based on the faith in the pledge and word of honor of an American General representing the highest government authority." Thus, islanders demanded that Puerto Rico "be instantly declared an integral Territorial district and not a mere tributary; her citizens in reality citizens of the United States and not subjects of an arbitrary and imperialistic power" (Congressional Record 1900, 2232).

When Congress dismissed these requests in 1900, the cynicism and skepticism of many Puerto Ricans grew. General Miles's pledge is simply a potent symbol of the battle between those who wished to keep the general's word and a majority who subscribed to the February 4, 1899, sentiments of United States Senator Horace Chilton: "We say to the powers of the Old World. We will not allow you to acquire further possessions in the Western hemisphere. Yet we will take Porto Rico and we reserve the right to take Haiti or Brazil or Cuba or any other part of North or South America when we think proper to do so" (Congressional Record 1898, 1448).

SUGGESTED READING

Congressional Record, Senate, February 4, 1898, especially pp. 1445–50; for the Memorial from the Puerto Rican representatives, see *Congressional Record*, Senate,

Jacobo Morales, 1994. (José Rodriguez and *El Nuevo Día*.)

February 26, 1900, p. 2232; William Dinwiddie, *Puerto Rico and Its Possibilities* (New York: Harper, 1899); Barbara Tasch Ezratty, *Puerto Rico: Changing Flags, an Oral History, 1898–1950* (San Juan, P.R.: Caribbean Stationery, 1986); Fernando Picó, *La guerra despues de la guerra* (San Juan, P.R.: Huracán, 1987); Kal Wagenheim, *Puerto Rico: A Profile* (New York: Praeger, 1972).

Mita, Church of   *See* **Church of Mita.**

Morales, Jacobo (1934–)   Born in Lajas, Jacobo Morales is a productive and talented writer and media personality. He attended high school at Román Baldorioty de Castro school in San Juan. From there he went to the **University of Puerto Rico** at Río Piedras where he studied theater and drama. He has had a long and successful career in Puerto Rican arts and letters, but above all he is best known for his work in the media. Morales began writing radio scripts and acting in radio soap operas as a young child. From radio, he moved on to television and was one of the early pioneers, starting to work in that medium during the 1950s. He wrote scripts for television programs and soap operas and also acted in many television programs. He is a good comedian, and Puerto Rican audiences still remember his many roles, both as writer and actor, in the comedy programs "Colegio de la alegria," "Ja Ji Ji Jo Jo con Agrelot" and "Desafiando a los genios." Morales also wrote scripts for many popular comedy programs of the 1960s and 1970s.

During the 1960s, Morales wrote the movie script for an adaptation of the popular Puerto Rican television programs "La criada malcriada" and "La palomilla." He also acted in several American films, including Woody Allen's *Bananas* and *Up the Sandbox*. In the 1970s, he produced such highly acclaimed Puerto Rican films as *Dios los cría, Nicolas y los demás, Lo que le pasó a Santiago* and, most recently, *Linda Sara*. These films were shot in Puerto Rico with Puerto Rican actors and themes. They have been a source of ethnic pride for many Puerto Ricans because Morales has proven that it is possible, with the island's talent and natural resources, to develop a high-quality Puerto Rican film industry.

Jacobo Morales is also an accomplished poet. His books of poems *100X35* and *409 metros de solar y cyclon fence* were well received by literary critics. As journalist and art and literature critic Pedro Zervigon said in a newspaper column praising Morales's work, "Jacobo Morales represents a renaissance spirit" (Zervigon 1990, 109).

SUGGESTED READING

Eric Landron, "Jacobo Morales o el poeta con palabras de dulzura y lente," *El Diario* (San Juan), December 14, 1995; Michael Singer, *Michael Singer's Film Directors: A Complete Guide* (Los Angeles: Lone Eagle Publishers, 1992); Pedro Zervigon, "Un merecido reconocimiento a Jacobo," *El Nuevo Día*, June 15, 1990, 109.

Mordaza, La   Literally the "gag law," *la mordaza* refers to the very controversial legislation passed by the Puerto Rican legislature in May 1948. The date is significant because conventional wisdom on the island suggests that the law was a response to the revolutionary insurrection initiated by the **Nationalist party** in October 1950. In truth, the law was passed two years before the violence occurred. The law stipulated that it was a *delito grave* (felony), punishable by a maximum of ten years in jail and/or a fine of $10,000, for anyone who "encouraged, pleaded, counseled, or preached the necessity, desirability or suitability, of overthrowing, paralyzing, or destroying the insular government, or any subdivision of it, by means of force or violence." It was also a felony to print, publish, circulate, sell or exhibit literature that suggested forceful threats to the island's government.

La mordaza was modeled after the Smith Act in the United States. Controversy arose because critics charged that the law grossly violated the right to free speech, and, of equal importance, that, on an everyday level, the law acted to silence many Puerto Rican supporters of independence. A climate of fear soon took hold of the island. People were afraid to say anything that could even be construed as advocating independence, and, ominously, people began to spy on one another. Thus, the slang expression, *la mordaza*—the gag law. Professor Ivonne Acosta argues that the law is best understood in the context of postwar Puerto Rico. In December 1945 a majority of the elected representatives of the dominant **Popular Democratic party** had asked Congress for independence. Congress, however, had refused to even allow a **plebiscite**, and that refusal moved Governor **Luis Muñoz Marín** to advocate what is today called a commonwealth. The island threatened to explode, and, for Muñoz and his associates, the gag law was one way to deal with the political opposition. The law was repealed in 1957, but its effects linger, particularly on the older generation who still speak guardedly when the issue is independence.

SUGGESTED READING

Ivonne Acosta, *La mordaza* (Río Piedras, P.R.: Edil, 1987); Luis Muñoz Marín, "Puerto Rico Does Not Want to Be a State," *New York Times Magazine*, August 16, 1945, 35–40; Ruth M. Reynolds, *Campus in Bondage: A 1948 Microcosm of Puerto Rico on Bondage* (New York: Centro de Estudios Puertorriqueños/Hunter College, 1989).

Morro, El This fort is a massive mound of concrete that sits at the edge of Old San Juan. Today one strolls to El Morro through a magnificent field of grass and on an endless walkway which, with the green grass carpet, perfectly displays one of the oldest military fortifications in the Western Hemisphere. Eager to attract tourists, modern designers deliberately created a park, but they nevertheless left signs emphasizing the fort's roots in the colonial struggles of the "Great Powers." Just before visitors enter El Morro, they read a sign that says—in English—that the fort is federal property, operated by the National Park Service of the United States of America.

The first El Morro was constructed in 1539. In 1590 Spanish engineers leveled the first structure, laid a footing of concrete five or six inches thick and then—using hundreds of slaves, convicts and any other body they managed to corral—they created a walled enclosure designed to keep the English, French and Dutch powers at bay. In 1595 Sir Francis Drake, after receiving word that a mangled Spanish treasure galleon lay at the bottom of San Juan harbor, attacked El Morro. The defenders fired twenty-eight separate salvos from the fort's battery of cannons. One ball interrupted Drake's dinner splintering the chair on which he sat. Presumably quite angry, Drake battled the Spanish for an hour. He lived, but many of his men died, and, this time, Drake retreated. But he and others of his kind always returned. Sir George Clifford, the third earl of Cumberland, led an English squadron that occupied the fort in 1598, and the Dutch invaded in 1625.

The fort changed hands many times, going from one colonial power to another. In time the power struggles ended and El Morro was left to decay slowly in the harsh Caribbean sun. In the late eighteenth century the fort was rebuilt, and once again El Morro became an instrument of political power. The crown shored it up to defend the new wave of colonists who, following the advice of **Alejandro de O'Reilly**, meant to turn isolated Puerto Rico into a large, Spanish sugar plantation.

El Morro contains a fascinating museum. Visitors see everything from mannequins in suits of armor to detailed drawings of the fort's construction and reconstruction. Next to the museum is a small chapel, and, across the stone corridor that separates one side of the fort from the other, is a walkway to the sea. It is dark and a bit treacherous, but if one turns to the left, one can see a tiny cell—perhaps three feet by five feet—secreted in the walls. It was the Spanish version of solitary confinement, and it remains a chilling reminder of the lives led by the slaves and soldiers who built, defended, lived and died in El Morro.

SUGGESTED READING

Albert Manucy and Ricardo Torres-Reyes, *Puerto Rico and the Forts of Old San Juan* (Riverside, Calif.: Chatham Press, 1973).

Moscoso, Teodoro (1910–1992)   Moscoso was the architect of **Operation Bootstrap**, the postwar plan designed to move Puerto Rico from an agricultural to an industrial nation. He played an important role in Puerto Rican economic and political affairs throughout his life. Born in Barcelona, Spain, he died in Puerto Rico on June 16, 1992. Moscoso studied at the Philadelphia College of Pharmacy and at Michigan State University. In the 1930s he worked in the family business, the Moscoso chain of pharmacies, still one of the largest in Puerto Rico. He also served as head of the Housing Authority of **Ponce**, until, during World War II, he became the architect of Operation Bootstrap. He also drafted the law that established Fomento, Puerto Rico's Economic Development Administration. Scholars generally argue that Moscoso was a pragmatist. In response to a congressman's question in 1943, he explained that "what we want to do is establish industry. Who does it, if it is the devil himself, I do not care" (U.S. Congress 1943, 845). By 1957 Moscoso had come to the conclusion that "private capital, the larger part of it from the United States, is the main ingredient [for success]" (Moscoso 1957, 3).

Moscoso left Fomento before the collapse of his theories became apparent. He worked for the Kennedy administration in two prominent positions. He was the ambassador to Venezuela, and then he became the first director of the highly publicized Alliance for Progress, an economic program designed to help Latin American economies achieve economic success through, among other things, industrialization. The alliance realized some success, but, as Moscoso told the president, it was resisted because it looked like a "made in the U.S.A. product." After he left the Kennedy administration, Moscoso served as a vice president of the Commonwealth Oil Refining Corporation. In 1973 he again took charge of Fomento and was involved in shaping the Puerto Rican economy until his death in 1992.

Ironically, a tribute to his leadership is now a subject of controversy in Puerto Rico. When a sparkling bridge leading in and out of the main airport was named in his honor, users complained about the high tolls. Today it is possible to find little traffic on a structure that saves all users a considerable amount of time.

SUGGESTED READING

Teodoro Moscoso, "Puerto Rico Chooses Free Enterprise," a speech delivered in New York City in 1957 (Kennedy Library, Boston, Massachusetts); David Ross, *The Long Uphill Battle: A Historical Study of Puerto Rico's Program of Economic Development* (San Juan, P.R.: Edil, 1969); U.S. Congress, House, Hearings before the Subcommittee on Territories and Insular Affairs, 78th Cong., 1st sess., June 14, 1943; Harvey S. Perloff, *Puerto Rico's Economic Future: A Study in Democratic Development* (London: University of Chicago Press, 1950).

Municipios   Municipalities are the basic form of political and geographical organization in Puerto Rico. The island is separated into seventy-eight municipalities, each of which is represented by a mayor and a municipal assembly. The number of people in the assembly is determined by the size of the population. Assemblies range in size from seventeen members for San Juan to twelve for Guánica to five for Culebra. Members of the municipal assembly do not receive a fixed salary; instead, they are paid for the meetings they attend.

Each and every municipality has its own flag and coat of arms, a custom that dates back to the Spanish period. Over each of the seventy-eight coats of arms there is a crown signifying to whom the municipality "belongs"—a king, a bishop or a marquee. The crown also signifies the security and protection that the municipality offers to its inhabitants. Also, at the very top of each coat of arms there are three, four or five castle-like towers. The number indicates whether the municipality is considered a village, a town or a city. Citizens take these coats of arms quite seriously. Even today, many Puerto Rican women and men owe their primary loyalty to their municipality, not necessarily to the Puerto Rican nation. It's not unusual that a Puerto Rican woman who has lived in the United States for thirty-five years has a license plate that reads Ciales, her spiritual home.

Municipalities are organized around local governments that oversee the general functioning of each town. This government consists of a mayor, a municipal assembly and various department heads. A municipal government earns revenues from property taxes and business permits to help defray the expenses of running school transportation, garbage disposal, local health centers, water and sewage services, town police and emergency services.

In contrast to the United States, where education and schools are left in charge of state and local governments, the Puerto Rican national government still controls the educational system.

Since municipal governments are elected along national party lines, there has been a great deal of party politics inside municipalities. Throughout the years, there have been substantial levels of corruption and political patronage in the municipal governments. Biased awards of municipal contracts and job placement are considered, by many, to be the rule rather than the exception.

The following list indicates the population of each municipality over the last century. Note how a mountain town like Adjuntas or Lares has remained virtually constant for one hundred years, while cities like Mayagüez, **Ponce** and San Juan have experienced phenomenal growth. The worldwide process of urbanization is also apparent in Puerto Rico.

Municipo	1898	1940	1990
Adjuntas	19,484	22,556	20,176
Aguada	10,581	17,923	36,620
Aguadilla	17,830	34,956	60,845
Aguas Buenas	7,997	14,671	25,691
Aibonito	8,596	16,819	25,551
Añasco	13,311	15,701	25,817
Arecibo	36,910	69,192	97,549
Arroyo	4,867	10,746	18,954
Barceloneta	9,357	18,545	22,320
Barranquitas	8,103	17,096	26,452
Bayamón	12,778	37,190	221,815
Cabo Rojo	16,154	53,356	39,887
Caguas	19,857	53,356	136,633
Camuy	10,887	18,922	29,490
Carolina	14,442	24,046	178,695
Cataño	2,737	9,719	35,369
Cayey	14,442	31,391	47,778
Ceiba	4,341	7,021	17,188

Municipo	1898	1940	1990
Ciales	18,115	22,906	19,437
Cidra	7,052	20,392	36,366
Coamo	15,144	22,772	35,062
Comerío	8,249	18,539	20,438
Corozal	11,508	20,458	33,961
Culebra	704	860	1,515
Dorado	3,804	9,481	32,326
Fajardo	9,505	20,405	37,036
Guánica	2,700	12,685	20,509
Guayama	12,749	30,511	43,039
Guayanilla	9,540	15,577	21,996
Guaynabo	6,957	18,319	92,997
Gurabo	8,700	15,870	29,436
Hatillo	10,449	18,322	33,283
Hormigueros	3,215	6,098	15,695
Humacao	14,313	29,837	56,210
Isabella	14,888	25,843	40,220
Jayuya	9,297	14,589	15,818
Juana Díaz	15,530	23,396	46,829
Juncos	8,249	19,464	30,967
Lajas	8,789	14,736	32,244
Lares	20,883	29,914	29,419
Las Marías	11,279	9,626	9,424
Las Piedras	8,602	15,389	28,739
Loiza	15,522	22,145	29,374
Loquillo	6,402	8,851	18,298
Manatí	13,989	29,366	39,659
Maricao	8,312	7,724	6,341
Maunabo	6,221	10,792	12,421
Mayagüez	35,700	78,487	103,259

Municipo	1898	1940	1990
Moca	12,410	19,716	33,414
Morovis	11,309	19,167	26,516
Naguabo	10,873	19,180	22,814
Naranjito	8,101	13,954	28,632
Orocovis	14,845	19,770	21,898
Patillas	11,163	17,319	19,891
Peñuelas	12,129	14,789	22,879
Ponce	55,477	105,116	195,217
Quebradillas	7,432	11,494	22,014
Rincón	6,641	9,256	12,653
Río Grande	10,061	16,116	45,860
Salinas	5,731	19,400	29,023
San Germán	20,246	26,473	35,133
San Juan	13,760	169,247	449,285*
San Lorenzo	13,433	26,627	35,394
San Sebastián	16,412	30,266	39,906
Santa Isabel	14,888	11,468	20,013
Savana Grande	10,560	14,146	23,285
Toa Alta	7,908	13,371	42,152
Toa Baja	4,030	11,410	89,413
Trujillo Alto	5,683	11,726	61,916
Utuado	31,939	42,531	37,192
Vega Alta	6,107	14,320	36,478
Vega Baja	10,305	23,105	58,124
Vieques	5,938	10,362	8,708
Villalva	12,366	12,871	24,197
Yabucoa	13,905	27,438	37,224
Yauco	27,119	30,533	43,078
TOTAL	**939,812**	**1,827,731**	**3,561,457**

*This includes the population of Río Piedras.

Source: José A. Toro-Sugrañes, *Nueva enciclopedia de Puerto Rico*, vol. 1, *Geografica, fisica y huamana* (Hato Rey, P.R.: Programa Educativo Lector, 1995).

Muñoz Marín, Luis (1898–1980)   Perhaps most Puerto Ricans would call Luis Muñoz Marín the most significant political figure in twentieth-century Puerto Rican history. He was born in San Juan on February 18, 1898, and he died in San Juan in 1980. Because of his father's political career (see **Luis Muñoz Rivera**), Muñoz Marín was raised in the United States. Later, even his opponents marveled at his command of both English and Spanish. He mastered the most obscure idioms in both languages and he used them skillfully with senators in Congress and **jíbaros** in the mountains of Puerto Rico. Muñoz Marín graduated from Georgetown University in Washington, D.C. He planned to attend law school, but his father's death caused him to return to the island. In the 1920s he worked with **Santiago Igslesias Pantín** to improve conditions for Puerto Rican workers.

His early speeches and writings led people to think that he was an ardent advocate of independence. In a 1929 article entitled "The Sad Case of Puerto Rico," he sounded as angry as the revolutionary **Pedro Albizu Campos**. Muñoz argued that, under American domination, "Porto Rico had become a land of beggars and millionaires, of flattering statistics and distressing realities." Indeed, the island

is a sweat shop that has a company store—the United States. American dollars paid to the peons are so many tokens, redeemable in the American market exclusively, at tariff inflated prices. The same tariff that protects the prices of sugar and tobacco, controlled by the few, skyrockets the price of commodities that must be consumed by all. (Muñoz Marín 1929, 139)

Muñoz often repeated this message as a member of the Liberal party during the 1930s. However, to help Puerto Rico survive the Great Depression, Muñoz met and courted a number of influential officials from the administration of President Franklin D. Roosevelt. By 1935 Muñoz actively promoted the New Deal in Puerto Rico. Indeed, whether in the **Chardón Plan** for the reform of the sugar industry or in the use of federal funds for the island's reconstruction, Muñoz depended, almost entirely, upon Washington for the funds needed to transform Puerto Rico's "sweat shop" economy.

In 1938 Muñoz created the Partido Popular Democrático (**Popular Democratic party**); as he later told Congress, "the Popular Democratic Party does not stand for independence or any other form of political status. It appealed to the people on the basis of their economic problems" (Nomination of Rexford Tugwell 1941, 49). And it succeeded. By 1945 the *Populares* controlled the island's government, but *not* Congress and *not* the members of Muñoz's own party. For example, in 1945, Senator Millard Tydings and his colleagues said "absolutely not" to both statehood and

Luis Muñoz Marín and his wife, María Inés Mendoza. (*El Nuevo Dia.*)

independence; meanwhile, in Puerto Rico, the Popular Democratic party's 1944 convention clamored to make independence the key issue of postwar Puerto Rican politics.

It was at this point—1946 to be precise—that Muñoz Marín began to talk openly of a third way—what is today called the commonwealth, or Estado Libre Asociado (**Free Associated State**). Whatever his motives—and debate on those motives still rages in 1996—Muñoz accepted the will of Congress by agreeing to accept a status that, as the House and Senate made quite clear, "changed nothing fundamental in the relationship between the United States and Puerto Rico." Meanwhile, Luis Muñoz Marín became the island's first elected governor (1948) and remained governor until 1964.

Through the 1950s Muñoz worked on two separate fronts. At home he pushed **Operation Bootstrap**, a program that dramatically transformed Puerto Rico and its economy; in Washington, the governor tirelessly lobbied for a significant increase in the powers of his own government. In 1962 he even submitted requests to President John F. Kennedy that, as aides told the president, would make Puerto Rico "free to wage war independently or together with the United States or allied with the United States or against the United States" (Kennedy Library 1962, 14–15).

This was too much for Kennedy. Without first telling Muñoz, the president reneged on a promise to permit a **plebiscite**, and he even allowed the governor to be humiliated in Congress. In 1963 during hearings in the House of Representatives, Representative John Saylor reminded the governor that Congress had said that commonwealth status changed nothing fundamental in the status of Puerto Rico. Governor Muñoz was then forced to admit that if that is what Congress said, then, "Puerto Rico is still a colony of the United States. If it is still a colony of the United States it should stop being a colony as soon as possible for the honor of the United States and the self respect of the people of Puerto Rico" (Congressional Hearings 1963, 50).

A reporter noted that this was the "death" of the commonwealth. That was an exaggeration; this creation of Luis Muñoz Marín, the commonwealth, won the status referendum in Puerto Rico. But, for Governor Muñoz, 1963 was nevertheless a turning point. As a result of his defeat at the hands of congress and President Kennedy, he lost a good deal of political credibility in Puerto Rico. The governor refused to run for a fifth term in 1964, but Muñoz helped lead the forces that split the Popular Democratic party's vote in the 1968 elections when he did not like the direction taken by his political successor, Roberto Sánchez Vilella. Ironically, the result of these efforts was the election of the first pro-statehood governor in Puerto Rican history, Luis Perre.

From 1968 until his death, Muñoz remained the elder statesman of Puerto Rican politics, consulted by both island and Washington officials.

His numerous honors included honorary doctorates from Harvard and Rutgers universities, the French Legion of Honor, the Peruvian Orden del Sol, and, from President Kennedy, the United States Medal of Freedom, awarded in 1963.

SUGGESTED READING

Thomas Aitken, *Luis Muñoz Marín: Poet in the Fortress* (New York: Signet Books, 1965); Rafael Alberto Bernabe, "Prehistory of the 'Partido Popular Democratico,' " (Ph.D. diss., State University of New York at Binghamton, 1989); Wenzell Brown, *Dynamite on Our Doorstep* (New York: Greenberg, 1945); Juan Manuel García Passalacqua, *La crisis politica en Puerto Rico*, 2d ed. (Río Piedras, P.R.: Edil, 1983); John F. Kennedy Library, Boston, Mass., White House Central Files, Box 18; Thomas Matthews, *Luís Muñoz Marín: A Concise Biography* (New York: American R.D.M. Corporation, 1968); Luis Muñoz Marín, "The Sad Case of Puerto Rico," *American Mercury* 16, no. 62 (February 1929): 136–41; Luis Muñoz Marín, "Breakthrough from Nationalism: A Small Island Looks at Big Trouble," *The Godkin Lectures* (Cambridge, Mass.: Harvard University, 1959); Nomination of Rexford Tugwell as Governor, Senate, Committee on Territories and Insular Affairs, 77th Cong., 1st sess. (Washington, D.C., 1941); Puerto Rico, Hearings before Subcommittee on Territorial and Insular Affairs, House, 88th Cong., 1st sess., 1963; Rexford Tugwell, *The Art of Politics* (New York: Doubleday, 1958).

Muñoz Mendoza, Victoria (1940–)   Popularly known as Melo, Muñoz Mendoza was the gubernatorial candidate for the **Popular Democratic party** (PPD) in 1992. The daughter of **Luis Muñoz Marín** and **Inés Mendoza de Muñoz Marín**, she grew up in the governor's mansion, **La Fortaleza**, in the heart of the political arena where she witnessed the inception and development of the commonwealth.

Muñoz Mendoza graduated from the **University of Puerto Rico** in 1964 and later continued her graduate work in psychology at the Caribbean Institute for Post-Graduate Studies. From 1965 to 1967, she worked as a social worker in Spanish Harlem, New York, where she developed liaisons between private enterprise and community leaders to develop projects that would improve the community. In 1965 she left for Greece where she worked as a teacher and met her husband, Minás Papadakis.

From the early 1960s Muñoz Mendoza was active in politics, particularly in activities involving the PPD and her father's political campaigns. In 1974 **Rafael Hernández Colón** appointed her to the Commission on Educational Reform, where she was responsible for research and evaluation of preschool education. During the 1980s her service on the Senate's Agricultural and Natural Resources commissions, as well as her work with the Commission on Legal Affairs revising the penal code that dealt with minors, began to propel her into the political sphere.

In 1983 the PPD recruited her as their mayoral candidate for the municipality of San Juan and elected her president of the PPD's San Juan

Central Municipal Committee. The mayoral campaign was unsuccessful, but opened the door for her career in electoral politics. In 1986 she resigned her post with the Central Municipal Committee and successfully campaigned for a Senate seat, which she held until 1992. In 1992 she was again elected president of the PPD and became their candidate for governor. Even though she did not win the governorship, she made history by being the first woman to run for the highest political office on the island.

SUGGESTED READING

Biografía concisa de Victoria Mendoza Muñoz (San Juan: Fundación Luis Muñoz Marín, 1992); Tomás Sarramía, *Nuestra gente* (San Juan: Publicaciones Puertorriqueñas, 1993).

Muñoz Rivera, Luis (1859–1916)   One of the most prominent political figures in Puerto Rico, Muñoz Rivera's political career spanned from the end of Spanish colonialism through the beginning of U.S. colonialism. He was born in Baranquitas, and he died in San Juan. On a street in Old San Juan there is a small plaque that commemorates one of Muñoz's greatest achievements—the newspaper *La Democracia*. Founded as a triweekly in 1890, *La Democracia* became a daily in 1893. Throughout Muñoz Rivera's life, it was arguably the island's most influential newspaper, and it maintained "the battle cry of autonomy and regionalism during the last years of Spanish rule and during the American occupation and control of the island" (Velez Aquino 1968, 117). When Muñoz Rivera criticized the way in which Republican forces were corrupting the island's electoral processes in 1902, his house was attacked and his own life was threatened. In 1902 he temporarily exiled himself to the United States.

Under the Spanish, Muñoz was instrumental in securing the **Autonomic Constitution**, which while representing a terrible compromise for the *independentistas*, was a significant achievement for a man who practiced a politics rooted in compromise. Muñoz was a leader of the **Union party** from 1900 until his death, a time when it dominated island politics. Even though he is often criticized for taking the road of least resistance, he is also responsible for one of the most eloquent speeches ever given by a Puerto Rican patriot. On May 5, 1916, with Congress once again trying to impose **United States citizenship** on the Puerto Rican people, Muñoz reminded all present that "for sixteen years we have endured this system of government, protesting and struggling against it, with energy and without result." Muñoz knew his adversary; he expected little, but, stressing that Puerto Ricans were "the southerners of the Twentieth Century," Muñoz courageously asked Congress to abide by its own political principles and let the Puerto Ricans decide the citizenship issue. Let them have a **plebiscite** because "it would be strange if, having refused citizenship for so long as the majority asked for it, you should decide to impose it by force now that the majority of the people decline it" (*Congressional Record* 1916, 7471).

This was the speech of a Puerto Rican with great pride in himself and his people. It is sometimes forgotten by critics who stress only Muñoz's admitted willingness to compromise with U.S. colonial authorities.

SUGGESTED READING

Congressional Record, House of Representatives, 64th Cong., 2d sess., May 5, 1916; for a fine summary of *La Democracia*'s activities, see Luis Antonio Velez Acquino, "Puerto Rican Press Reaction to the Shift from Spanish to United States Sovereignty, 1898–1917" (Ph.D. diss., Teacher's College, Columbia University, 1968).

N

Nationalist Attack on Congress This event occurred on March 1, 1954, when four members of the **Nationalist party** attacked the U.S. House of Representatives and wounded five congressmen. The four Puerto Ricans were **Lolita Lebrón**, Rafael Cancel Miranda, Irwin Flores, and Andrés Figueroa.

The Nationalists expected to die. They had bought one-way tickets to Washington and chose the House, rather than the Senate, because it provided easier access to visitors. Carrying weapons, the four entered the visitors' gallery during a debate on Mexican wetbacks. One congressman was accusing his fellow Americans of practicing "modern slavery" when Lolita Lebrón unveiled the **flag of Puerto Rico**, shouted "Viva Puerto Rico libre" and fired her gun at the ceiling. Andrés Figueroa's pistol would not fire, but Cancel Miranda and Flores wounded five congressmen when they opened fire on the House floor.

The aim of the attack was, as with the assault on **Blair House** in 1950, to protest and call the world's attention to the colonial status of Puerto Rico and its people. On November 27, 1953, the **United Nations** had removed Puerto Rico from its list of non-self-governing territories; to the Nationalists, this was both a lie and a farce. They believed that the attack was one way to finally get the world to understand the colonial essence of a commonwealth.

In the United States the four Nationalists were labeled fanatics. Meanwhile, as indicated by the entry on U.S. Ambassador to the United Nations **Henry Cabot Lodge**'s documents, the same high-ranking U.S. officials who called the Nationalists fanatics were simultaneously trying to convince Governor **Luis Muñoz Marín** to accept that same independence desired by the

Nationalists. The four Nationalists each spent twenty-five years in federal prisons. They committed the attack for political reasons, and they were released in 1979 for political reasons. As national security advisor Zbigniew Brzezinski pointed out to President Jimmy Carter in a 1978 confidential memo, the four had already served twenty-four years in prison, "and no other woman in the hemisphere has been imprisoned on such charges for so long a period; a fact which Communist critics of your human rights policy are fond of pointing out" (Fernandez 1994, 195–201).

SUGGESTED READING

Ronald Fernandez, *Prisoners of Colonialism: The Struggle for Justice in Puerto Rico* (Monroe, Me.: Common Courage Press, 1994); Antonio Gil De La Madrid Navarro, *Los Indomitos* (Río Piedras, P.R.: Editorial Edil, 1981).

Nationalist Insurrection of 1950   This violent, revolutionary insurrection was planned and carried out by the **Nationalist party** in Puerto Rico and in the United States, primarily between October 30 and November 1, 1950. The insurrection was a deliberate attempt to foil the referendum that would, in 1952, approve or disapprove of Public Law 600, the congressional legislation that legitimated the creation of El Estado Libre Asociado (**Free Associated State**). **Pedro Albizu Campos,** the leader of the Nationalist party, made no secret of his party's revolutionary intent. Speaking at Lares on September 23, 1950, Albizu ardently criticized the **migration** that condemned Puerto Ricans to be "slaves" for powerful North American business interests. He also harshly condemned the **blood tax** that sent Puerto Rican men to die in Korea, but he reserved his strongest criticism for Public Law 600. He said that the law left sovereignty over Puerto Rico in U.S. hands—after all, no matter what Puerto Ricans said or did, the Puerto Rican constitution still had to be approved by the U.S. Congress. "Why all the enthusiasm for such an illusory power. This was a law that would affirm U.S. despotism over Puerto Rico. So, we have to defy them and we have to do like the men of Lares did it, with revolution" (Acosta 1993, 175).

The Nationalists knew that, under the best of circumstances, their chances of success were quite slim. Those slim chances were reduced to almost none when they were forced to act weeks before their final preparations had been completed. On October 27, 1950, police officers stopped one of the cars used to escort and guard Albizu Campos on his travels about the island. When police discovered guns, ammunition and bombs in the car, its four occupants were immediately arrested. That left the Nationalists with only two alternatives—take the initiative weeks before they were ready or allow colonial authorities to arrest Nationalists all over the island. The Nationalists chose to act. They assaulted **La Fortaleza** in an attempt to assassinate Governor **Luis Muñoz Marín;** in Santurce, Nationalists tried to attack the military barracks; in Jayuya, **Blanca Doña Canales** and her Nationalist colleagues declared the existence of a republic; in San Juan, the police surrounded and attacked the residence of Albizu Campos; in Utuado, **Ponce** and Naranjito, the revolutionaries also made an appearance; and in Washington, Oscar Collazo and Griselio Torresola attacked Blair House, then the residence of President Harry Truman.

The insurrection failed. Within days the island's National Guard, supported by U.S. soldiers, put down all attempts to overthrow the colonial government of the United States. Historians now estimate that 140 Nationalists participated in the revolutionary outbreaks, including people from all parts of the island. Fourteen percent of the participants were either attending or had graduated from college, but close to 70 percent were *obreros* (workers), individuals who were not otherwise out of the ordinary in Puerto Rican society. Only three of the participants were women. Reaction to the violence was both immediate and strong. In general, the Puerto Rican people did not support the use of violence to achieve social change, however, the political motives of the Nationalists were well understood, and people from all political persuasions requested that, despite the insurrection, Albizu Campos be granted an unconditional amnesty.

SUGGESTED READING

Ivonne Acosta, ed., *La palabra como delito* (San Juan: Editorial, P.R. Cultural, 1993); Juan Angel Silén, *We, the Puerto Rican People: A Story of Oppression and Resistance* (New York: Monthly Review Press, 1971); Miñl Seijo Bruno, *La insurrección nacionalists en Puerto Rico—1950* (Río Piedras, P.R.: Editorial Edil, 1989); Pedro Aponte Vázquez, ed., *El ataque nacionalists a La Fortaleza* (San Juan, P.R.: Publicaciones Prené, 1993).

Nationalist Party   This Puerto Rican political party has advocated revolutionary change. It was most active from 1930 to the mid-1950s, but it still exists as a functioning political party in Puerto Rico. The Nationalist party was founded on September 17, 1922, in Río Piedras. Like so many other political developments of the period, the Nationalists were a response to the prohibition of independence by U.S. Governor **E. Montgomery Reilly**.

In its early years, the party expressed little of the revolutionary fervor with which it is associated today—that came when **Pedro Albizu Campos** assumed the party's presidency on May 11, 1930. Asked about the party's platform, Albizu replied,

Our program, our general thesis is to recreate in the Puerto Rican people the moral situation that was found in 1868, when Betances, Hostos, etc. preached the revolutionary creed. We want to express that creed in every form of resistance that one is able to use against the foreign [U.S.] colonialism. (Albizu Campos, *OBRAS* 1: 1975, 50)

Thus, whether it was the creation of a military force called the Cadets of the Republic or the sale of bonds to underwrite the proposed Republic of Puerto Rico, the aim was always the same—create the sense of mission that existed in 1868.

The party also had an economic program. It sought to organize sugar and tobacco workers and obtain for them a much greater share of the profits that then went to absentee American landowners. The Nationalists favored exclusively native industries, where they existed, and the creation of new ones where, as a result of U.S. colonialism, they had disappeared. They also demanded an end to the **coastwise shipping laws** that substantially increased the costs of Puerto Rican exports and imports.

The Nationalists also preached what Albizu called the *Concepto de la Raza*. This is translated into English as race, but he was really referring to ethnicity. He sought to create the desired sense of moral fervor by promoting in Puerto Ricans pride in the achievements of Spain, *La madre patria* (the mother country). To the Nationalists, Spain was the source of a wonderful set of discoveries that had opened the Caribbean to Spanish political, cultural and religious influences. Thus, many Nationalist meetings began with a prayer.

Many Puerto Ricans found the *Concepto de la Raza* hard to accept. They remembered the brutalities of **Ponce de León** and the terrible injustices of **slavery** and **La Libreta de Jornalero**. Nevertheless, the Nationalists continued to praise Spain and its first envoy, Christopher Columbus.

The Nationalists initiated the revolutionary insurrection of October 1950 (see **Nationalist Insurrection of 1950**) and the attack on the House of Representatives on March 1, 1954 (see **Nationalist Attack on Congress**). The party collapsed in the 1950s because of the arrest and incarceration, not only of Albizu Campos, but of the entire party leadership.

In recent years, both the Nationalists (led by Laura Meneses, an attorney and a granddaughter of Albizu Campos) and Albizu Campos have received a second, very positive, reading from Puerto Ricans of all political persuasions. One result has been a marked increase in the party's membership.

SUGGESTED READING

Pedro Albizu Campos, "The Concept of Race," in *Borinquen: An Anthology of Puerto Rican Literature*, ed. María Babín and Stan Steiner (New York: Vintage, 1981); for an understanding of the party, see Pedro Albizu Campos, *Obras escogidas*, vols. 1, 2, 3 (San Juan, P.R.: Editorial Jelofe, 1975); for the U.S. government's point of view, see U.S. Congress, House, Committee on Interior and Insular Affairs, *Nationalist Party* (Washington, D.C.: 1951); Trumbull White, *Puerto Rico and Its People* (New York: F. A. Stokes, 1938).

Naveira, Miriam (1937–   )   Justice Naveira, a lawyer and an associate justice of the Supreme Court of the Commonwealth of Puerto Rico, has become one of the most distinguished lawyers and jurists on the island of Puerto Rico. Born in Santurce, she obtained an undergraduate degree in chemistry at the College of Mt. Saint Vincent in New York City in 1956 and her law degree at the **University of Puerto Rico** in Río Piedras. In addition, she has received a master's degree in law from Columbia University (1969) and has pursued advanced studies at the University of Leyden School of Law in Holland.

During her professional life, Judge Naveira has successfully progressed through some of the most prestigious judicial positions in Puerto Rico. She has litigated in both local and federal courts, including the Circuit Court for the First District and the United States Supreme Court. In addition, she has worked for the Department of Justice in Puerto Rico. In 1966 Naveira was the first woman to be appointed assistant attorney general, and in 1973 she was the first woman to be appointed solicitor general of Puerto Rico. During the 1970s and 1980s, she worked as a law professor at the **Interamerican University** Law School. In 1985 **Rafael Hernández Colón** appointed her the first woman associate justice of the Puerto Rican Supreme Court where she continues to serve.

Judge Naveira has been awarded many honors during her successful career. In 1990 Georgetown University awarded her a Doctor of Law degree, Honoris Causa. Her undergraduate alma mater, the College of Mt. Saint Vincent, also presented her with an Honoris Causa Doctor of Law degree. She has recently been appointed to preside over a newly created commission on gender biases charged with examining sexism on Puerto Rican courts. She was married in 1961 and has two children and two granddaughters.

SUGGESTED READING

"N. J. Marquis," *Who's Who in America, 1992–1993* (New York: R. R. Bowker, 1992); "N. J. Marquis," *Who's Who in American Politics, 1993–1994* 14th ed. (New York: R. R. Bowker, 1994); "Personal Semblance," provided by her office at the Supreme Court of the Commonwealth of Puerto Rico, October 10, 1996.

Negrón Muñoz, Angela (1892–1961)   A journalist, originally from Barranquitas, Negrón Muñoz was one of the first women to have a regular column in *El Mundo*, the largest newspaper in circulation at the time. She began her journalistic career in 1917, writing under the pseudonym of Ana María Aldana. Under that pseudonym, she also wrote for the **Ponce** newspaper *El Día*. The defense of women's and children's rights was a theme that would permeate her writings throughout her life. Her work for children won accolades and numerous awards both on the island and around the world. From France she received the Medal D'Honneur du Mérit Français, and she received the journalistic award of the Puerto Rican Institute of Culture in 1944 for her article titled "The Tragedy That Lives in the Innards of San Juan." In this article, she exposed the disgraceful conditions of poor, homeless children. Her journalistic work in this area led her to establish the Society Pro-defense and Welfare of Children, an organization through whose efforts Children's Town (*El Pueblo del Niño*) was later established to provide shelter for homeless and orphaned children. Muñoz Negrón spent her lifetime writing about and working for this cause.

Muñoz Negrón also distinguished herself as one of the most activist feminists on the island. Through her newspaper column, she provided a forum to the feminist cause by announcing their news and their schedule of activities. As part of her column in the journal *Puerto Rico Illustrado*, she began to publish a series of biographies of outstanding Puerto Rican women. This collection was published in book form in 1935 as *Mujeres de Puerto Rico*, and the book continues to be an important source of information about Puerto Rican women's participation in the island's political, historical and artistic development. In the preface, describing how women as well as men had contributed to Puerto Rico's development, she states:

When I started to collect the data for this book, I never thought that at the end of this task, I would be able to say, with feminist jubilation: there has been not one meritorious endeavor in Puerto Rico where women have not collaborated, in many cases as principles, as fortuitous initiators or as successful founders. (Negrón Muñoz 1935, 7)

She was the daughter of distinguished poet Quintín Negrón Sanjurjo and niece of **Luis Muñoz Rivera**, and the sister of **Mercedes Negrón Muñoz**, who distinguished herself in the genre of poetry. Angela Negrón Muñoz left a legacy of writings and institutions that are still serving the people of the island today.

SUGGESTED READING

Angela Negrón Muñoz, *Mujeres de Puerto Rico* (San Juan, P.R.: Imprenta Venezolana, 1935); "En Ponce, Angela Negrón Muñoz muere a los 64 años," *El Mundo*, July, 15, 1961, 2; Josefina Rivera de Alvarez, *Diccionario de literatura puertorriqueña* (Rio Piedras, P.R.: Ediciones la Torre, UPR, 1955).

Negrón Muñoz, Mercedes (pseudonym: Clara Lair) (1895–1973)   Originally from Barranquitas, Negrón Muñoz, a member of a family of writers, was the niece of **Luis Muñoz Rivera** and sister to Angela Negrón Muñoz. Educated as a librarian at the **University of Puerto Rico**, she made writing her profession. All of her literary work was written under the pseudonym Clara Lair.

She is a contemporary of **Julia de Burgos** and **Amelia Ceide**, who also were known for outstanding lyricism. Like Burgos, nature and love—as well as the pain they can cause—play important roles in much of her poetry.

In her review on Puerto Rican poets, **María Teresa Babín** described Clara Lair as a poet "full of passion, one who writes about love without vacillating and with a desperate dignity, full of anguish, bitterness and intimate torture" (Babín 1958, 397). The descriptions of love in her poetry portray great love affairs that end tragically; the woman is left alone, hurt and nostalgic. Some of her descriptions of love are daring and graphic, at times, even sensuous. She is considered an excellent exponent of the femme fatale both in her work and in her life. In the literary world of those times, Clara Lair was one of the few writers who dealt with taboo subjects. "Arras de cristal" (1937) and "Trópico amargo" (1950) are examples of her poetry that capture her lyrical description of love. At the time of their publication, both these works received awards for excellence from the Puerto Rico Institute of Culture.

SUGGESTED READING

Sandra María Esteves, "The Feminist Viewpoint in the Poetry of Puerto Rican Women in the United States," in *Images and Identities: The Puerto Rican in Two World Contexts*, Asela Rodríguez de Laguna, ed. (New Brunswick, N.J.: Transaction Books, 1987); Yamila Azize Vargas and Sonia Crespo Vega, "A Commentary on the Works of Three Puerto Rican Women Poets in New York," in *Breaking Boundaries: Latina Writing and Critical Readings*, Asunción Horno-Delgado et al., eds. (Amherst: University of Massachusetts Press, 1989); *Panorama de la cultura puertorriqueña* (New York: Las Americas Publishing, 1958).

New Progressive Party (Partido Nuevo Progresista) Officially established on August 20, 1967, the New Progressive party's "Declaration of Principles" states that

it recognizes as a permanent union (with the United States) only that legal relationship granted by the U.S. Constitution to each of the sovereign states of the Northamerican Union; and it advocates Statehood as the only solution for the political inferiority to which we (the Puerto Rican people) have been submitted for a space of five centuries.

The party principles specifically indicate that statehood is the only means to ensure U.S. citizenship permanently and that the party supports all legitimate means for the "decolonization of Puerto Rico." Closely following the position of one of its foremost leaders, **Carlos Romero Barcelo**, the party seeks to promote Puerto Rican culture, united to the Spanish language as the primary public and private vernacular of Puerto Rico. As Romero Barcelo noted in *Statehood Is for the Poor*, "Our language and our culture are not negotiable" because "we are, above all else, a *people*, which is to say that we possess a culture—or way of life—which, though similar in certain ways to those of some other societies, is nevertheless uniquely our own" (Romero Barcelo 1978, 9). Although officially created in 1967, the roots of the party date back to a conflict over participation in the **plebiscite** signed into law on December 23, 1966. This plebiscite offered a choice of commonwealth, statehood or independence; but, because the U.S. Congress refused to agree to accept the will of the Puerto Rican people as expressed in the plebiscite, many advocates of statehood argued that they should boycott the plebiscite. The controversy produced so much political heat that, on January 22, 1967, statehood advocates met in the Hotel San Geronimo (now the Condado Plaza) to discuss the appropriate course of action. Many spoke in favor of or against participation, but, finally, **Luis Ferré** gave an ultimatum—he would resign his position in the group unless they agreed to participate in the plebiscite. When the assembly then was asked if they were in favor of Ferré's suggestions, shouts of "no" came from the audience. The chair took this as a vote, closed the proceedings and Luis Ferré and a number of his colleagues left the hall. They participated in the plebiscite and were buoyed by the results—statehood won 39 percent of the votes.

Thus, in a move with deliberate symbolism of the famous "tennis court oath" of the French revolution, the statehood advocates formally declared their existence on August 20, 1967, at the Manuel Carrasquillo Herpen tennis court in a country club in Carolina, Puerto Rico. In 1968 the New Progressive party elected Luis Ferré as the first statehood governor of Puerto Rico. A bitter spilt among the advocates of commonwealth was a major reason for Ferré's election, but the party nevertheless achieved a status it still enjoys—one of the two principal political parties supported by the Puerto Rican people.

When Luis Ferré lost his bid for reelection in 1972, Carlos Romero Barcelo became president of the party. Under his direction, the party has emphasized economic themes. Romero Barcelo argued that

regardless of where you look, the bitter truth is that Puerto Rico is even poorer than the very poorest of the fifty United States: Mississippi. And it is precisely because of this agonizing fact that I keep saying that no true Puerto Rican can stand idly by and tolerate a situation of that kind. (Romero Barcelo 1978, 36)

Thus, Puerto Rico needed to achieve statehood because

the per capita benefits we'd reap from federal aid programs would be greater than any other state in the Union. On top of this, we'd also have seven or eight Puerto Ricans serving as full voting members of Congress, working up in Washington at all times to help draft and pass new and improved social welfare legislation. (Romero Barcelo 1978, 87)

This message—Statehood Is for the Poor—caught on. Romero Barcelo won the governorship by nearly 50,000 votes in 1976 but (after **Cerro Maravilla**) by only 3,000 votes in 1980. When he was challenged for the party's nomination in 1984 by Dr. Hernán Padilla, the party split, and Padilla helped organize another political entity.

In 1992 **Pedro Rosselló González** won the governorship under the banner of the New Progressive party; meanwhile, Carlos Romero Barcelo won election as **Resident Commissioner**. Although the two men have had a number of public disagreements, they are nevertheless united in their drive to achieve statehood as soon as possible. The most recent initiative promises a plebiscite for 1998, but Congress has not yet said that it would abide by the expressed will of the Puerto Rican people. Arguably the biggest obstacle to statehood is the point raised by Resident Commissioner Romero Barcelo: With its 3.5 million people, Puerto Rico would be entitled to at least six representatives in the U.S. House of Representatives. That alone would immediately make the island the twenty-eighth most powerful state in the union. Wyoming, Montana, Vermont, New Hampshire, West Virginia, Rhode Island and Delaware, along with many other states, would have to accept less power in order for Puerto Rico to enter the union. Indeed, some skeptics note that, if you include the 2.5 million Puerto Ricans who live in the United States—and the three existing representatives justified by this population—the island would be too powerful a political force for many sister states to countenance.

Meanwhile, the New Progressive party continues its efforts, united by the sentiments expressed by New Progressive party leader Senator Oreste Ramos:

The people of Puerto Rico presently express to the Government and people of the United States and to the international community, their profound dissatisfaction with the actual state of their relations and they request that all concerned united [*sic*] to begin the immediate decolonization of Puerto Rico. (Gamaliel Ramos 1987, 153)

SUGGESTED READING

Aarón Gamaliel Ramos, *Las ideas anexionistas en Puerto Rico bajo la dominación norteamericana* (San Juan, P.R.: Huracán, 1987); Edgardo Melendez, *Puerto Rico's Statehood Movement* (Westport, Conn.: Greenwood Press, 1988); Partido Nuevo Progresista, *Desarrrollo del Partido Nuevo Progresista* (San Juan, P.R.: n.p., 1996); Carlos Romero Barcelo, *Statehood Is for the Poor* (San Juan, P.R.: n.p., 1978).

Nieves Falcón, Luis (1929–)   Born in Bayamón on December 29, 1929, Nieves Falcón received a B.A. from the **University of Puerto Rico**, a master's degree from New York University and a Ph.D. in sociology from the London School of Economics. Nieves Falcón is one of Puerto Rico's most distinguished educators. He began teaching at the University of Puerto Rico in 1956 and was instrumental in creating two of its best research organizations—the Center for Social Research and the Institute for Caribbean Studies. Nieves Falcón directed each of these organizations for many years and was also director of the Curriculum Division of Puerto Rico's Department of Public Instruction from 1963 to 1967.

Nieves retired from the University of Puerto Rico in 1990 in order to devote all of his time to efforts directed toward freeing Puerto Rican **political prisoners**. At his own expense, he has visited prisoners at facilities in California, Oklahoma, Illinois, Wisconsin and Pennsylvania.

SUGGESTED READING

Luis Nieves Falcón, *Diagnóstico de Puerto Rico* (Rio Piedras, P.R.: Editorial Edil, 1970); Luis Nieves Falcón, *Puerto Rico, grito y mordaza* (San Juan, P.R.: n.p., 1981); Luis Nieves Falcón, *Fabián: Historia de un niño campesiño pueretorriqueño* (San Juan: Ediciones Libreria Internacional).

Nuyorican   This word, sometimes spelled *Neorican*, is a word full of double meanings, normally accompanied by doses of pain, longing and alienation.

On the island, a Puerto Rican who was born in the United States and then comes to live in Puerto Rico is a *Nuyorican*. Generally, the word is used in a derogatory sense. The *Nuyorican* is nothing like a real Puerto Rican who, if only because he or she was born on the island, claims a level of authenticity the *Nuyorican* can never enjoy. It is common to hear negative comments about the newcomer's use of Spanish and even his or her "strange" accent.

In the United States, the term *Nuyorican* evokes a never-finished adaptation to mainland beliefs, values and practices. The *Nuyorican* often experiences a profound sense of alienation especially if he or she migrated to New York or Chicago after growing up in Puerto Rico. It could be the racism that so troubled Piri Thomas in his autobiographical *Down These Mean Streets* (1967) or Martín Espada in *Trumpets from the Islands of Their Eviction* (1994).

One reaction to the trumpets is to idealize them, to live with a profound longing for the islands of eviction. However, for the 2.5 million Puerto Ricans living in the United States, a more typical reaction is "branching out, the selective connection to and interaction with the surrounding North American society" (Flores 1993, 101). *Techo* (the Spanish word for roof) becomes *roofo*, and, instead of a bastardization of standard English, it is a creative manifestation of something new and different—the world of the *Nuyorican* in which, "rather than being subsumed and repressed, Puerto Rican culture contributes, on its own terms and as an extension of its own traditions, to a new amalgam of human experience" (101).

SUGGESTED READING

Martín Espada, *Trumpets from the Islands of Their Eviction* (Tempe, Ariz.: Bilingual Press, 1994); Martin Espada, *Imagine the Angels of Bread* (New York: Norton, 1996); Juan Flores, *Divided Borders: Essays on Puerto Rican Identity* (Houston: Arte Público, 1993); Piri Thomas, *Down These Mean Streets* (New York: Doubleday, 1967).

O

Ojeda Ríos, Filiberto (1933–) A Puerto Rican revolutionary, a founder of the revolutionary group **Los macheteros**, and a legend (famous to some infamous to others) in contemporary Puerto Rican society, Ojeda Ríos was born in Naguabo. As of August 1996, he was living clandestinely somewhere in Puerto Rico.

As a child, Ojeda Ríos spent time in New York City, where he won a school contest for best class essay; his was on the **Three Kings** (*Los Tres Reyes*). He returned to Puerto Rico in the late 1940s and quickly combined a career in revolutionary politics with a career in music (Ojeda played trumpet in some of the best Caribbean bands). A Communist with a high regard for the achievements of Fidel Castro, Ojeda is first and foremost a Puerto Rican nationalist, committed, like **Pedro Albizu Campos**, to the overthrow of the U.S. colonial regime.

In 1989 Ojeda stood center stage as the key defendant in one of the most celebrated court cases in recent Puerto Rican history. When the FBI tried to arrest him on August 30, 1985, for his alleged involvement in a Wells Fargo robbery of $7.1 million in West Hartford, Connecticut, in September 1983, Ojeda used a machine gun and a pistol to prevent the FBI from entering his apartment. He was tried on these charges in 1989 and, to the amazement of many, he was found not guilty even though he never denied using force to resist the FBI. In his closing arguments to the jury (Ojeda acted as his own attorney), Ojeda called the FBI everything from oppressors to assassins, from terrorists to members of a *foreign army*. Nevertheless, the twelve jurors found a man praising Fidel Castro in a federal court not guilty of using the violence he said he used. It was an outcome that brings to mind an old Puerto Rican adage: Give somebody three drinks and he becomes an *independentista*. Although no one knows what the verdict actually indicated, a jury of his Puerto Rican peers accepted that Filiberto Ojeda was a patriot, a man who used violence to defend his wife and himself from an invading colonial army.

SUGGESTED READING

Ronald Fernandez, *Prisoners of Colonialism: The Struggle for Justice in Puerto Rico* (Monroe, Me.: Common Courage, 1994); Juan Manuel García Passalacqua, "El juicio de la historia," *El Nuevo Día*, September 12, 1988, 132; Filiberto Ojeda Ríos, *Statement to the Court* (San Juan: Movimiento de Liberación Nacional Puertorriqueño, 1990).

Oller, Francisco (1833–1917)   Oller was one of the most significant Puerto Rican artists of the nineteenth century. He was born in Bayamón. Oller, who exhibited great abilities to paint in his childhood, was exposed to and trained by some of the best European painters of his time.

In Spain, he studied under the tutelage of noted painter Federico de Madrazo. Then, he moved to France, where he came in contact with some of the realist painters such as Gustave Courbet and Edouard Manet. He was also exposed to the works and techniques of impressionist painters like Camille Pissarro and Paul Cézanne (Riutort 1994, 146).

Oller's sharp eye and sophisticated style made him a pioneer in the plastic arts on the island. He gave contemporary audiences the opportunity to view the qualities of Puerto Rico's landscapes. The artist vividly revealed a myriad of customs, traditions and folklore of Puerto Rico at that time. One of his most important works is, without doubt, *El Velorio*. Completed in 1893, this realistic painting portrays the ceremonial wake traditionally held for infants who died in the island. The picture is in a permanent exhibit at the Art and History Museum at the **University of Puerto Rico.**

Oller painted scores of other pictures, such as *Mesa de rico, Mesa de pobre, Una chula*, and *El maestro Rafael*. His painting *El estudiante* is exhibited at the Louvre Museum in Paris. Oller received many awards during his lifetime. His most important distinction was being appointed chamber painter for King Amadeus I of Spain.

SUGGESTED READING

Ponce Art Museum, *Colección de Arte Latinoamericano* (Ponce, Museo de Arte de Ponce, n.d.); Ana Ruitort, *Historia breve del arte puertorriqueño* (Madrid: Editorial Playor, 1994); Edward J. Sullivan, "Paris/San Juan: Francisco Oller," *Arts Magazine* 58 (1984): 120–124.

Olmstead Act   This law, passed by the U.S. Congress in 1910, stipulated that if the Puerto Rican House of Delegates did not pass a government

Francisco Oller, "Hacienda Aurora." (Museo de Arte de Ponce, The Luis A. Ferré Foundation, Inc., Ponce, Puerto Rico.)

Francisco Oller, "El Velorio" ("The Wake"), 1893. (Museo de la Universidad de Puerto Rico.)

budget in any particular calendar year, the island's government would receive the amount of money allocated in the preceding year.

By 1909 the Puerto Rican House of Delegates had, from their point of view, exhausted every conceivable option for school and political change. Neither public complaints to Congress, nor pleas to the president had had any effect. The House of Delegates contended that it remained as powerless in 1909 as it had been in 1900. Therefore, in 1909, the House of Delegates deliberately created a government crisis. They refused to pass a budget; their hope was to draw attention to the island's colonial status. Instead the Olmstead Act was passed, which stipulated that, in the event the Puerto Rican House of Delegates refused to pass any particular budget, the figure from the previous year would be used.

The debate that preceded the bill's enactment was hard for any Puerto Rican to hear. Representative James Slayden called the islanders a bunch of "mongrels"; Representative Atterson Rucker said that "the country ones are naked until they reach the age of 10 or 12 years"; and Representative Michael Kennedy summed up the attitudes of many when he said that "the great mistake we made was in assuming that the Porto Ricans [*sic*] had any capacity for self government whatever" (*Congressional Record* 1909, 2923).

These debates had a significant ripple effect on the island. Indeed, when the dominant **Union party** removed statehood from its list of status alternatives in 1913, one of the reasons for the change was the congressional reaction that had produced the Olmstead Act.

SUGGESTED READING

Congressional Record, House, 61st Cong., 1st sess., June 7, 1909; Robert Hunter, *Historical Survey of the Puerto Rico Status Question*, Status of Puerto Rico, Selected Background Papers Prepared for the United States–Puerto Rico Commission on the Status of Puerto Rico (Washington, D.C.: U.S. Government Printing Office, 1966).

Operación Manos de Obra   *See* Operation Bootstrap.

Operation Bootstrap (Operación Manos de Obra)   This catchall phrase for the industrial development of Puerto Rico pertains to the period from 1945 to 1964. Led by **Luis Muñoz Marín** and **Teodoro Moscoso**, the effort to transform the economy began during World War II but accelerated after the end of the war. For example, between 1952 and 1961, literally hundreds of firms flocked to the island, investing nearly half a billion dollars of their own money. By 1957 the United States boasted that Puerto Rico was the Showcase of the Caribbean, a model of how free enterprise capitalism could transform a nation once thoroughly rooted in agriculture. However, despite the emigration of 25 percent of the Puerto Rican people

between 1947 and 1960, unemployment actually increased during the heyday of Operation Bootstrap: 11.2 percent in 1948, 12.9 percent in 1958,
and 12.8 percent in 1963.

Scholars explain the apparent contradiction—high rates of economic
growth linked to continuing high levels of unemployment—by noting that
businesses came to Puerto Rico because they were lured by the prospect of
no local and no federal taxes. Profits skyrocketed in Puerto Rico, but the
law mandated that a firm could bring its profits to the United States, tax
free, only when it liquidated the corporation. Thus, as early as 1950, ac-
countants representing the island government told businesses about this
loophole: The corporate activities of the subsidiary should be carefully
conducted with a view to liquidation rather than continuation of operations. In practice, many firms left as soon as they had exhausted their local
and federal tax benefits. By 1960 to 1965, many new firms only replaced
those that had liquidated; meanwhile, the island government never received
the tax revenue required for everything from education to roads.

Another major problem was what island planners called the "fishing net
approach" to industrialization. They took whatever the nets gathered. Critics argue that no one devoted enough attention to a strategic analysis of
the possible contribution of the new firms to the creation of a self-sustaining
Puerto Rican economy; equally important, many of the industrial investors
lured to the island had no interest in Puerto Rico's long-term development.
A study conducted by Harvard University (Barton 1959) stressed that businesses came to the island "to make a killing." They stayed if they found
gold; they left if they did not.

Also significant was the island's political status. From 1947 to today,
U.S. unions have loudly complained if businesses that went to Puerto Rico
equaled fewer jobs on the mainland. Thus, the island's economic development administration agreed to take the crumbs that fell off the U.S. table.
Even when an industry with great potential came to the island, for example,
petroleum in the 1960s, oil companies on the mainland demanded restrictions be placed on Puerto Rican production. Thus, the island had to contend with powerful U.S. lobbies committed to limiting severely whatever
petroleum success Puerto Rico enjoyed.

In 1975 **Resident Commissioner** Jaime Benítez complained to Congress
that "Puerto Rico is essentially a trading post where we import what we
consume and export what we produce." Two years later, Senator Frank
Church of Idaho echoed Benítez when he offered this succinct, albeit tragic,
assessment of Puerto Rico's economic development: "Anyone who can accept the proposition that the investment of the big multinational companies
is a boon to the host countries, who does not thoroughly look at Puerto
Rico, is not serious" (Fernandez 1994, 365). After nearly thirty years of
industrialization by invitation, the 1973 oil crisis had helped pushed official
unemployment to nearly 20 percent of the workforce.

One final point: Operation Bootstrap did help create one of the best educated labor forces in Latin America. No one doubts that, like the people of Singapore, Puerto Ricans have the intelligence, experience and skill required to transform the economy. Those seeking new routes to economic development argue that what the island lacks is power, as well as a comprehensive strategy for attaining self-sustaining economic growth.

SUGGESTED READING

H. C. Barton, *Puerto Rico's Industrial Development Program, 1942–1960* (Cambridge, Mass.: Harvard University, 1959); Ronald Fernandez, *Cruising the Caribbean: U.S. Influence and Intervention in the 20th Century* (Monroe, Me.: Common Courage, 1994); Emilio Pantojas Garcia, *Development Strategies as Ideology: Puerto Rico's Export-Led Industrialization Experience* (Boulder, Colo.: Lynne Riener Publishers, 1990); David F. Ross, *A Historical Study of Puerto Rico's Program of Economic Development* (San Juan, P.R.: Editorial Edil, 1969); U.S. Congress, Senate, *Tax Treatment of U.S. Concerns with Puerto Rican Affiliates*, 88th Cong., 2d sess., 1964; "Puerto Rico's Program of Industrial Tax Exemption," *George Washington Law Review* 18, no. 4 (June 1950): 443–73.

O'Reilly, Alejandro de (1715?–1780?)   This envoy of the Spanish crown devised economic plans that changed Puerto Rico's economy in the late eighteenth century. Under Spanish rule, Puerto Rico was a neglected part of the empire. It served as a military bastion and received little economic assistance or encouragement. As late as 1765, the island's population totaled only 44,000 people. The English consistently inflicted damage on Spanish traders, and the Puerto Rican economy relied on a significant amount of contraband. Because islanders openly bartered with a variety of "forbidden" (by the Spanish) traders, the mother country eventually sent an emissary to investigate conditions in its Puerto Rican colony.

The emissary was Alejandro de O'Reilly. After sailing on a frigate called *The Eagle*, he arrived in Puerto Rico on April 8, 1765. In his report to the Spanish Crown—*La memoría*—O'Reilly described a colony that contained only two schools and a population that calculated age by the visits of a bishop or a change in government. However, where contraband undermined the economy of other Caribbean colonies, in Puerto Rico it seemed to be the only means of economic progress. O'Reilly suggested that the crown dramatically change its policies toward Puerto Rico: expropriate land that was uncultivated and give it to the people willing to use it, stimulate immigration and, above all, resurrect the dormant sugar industry. Although O'Reilly also offered a number of important suggestions in relation to the island's fortifications, he is best remembered as the catalyst who brought about significant changes in the island's development; for example, by 1799 the population had almost quadrupled, to more than 150,000 inhabitants.

SUGGESTED READING

Loida Figueroa Mercado, *History of Puerto Rico* (New York: Anaya Books, 1974); Fernando Picó, *Historia general de Puerto Rico* (San Juan, P.R.: Ediciones Huracán, 1988).

Ortiz del Rivero, Ramón (1909–1956)   This comedian, actor, composer and scriptwriter was best known as Diplo. He was an extremely popular comedian in Puerto Rico. He helped to define an era during the early history of radio, television and film in the island. Born in Naguabo, he graduated from Central High School in Santurce. With an eclectic background, he tried many different careers such as studying law, playing professional basketball and even teaching physical education before settling in the arts (Sarramía 1993, 158).

The importance of Diplo in Puerto Rican art lies in the fact that through his many roles he pioneered the genres of situational and stand-up comedy. Diplo became a central figure in the artistic landscape of Puerto Rico. His versatility as an actor was proven by his ability to transition across multiple platforms and media such as theater, radio, television and film. He was one of the first comedians to appear in Puerto Rican radio by participating in programs such as "Los embajadores del buen humor" and "La tremenda corte radio program." He achieved his greatest popularity through his television role in "La taberna India." Diplo acted with Miriam Colón in the famous film *Los peloteros* produced by **Jack Delano** for the **Community Education Division** of the Department of Education. He was also a music composer. He is best remembered by his development of Chico Mambí, a minstrel character.

SUGGESTED READING

Ramón Ortiz del Rivero, *¿Porqúe se rié la gente?* (San Juan: Biblioteca de Autores Puertorriqueños, 1980); Tomás Sarramía, *Nuestra gente* (San Juan: Publicaciones Puertorriqueñas, 1993).

Osuna, Juan José (1884–1950)   Born in Caguas, Osuna became a pioneer in the field of education in Puerto Rico during the first part of the twentieth century. He received a teaching certificate from Bloomsburg State College in Pennsylvania, a divinity degree from Princeton University and master's and doctoral degrees from Columbia University. Osuna had a distinguished career in education having worked as a teacher in the public school system in Mayagüez and the Polytechnic Institute in San Germán.

Dr. Osuna made lasting contributions to education and pedagogy from his position as director of the Department of Education at the **University of Puerto Rico** at Río Piedras. Osuna, although trained in the United States, was a severe critic of the methods used to educate children in the public school system in Puerto Rico. Since 1898, American cultural concepts and the English language had been at the center of the educational philosophy stressed in the public schools. He worked hard to foster values and ideas relevant to the culture of the island and move away from the emphasis on the United States and their imposed values. Supported by the Teachers' Association, he launched a vigorous campaign against the plans of Commissioner of Education Juan B. Huyke to further Americanize Puerto Rican children undergoing their public education (Negrón de Montilla 1977).

Although Osuna favored statehood status for the island, he was a leading proponent of developing a cultural objective that would guide the school system (Negrón de Montilla 1977). His vision was to stress and bring knowledge about Puerto Rican civilization, history, ideas and language into the educational curriculum. His book, *A History of Education in Puerto Rico* (1949), is considered to be one of the most important chronicles of education in Puerto Rico since the Spanish regime gave way to the American one.

SUGGESTED READING

Aida Negrón de Montilla, *La Americanización en Puerto Rico y el sistema de instrucción pública: 1900/1930* (Río Piedras: Editorial Edil, 1977); Juan José Osuna, *A History of Education in Puerto Rico* (Río Piedras: Editorial de la Universidad de Puerto Rico, 1949).

Otero, Ana (1861–1905)   Puerto Rico's first internationally acclaimed concert pianist was born in Humacao, where from an early age and under the tutelage of her father, a well-known piano teacher, she began to develop a talent that would take her all over the world, to the largest, most famous concert halls.

All the articles written about Ana Otero point to her self-confidence, tenacity and determination. Throughout her youth, she dreamed of going abroad to study at a conservatory of music. However, economically, this goal was out of reach. In 1886 she began an island-wide tour performing in all the major towns—**Ponce**, Mayagüez, San Germán and Yauco, among others—a feat not at all common for a woman during the nineteenth century. Her concerts were very well received not only by the people, but also by the critics. She was hailed for her technical ability and precision and as well as for the ease with which she interpreted difficult scores.

By July 1887, she was in Barcelona participating in a festival of that city's Society of Writers and Artists. Her interpretation of Pujols's *Faust* was described as "virtuoso" by the critics, including Pujols himself who was in the audience. The following month she was in Paris to participate in a contest of 224 musicians; the best eight pianists were to be awarded admission to the Paris Conservatory of Music. Her outstanding performance helped her realize her dream when she was accepted to the conservatory. Under the tutelage of renowned piano masters Fissot and Todou,

Otero completed her first year of training successfully, but she found herself unable to offset the expenses for the coming year at the conservatory. When she learned of the gifted pianist's hardship, feminist leader **Ana Roqué de Duprey**, with the support of some friends, launched a literary magazine, *Euterpe*, and with the profits, sponsored Otero's musical studies. Otero was thus able to continue at the conservatory. In 1888 one of her mentors, the well-known French pianist Marmontel, praised her work and encouraged her to engage in a concert tour of Europe's major cities and promised to write the first concert program of the tour. Puerto Rico began to hear of Otero's successful tour through articles printed in the Paris newspapers *L'Echo* and *Le Figaro*.

After her European tour, she returned to Puerto Rico and once more gave a series of concerts in the cities she had performed in earlier. Then she departed for tours in the rest of Latin America and the Caribbean as well as New York City where she remained for some time. Although it is known that Otero lived and performed in New York for a number of years, the precise dates are not known. Due to failing health, however, she returned to Puerto Rico in the early 1900s, by this time a world-renowned pianist who was fluent in French, English and Italian. She founded the Academy Ana Otero and began to mentor and train other promising pianists. On April 4, 1905, at the age of forty-three, she died. Accounts of those days state that her death was caused by a combination of her longstanding health problems and excessive work, which took a toll on her energy. Described by the Latin American poet Rubén Darío as "the artist of America," she holds a place of honor at the Puerto Rican Athenaeum and in Puerto Rico's history.

SUGGESTED READING

María Luisa de Angelis, *Mujeres puertorriqueñas que se han distinguido en el cultivo de las ciencias, letras y las artes desde el siglo XVIII hasta nuestros días* (San Juan, P.R.: Topografías de Boletín Mercantil, 1908); Angela Negrón Muñoz, *Mujeres de Puerto Rico* (San Juan, P.R.: Imprenta Venezolana, 1935).

P

Pagán, Genara (?–1963)   Until 1979, the name Genara Pagán was missing from all the history books. She was, however, the first Puerto Rican woman to challenge legally the system that denied women the right to vote.

Pagán, a tobacco worker and an active member of the Tobacco Union of Puerta de Tierra (itself an affiliate of the Free Federation of Labor, or La federación libre de trabajadores), was a founding member and leader of the federation's Women's Organization Committee. In 1920, at the Tenth Congress of the Free Federation of Labor, and as a representative of the Women's Committee, she presented a motion that included instituting a minimum salary for women.

In 1920, recognizing the need for feminist consciousness raising among the rank and file as well as the necessity for helping women develop the activism and skills that would be needed in order to obtain universal voting and human rights, Pagán helped found the Popular Feminine Association.

That same year, passage of the Nineteenth Amendment to the U.S. Constitution established the right of American women to vote. The question for Puerto Rican feminists was whether this law would be applicable to Puerto Rico. The test case was presented by Genara Pagán. When she was denied the right to register to vote, Pagán took the unprecedented step of challenging the system. She launched a legal case against the Joint Board of Elections of San Juan that challenged the constitutionality of denying women the right to vote. Shortly thereafter, the U.S. Bureau of Internal Affairs ruled that the Nineteenth Amendment did not apply to Puerto Rico. The importance of this decision, according to feminist scholar Yamila Azize, was that it very clearly illustrated the powerlessness of Puerto Rico under colonial status and signaled to the feminist movement the need to rethink their strategies in their struggle for the right to vote.

As early as 1914, Pagán had been active in the labor movement, particularly in the union that represented tobacco workers. However, Pagán's feminist and labor activism was not limited to Puerto Rico. As early as 1917, when she lived in New York City, she became active in the union activities of New York's garment district. The feminist struggles occurring in the United States at the time, particularly the suffragist movement, influenced and later sustained her commitment to the Puerto Rican feminist cause. That is why, right after the American suffragettes obtained the right to vote, Pagán returned to Puerto Rico in 1920.

SUGGESTED READING

Edna Acosta-Belen, *The Puerto Rican Woman: Perspectives on Culture, History, and Society* (New York: Praeger, 1986); Yamila Azize, *La mujer en la lucha* (San Juan, P.R.: Editorial Cultural, 1985).

Palés Matos, Luis (1898–1959)   Palés Matos was born in Guayama, a town in the southeastern corner of Puerto Rico. He was a groundbreaking poet and his work represents some of the best modernist poetry in Puerto Rico during the first part of the twentieth century. The work of Palés has extraordinary importance not only on the island but also in the Caribbean and Latin America where it defined literary trends. Palés's biggest contribution to poetry was in the area of African-Antillean, or black, poetry (*poesía negroide*). Although his poetry is diverse, his Afro-Antillean verses define the literary movement known as *negrismo*. In fact, many critics and scholars have credited him, along with Nicolás Guillén from Cuba, with being the creators of this genre (González-Pérez 1989, 821).

Palés's poetry reflects on the characteristics, lives, experiences and heritage of black Puerto Ricans (see **African Roots**). He used poetry to exalt the beauty of African culture and black people in the Caribbean. Moreover, it brought the many ethnic and cultural traits that characterized these people to the forefront of the public mind. As a native of Guayama, a town with a large population of African descent, Palés had a wealth of observations and experiences that he could use to generate his poetry. He also had a rich literary and poetic production outside the Afro-Antillean canon.

Pales's literary technique was rich and complex. He developed a unique onomatopeic style, known as *diepalismo*. His poems imitate the sounds of people, animals and the environment. His verses, filled with short syllables resembling sounds, were structured with a highly rhythmic style that duplicates the essence of the Afro-Antillean beat. Many of his poems have a distinct comedic and satiric tone that gives a platform for the voices of the African element present in Puerto Rican society. While his poetry was not political in nature, it made clear the racial divide between Puerto Ricans who identified themselves with their Hispanic heritage versus those who preferred their African roots. According to critic Anibal González-Pérez, Palés saw "Hispano-Caribbean culture as the product of the fusion of the Spanish and African cultures on Caribbean soil" (1989, 823).

Palés wrote three books of poetry during his lifetime. They were *Azaleas* (1915), *Tuntún de pasa y grifería* (1937) and *Poesía 1915–1956* (1957). He also left multiple unpublished manuscripts of poetry. He wrote the novel *Litoral: Reseña de una vida inútil* (1949). His complete works have been published in a collection known as *Poesía completa y prosa selecta* (1978).

SUGGESTED READING

Jeanette Bercovici Coin, *Social Aspects of Black Poetry in Luis Palés Matos, Nicolás Guillén y Manuel del Cabral* (Ann Arbor, Mich.: University Microfilms International, 1976); Arcadio Díaz Quiñones, "Luis Palés Matos en la Biblioteca Ayacucho," *Revista Sin Nombre* 10, no. 2 (1979); Luis F. González-Cruz, "Nature and Black Reality in Three Caribbean Poets: A New Look at the Concept of Negritude," *Perspectives in Contemporary Literature* 5 (1979); Anibal González Pérez, "Luis Palés Matos" in Carlos A. Solé, ed. *Latin American Writers* (New York: Scribners, 1989); Luis Palés Matos, *Tun tun de pasa y griferia: poemas afroantillanos* (San Juan: Biblioteca de Autores Puertorriqueños, 1937); Lucy Torres, *The Black Poetry of Luis Palés Matos and Its Sources* (Ann Arbor, Mich.: University Microfilms International, 1970).

Paoli, Antonio (1871–1946)   Antonio Paoli was a famous opera singer and dramatic tenor of the late nineteenth and early twentieth centuries. Paoli was born in **Ponce** to a Corsican father and to a Venezuelan mother. He received his primary education in Ponce. As a young boy, his family recognized that he had musical talents and sent him to Spain so that he could enhance his music training and broaden his education. In Spain, Queen María Cristina de Habsburgo awarded Paoli scholarships to study music at the Royal Academy of El Escorial and specialized studies at La Scala in Milan, Italy. He also pursued military studies at the Toledo Military Academy and served on behalf of Spain in the War of Independence in Cuba.

Paoli was the first Puerto Rican to develop a brilliant career as an opera singer in Europe. His music and performances entertained many members of the European royalty and he became known as *el tenor de los reyes y el rey de los tenores* (The tenor of the kings and the king of tenors). His voice and dramatic performances were judged to be of superior quality. Giuseppe Verdi, whose *Otello* Paoli represented more than five hundred times, said that Paoli was the best and most humane interpreter of the role (Fundación Santillana and Universidad Interamericana 1994, 1).

Paoli's artistic representations were vast. During his lifetime, he gave thousands of performances. Among them were Paoli's debut in Valencia, Spain, in Gaetano Donizettis Lucia de Lamermoor in 1897 and his debut at the Great Opera in Theater in Paris in 1899. After that, Paoli toured the world and performed at the most prestigious theaters, such as Teatro Colón in Buenos Aires, Covent Garden in London, Rome's Opera, and the Metropolitan Opera House in New York, among others. Paoli returned briefly to Puerto Rico in 1901 and gave many recitals that were highly acclaimed and received. When he returned to the island in 1922, however, he was ostracized and ignored in his native Ponce. Paoli was accused of denying his Puerto Rican ethnicity while he was abroad. The tenor had to defend himself against this allegation for the rest of his life. He attributed this claim to the fact that he had retained his Spanish citizenship when Puerto Rico was transferred to the United States in 1898 because he could not relate to the Americans, but to the Spaniards who had sponsored his career (López 1994; Murray Irizzary 1994).

Paoli's legacy to Puerto Rican history is perhaps not well understood in Puerto Rico today. Although he worked hard to develop a music academy and a conservatory on the island, his contributions to the culture are not widely known. His native city has rendered tribute to this artist by recognizing *Casa Paoli*, located at Mayor Street, as a historic place dedicated to the study and preservation of his legacy. *Casa Paoli* also serves as the headquarters for the Puerto Rican Center for folkloric and historic research.

SUGGESTED READING

Jesús M. López, *Antonio Paoli (1871:1946): El hombre . . . el artista* (Ponce, Casa Paoli, 1994); Néstor Murray Irizarry, *Puerto Rico, Antonio Paoli y España: Aclaraciones Críticas* (Ponce: Fundación Santillana, 1994); Fundación Santillana and Universidad Interamericana de Puerto Rico, *España en Puerto Rico: Exposición Cien Años de Convivencia* (Ponce: Fundación Santillana, 1994); H. Wiley and Stanley Sadie, eds., *New Grove Dictionary of American Music* (London: Macmillian, 1986).

Parque de Bombas   One of the most well-known buildings in Puerto Rico, the "firehouse" in **Ponce**, is an architectural delight. Victorian catches its eccentric spirit, but the octagonal towers (perfect for spotting fires) call to mind a castle, and the red and black stripes remind some tourists of a circus. The building, constructed in 1882, has a distinct charm, which is enhanced by its location in the Plaza de Ponce. Surrounding the firehouse are some of the finest examples of stone buildings in the Caribbean. Because so many are painted in the vibrant pastels for which Ponce is justly famous, the garish red and black of the Parque de Bombas stands out all the more.

SUGGESTED READING

Loretta Phelps de Córdova, *Ponce: Rebirth of a Valuable Heritage* (San Juan, P.R.: Publishing Resources, 1991); Angel G. Quintero Rivera, *Patricos y plebeyos: Burgesses, hacendados, artesanos y obreros* (San Juan, P.R.: Huracán, 1988).

Parquera, La   Located in the municipality of Lajas, La Parquera is home to one of Puerto Rico's two bioluminescent bays; the other is in **Vieques**. As if by delightful accident, the precious balance between fresh water and the sea breathes life into millions of microscopic creatures, called dinaflagellates, which literally burst into light when disturbed. They are best seen in the dark of night. It is possible to throw a bucket into the water, retrieve the water and thrust one's hands into an explosion of light. Or, one can experience this by jumping into the water: "It is as though a million stars were caught in the sea. Softly their light flows over the body of a swimmer. To dive is to share universal fires" (Langhorne 1987, 88). Although this quotation describes Vieques, where the absence of street or other lights makes the experience all the more remarkable, La Parquera's easier access has turned it into a tourist mecca. On dark nights, several boats motor out into the bay allowing as many people as the boats will hold to enjoy this natural wonder.

SUGGESTED READING

Elizabeth Langhorne, *Vieques: History of a Small Island* (Vieques, P.R.: Vieques Conservation and Historical Trust, 1987); Neal Sealey, *Caribbean World: A Complete Geography* (London: Cambridge University Press, 1995).

Parrandas   Also referred to as *asalto*, it is one of the leading social activities of the Christmas holiday season on the island. Groups of friends, coworkers and acquaintances get together and serenade people they know with **aguinaldos** and typical Christmas music during the middle of the night. Accompanied by amateur musicians, they knock on someone's door and then serenade the person. The host is supposed to wake up, open the doors welcome these people into the household and serve them food and beverages. They continue playing songs until the early hours of the morning and then move on to another house and party until dawn.

Partido Nuevo Progresita   *See* **New Progressive Party.**

Partido Unión de Puerto Rico   *See* **Union Party.**

Pedreira, Antonio (1899–1939)   A member of the **Generation of the Thirties**, Pedreira wrote influential books about Puerto Rico's history and culture. He received his B.A. from the **University of Puerto Rico**, his master's degree from Columbia University and his Ph.D. from the University of Madrid. He was the founder of the University of Puerto Rico's Hispanic Studies program, and he taught at the university until his untimely death.

During the 1930s Pedreira published a number of books, among them a biography of **Eugenio María de Hostos** and a still valuable compilation of Puerto Rican culture. However, he is best known for *Insularismo*, published in 1934. According to Pedreira, there were "three supreme moments in the development of our people" (Pedreira 1934, 25). The first began with the discovery and conquest of the island by the Spanish. This period ended in the late 1700s when the economic development of the island took precedence over other concerns. The Spanish-American War initiated the third stage, a period of indecision and transition. Pedreira argued that the U.S. influence had "superimposed" itself on the development of a purely Puerto Rican culture and outlook. The war cut short a work in progress: "We were born, and we grew but we never had a renaissance." Although Pedreira is at times optimistic—to finish the creation of Puerto Rican culture is a task for the young—the book is nevertheless suffused with a heavy dose of pessimism. "In proportion to its size, a nation develops its riches and therefore its culture. Puerto Rico was a tiny island—of the Lesser, not the Greater, Antilles—and its size and location helped produce the defeatism that was born of a pernicious sentiment, our inferiority complex" (Pedreira 1934, 43–44). It was this sense of inferiority that had to be overcome if Puerto Rico were to produce the rebirth so necessary for its cultural and political well-being. At the conclusion of *Insularismo*, the author stresses that his views represented a hypothesis, not a dogma. Nevertheless, many readers have used Pedreira's thoughts to explain the often unhappy course of Puerto Rican history.

SUGGESTED READING

Juan Flores, *Divided Borders: Essays on Puerto Rican Identity* (Houston, Tex.: Arte Público Press, 1993); Gordon Lewis, *Puerto Rico: Freedom and Power in the Caribbean* (New York: Harper, 1963); Sidney Mintz, *Caribbean Transformations* (New York: Columbia University Press, 1989); Antonio S. Pedreira, *Insularismo* (Río Piedras, P.R.: Edil, 1934, 1985).

Pérez Marchand, Ana Dolores (1888–1983)   Ponce's first female physician, Ana Dolores Pérez Marchand was born on a coffee plantation, *Hacienda Gripiñas*, in Jayuya. She moved to Ponce at a very early age, and there distinguished herself as an outstanding honor student throughout elementary and high school, where she graduated first in her class.

Bolstered by a scholarship to the University of Pennsylvania, she graduated with high honors from her pre-medical training and was admitted to the Women's Medical College of the University of Pennsylvania, and graduated in 1911. At Johns Hopkins University and Boston Medical School she continued her studies, specializing in obstetrics, gynecology and pediatrics. Upon completing her specializations, she passed licensing exams to practice medicine in Pennsylvania, New York, Boston, Washington, D.C., and Virginia.

In 1914, she began to work as a physician in Ponce's Damas Hospital. Her main focus was always the health of women and children. An ardent supporter of women's rights, she was one of the pioneers of the feminist movement in Ponce. In the 1920s Pérez Marchand was elected to the feminist Ponce Committee, and was a member of the Commission of Puerto Rican women who in 1927 traveled to Washington to advocate for women's right to vote. Once women's right to vote was obtained, Pérez Marchand declined a nomination as representative to the island's legislature.

Pérez Marchand continued her dedication to women and children's health even after retirement. When she retired, she requested the Puerto Rican government assign her to the Children's Dispensary in the Playa de Ponce, a very poor section of the city at that time. There she served as an unpaid physician for many years.

She has been honored on the island and in the United States. In 1961 on the 50th anniversary of her entering the medical profession The Women's Medical College of the University of Pennsylvania, her alma mater, honored her with a gold medal and dedicated that year's graduation ceremony to her. During the inauguration of the new facilities of the Ponce School of Medicine the street where the school is located was renamed in her honor: Avenue Ana Dolores Pérez Marchand.

SUGGESTED READING

Ana Dolores Marchand, Primera Doctora en Medicina (Personal biography provided by the Perez Marchand family, 1997); Angela Negrón Muñoz, *Mujeres de Puerto Rico* (San Juan, P.R.: Imprenta Venezolana, 1935).

Personalismo   This word signals one of the most distinctive characteristics of Puerto Rican culture. In the United States people say, "Don't take it personally." In Puerto Rico this admonition makes little sense. People take everything personally; it is a hallmark of the culture that you matter and that my assessment of you as a personality can make or break even the most advantageous (to me, to you, to others) political or economic relationship.

Five hundred years of colonialism help explain Puerto Rico's focus on the individual as the axis of social relationships. In politics, in the economy, in social gatherings, the colonized deferred to their "superiors" or were humiliated by Spanish soldiers and American officials. As the wives of U.S. colonial officials bragged, they had been on the island for years and, except as servants, "no Puerto Rican had ever entered their home" (Hanson 1955, 75). One consequence of such subordination is a sensitivity to personal slights; another is a refusal to work with people one does not like. Especially in the island's independence movement, it is possible to come across people who share the same political beliefs and values but refuse to be in the same room with those they dislike or, more often, despise as personalities. In the United States, people who dislike each other can still work for the same or similar goals. In Puerto Rico, *personalismo* erects a barrier that makes lifelong enemies of even people who agree politically.

Another side of *personalismo* is the "habit of deference to and dependence upon personal authority" (Wells 1955, 28). The incredible influence of **Luis Muñoz Marín** was tightly linked to the positive, personal qualities that produced in others everything from admiration to willing obedience. *Personalismo* has similarities to what Americans call charisma, but in Puerto Rico its deepest roots are in colonialism. For their survival, the *macheteros* in the sugar fields or the *jornaleros* (day workers) on the docks relied on individuals rather than on the state, on personalities instead of a Bill of Rights.

SUGGESTED READING

Earl Parker Hanson, *Transformation: The Story of Modern Puerto Rico* (New York: Simon and Schuster, 1955); Gordon Lewis, *Puerto Rico: Freedom and Power in the Caribbean* (New York: Harper, 1963); Henry Wells, "Ideology and Leadership in Puerto Rican Politics," *American Political Science Review* 49 (1955): 22–39.

Picó, Fernando (1941–)   Picó is one of Puerto Rico's most respected and insightful historians. Born in San Juan, Picó received his Ph.D. in history from Johns Hopkins University. Also a Jesuit priest, he is one of the most prolific historians in Puerto Rico.

Picó's work is characterized by extensive research into primary sources; he first completes an exhaustive examination of official and unofficial documents and then weaves the hundreds of details into books that focus on supposedly ordinary yet, in reality, very significant aspects of Puerto Rican life. In *Los gallos peleados* (The Fighting Cocks) (1984), he explains the Puerto Rican people's continued dislike of the police by focusing on the early twentieth-century imposition of central authority. When officers rigorously enforced new regulations for the production of everything from milk to cigarettes to liquor, they laid the groundwork for a lingering resentment of police authority. In his analysis of family violence, Picó used local criminal records to show that the level of family violence preceded the introduction of U.S. authority. Colonialism cannot be blamed for every problem of the Puerto Rican people.

Picó's other work ranges from *La guerra despues de la guerra* (1987), a detailed examination of Puerto Rican responses to the U.S. invasion, to *Vivir en Caimito* (1989), a sociological and historical analysis of life in a San Juan barrio. In his examination of the attitudes of young men toward the children they have fathered, Picó shows the everyday impact of **machismo** on the daily life of many Puerto Rico children—and their mothers.

SUGGESTED READING

Fernando Picó, *Libertad y servidumbre en el Puerto Rico del siglo XIX* (San Juan: Huracán, 1979); Fernando Picó, *Historia general de Puerto Rico*, (San Juan, P.R.: Huracán, 1986).

Piñero, Jesús (1897–1952)   A prominent politician throughout his lifetime and the first Puerto Rican governor of the island, Piñero was born in Carolina and died in his hometown on November 16, 1952. He studied at the University of Puerto Rico and at the University of Pennsylvania for an engineering degree. With **Luis Muñoz Marín**, he was a founder of the **Popular Democratic party**; in 1945, at a crucial moment in the island's history, he served as **Resident Commissioner**. However he is best remembered for being the first Puerto Rican governor of the island. He was appointed by President Harry Truman in 1946 and served until 1948. Working behind the scenes, but with great passion and determination, Piñero successfully fought with the U.S. Navy to return lands confiscated during World War II. And, at a time when U.S. officials seriously proposed sending citizens of **Vieques** to live and work in Alaska, then a U.S. territory, Piñero was able to restrain the Navy's desire to expand its bases in Puerto Rico.

SUGGESTED READING

Thomas Matthews, *Puerto Rican Politics and the New Deal* (Gainesville: University of Florida Press, 1960); Vincenzo Petrullo, *Puerto Rican Paradox* (Philadelphia: University of Pennsylvania Press, 1947); Rexford Tugwell, *Puerto Rican Public Papers* (San Juan, P.R.: n.p., 1945); Rexford Tugwell, *The Stricken Land* (New York: Doubleday, 1947).

Pitirre   This small, native bird has a significance beyond its size. Puerto Rico is one of the most densely populated places on earth. However, despite its population density, the island somehow remains home to more than 149 classes and 239 species and subspecies of birds. One of the best known is the brown and white pitirre. Its face sports a long, sharp beak, and, by any standards, the pitirre is small but fierce. With its *alardes de guapo* (bold displays of courage), the pitirre attacks much larger birds. Fear is not in the bird's vocabulary; courage is.

The pitirre is a political symbol to many Puerto Rican *independentistas*. With tenacity and courage, the small can defeat even a giant like the United States. The revolutionary group **Los macheteros** used the pitirre as a code name for their attacks on military bases and military personnel.

SUGGESTED READING

José A. Toro-Sugrañes, *Nueva enciclopedia de Puerto Rico: Geografíca, fiscia y humana* (Hato Rey, P.R.: Lector, 1995).

Plebiscite   A plebiscite is a voters' referendum on a particular social issue; in Puerto Rico, the issue has been the political status of the island. While U.S.-sponsored plebiscites have been a political possibility in Puerto Rico throughout the twentieth century (see **Luis Muñoz Rivera**), the issue has come to a head on only three occasions. In late 1945, close to 60 percent of the **Popular Democratic party**'s elected representatives publicly told the U.S. Congress that they wanted independence. To achieve their goal, they passed a plebiscite bill which was vetoed by Governor Rexford Tugwell. In January 1946, the Puerto Rican legislature passed the plebiscite bill over Tugwell's veto, which brought the bill to President Harry Truman's desk. He also vetoed the bill because Congress had clearly ruled out either independence or statehood as status possibilities. Thus, in order to avoid the international embarrassment of refusing to accept the will of the Puerto Rican people, President Truman never allowed that will to be expressed.

In the 1967 plebiscite, 60 percent of the voters expressed their preference for commonwealth status. This appeared to be an overwhelming endorsement, but the history of this vote is both complicated and controversial. Remembering the previous plebiscite, Puerto Ricans of all political persuasions told Governor Muñoz that they would participate only if Congress agreed to abide by the expressed will of the people. Congress refused, and the plebiscite planned for 1963 was forgotten. Thus, in 1967, a substantial portion of both statehood and independence voters boycotted the election because they thought its results would be meaningless. There is also the confirmed fact (see **Las Carpetas**) that the FBI illegally interfered in the 1967 plebiscite.

In 1991 Congress again considered the possibility of a plebiscite, but this time the vote was denied because the House of Representatives refused to detail the specifics of any status option. The Senate had provided details about everything from the tax laws to citizenship. The House of Representatives refused to do the same thing; in the words of the powerful representative Morris Udall, "While we can assure through this legislation that a winning status will be considered by both Houses of Congress, we cannot assure enactment or that the bill will be what the winning political party will prefer" (*Congressional Record* 1990, E 1439). On November 13, 1993, islanders held their own, nonbinding plebiscite. Both the Popular Democratic and Statehood parties used ads that made claims they could never substantiate. Nevertheless, in a manifestation of their commitment to the democratic process, more than 75 percent of Puerto Rico's eligible voters expressed themselves in this way: 48.4 percent for commonwealth, 46.2 percent for statehood and 4.4 percent for independence.

As this is written more calls for more plebiscites appear in both island and mainland periodicals. However, experience would seem to indicate at least two things. First, for Puerto Ricans to take any plebiscite seriously, Congress must agree to abide by the expressed will of the Puerto Rican people. Second, unless the specifics of each option are cited—for example, the language of public discourse in Puerto Rico—any vote will leave the status issue as confused and as unresolved as it was in 1945, and as it is in 1997.

SUGGESTED READING

Juan Manuel García Passalacqua, *The 1993 Plebiscite in Puerto Rico* (New York: Institute for Puerto Rican Policy, 1993); Carmen Gautier Mayoral, ed., *Poder y plebiscito* (San Juan, P.R.: Centro de Investigaciónes Sociales, 1990); Jorge Heine, ed., *Time for Decision: The United States and Puerto Rico* (Lanham, Md.: North-South Publishing, 1983); U.S. Congress, House, *Congressional Record*, 101st Cong., 1st Sess., May 9, 1990; U.S. Congress, Senate, *Political Status of Puerto Rico*, Hearings before the Committee on Energy and Natural Resources, 102d Cong., 1st sess. (Washington, D.C.: U.S. Government Printing Office, 1991).

Plena   Controversy rages about the origins of this popular music and dance form, which was virtually unknown in Puerto Rico until from 1915 to 1920. It is a simple music considered to be typical of Puerto Rico. Commonly associated with the Afro-Antillean elements in Puerto Rico, the origins of *plenas* can be traced back to the coastal areas of the southern, southeastern and eastern regions.

Ponce and its people have historically claimed proprietorship over the origins of *plena*. They argue that the rhythm originated in the San Antón area of that municipality (a poor area inhabited by black sugar cane workers). Meanwhile, music scholars, such as Francisco López Cruz, argue that, while *plenas* were highly popular in Ponce, the rhythm originated elsewhere. He cites examples of music found in other regions of the island and even in the Dominican Republic during the nineteenth century. He reaffirms, however, that, today, *plenas* are found only in Puerto Rico.

Plenas have stylistic elements of many other Caribbean and Latin American music forms, such as Trinidad's calypso, Mexico's corridos, the Dominican Republic's *merengue* and even English ballads (López Cruz 1967, 66). The music discourse of *plena* alternates between a soloist and a chorus and uses the format of the *cuarteta* (four verses) or *sextilla* (six verses).

Plenas are popular, not classical, music. They use everyday experiences as the basis for lyrics. The themes explored by *plena* generally concern everyday experiences of the working class; for example, the local woman, Elena, who gets stabbed and taken to the hospital (in "Cortaron a Elena"), the huge shark that lurks in the sea (in "Tintorera del mar"), the arrival of a bishop in the city (in "Mamita llegó el obispo") and the origins of *plena* itself (in "Plena de San Antón").

Plenas are often danced to the beat of percussion instruments, including the conga, drums, and tambourines. They are danced by couples in a closed position with simple backward and forward steps. During the past fifteen years, *plenas* have regained extraordinary popularity among Puerto Ricans partly due to the efforts of many civic organizations and cultural groups which have revitalized them. Groups such as Los Pleneros de la 23 Abajo and Los Pleneros del Quinto Olivo have popularized this dance form again.

SUGGESTED READING

Fransisco López Cruz, *La música folklórica de Puerto Rico* (Sharon, Conn.: Troutman Press, 1967).

Political Prisoners   This topic spans three generations of Puerto Rican revolutionaries. In the 1930s a number of Nationalists received long prison sentences for **seditious conspiracy**. U.S. officials generally refused to call them political prisoners, but a typical Latin American perspective was offered to President Franklin D. Roosevelt in 1942. In a plea that went unheeded, the powerful Argentinean politician Alfredo Palaciós wrote about the imprisonment of **Pedro Albizu Campos**. The Argentinean said that a man of Albizu's stature reminded him of a great American, Abraham Lincoln. So, "invoking Lincoln's memory, which is sacred for all the oppressed throughout the world, I ask of you the freedom of Albizu Campos, the imprisoned liberator . . . the first Hispano-American" (Roosevelt Library 1942, 2).

In 1950 and 1954, a second generation of revolutionaries began to serve prison terms that exceeded twenty-five years in jail. Although these individuals were convicted of specific acts (e.g., the **Nationalist attack on Congress** in March 1954), White House documents show that the Carter administration recognized the political nature of the actions. The White House memos discussing the prisoners' release are titled, "Release of the Puerto Rican Independence Fighters," "Clemency for the Four Puerto Rican Nationalists," and "Puerto Rican 'Political' Prisoners Situation."

As of mid-1996 fifteen members of the **FALN** and **Los macheteros** were in U.S. prisons. Convicted of seditious conspiracy in 1981, many members of the FALN received seventy-year prison sentences. The conditions of their incarceration are so extreme that Amnesty International filed a brief on behalf of, among others, Alejandrina Torres when she was incarcerated in Lexington, Kentucky.

Amnesty International considers that the conditions of confinement and the transfer of prisoners to the Lexington High Security Unit on the basis of their political beliefs constitute cruel, inhuman and degrading treatment in contravention of Article 5 of the Universal Declaration of Human Rights. (Fernandez 1994, 287)

Oscar López, in a "maxi, maxi" unit in Colorado, recently had his first meal with other prisoners after five years.

What did these Puerto Ricans do? To put an end to U.S. colonialism, they blew up buildings and killed people. In the FALN attack on Frances Tavern in Manhattan in 1975, five people died and sixty-two were wounded. These are serious offenses by any standard; on the other hand, if they are regarded as terrorists in the United States, at home, the political nature of their actions is understood. Thus, the third generation of revolutionaries poses a question that is both morally difficult and politically explosive: What is justifiable when, only months before the attack on Frances Tavern, Senator Henry Jackson explicitly and publicly told Governor Rafael Hernández Colón that "neither developed commonwealth, independence or statehood can be had. Puerto Rico must remain a colony"? (Nixon Project 1974, 1).

Since many of the prisoners are now entering their sixteenth year of prison time, many people have answered this question by requesting that the prisoners be released as a first step toward the decolonization of the island. The diverse and extensive list of people supporting the release of the imprisoned Puerto Ricans includes two former governors (Rafael Hernández Colón and Roberto Sánchez Veliella) and three U.S. congressional representatives (Luis Guitiérrez, José Serrano and Nydia Velásquez).

SUGGESTED READING

Amnesty International, *The High Security Unit, Lexington Federal Prison, Kentucky* (New York: Amnesty International, August 1988); Ronald Fernandez, *Prisoners of Colonialism: The Struggle for Justice in Puerto Rico* (Monroe, Me.: Common Courage Press, 1994); Franklin Roosevelt Library, Hyde Park, New York, Papers of Rexford Tugwell, Box 47, May 1942; Nixon Project, Alexandria, Virginia, White House Central Files, ST51–21 (April 30, 1974); Jan Sussler, *Conditions of Incarceration* (Río Piedras, P.R.: Ofensiva '92, 1992).

Ponce   In a splendid essay about San Juan and Ponce, historian **Angel G. Quintero Rivera** makes this point: Even today it is common for a person leaving San Juan to say, "Me voy para la Isla" (I am going to the island). This continuing distinction between the walled city of San Juan and the rest of the island is fundamental to any understanding of the significance of Ponce in Puerto Rican life.

To its critics, San Juan represents creativity in chains, minds locked up by military discipline. Ponce, however, is the real Puerto Rico because it is here that *los criollos* (the native residents) have had free rein to create a world that shines with individuality. *El orgullo* (the pride) of *Los Ponceños* is legendary. Locals are rarely overbearing or obnoxious; instead, a *Ponceño* will simply ask one to look at the colors of the houses: Can one see such a wonderful mixture of brown, orange and aquamarine anywhere else? In Ponce people have created homes—one next to the other—that incorporate the pastoral image of a hacienda in an urban setting. The balconies, the stonework, the doors, the wrought iron twisted into so many inviting shapes—everything bears the stamp of a people who used Ponce to declare cultural independence.

Although this is an exaggeration, *Ponceños*, nevertheless, have great cause for civic pride. The central plaza remains one of the most exquisite in the Caribbean. Even the Burger Kings (with small signs) do not mar the beauty of the sculptured trees surrounding a fountain guarded by four stone lions who, with their heads erect, protect the city center. The Art Museum (generously endowed by the Ferré family) contains a superb collection of painting and sculpture; and the renovated La Perla Theater provides a dramatic setting for everything from opera to salsa.

Finally, Ponce is and always has been a center of commercial activity in Puerto Rico and the Caribbean. Historically, the city's wealth rested with sugar; however, today, the Chamber of Commerce is both ambitious and successful. Industrialists have made a commitment to remain competitive in the global economy, and, although the island's colonial status sometimes limits its economic possibilities, the city and its environs are nevertheless filled with representatives of many world-class corporations.

SUGGESTED READING

Loretta Phelps de Córdova, *Ponce: Rebirth of a Valuable Heritage* (San Juan, P.R.: San Juan Publishing, 1991); Angel G. Quintero Rivera, "La capital alterna," in *Patricios y plebeyos* (San Juan, P.R.: Huracán, 1988); Francisco A. Scarano, *Sugar and Slavery in Puerto Rico: The Plantation Economy of Ponce* (Madison: University of Wisconsin Press, 1984).

Ponce de León, Juan (1460–1521)   This Spanish explorer also served as the Spanish governor of Puerto Rico from 1510 to 1512. Born in Spain in 1460, Ponce de León died in Cuba in 1521. His Caribbean career began in the Dominican Republic; he was one of the Spanish explorers who "pacified" the Indians of the island. In 1508, lured by tales of gold in **Boriquen**, Ponce de León founded the settlement of Caparra, named after a place in his native León. Since this settlement was established a century before Jamestown was founded in Virginia, islanders with a sense of history stress that its Western development began a hundred years before that of the United States!

From Ponce de León's perspective, the change of name—from Boriquen to Puerto Rico (rich port)—was perfect. His principal aim was to extract gold for the crown and for himself; he never received a salary, simply a substantial share of what he sent back to Spain. Caparra was therefore ruthlessly organized around the extraction of the gold and the exploitation of the Indians who mined it. Ultimately, the Indians balked. **Urayoán** initiated the uprising that led to the destruction of **los Taínos**. Led by Ponce de León, the Spanish used their skills and technology to crush the Indians. De León burned their villages, made captives of the survivors, and branded them with an F on their foreheads: for Fernando de Aragón.

In reaction to the "civilization" brought from Spain, many Taínos escaped to the remotest parts of Puerto Rico. Scholars suggest that it is still possible to see Indian characteristics in the faces of people who live, for example, in Indiera Fria, near Maricao.

Most of the Indians perished under the harsh domination of the Spanish. Ironically, the Taínos were already dying while Ponce de León was seeking the legendary fountain of youth in Florida. In 1521 Indians attacked his landing party, his troops withdrew, and the wounded de León died soon afterward in Cuba. How ironic that the city of **Ponce**, for many the spiritual capital of the Puerto Rican people, bears the name of the man who helped eradicate the original inhabitants of Puerto Rico.

SUGGESTED READING

Arturo Morales Carrion, *Puerto Rico and the Non-Hispanic Caribbean* (Río Piedras: University of Puerto Rico Press, 1971); Fernando Picó, *Historia general de Puerto Rico* (San Juan, P.R.: Huracán, 1988).

Ponce Massacre   During this tragedy, which occurred on March 21, 1937, 20 people died and more than 100 were wounded in one of the worst political confrontations to ever occur in Puerto Rico. During the 1930s many analysts, including President Franklin Roosevelt, agreed that a substantial number of Puerto Ricans wanted independence. This desire had produced revolutionary violence from the **Nationalist party** as well as a violent response from the island's colonial administration. Governor Blanton Winship assured his superiors in Washington, he could handle any military show of force or mob violence.

The governor kept his word. However, instead of quelling a violent mob, his subordinates murdered unarmed men and women. The Nationalists had planned a parade for March 21. They asked for and received a permit from the mayor of **Ponce**. But, under orders from the governor, soldiers convinced the mayor to rescind his permission. The Nationalists, realizing that people were arriving from all over the island, decided to march despite the revocation of the parade permit. Photos taken on that day show that the Nationalists were unarmed but loosely surrounded by large numbers of police. The march began with the singing of "La Borinqueña," the Puerto Rican national anthem, and, soon after the parade began, a shot rang out. To this day, no one knows who fired that first bullet, but the police, with their guns already drawn, began to fire at will. Minutes later, twenty Puerto Ricans (including two police officers) were dead. A variety of investigations were held; one of the most impartial, chaired by Arthur Garfied Hays, general counsel for the American Civil Liberties Union, drew this conclusion: "The facts show that the affair of March 21st in Ponce was a 'Massacre' . . . due to the denial by the police of the civil rights of citizens to parade and assemble. The denial was ordered by the Governor of Puerto Rico" (quoted in López 1977, 107).

SUGGESTED READING

Wenzell Brown, *Dynamite on Our Doorstep* (New York: Greenberg, 1945); "Hays Report," *Report of the Commission of Inquiry on Civil Rights in Puerto Rico*, in *Puerto Rican Nationalism*, ed. José López (Chicago: Editorial Coquí, 1977); Alfredo López, *The Puerto Rican Papers* (Indianapolis: Bobbs Merrill, 1973).

Popular Democratic Party   One of the two most powerful political parties in Puerto Rico, it advocates that commonwealth should be the permanent status of the island but it has also asked, since 1952, that the powers (e.g., over the economy) granted to Puerto Rico via the commonwealth be significantly enhanced.

Luis Muñoz Marín and the other Puerto Ricans who founded the party in 1938 wanted to create a party with a new emphasis. As Muñoz told Congress shortly after his party had won their first election,

The program of the Popular Democratic Party was made clear during the [1940] campaign; that is, the political question was not an issue. We said to the voters: "We will not interpret your votes in favor of our party as votes either for or against any political status but only as votes against the present economic situation, if you are against it." (Hearings 1941, 41)

To achieve growth and prosperity, the party relied on the federal government for everything from funding to the legal assistance required to break up the plantations owned by U.S. absentee corporations. In the early years, the party set up grassroots organizations in every municipality and in 786 rural barrios. The party's newspaper was *El Batey* (the *batey* was the ballfield used by the Taíno Indians—see **los Taínos**—in precolonial times), its slogan was "Bread, land and liberty," and its emblem was the profile of a *jíbaro*, a poor, rural Puerto Rican dressed in a straw hat, or *la pava*.

Despite the party's specific claims that it offered no political status preference, scholars like Robert Anderson correctly argue that "it was commonly recognized that the leadership of the party favored independence" (Anderson 1965, 53). This unstated assumption produced controversy when, after World War II, party leaders pressed for independence. However, led by Muñoz, the Popular Democratic party offered this compromise: It would focus on the economy and offer the Puerto Rican people a **plebiscite** in which they could freely express their own preference for statehood or independence. The promised plebiscite between alternatives never took place. Instead, in 1952, the people were offered a chance to say yes or no to commonwealth status, with the result that commonwealth won by an overwhelming margin. The party won election after election and, with **Operation Bootstrap,** it attempted to create a self-sustaining economy.

Meanwhile, Governor Muñoz tried to convince U.S. presidents and the U.S. Congress to enhance the powers granted to the commonwealth government. Congress refused to make any changes, citing the U.S. Constitution, which grants to Congress the power to make all rules and regulations for all U.S. possessions. In 1967, with many islanders refusing to vote because Congress never agreed to accept the will of the Puerto Rican people, commonwealth again won overwhelming support in a plebiscite. But, by 1967, the party was split between those who supported the commonwealth with or without any changes, and those who felt that after fifteen years of requests, it was time to seek other ways to improve Puerto Rico's political status. In 1968 these fractures in the party's solidarity produced two candidates for governor, with the result that the **New Progressive party** (which advocated statehood) won its first gubernatorial election.

In 1972, and again from 1984 to 1992, **Rafael Hernández Colón** led the party to victories in the gubernatorial elections. With his "New Theses," he tried to obtain the enhanced powers denied Muñoz Marín but, like his predecessor, Hernández Colón never succeeded in obtaining from Congress the powers that might substantially increase the party's support. In the November 1993 referendum, the Popular Democratic party narrowly defeated (49 percent to 47 percent of the vote) the statehood party but, as Congress emphasized, the ads run by *Los Populares* claimed political and economic powers that Congress would never concede.

In 1996 the party still claims those powers but, since political status is only one of the many issues that determine how voters vote, it is entirely possible that, once again, **La Fortaleza,** will be in the hands of the Popular Democratic party.

SUGGESTED READING

Robert W. Anderson, *Party Politics in Puerto Rico* (Stanford, Calif.: Stanford University Press, 1965); Ronald Fernandez, *The Disenchanted Island: Puerto Rico and the United States in the Twentieth Century,* 2d ed. (Westport, Conn.: Praeger, 1996); U.S. Congress, Senate, *Political Status of Puerto Rico,* Hearings before the Committee on Energy and Natural Resources, 102d Cong., 1st sess., 1991; U.S. Congress, Senate, Hearings before the Committee on Territories and Insular Affairs, 77th Cong., 1st sess., 1941.

Porto Rico   This spelling was used by U.S. officials and writers to refer to Puerto Rico from 1898 until 1932. When **General Nelson Miles** invaded the island in July 1898, he took charge of everything—from the exchange rate for Puerto Rican currency to the spelling of the island's name. In the general's mind, Puerto became Porto; it did not matter that no such word existed in the Spanish language. The general was in command, and so, for thirty-four years, Puerto Ricans were forced to misspell the name of their own country. Congress finally rectified the general's mistake in 1932 when, as a result of "a unanimous request from the Porto Rican legislature" in April 1930, it agreed "to restore to the island its true name of Puerto Rico . . . because it is considered that full justice will thus be done to our [Puerto Rican] history, our language, and our traditions."

SUGGESTED READING

U.S. Congress, 72d Cong., 1st sess., Report 58, February 20, 1932; Knowlton Mixer, *Porto Rico: History and Conditions* (New York: Macmillan, 1926).

Public Law 600   Approved on July 3, 1950, this law, "in the nature of a compact," allowed Puerto Ricans "to organize a government pursuant to a constitution of their own adoption." That constitution, including a Bill of Rights, would be submitted to the people of Puerto Rico for a vote and, if adopted by the people, would "become effective in accordance with its [the U.S. Congress] terms."

The law had its roots in the refusal of Congress to consider either statehood or independence as possible status alternatives. For example, after ruling out statehood, Senator Howard Ellender had this exchange with **Luis Muñoz Marín** in May 1945.

Senator Ellender: "You cannot hope to obtain full independence. You would have to depend on something or may I say some preference accorded to you by us. In other words certain relationships must be maintained between you and us that would exclude complete independence, as we know it."

Luis Muñoz Marín: "We are always glad to do things that you ask us to do anyway." (Hearings 1945, 387)

Historians debate why Muñoz agreed to compromise; whatever the factors involved, he and his colleagues in the **Popular Democratic party** accepted the "preference" (i.e., commonwealth or **Free Associated State**) accorded by Congress and then artfully argued that the phrase "in the nature of a compact" meant that Congress could never unilaterally change laws enacted by the government Puerto Rico would create. The debate was settled when, after the Puerto Rican people voted to accept it, Muñoz submitted what analysts called a very progressive constitution to Congress. Section 20 in the Bill of Rights guaranteed the right to work, and another article mandated compulsory school attendance. Congress first criticized and then unilaterally eliminated these sections of the already approved constitution. As Congressman Fred Crawford stressed in the debate about Section 20, "We do not want people referring to this here later on to the effect that Puerto Rico is a free and independent country . . . the people of Puerto Rico are still definitely tied in under the supervision of Congress and the protection" (*Congressional Record* 1952, 6179).

In July 1952 the Puerto Rican people accepted the corrected constitution in another vote and, as a consequence of Public Law 600, Governor Muñoz declared the island a commonwealth on July 25, 1952. This was the fifty-fourth anniversary of the U.S. invasion. However, in a gesture underlining his interpretation of the law, Governor Muñoz raised the **flag of Puerto Rico** beside the American flag. On the island, the two banners flew as equals.

SUGGESTED READING

U.S. Congress, House, *Puerto Rico Constitution*, Hearings before the Committee on Public Lands, 81st Cong., 1st sess. (Washington, D.C.: U.S. Government Printing Office, 1950); U.S. Congress, Senate, *Independence for Puerto Rico*, Hearings before the Committee on Territories and Insular Affairs, 79th Cong., 1st sess., May 1945; *Congressional Record*, House of Representatives, 82nd Cong., 1st sess., May 28, 1952.

Puerto Rican Independence Party   Now led by **Rubén Berríos Martínez**, this party works within the political system established by the colonial authorities. It is dedicated to making Puerto Rico an independent nation, and it is firmly rooted in these beliefs: "Puerto Ricans are a people; they constitute a distinct nationality, inhabiting a separate and distinct territory; they speak a different language, they aspire to maintain a separate identity, and they happen, through no fault of their own, to be citizens of the United States" (Hearings 1991, 176).

The party's origins date back to the mid-1940s when many members of the **Popular Democratic party** organized El Congreso Pro-Independencia; the aim was to put pressure on **Luis Muñoz Marín** and other *populares* to declare their support for independence as the preferred status of the future. When Muñoz instead advocated what was later called a commonwealth, the Independence party was established in 1946. It has enjoyed a measure of electoral success. In 1952, for example, the Independence party won 19.6 percent of the popular vote. The *populares* won 67 percent of the vote and the statehooders, 13 percent. Remembering that **La mordaza** (the gag law) was in effect during these years, and that the country was also dealing with the revolutionary activities fomented by the Nationalists, winning nearly 20 percent of the vote was a political achievement.

In terms of votes, 1952 was the high point for the Independence party. For more than thirty-five years, it has achieved roughly from 3 to 5 percent of the electoral vote. This has moved some analysts to argue that the *independentistas* are irrelevant in any future negotiations about Puerto Rico's political status. However, in analyzing the validity of such a judgment, at least four factors must be considered. First, as the statehooder **Resident Commissioner Carlos Romero Barceló** stresses, "The results of the general elections held every four years hinge on a great many issues, most of which have little or no bearing on the ultimate resolution of Puerto Rico's political status question" (Romero Barcelo 1978, 104). Second, many advocates of independence refuse to vote. Arguing that the colonial system is a farce, they contend that casting any vote is participating in an illegal system. Third, the Independence party has been controlled by the same group of leaders for more than thirty years; critics suggest that new leadership could reinvigorate the party. Finally, and most important, an unspecified number of those who vote for the Popular Democratic party actually support independence. Called *melones* on the island (because, while the color of the Independence party is green, they vote with the *populares*, whose color is red), some of these voters support the *populares* for reasons of self-interest, others because they fear that a split in the vote between independence and commonwealth could produce a result too favorable for the statehooders.

These caveats suggest this point: It is not wise to make any snap judgments about the status politics of Puerto Rico and its people. The island's political situation, which is very complicated, has always been affected by decisions made in Washington. For example, it is easy to imagine a very different outcome if the United States were to insist that English would be the number one language if Puerto Rico were to become the fifty-first state.

At the United Nation's hearings on decolonization held in July 1996, the spokesperson for the Independence party indicated support for the bill recently proposed by Congressman Donald Young of Alaska (see **Young Bill**). This bill advocates a **plebiscite** with two options: independence or statehood. The Independence party appears to be betting that statehood will win but that the U.S. Congress will never concede statehood no matter how the Puerto Rican people vote. Thus, independence will win by default. The bill is still in committee as of the fall of 1996. The plebiscite it proposes would occur in the late 1990s.

SUGGESTED READING

Robert W. Anderson, *Party Politics in Puerto Rico* (Stanford, Calif.: Stanford University Press, 1965); Carlos Romero Barcelo, *Statehood Is for the Poor* (San Juan, P.R.: n.p., 1978); Statement of Rubén Berriós Martínez, *Political Status of Puerto Rico*, Hearings before the Committee on Energy and Natural Resources, U.S. Senate, 1991.

Q

Quintero Rivera, Angel G. (1947–) A distinguished writer, professor and one of the founders of highly successful El Centro de Investigaciónes Sociales at the **University of Puerto Rico**, Quintero Rivera was born in San Juan, attended the University of Puerto Rico and earned his doctorate at the London School of Economics and Political Science.

Quintero Rivera has written books that are both provocative and insightful. In *Conflictos de clase y política en Puerto Rico* (Class and political conflicts in Puerto Rico) (1977), he uses the image of a triangle to understand the political and economic conflicts at the beginning of the twentieth century. He discusses the class of traditional landowners, the workers adjusting to the harsh realities of capitalism and the Americans and Puerto Ricans who, together, sought to eclipse the traditional landowners while they "disciplined" the workers.

Another volume, *Patricios y plebeyos* (Patricians and proletariats), (1988), underlines Quintero's passion for Puerto Rico, rooted in the meticulous scholarship that characterizes his work. The essay that compares San Juan and **Ponce** says as much about Puerto Ricans as it does about the realities and architecture of these cities.

Quintero Rivera is now teaching at the University of Puerto Rico and working in the research center he helped to establish.

SUGGESTED READING

Gervasio L. García and Angel Quintero Rivera, *Deasafío y solidaridad: Breve historia del movimiento obrero puertorriqueño* (San Juan, P.R.: Huracán, 1986); Angel G. Quintero Rivera *La historia de Puerto Rico desde su cara obrera 1800–1825* (San Juan: Huracán, 1984).

R

Radio There is a significant radio industry in Puerto Rico. There are 118 radio stations on the island. Sixty percent of the stations are AM and 40 percent are FM. Estimates from the Puerto Rican Association of Broadcasters indicate that there are approximately 4 million radios on the island: 2.3 millions sets are operated from households, 1.6 million from automobiles. In addition, estimates indicate that there are 80,000 radio sets operating within businesses and industries throughout the island (Asociación Puertorriqueña de Radiodifusores 1997, 13).

Listening to the radio is an important activity for Puerto Ricans of all social levels. Forty-seven percent of all time spent using communications media is devoted to listening to radio. The largest segment of the listening audience, 45 percent, uses the radio between 6:00 A.M. and 8:00 A.M. on weekdays (Asociación Puertorriqueña de Radiodifusores 1997, 15). Radio is a profitable business. Publimedia, a media accounting firm, in its 1996 *Annual Report*, estimates that 57.9 million dollars were spent by businesses in radio advertising in 1995.

The first Puerto Rican radio station, WKAQ, began operations on the island in 1922. WKAQ was the fifth commercial station to go into service in the world. It was installed and owned by the Behn Brothers who also were owners of the Radio and Telephone Corporation of Puerto Rico. In 1949 it was acquired by Angel Ramos, who was the owner of *El Mundo* newspaper and later founded WKAQ-TV. The station, which now has an all-news format, became a cultural landmark of Puerto Rico and has contributed to the formation of public opinion, information and entertainment for millions of Puerto Ricans throughout the years. WKAQ was followed by WNEL in 1934, WPRP from Ponce in 1936, WPRA from Mayagüez in

1937, WPAB from Arecibo in 1940 and WVKM from Arecibo in 1943 (Aguilar 1991).

In historic terms, the advertising industry has been very important in shaping the nature of radio because it has funded the production of specific kinds of programs. By 1930 two advertising agencies, Publicidad Badillo and West Indies Advertising, were sponsoring particular types of programming such as dramatic productions, comedy and entertainment. Radio productions during the early days of radio in Puerto Rico, characterized by their high aesthetic, social, entertainment and political values, served as a platform for the later introduction of television. Programs such as "La abuelita Borinqueña," a children's program that started in 1930, "Los jibaros de la radio," a political satire program and "Los embajadores del buen humor," a comedy program, were very popular. These programs were supported by commercial advertisements.

There are no doubts that the most important and strongest segment of radio programming during the early years was made up of the locally produced "radio novelas." This was a programming genre similar to the American soap operas but with a close-ended narrative and a limited duration. Sponsored by soap manufacturers' advertising, the radio novelas were carefully crafted productions developed in installments. Many of the early radio novelas were produced by "La escuela del aire," a governmental institute that sponsored the production of radio programming for educational purposes. Radio novelas served as a training ground for some of the most capable directors and actors and actresses of the time. People such as José Luis Torregrosa, **Lucy Boscana**, Madeline Williemsen and Edmundo Rivera Alvarez were key players in the production of such dramatic soaps as "Las gaviotas," "El derecho de nacer," "Los tres Villalobos" and "Entre monte y cielo," which captured the attention of scores of Puerto Ricans through the airwaves.

Radio programming today is varied. It has been heavily influenced by American radio, and there is a wide representation of most American radio formats, such as top 40, adult contemporary, easy listening and all news/talk radio. The American influence on Puerto Rican radio is clearly seen in American music and the production values that are followed. American innovations, such as "shock radio," have become very popular on the island, and radio personalities, such as "El Ganster," are as popular and as controversial as Howard Stern is in the United States.

Contrary to the **television** industry, where stations are mostly owned by American corporations, the radio industry remains Puerto Rican in nature. J. Ribas Domminici, from the Puerto Rican Association of Broadcasters, estimates that approximately 90 percent of the radio stations on the island are owned by Puerto Ricans who operate them as family businesses (Personal interview 1997).

SUGGESTED READING

Charlie Aguilar, *La Radio antes de la TV* (Quebradillas: Imprenta San Rafael, 1991); Asociación de Radiodifusores de Puerto Rico, *La radio: medio primario* (San Juan: Asociación de Radiodifusores, 1997); Publimedia, *Annual Report* (San Juan: Publimedia, 1996); J. Ribas Domminici, personal interview (March 20, 1997).

Reilly, E. Montgomery (1866–1934) A U.S. governor of Puerto Rico, Reilly was born in Sedalia, Missouri, in 1866. Reilly was appointed governor of **Porto Rico** [*sic*] by President Warren Harding. He served as governor from July 1921 until April 30, 1923. He is easily the most controversial American governor in Puerto Rican history and is important here because his policies helped transform island politics. Reilly sent a draft of his inaugural address to President Harding. In it he stated that he meant to "rule" Puerto Rico. Harding changed "rule" to "administer," but he did not expunge other statements that later ignited a firestorm of protest in Puerto Rico. Since the passage of the **Jones Act** in 1917, many islanders had expressed a desire for independence. In his first speech to the island, Reilly said that the president "would be deeply distressed to see any feeling or growing sentiment on these islands tending toward any thought or idea of independence . . . as long as Old Glory waves over the United States, it will wave over Porto Rico, and it will never be hauled down" (Fernandez 1996, 87).

After this speech, Reilly told Harding, "I received a number of letters threatening my life, others telling me that if I did not leave the island in 48 hours I would be killed, and if I drove through the streets I would be murdered" (Fernandez 1996, 88). Reilly also openly antagonized Puerto Rico's major politicians. Traditionally, American governors perfunctorily approved the appointments made by island leaders. Reilly not only refused to do that, but he told Antonio R. Barceló, the head of the Union party, to "sever your connection with the independence party and become a loyal Porto Rican or we cannot have any friendly relations" (Reilly 1920). Eventually island politicians accepted this requirement. They removed independence from their political platforms and, in 1924, formed *La alianza* (the **Alliance party**) and *La Coalición* (the **Coalition party**).

Meanwhile, in **Ponce**, members of the **Nationalist party** began to speak openly of revolution as the only way to change the island's status. President Harding removed Governor Reilly in 1923, but his refusal to countenance any thought of independence helped shape Puerto Rican politics to the present day.

SUGGESTED READING

Truman Clark, *Puerto Rico and the United States, 1917–1933* (Pittsburgh: University of Pittsburgh Press, 1975); Ronald Fernandez, *The Disenchanted Island: Puerto Rico and the United States in the 20th Century*, 2d ed. (Westport, Conn.: Praeger

1996); Papers of Montgomery Reilly, Manuscript Division, New York Public Library, 1920; Roberto H. Todd, *Desfile de gobernadores* (San Juan: n.p., 1943).

Republican Mobs (Las Turbas Republicanas)   This entry refers to a series of sometimes violent, pro-statehood disturbances that occurred during the first years of U.S. colonial control. The leader of many of the disturbances was José Mauleón y Castillo. In 1901 he directed an organization formally known as the Committee for the Defense of the Republican Party, and he used San Juan as his base of operations. In February 1901 Mauleón ran through the streets of San Juan dressed as a madman carrying a sign that ridiculed the head of the Federal party, **Luis Muñoz Rivera**. He was accompanied by a crowd that proudly carried signs saying *las turbas* (the mobs) *de San Juan*. Some of the members of the mob were dressed as police officers. They would try to capture the madman, but he always escaped, signifying that Muñoz operated outside the control of the government. As he escaped the crowd's grasp, a group in a nearby ox cart chanted, "long live the people's rights! Down with the despots."

This outburst was one of a series of often violent attempts that occurred over a four-year period to resolve political problems through intimidation. The Federal party (later the **Union party**) decisively won the municipal elections that were held in 1899. The Federalists advocated annexation by the United States, but they nonetheless pressed for a significant degree of local control by Puerto Ricans. They were particularly distressed by the efforts of the colonial government to eliminate powers held by the municipalities and transfer them to Americans based in San Juan.

The Republicans also favored annexation; moreover, led by **José Celso Barbosa**, they advocated a variety of very liberal, democratic measures that were modeled after political practice in the United States. Problems between the island parties first arose on June 28, 1900, at the inaugural organizational meeting called by the first U.S. governor of Puerto Rico, Charles Allen. The Federal party, stressing that it had the support of the island's voters (it had won majorities in forty-four of sixty-six municipalities) wanted more power for the local governments. Allen said no. The Republicans immediately supported Allen and the United States. The result was four years of tacit support, both by Governor Allen and the Republican party, for widespread intimidation of the political opposition. Muñoz Rivera legitimately feared for his life and subsequently exiled himself to New York. Until the residents of San Juan finally pressured Allen to stop the mob activity, Mauleón enjoyed Allen's support. When Mauleón was seriously wounded during mob activity that occurred in Río Piedras, Governor Allen constantly asked Republican leaders about the state of his health because "Allen knew that Mauleón was a popular leader of the Republican Party" (Todd, 1943, 17).

Las turbas republicanas mocked the high ideals and genuine concerns of many island Republicans. After all, the will of the people (or, more accurately, of those people permitted to vote in 1899) had been democratically expressed. To use mob intimidation as a democratic tool was a contradiction in terms. But the Republicans apparently believed that the United States offered the only route to a "modern" Puerto Rico. Meanwhile, with the creation of such agencies as the **Executive Council**, the United States had deliberately designed and imposed an administrative apparatus that was, in the words of one its creators, "an autocratic government" (Willoughby 1932, 106).

SUGGESTED READING

Mariano Negrón Portillo, *Las Turbas Republicanas* (San Juan, P.R.: Huracán, 1990); A. G. Quintero Rivera, *Conflictos de clase y política en Puerto Rico*, 4th ed. (San Juan, P.R.: Huracán, 1984); Roberto Todd, *Desfile de gobernadores* (San Juan: n.p., 1943); W. F. Willoughby, *The Government of Modern States* (New York: D. Appleton-Century, 1932).

Resident Commissioner   This title is given to the Puerto Rican official who is a nonvoting member of the United States House of Representatives. When Hawaii, Alaska, Arizona and New Mexico became U.S. territories, they were always incorporated parts of the United States because they had received explicit promises of eventual statehood. Puerto Rico is the first *unincorporated* territory in U.S. history. Citing everything from racism to the island's level of economic development, Congress refused to promise the islanders a specific political status. Puerto Rico might be a state in several generations; it might remain a colony; it could become autonomous. The only certainty was ambiguity—and a decided reluctance to make Puerto Rico an integral part of U.S. political life.

When Congress debated what to call Puerto Rico's nonvoting member of Congress, it rejected the label "delegate." As Senator Carl Spooner reminded his colleagues on April 2, 1900, that designation "has always been considered a pledge of statehood" (*Congressional Record* 1900, 3632). The Puerto Rican representative was called a resident commissioner to emphasize that he or she lacked the rights and privileges accorded to other territorial representatives. For example, a delegate could appear on the floor of the House and speak before the chamber. Until 1902 the resident commissioner of Puerto Rico was not even allowed on the floor of the House, and, until 1904, he could not speak before his colleagues. In 1996 the resident commissioner still lacks any voting rights, and a 1970 provision that he or she be allowed to vote in committees was rescinded by Congress in 1994.

SUGGESTED READING

Congressional Record, Senate, April 2, 1900, 3632; *Congressional Record*, House of Representatives, February 2, 1904, 1523–29, especially 1525.

Rexach, Sylvia (1922–1964)   The songs of this premier female composer—simple romantic ballads—are filled with a nostalgic and nonconformist tone that has enchanted the people of Puerto Rico for decades, and her Bohemian escapades have transformed her into a figure of almost mythical proportions within the musical circles of the island. Her music has been recorded by countless performers from Puerto Rico, Latin America and the Caribbean.

She lived an eclectic life. She attended the **University of Puerto Rico** law school but left it to join World War II. After the war, she launched her own musical group, made up almost entirely of women. Although she died at an early age, she left a substantial legacy of songs, many of which became popular after her death. Among her best-known compositions are "Idilio," "Y entonces," "Alma adentro," "Anochecer" and "Una vez."

Her work is so important because as a music composer she broke away from many preconceived and stereotypical notions about the role of women in Puerto Rican society. Similar to the works of poet **Julia de Burgos** and singer **Luz Esther Benítez**, Rexach's music gave a voice to and empowered the experience of Puerto Rican women who had been isolated, rejected and undervalued by the artistic establishment. There were thematic elements in her songs that legitimized women's experiences, including sensuality, womanhood, romance and the uniqueness of a woman's feelings. These themes ran through most of her compositions. She is perhaps the most distinct and powerful voice representing the experience of women in Puerto Rican popular music of the 1950s.

SUGGESTED READING

Centro de Investigaciones y Ediciones Musicales de Puerto Rico, *Compositores contemporaneos puertorriqueños* (San Juan, P.R.: El Instituto, 1981).

Rincón de Gautier, Felisa (1897–1995)   One of the first female political leaders on the island, Felisa Rincón was affectionately known as Doña Fela by the Puerto Rican people.

Originally from the town of Ceiba, her family moved to San Juan—the city she would one day lead as mayor. After only a year in San Juan, eleven-year-old Felisa and her ten siblings found themselves effectively orphaned. After her mother's death and with her father in a state of deep depression and despair, the children were each sent to live with different relatives. Felisa went to live with her aunt and uncle in the town of San Lorenzo, and it was there that Felisa's political education began. Following a tradition that is island wide, her uncle's pharmacy served as a central meeting place where townspeople (mostly men) debated local politics—particularly the new relationship between Puerto Rico and the United States. It was through these discussions that, in addition to politics, Felisa learned about **machismo** and the prevailing double standard for women on the island.

Former mayor of San Juan, Felisa Rincón de Gautier, 1974. (*El Nuevo Día.*)

Her political savvy was developed by playing hostess to the gatherings of intellectuals and politicians at the Rincón household, where she lived with her father during the late 1920s and early 1930s. In 1932, against her father's wishes, she registered to vote, and she also became a representative to the Liberal party. Shortly thereafter, she met and campaigned for the Liberal party's principal candidate, **Luis Muñoz Marín**.

With her Felisa's Style Shop in Old San Juan, Felisa became a very successful businesswoman. At the same time, she was eagerly helping Muñoz Marín form the **Popular Democratic party** and prepare for the upcoming elections in 1940. In 1938, at the behest of Muñoz and other political friends, she sold her business and began to work full-time on the Popular Democratic party's campaign. During this period she met her future husband, Jenaro Gautier, a source of support who believed that she should "use [her] talents to help the party and the poor. Others can do the cooking" (Gruber 1972, 103). Indeed, she would use her talent as the newly appointed president of the San Juan Committee of the Popular Democratic party, which was gearing up for the 1940 elections, and would hold that position for the next thirty years. The Popular Democratic party lost the city of San Juan but won the Senate (with Muñoz Marín presiding) and eighteen of thirty-nine seats in the House. Rincón de Gautier continued to work tirelessly for the party and helped the citizenry improve their quality of life through housing, health and education projects. During the party convention leading to the 1944 elections, the delegates declared Felisa their candidate for mayor of San Juan. It was then that her husband's true colors came to light—he looked at her and shook his head. Felisa, in many ways a traditional woman, acquiesced and did not run for office. As she continued her work with the party, she began to encounter and become aware of the high level of sexism that existed in the system and realized that her present position lacked true power.

In 1946, the mayor of San Juan, Roberto Sánchez Vilella, resigned to take on another political appointment. This time, without giving it a second thought, Felisa Rincón de Gautier accepted the position and became the first woman mayor in Puerto Rico's history and the first Puerto Rican woman to hold such a high political post. From that time on she, with her trademark upswept hairstyle, became known as Doña Fela. She made city hall the "house of the people," and every Wednesday she would set aside her regular governing duties and open the doors of city hall to droves of people who would come to tell her their problems.

One of Doña Fela's major concerns was cleaning up the city of San Juan, and she had no qualms about personally calling up the sanitation department to inform them that they had not cleaned a certain street. She tirelessly crusaded to improve San Juan's quality of life everywhere she went—particularly in Washington, D.C., where she lobbied for such initiatives as **Operation Bootstrap** and **commonwealth** status. Doña Fela served five terms and retired from city hall in 1968 at the age of seventy-one. She remained politically active throughout her retirement, participating in elections and serving as a delegate to the U.S. Democratic party conventions until 1992, where, at the age of ninety-five, she was the oldest delegate.

SUGGESTED READING

Ruth Gruber, *Felisa Rincón de Gautier: The Mayor of San Juan* (New York: Thomas Y. Crowell, 1972); *Beginning Biographies of American Women*, audiovisual, six books plus six teaching companions and posters (Morristown, N.J.: Modern Curriculum Press, 1995); Magali García-Ramis, *Dona Felisa Rincón de Gautier: Mayor of San Juan* (Morristown, N.J.: Modern Curriculum Press, 1995); *Global Hispanic Biographies* (Englewood Cliffs, N.J.: Globe Book Company, 1989).

Rivera, Carlos Raquel (1923–   )   Carlos Raquel Rivera's art is expressed through prints, paintings and drawings that fall within the realm of the fantastic and surreal. A native of Río Prieto, a remote neighborhood in the coffee heartland of Yauco, he studied at the Academia de Arte Edna Coll in San Juan. In 1949 he moved to New York City where he studied with John Marsh and John Corbino at the Art Students League. He joined the art workshop at the Education Department's **Community Education Division** and worked there for several years. A committed *independentista*, his work has explored the mores and traditions of Puerto Rican culture within a nationalistic and patriotic framework that examines nature and the Puerto Rican landscape. For instance, his drawings and prints have appeared as illustrations in books written by **Juan Antonio Corretjer** and **Pedro Juan Soto**. He also painted a picture on the **Ponce Massacre**.

Rivera has participated in numerous individual and collective exhibits in Puerto Rico, the United States and Latin America. His works are part of the collection of the Ponce Art Museum and the Museum of the Institute of Puerto Rican Culture.

SUGGESTED READING

Juan Antonio Gaya-Nuño, *La pintura puertorriqueña* (Soria, Spain: Centrode Estudios Sorianos, 1944); Museo de Arte de Ponce, *Colección de Arte latinoamericano* (Ponce: Museo Arte de Ponce, n.d.).

Rivera, Graciela (1921–   )   Graciela Rivera was the first Puerto Rican woman to have a successful career in the highly competitive and exclusive world of international classical opera. She was born in **Ponce** but studied in San Juan. While she was a student at Central High School in Santurce, Dwight W. Hiestand, one of her teachers, listened to her singing and discovered the formidable quality of her coloratura soprano voice. He started promoting her musical education and nurtured her talents by organizing student productions that would give her some musical training and experience.

After high school, Rivera was accepted by the Jiulliard School of Music where she received advanced musical training and graduated in 1943. Assisted by her husband, Joseph Zumchak, she launched a successful career that took her to some of the most important stages of the world. She made her American professional operatic debut in 1945 as Adele in *Rosalinda*. During the war years, she was an active supporter of the U.S.O. and played for American soldiers on the USS *Missouri* and the USS *Philippine Sea* as well as in many hospitals and bases of the U.S. armed forces.

In February 1952 Graciela Rivera became the first Puerto Rican woman to be invited to perform at the Metropolitan Opera House in New York City. There she interpreted Lucia's part in Gaetano Donizetti's *Lucia di Lammermoor*. After a performance that the *New York Times* labeled "pure, clear and beautifully modulated," she won seven curtain calls (*New York Times* 1952). In 1952 she became the first woman to sing with the chorus of Mexico's Church of the Guadaloupe in its 500-year history. She also sang with many operatic companies throughout the United States and Europe, where she sang in England, Italy, Germany, France and Portugal. In 1950, after a performance of Rossini's *Barber of Seville* at the Royal Theater in Rome, she was received by the pope. In 1952 Donald Vail Allen of the *Times Herald* labeled her the best coloratura soprano of all time.

During her long career, Rivera was a pioneer who opened doors to the music field for many other Puerto Ricans. She appeared in the most prestigious and popular halls of New York—Lewisohn Stadium, Madison Square Garden, the Met and Radio City Music Hall—and was heard on American radio through the "CBS Concerts." For five years, Rivera had a Spanish radio show on station WHOM titled "Graciela Rivera Sings." She was a guest on television shows such as "Name that Tune" on CBS as well as "Your Show of Shows" and "The Jack Paar Show" on NBC. She was an assistant professor of music at Hostos Community College in New York for seventeen years, nurtured new talent through her Graciela Rivera Opera Workshop and was the artistic director of the Puerto Rico Opera Company.

Rivera was always proud of her humble beginnings and that she had paid for her own education at Jiulliard using her own talents and voice.

SUGGESTED READING

Rubén Alejandro Moreira, "Memorias de una voz," *El Mundo*, May 6, 1990; Adrian Gaster, *International Who's Who in Music and Musicians Directory* (Cambridge, England: International Who's Who in Music, 1980); "Graciela Rivera: Puerto Rican Soprano Wins 7 Calls before Curtain as Lucia in Her 'Met' Debut," *New York Times*, February 5, 1952; Joseph Zumchack, *Graciela Rivera: la diva puertorriqueña* (Rio Piedras: Joseph Zumchack 1990).

Rivera, Ismael (1931–1987)   This popular singer, band leader, composer and percussionist was born in Loíza Aldea and raised in Santurce. He started his musical career when he was thirteen years old and became a fixture on the popular music scene, first through his participation in Orquesta Panamericana but, above all, through the Cortijo y su Combo group. As a singer who brought **bomba** and **plena** to the highest levels of popularity and recognition in Puerto Rico and Latin America, he had a powerful and resonant voice that could adapt and improvise to the beat of most Latin music.

During his childhood, he lived in very poor and limited conditions in one of the most deprived areas of Santurce. He worked as a mason, but his singing and percussion abilities were discovered by another talented musician, **Rafael Cortijo**. Together they formed a lasting musical partnership. Although he had his own band, Ismael Rivera y sus cachimbos, he is best remembered for his association with Cortijo. Unique characteristics of Rivera's artistic genius included his improvisations and the musical games that he played with his voice during his interpretations. He recorded dozens of albums with many different bands and was widely acclaimed throughout Latin America. He is considered one of the great popular musicians of all times. During the 1970s, as he matured as a musician, Rivera successfully made the transition into the **salsa** genre. He recorded with artists from the Fania All Stars. Among the hits he interpreted and was famous for are "Quitate de la via perico," "El negro bembón" and "El Bombón de Elena." His fans called him El Sonero Mayor, which means the biggest of all!

SUGGESTED READING

Donald Clarke, *Penguin Encyclopedia of Popular Music* (New York: Penguin, 1989); César Pagano, *Ismael Rivera: El sonero mayor* (Bogotá, Colombia: Ediciones Antropos, 1992).

Rockeros   This fairly new slang term of the Puerto Rican language refers to one of the different subcultures that has emerged in Puerto Rico around American rock music and musicians. A *rockero* is a cultural composite that groups upper middle-class and upper-class youth from the island of Puerto Rico. It refers to the many fans and followers of American rock music that has progressively influenced the native musical establishment since the sixties but that grew in popularity and gained support during the eighties. *Rockeros* are individuals who adopt the demeanor, looks, and behavior of American rock musicians. A stereotypical *rockero* is a Puerto Rican young man who is highly Americanized. They wear the latest American fashions and designer clothes, attend rock concerts around the island, play rock music in their expensive European sports cars, and are fond of being associated with almost every popular cultural form that comes from the United States. *Rockeros* tend to see themselves as white, pro-American and are generally in favor of statehood for the island. They also tend to see rock music as an elite art form.

Some island sociologists suggest that *Rockeros* are a reflection of the process of hegemony at work. These are individuals who have adopted the mores, beliefs and traditions of American culture and who have accepted or created a false consciousness modeled after Americans. This term is a reflection of the powerful cultural and social dynamics that have taken place as a result of U.S. influence on the island. As a subculture, the *rockeros* are important, not because of the values and beliefs they hold, but because of the cultural distance they have established between themselves and poorer, island-oriented adolescents and teenagers.

SUGGESTED READING

Jorge Duany, "Popular Music in Puerto Rico: Toward and Anthropology of Salsa," in Vernon Boggs, ed., *Salsiology: Afro-Cuban Music and the Evolution of Salsa in New York City* (New York: Excelsior Music Publishing House, 1992); Javier Santiago, *Nueva ola portorricensis: la revolución musical que vivió Puerto Rico en la decada del 60* (Santurce: Editorial del patio, 1994).

Rodón, Francisco (1934–   )   Born in an upper-class family in San Sebastián, Rodón is one of the best-regarded Puerto Rican painters of today and perhaps one of the best painters in the nation's history. Rodón expressed an interest in painting in his youth, and his talents were immediately recognized by his teachers in San Sebastián. In the seventh grade, rather than having to write papers and critiques about books and stories, he would negotiate with his English teacher to create original illustrations for them. When he was eighteen, he started a long trip that took him through Costa Rica, San Salvador and Mexico (Gaya-Nuño 1994, 149–50). He went on to study at the Academie Julian in Paris but had difficulties operating under their academic constraints. He also studied at the Real Academia de Bellas Artes San Fernando in Madrid. Eventually he won a scholarship to study at the Academia la Esmeralda in Mexico where he spent a year. He also studied at the Student Arts League in New York and at the Graphic Arts Workshop at the Institute of Puerto Rican Culture, directed by **Lorenzo Homar.**

His art is eclectic. Critic Gaya-Nuño has labelled his art as fauve or someone in love with color (1994, 149). He has painted still-life pictures, but he is best known and regarded for his portraits. Through his paintings, Rodón pursues a quest for the identification and expression of beauty. However, he uses painting to explore the real "self" of his subjects, uncovering the complex emotional and private character that tends to stay hidden behind the public personas. During the past twenty years, Rodón's work has focused on personalities from the worlds of art and politics in Puerto Rico and Latin America. He has worked to bring to the surface the mythical and heroic dimensions of the artists and politicians of our time. His paintings of writer Jorge Luis Borges, Venezuelan president Rómulo Betancourt, famous Cuban ballerina Alicia Alonso, as well as his portrait

Francisco Rodón with one of his most well-known works, "Alicia Alonso," 1982–1983. (Ramon Korfe and *El Nuevo Día*.)

Francisco Rodón, "Penelope y el gallo." (Museo de Arte de Ponce, the Luis A. Ferré Foundation, Inc., Ponce, Puerto Rico.)

of former governor **Luis Muñoz Marín**, are all representative of this trend. Rodón's paintings are colorful, expressive and, above all, dramatic. They give the viewer a sense of the character and emotions of the subjects.

Rodón is a highly private person who focuses on his work. He has been awarded numerous prizes; among them are First Prize in Painting from the Puerto Rican Athenaeum (1969, 1963), Second Prize in Painting from the Puerto Rican Athenaeum (1961), Great Prize for Painting from the UNESCO Salon, Río Piedras (1972), Sole Prize from the UNESCO Salon, Río Piedras (1975) and the Franscico Oller Medal for painting (1983). His paintings are part of the most important collections in the United States, Europe and Latin America. They are exhibited at the Museum of Modern Art and the Metropolitan Musem of Art in New York City, the Bibliothèque National in Paris and the Chicago Art Institute.

SUGGESTED READING

Juan Antonio Gaya-Nuño, *La pintura puertorriqueña* (Soria, Spain: Centro de Estudios Sorianos, 1994); Veronica Gould Stoddart, "Art," *Américas* (January/February 1988); Museo de Arte de Ponce, *Colección de arte latinoamericano* (n.d.); Connie Underhill, "Portrait of a Portrait: The Evolution of the Portrait of Jorge Luis Borges by Francisco Rodón," *San Juan Star*, March 10, 1974.

Rodríguez Capó, Felix (1921–1989)   Born in Coamo and known as Bobby Capó, he was a talented composer and singer. Capó studied in Coamo and started his artistic career in 1937 through his participation in a radio talent show known as "Tribuna del arte." During the 1940s, he traveled to New York City and was the lead singer in **Rafael Hernández**'s Cuarteto Victoria and in Cuarteto Marcano. He was also the lead singer for the Xavier Cugat Orchestra. With this orchestra, he traveled through Cuba and Latin America, achieving the peak of his popularity. As a composer, he wrote more than 1,000 songs. Among his biggest hits were: "Piel canela," "Soñando con Puerto Rico," "Luna de miel en Puerto Rico," "El bardo," "Sin fe," "Jugete" and "De ti enamorado." One of his most transcendental compositions was the Christmas **aguinaldo** "De la montaña venimos." Capó was also a television producer and director for Channel 47 in New York, the Spanish-speaking television channel, where, for many years, he broadcast "El Show de Bobby Capó."

Capó was actively involved in Puerto Rican affairs in New York and for many years worked in the Puerto Rican Affairs Office in New York and on the New York parole board. He died at the age of sixty-seven of a heart ailment.

SUGGESTED READING

Melba Ferrer, "Entertainer Bobby Capó Dead at 67," *San Juan Star*, December 19, 1989, p. 3; Pedro Zervigón, "El regreso del hijo prodigo," *El Día,* September 14, 1987, p. 60.

Rodríguez de Tío, Lola (1843–1924)   A poet and writer, Rodríguez de Tío
is considered to be Puerto Rico's most distinguished nineteenth-century
poet. A woman of revolutionary vision, she was the author of Puerto Rico's
official anthem, "La Borinqueña." Rodríguez de Tío was born in San Germán to an upper-class family, where she was able to be educated by private
tutors. Among the resources available to her were her father's well-stocked
library, where she spent countless hours and where her initial literary awak-
ening occurred. Her parents were part of the political and intellectual elite
who believed in and sought out Puerto Rican autonomy from the Spaniards. This love of country guided her throughout her life as she wrote and
spoke in favor of Puerto Rico's independence. However, she was also very
much concerned about the lack of status for women, and her thoughts on
this issue unfold in some of her essays, including "Feminismo," "La in-
fluencia de la mujer en la civilización" (The influence of women on civilization) and an essay on the education of women.

In 1865 Lola Tío met and married Bonocio Tío Segarra, who shared
her belief in autonomy for the island. At this period of time in Puerto
Rico, women were very much subservient to men (perhaps to the extreme
of being outright property), and Rodríguez de Tío encountered tremendous sexism from her mostly male compatriots. This did not, however,
dissuade her from her continued work and struggle toward freeing political prisoners in Puerto Rican prisons, who shared with her the ideals of
nationhood for her country. One of her more defiant acts against the
sexism of the times, particularly the objectification of women as well as
dictates that women look like prim, pretty, mindless "ladies," was the
cutting off of her long hair. Cutting off her hair was not merely a capri-
cious act of rebellion, it enabled her (dressed as a man) to sneak into
nocturnal political meetings.

Thrice exiled owing to her political beliefs and her resistance to the political measures imposed by the Spanish colonial government, her family,
including her parents, lived in a number of different places, including Venezuela, Cuba and New York City. The first banishment of the family was
to Venezuela in 1877, nine years after she first recited the stanzas of "La
Borinqueña," which was later to become the national anthem, at a political
gathering.

After a few years in Venezuela, and after having met and formed a
close relationship with the renowned Puerto Rican leader, **Eugenio María
de Hostos,** she returned to Puerto Rico only to find herself again forced
into exile by the Spanish governor of the island, Segundo de la Portilla.
In 1887 de la Portilla gave Tío and her husband just a few hours to
leave the country. This time the banishment led them to Cuba, where
both she and her husband joined the growing revolutionary movement
for Cuban autonomy from the Spanish colonists. As in Puerto Rico, their
political activism resulted, in 1892, in their being forced to leave Cuba

for New York, where she and Bonicio Tío Segarra lived for the next six years.

It was during her years in exile that Rodríguez de Tío published some of her more outstanding literary work—"Mis cantares" (My songs, 1876), "Claros y nieblas" (Light and fog, 1885) and "Mi libro de Cuba" (My book about Cuba, 1893).

After the Spanish-American War in 1915, she returned to Havana and also visited Puerto Rico, where she was welcomed jubilantly by the people. Her visit to the island was considered a national event. She then returned to Cuba where she continued to write and publish, and, in 1924, she was invited to Europe for an extensive literary tour. She died upon her return to Cuba that same year.

Rodríguez de Tío's banishment from Puerto Rico on two separate occasions resulted in her traveling and living in a number of different countries. Her deep-seated feeling about her love for Puerto Rico and the reality of exile are best expressed in her poem "Autógrafo," in which she relates how, in the long run, she carries her country within her heart.

SUGGESTED READING

Loida Figueroa, "Lola Rodríguez de Tío," *Claridad*, September 16–22, 1983; Alfredo Matilla and Iván Silén, ed., *The Puerto Rican Poets* (New York: Bantam, 1972); "Notable Women Photo Display," presented by California: National Women's Project, 1989, 1994; Lola Rodríguez de Tío, *Poesías* (San Juan: Instituto de Cultural Puertorriqueña, 1960); Aurelio Tío, "Juicios sobre la obra de Lola Rodríguez de Tío," *Boletín de la Academia de Artes y Ciencias de Puerto Rico* 1 (1966): 97–114.

Romero Barceló, Carlos (1932–)   One of the most powerful and controversial politicians of his generation, he was governor of Puerto Rico from 1976 to 1984 and **Resident Commissioner** from 1992 to the present. Born in Santurce, he received his B.A. from Yale University and his law degree from the **University of Puerto Rico.** He has been actively and centrally involved in Puerto Rican politics throughout his adult life. Along with leaders like **Luis Ferré,** Romero was a founder of the **New Progressive party** (Partido Nuevo Progresita) in 1967, and he achieved electoral success when he became mayor of San Juan in 1968. Today he serves as resident commissioner to Washington, D.C., under the administration of Governor **Pedro Roselló González.**

Romero is one of the island's most controversial politicians. The police murders at **Cerro Maravilla** occurred during his first term as governor, and he has never shaken the impression that he lied during the many investigations of the incident at Cerro Maravilla. In the 1990s he has been involved in a variety of public squabbles with the members of his own party.

The governor is perhaps best known for a book, *Statehood Is for the Poor*, which is still the backbone of the Statehood party's platform. He stresses that "the State of Puerto Rico will qualify for a great deal of federal aid money" that is denied to the island under either **commonwealth** or independence. Moreover, to those who remind Puerto Ricans that they will pay federal income tax under statehood, Romero emphasizes that "Puerto Rico's per capita contribution to the Federal treasury, were we a state, would come to less that of any other state in the Union. At the same time, the per capita benefits we'd reap from federal aid programs would be greater than those of any other state in the Union" (Romero Barceló 1978, 87).

Romero is also an insightful observer of Puerto Rican life. For example, to those who cite the low vote of the Independence party as an indication of status sentiment, Romero notes that "the results of the general elections held every four years hinge on a great many issues, most of which have little or no bearing on the ultimate resolution of Puerto Rico's political status question" (104).

Whether at home or in Washington, the resident commissioner is a staunch defender of Puerto Rican culture, who reminds his many *independentista* critics that "you say English is a threat to our Puerto Rican culture. But the majority of the independence advocates are fluent in English and their feeling for Puerto Rican culture has not diminished at all. In fact, they consider themselves the purest of the Puerto Rican patriots" (Barceló 1987, 137). In November of 1996, Romero Barceló was once again elected resident commissioner of Puerto Rico. In a close vote, he defeated Celested Benítez; he received 49.9 percent of the votes to Benítez's 46 percent.

SUGGESTED READING

Carlos Romero Barceló, *Statehood Is for the Poor* (San Juan, P.R.: n.p., 1978); Carlos Romero Barceló, "La estadidad para Puerto Rico," in *Las ideas anexionistas en Puerto Rico bajo la dominación Norteamericana*, ed. Aarón Gamaliel Ramos (San Juan, P.R.: Huracán, 1987); Manuel Suarez, *Requiem on Cerro Maravilla* (Maplewood, N.J.: Waterfront Press, 1987).

Roosevelt Roads   Situated on the eastern tip of the Puerto Rican mainland, near the city of Ceiba, the Roosevelt Roads Naval Station is the largest naval station in the world. It includes the 29,000 acres of land owned by the U.S. Navy on the adjoining island of **Vieques**, and, with that land, Roosevelt Roads serves as the key U.S. facility in the Atlantic Ocean. It also serves as the coordinating center for the Navy's annual Caribbean wintertime maneuver during which all weapons systems of the Atlantic Fleet Weapons range are used. NATO forces have often trained at Roosevelt Roads, and the facility was essential to the United States when it invaded Grenada in 1983 and Panama in 1989. When President Ronald

Reagan sponsored the Contras in their war against the government of Nicaragua, the Nicaraguan counterrevolutionaries trained at Roosevelt Roads. Despite the end of the Cold War, the Navy has consistently maintained that Roosevelt Roads is essential to the well-being of the United States. The facility was formally commissioned in 1943 when President Franklin Roosevelt made a statement that still receives substantial support in U.S. military circles—that Puerto Rico was the center of a vast island shield, and "Its possession or control by any other foreign power—or even the remote threat of such possession—would be repugnant to the most elementary principles of national defense" (Roosevelt 1943, 2).

SUGGESTED READING

Paola Coletta, ed., *United States Navy and Marine Corps Bases, Overseas* (Westport, Conn.: Greenwood Press, 1986); Georges Fauriol, *Puerto Rico and the United States: Understanding the Foundations of a Strategic Relationship* (Washington, D.C.: Georgetown University Center for Strategic and International Studies, 1985); Message from the President of the United States, *Report on the Progress of Puerto Rico*, House of Representatives, 78th Cong., 1st sess., Document 304 (Washington, D.C., September 28, 1943).

Roqué de Duprey, Ana (1853–1933)   A writer and feminist leader, Ana Roqué de Duprey played an important role in laying the groundwork for bringing about the passage of women's suffrage in Puerto Rico. Her privileged upbringing provided her with many options. She completed her college career in elementary and secondary teaching and was an avid student of literature and astronomy, achieving the distinction of being named honorary member of the Paris Society of Astronomers. However, she devoted an increasing amount of her work to literary and political writing as well as the suffragist movement (see **Feminism**) in Puerto Rico.

In her research on Puerto Rican women, Edna Acosta-Belén distinguishes between two major trends in the feminist movement on the island: "the petit bourgeois and the proletarian" (1986, 7). As a product of the middle class, Roqué de Duprey's work, including the establishment of the first feminist newspaper in Puerto Rico and being a founding member of the Puerto Rican Feminine League, focused almost exclusively on women's suffrage at the expense of other important issues that were germane to working-class women. Nevertheless, in 1894, she is credited with publishing the first feminist newspaper on the island, *La mujer del siglo XX*, which opened opportunities for other literate women to promulgate their own ideas. In 1893 she began to publish *La Evolución*, another journal, targeted at the female elite, dedicated to exposing the discrimination against women. Unlike the publications of her counterparts in the labor movement, which urged women to become active in the social and political struggles of the day, Roqué de Duprey's periodicals were in more of a literary vein, where the issues surrounding women were discussed from the perspectives of bibliographic and literary reviews, essays and other literary genres.

In 1921, after the defeat in the legislature of three bills that would have emancipated women and given then the right to vote, Roqué de Duprey, in a letter to Félix Matos Bernier, known as one of the most antifeminist legislators in that debate, blamed the bill's defeat on the fear that the poor would prevail and the bourgeois were afraid. She had realized that unleashing the political power of 300,000 women was threatening to the establishment. In 1932, a year before her death, her lifetime struggle for women's suffrage in Puerto Rico was realized.

In the literary arena, Ana Roqué de Duprey's work includes *Explicaciones de gramática castellana* (1889), *Geografía universal* (written with Alejandro Infiesta in 1894), *Pasatiempos* (1894), *Novelas y cuentos* (1895) and *Luz y sombra* (1903).

SUGGESTED READING

Edna Acosta-Belén, *The Puerto Rican Woman: Perspectives on Culture, History, and Society* (New York: Praeger, 1986); Yamila Azize, *La mujer en la lucha* (San Juan: Editorial Cultural, 1985); María Teresa Babín, *Panorama de la cultura puertorriqueña* (New York: Las Americas Publishing, 1958).

Rosselló González, Pedro (1944–)   The governor of Puerto Rico since 1992, Rosselló was born in Santurce, graduated from Norte Dame University and received his medical degree from Yale University. In Puerto Rico, Rosselló was a faculty member at the **University of Puerto Rico** School of Medicine. While there, he became chief of the Department of Pediatric Surgery and chief surgeon at Children's Hospital. In 1985 Baltazar Corrada del Río, then mayor of San Juan, appointed Rosselló to the directorship of the Department of Health in San Juan. He occupied that position until 1988. Later he became the medical director of Hospital San Jorge, a pediatric hospital in Santurce.

In 1988 Rosselló launched a career in politics when he accepted the **New Progressive party**'s nomination to run as a candidate for **resident commissioner** in Washington, D.C. He lost that election but, in 1991, Rosselló became the president of his party. In 1992 he became governor of Puerto Rico when he won the election by the biggest margin of any candidate in the past twenty years. His achievements include the passing of a comprehensive health reform package and a vigorous anticrime offensive to control **crime** and **drugs** that included sending the National Guard into public housing complexes to patrol and regulate criminal activity. His critics have charged that these efforts violate basic political rights.

One of Rosselló's most ambitious proposals would provide low-income and underprivileged Puerto Ricans with a **health** plan. His program, known as "La Tarjetita," has been vigorously implemented by his Secretary of

Governor Pedro Rosselló with former governor Romero Barceló, 1995. (Juan Rivas and *El Nuevo Día*.)

Health Carmen Feliciano de Melecio. It has been perceived by the voters and the public as a huge success even while Rosselló's oponents argue that it will throw the island unto debt.

Keeping a campaign promise, in 1993, Governor Rosselló sponsored a referendum on the island's future political status. His preferred alternative, statehood, was narrowly defeated. Rosselló has worked hard to eliminate the 936 tax laws (see **Tax Laws and Exemptions**) that are crucial to many of the island's manufacturing facilities. Critics charge that he wants to create an economic crisis that will force Congress to admit Puerto Rico as the fifty-first state.

In November 1996 Governor Rosselló overwhelmingly won the gubernatorial elections, receiving 51.2 percent of the vote. His principal opponent, Luis Acevedo, received 44.4 percent of the vote. With his total of 1,000,940 votes, Rosselló was the first gubernatorial candidate in Puerto Rican history to receive more than 1 million votes. In a remarkable commentary on the commitment of Puerto Ricans to the democratic process, more than 82 percent of the registered voters went to the polls.

SUGGESTED READING

Pedro Rosselló, *Who's Who in America*, 48th ed. (New Providence, N.J.: Marquis Who's Who, 1994).

S

Sáez, Antonia (1889–1964)   This educator and scholar spent her career teaching, researching and publishing in the field of Spanish language and literature. She began teaching in her native town of Humacao in 1908, and seventeen years later, upon her completion of a B.A. degree in secondary education, she moved to Central High School, the largest secondary school in metropolitan San Juan, where she taught commercial Spanish. In 1930 Sáez completed a master's degree at the **University of Puerto Rico,** and by 1931 she had finished her doctoral studies in Madrid, Spain. Her doctoral dissertation, titled "El teatro en Puerto Rico" was considered, at the time, to be the most comprehensive scholarly work on Puerto Rican theater. In addition to the research focusing on theater as a genre, she includes a historical perspective on theater in Puerto Rico, including all the native theatrical companies and their productions, the artists, the local stages where plays were produced and narratives on the events surrounding these presentations. It was the first publication of its type and was lauded as a contribution to Puerto Rican culture during a time when other colleagues of Sáez (e.g., **Concha Meléndez, Carmen Gómez Tejera** and **Margot Arce de Vázquez**) were focusing on topics germane to Puerto Rican culture and literature.

After completing her doctoral degree, Sáez dedicated a quarter of a century to training teachers at the University of Puerto Rico's School of Education. Among her publications during this time, there are two in particular that, for a very long time, served as basic textbooks in Spanish language arts courses. These books, *Las artes del lenguaje en la escuela elemental* (1944) and *La lectura, arte del lenguaje* (1948) won the Puerto Rican Institute of Culture annual award for literary and pedagogical excellence.

These books, in particular, have been lauded, not only for the clarity of writing given their didactic nature, but also for the contribution they made to creative teaching and to the use of the vernacular in the classroom.

SUGGESTED READING

Julita Córdova, "Antonia Sáez, mujer y maestra" *Boletín de la Sociedad de Autores Puertorriqueños*, (July 1979): 27–34; Cesáreo Rosa Nieves and Esther Melón, *Biografía Puertorriqueñas: Perfil histórico de un pueblo* (Sharon, Conn.: Troutman Press, 1970); Antonia Sáez, *El teatro en Puerto Rico* (San Juan: Editorial Universidad de Puerto Rico, 1950).

Salsa   This highly popular Puerto Rican music and dance form has been evolving during the last twenty-five years. Salsa is the cultural product and artistic contribution of Puerto Ricans living in New York City. Although it is not exclusively interpreted or produced by **Nuyoricans** (Cubans, Venezuelans, Panamanians and other Latin American groups also produce it), it has been historically performed and developed by them. As a music genre, salsa is a hybrid that represents many of the cultures and nationalities interacting together in the barrio of New York as well as many of their indigenous music forms.

Salsa has its roots in the Cuban rhythm known as the *son*; however, it combines elements of Afro-Antillean music such as the Puerto Rican **bomba** and **plena**. Salsa is the most significant artistic import from the 2.5 million Puerto Ricans who live in the United States. Its highly rhythmic music uses a similar song and response structure, with a singer and a chorus, as *bomba* and *plena*. Salsa, which is interpreted by orchestras, has strong percussion and brass elements. It uses a four-by-four, or six-by-eight percussion pattern known as *la clave*—the key or recipe. It lays on popular themes that are of relevance to groups of Puerto Ricans and Latinos in the United States, Puerto Rico and Latin America.

During the 1970s, salsa music received an enormous economic and commercial boost from music producers in the United States who recognized the commercial potential and impact of this music and brought it to the public. Lawyer and entrepreneur Jerry Masucci from Fania Records is one example. Puerto Rican singers, such as Andy Montañez, Hector Lavoe and Willie Colón, took it from New York to the island and popularized it there. Salsa music is very prevalent in contemporary Puerto Rican society, and scores of radio stations, such as Salsa 93 (*La Zeta*), use salsa as the basis of their programming. Salsa groups are a fixture of concert halls and television programs in Puerto Rico. A new trend is blending salsa with American jazz and trying to fuse the two genres.

SUGGESTED READING

Jorge Duany, "Popular Music in Puerto Rico: Toward an Anthropology of Salsa," in *Salsiology: Afro-Cuban Music and the Evolution of Salsa in New York City*, ed.

Vernon Boggs (New York: Excelsior Music Publishing Company, 1992); Charley Gerard and Marty Sheller, *Salsa!: The Rhythm of Latin Music* (Crown Point, Ind.: White Cliffs Media, 1989); Peter Manuel, "Puerto Rican Music and Cultural Identity: Creative Appropriation of Cuban Sources from Danza to Salsa," *Ethnomusicology*, 38 (2), 1994; Brittmarie Pérez, "Political Facets of Salsa," *Popular Music*, Vol. 6 (2), 1987.

Sánchez Erazo, Jesús (1900–1979)　　This singer, composer and musician was known by the artistic name of Chuito el de Bayamón. He was born in the Bayamón area into a very poor family. He worked in agriculture (sugar cane plantations and cigar making) during his youth. While he was working, he learned to interpret the songs and music forms of the countryside. He was a master of *décimas*, **seis**, **aguinaldos** and controversies (a musical/rhetorical challenge undertaken by two musicians interpreting native folk tunes with **cuatros** or guitars). Chuito started to write songs early in his youth, and his career skyrocketed with the introduction of radio and television to the island. Along with Felipe Rosario Goyco (Don Felo), another icon of native music, he participated in many media programs and was one of the best-regarded interpreters of native music.

Dressed in white clothes, much like those worn by **jíbaros**, and wearing a wide-brimmed palm hat and a colorful handkerchief around his collar, he traveled throughout the world carrying his Puerto Rican music. He contributed to the musical folklore of the island through his singing and writing; his compositions are still part of the music repertoire used by Puerto Ricans during the Christmas season. He won many awards, and during his long career as a musician he recorded more than forty records. Some of his most popular compositions are "Yo me tomo el ron," "La vieja voladora" and "El cotorro y el leal."

SUGGESTED READING

José Toro Sugrañes, *Nueva enciclopedia de Puerto Rico* (Hato Rey, P.R.: Editorial Lector, 1995).

Sánchez, Luis Rafael (1936–　)　　Sánchez, who writes primarily in the genres of theater and the novel was born in Humacao. He received his education at the **University of Puerto Rico**, New York University and the Universidad Complutence de Madrid.

Sánchez, an insightful observer of Puerto Rico's modern society and its culture, is one of the most respected contemporary writers in Puerto Rico. Highly concerned with popular culture, Sánchez wants to explore its manifestations in society and the way it reflects and affects the national thinking. He is particularly interested in revealing the natural processes by which Puerto Rican society, through its people and institutions, creates, generates and exalts its own people into icons or heroes. He accomplishes this by

Luis Rafael Sánchez, 1991. (*El Nuevo Día*.)

using celebrities, by immersing his readers in the most "mundane" plots and by making the readers relate to the sometimes vulgar elements of the popular culture. Sánchez exposes the fragile side, the inconsistencies and weaknesses of popular discourse, by underlining Puerto Ricans' quest for popular heroes. This can be appreciated in a small fragment of his biographic novel *Importancia de llamarse Daniel Santos*:

Readers, I present Daniel Santos' other public, the one that is not accounted for among the proletarian multitudes across the Andes, Costa de los Mosquitos, from Veracruz to Darién, from Pinar del Río to Vieques, from *Punta de Gallinas* to *Tierra del Fuego*. Daniel Santos rewards the expectations of marginalization. But only, marginalization that stops the ones those who make them exist seeking happiness in hell. (Sánchez 1988, 87)

Sánchez's work suggests, or at least leaves the door open for the reader and critic to believe, that these weaknesses may be the cause, or effect, of many of Puerto Rico's other social and political illnesses, perhaps as a result of the colonial status. He is concerned with the hegemonic process and its devastating effects on the public mind. Sánchez's style is impeccable, and he is a sophisticated technician who masters language like few other contemporary writers. His command of intertextual techniques is absolute. Among his most prominent theater works include *Farsa de amor compradito* and *La pasión según Antigona Pérez: O acs el alma*. His novel *La guaracha del Macho Camacho* (1986) has been one of his most critically acclaimed pieces. Sánchez teaches at the University of Puerto Rico and in the United States.

SUGGESTED READING

Marie-Lise Gazarian Gautier, *Interviews with Latin American Writers* (Elmwood Park, Ill.: Dalkey Archive Press, 1989); Nelida Hernández Vargas and Daisy Caraballo, *Luis Rafael Sánchez: Crítica y bibliografía* (Río Piedras: Editorial U.P.R., 1985); William Luis and Ann González, *Dictionary of Literary Biography: Modern Latin-American Fiction Writers* (Detroit: Gale Research, 1994); "Luis Rafael Sánchez," *Who's Who among Hispanic Americans* (Detroit: Gale Research, 1994); Luis Rafael Sánchez, *La guaracha del Macho Camacho* (Ciudad de la Habana, Cuba: Casa de las Americas, 1986); Luis Rafael Sánchez, *La importancia de llamarse Daniel Santos* (Hanover, N.H.: Ediciones del Norte, 1988).

San Juan Star   The *San Juan Star* is the only English-language daily newspaper published on the island of Puerto Rico at the time of this writing. The *Star*, as it is commonly known, has been published on the island since 1959. Although it has a very small circulation when compared to the other newspapers—it publishes only 35,000 papers daily—it has gained substa]ntial levels of credibility and respect from the public. This has been made possible by its highly independent editorial policy which submits government, business and the political establishment to close scrutiny. Throughout the years, the *Star* has been able to recruit a body of skilled and talented reporters who have brought distinction to its pages. In addition, it has published columns from some of the most important public and intellectual figures of the island. It has assumed a tough stance against government corruption. The *Star* has been praised for the quality of its cultural, artistic and literary reviews. It is considered to be the newspaper of the privileged class or the power elite in Puerto Rico. In 1961 the *Star*'s editor, William Dorville, won a Pulitzer Prize for editorial writing.

SUGGESTED READING

Gary Braun, *Gale Directory of Publications and Broadcast Media* (New York: ITP, 1996); José A. Romeu, *Panorama del periodismo puertorriqueno* (Rio Piedras: VPREX, 1985).

Sanromá, Jesús María (1902–1982)   Sanromá, who was born in Carolina but raised in Fajardo by his Catalonian parents, is the most famous pianist ever to come out of the island and one of the best-regarded pianists in the United States. He enjoyed a long and fruitful professional life. He studied with Antoinette Szumowska at the New England Conservatory in Boston with funds from a scholarship given to him by the government of Puerto Rico. He also studied with piano masters Alfred Corlot in France and Arthur Schnabel in Berlin.

As a pianist, Sanromá had an impressive career. His specialty was contemporary music, and he premiered Walter Piston's *Concertino* in 1937 and Paul Hindemith's *Concerto* in 1947. He traveled the world giving concerts and was showcased in the leading European capitals. From 1926 to 1944 he was a pianist with the Boston Symphony Orchestra. He taught at the New England Conservatory from 1930 to 1941, was chair of the music department at the **University of Puerto Rico** at Río Piedras from 1951 to 1959 and held the chairmanship of the piano department at the Puerto Rico Conservatory of Music from 1959 to 1980.

He was a prominent personality in Puerto Rican society. For example, he was the protagonist of the poetic biography *El niño Sanromá*, by noted writer **Emilio S. Belaval**. Sanromá was also very active in cultural and public life in Puerto Rico and often participated in public concerts and recitals on the island. He recorded many albums of Puerto Rican music—**danzas**. He gave several piano concerts with amateur players and even with former governor **Luis Ferré**, a close friend of his.

SUGGESTED READING

Emilio Belaval, *El niño Sanromá* (San Juan, P.R.: BAP, 1952); H. Wiley Hitchcock and Stanley Sadie, *New Grove Dictionary of American Music* (New York: Groves Dictionary of Music, 1986); Arthur Jacobs, *Penguin Dictionary of Musical Performers* (New York: Penguin, 1990); Stanley Sadie, *New Grove Dictionary of Opera*. London: Macmillan, 1992); Nicolas Slonimsky, *Baker's Biographical Dictionary of Musicians* (New York: Schirmer Books, 1992).

Santería   This religion arrived on the shores of Puerto Rico and other Caribbean islands with the slave trade (see **Slavery**). The slaves came from West Africa, what is today Nigeria, from a tribe called the Yoruba (see **African Roots**). As slaves, the Yoruba people were forced to learn the Spanish language and to worship Catholic saints and the Catholic God. In their desire to maintain their own traditions, the Yoruba found similarities between their deities and the Catholic saints. This connection, if superficial, gave the new religion the name Santería, or worship of the saints. The Yorubas' deities became represented by Catholic saints. In this way, when their Spanish masters saw them worshipping Santa Barbara, for example, they were actually secretly worshipping Changó, the god of thunder. Be-

Botánica with artifacts used in the practice of Santería. (*El Nuevo Día.*)

cause of this mixture of the Spanish and Yoruba languages, today Santería has both Spanish and African terminology. In addition to the main god, known as Olorun or Olodumare, there are many other *orishas* or deities; the seven most popular are sometimes referred to as the Seven African Powers or *Seite Potencias*.

The traditions of Santería are still preserved today, and anyone engaged in this religion is required to know the rituals, songs and language of the religion. Initiates, who follow a rigorous regimen, are answerable to their god Olorun. During the first year of the initiation the initiate, or *Iyawó*, must dress in white. The initiate cannot look into a mirror, touch anyone or allow himself or herself to be touched; the initiate may not wear makeup or go out at night for the entire year. When he or she becomes a priest or priestess, he or she is received and comes under the protection of one of the *orishas*.

The rituals of Santería typically begin with an invocation to Olorun, while drums play African rhythms. The *Óru*, or rhythm, changes to that associated with a specific *orisha*, who is invoked at this time. At times, animals, most commonly chickens, are sacrificed. Practioners of Santería, often criticized by animal rights groups, have been quick to point out that these animals are killed in a humane manner and are later eaten.

It is believed that there are many hundreds of thousands of believers of Santería throughout the Caribbean and Latin America. In Puerto Rico, the practice of Santería coexists with the main religion, Catholicism. For many years, the Catholic Church banned Santería. Many Puerto Ricans see nothing contradictory in being devotees of several creeds, although the Catholic Church is preferred for solemn occasions such as weddings and baptisms.

SUGGESTED READING

George Brandon, *Santería from Africa to the New World: The Dead Sell Memories* (Bloomington: Indiana Press, 1993); Joseph M. Murphy, *Santería: African Spirits in America* (Boston: Beacon Press, 1993).

Seditious Conspiracy   Seditious conspiracy is essentially treason; however, prosecutors need only show that a defendant *planned* to do something—that he or she "conspired to overthrow, put down or destroy by force the government of the United States" (*U.S. vs. Jose Rodriguez*, 1986). With few exceptions in the entire twentieth century, the only people federal prosecutors have tried for seditious conspiracy were Puerto Ricans. The most famous case was that of **Pedro Albizu Campos** in 1936.

Conventional wisdom in Puerto Rico argues that federal prosecutors decided to try Albizu and eight other leaders of the **Nationalist party** because of their involvement in the assassination of the U.S. chief of police in San Juan in February 1936. In fact, Justice Department investigators had already left San Juan weeks before the assassination. In what Federal District

Attorney Cecil Snyder called "the most important criminal case ever tried in Puerto Rico," the government meant to show that Albizu did in fact conspire to overthrow the government of the United States (Roosevelt Library 1938, 3).

The problem was that Albizu never denied the charge. He was an open revolutionary, with a great deal of popular support. The heads of the island's Republican (statehood) and Liberal (independence one day, autonomy the next) parties had both sent President Franklin Roosevelt requests to stop the trial; and, throughout island, one municipality after another echoed the requests of their political leaders: Free Albizu. The first trial ended in a hung jury. The seven Puerto Ricans said not guilty; the five Americans said guilty as charged. Disgusted with the verdict, Prosecutor Snyder called another trial within a week. This time, with only 5,000 Americans on the entire island, the ten North American and two Puerto Rican jurors all voted to convict Albizu and his Nationalist colleagues.

Two years later, President Roosevelt received a letter (dated October 17, 1938) from Elmer Ellsworth, one of the U.S. jurors. He supported efforts for an immediate grant of clemency because

I can't refrain from saying that my associates on the jury all seemed to be motivated by strong if not violent prejudice against the Nationalists and were prepared to convict them regardless of the evidence. Ten of the jurors were Americans resident in Puerto Rico and the two Puerto Ricans were closely associated with American business interests. It was evident from the composition of the jury that the Nationalists did not and could not get a fair trial. (Files of the American Civil Liberties Union 1938, vol. 2053)

In response to this letter, President Roosevelt did nothing. The Nationalists remained in jail and, when he was later offered a pardon, Albizu refused it. To accept the pardon was to accept the legitimacy of U.S. authority over Puerto Rico and its people. Since that was out of the question, Albizu remained in prison.

The case represents a sore spot in Puerto Rican history, not only because of the kangaroo court assembled by Cecil Snyder. The deeper issue is the alleged impossibility of treason if, following the precedent set in Congress by **Luis Muñoz Rivera** in 1914 and 1916, a Puerto Rican refuses to accept American citizenship. Is it possible to commit treason against a government one does not recognize?

SUGGESTED READING

Albizu et al. vs. United States, no. 3174, *Federal Reporter*, 2d series, vol. 88, February 12, 1937; Ronald Fernandez, *The Disenchanted Island: Puerto Rico and the United States in the Twentieth Century*, 2d ed. (Westport, Conn.: Praeger, 1996); Files of the American Civil Liberties Union, Princeton University Library, Vol.

2053, letter dated October 17, 1938; Roosevelt Library, Official File 400, Box 24, Folder marked Puerto Rico, 1938, p. 3.

Seis *Seis* is one of the most popular forms of native Puerto Rican music. According to Francisco López Cruz, a former professor of the **University of Puerto Rico** and the foremost authority on Puerto Rican folkloric music, the *seis* constitutes "the backbone" of Puerto Rican native music (López Cruz 1967, 3). *Seis* is a very broad term. It encompasses a wide array of musical verse forms that can be found in the Puerto Rican countryside and are interpreted by the **jíbaros** and people from the mountains.

The origins of this rhythm are not known. While it has some similarities to some Andalusian rhythms, it seems that the origins of the name *seis*, which means six, reflects the number of people that initially danced it. However, the *seis* has elements of most universal dances. López believed that the origins of this rhythm were in Spanish music that has evolved from other rhythms and was changed slowly by its Puerto Rican interpreters through generations. *Seis* is characterized by a two-by-four music compass with frequent triplets and syncopations. It is played by **cuatros**, or guitars, **guiros** and other popular instruments. It is characterized by having a simple melody and harmony with elements that repeat themselves in a monotonous way. The *seis* serves as the backdrop for troubadours who either sing by themselves or sing in couples (i.e., they sing verses back and forth challenging each other in a form called a controversy). It generally has verses of ten lines (*décimas*), and each one them has eight syllables.

Seis are always untitled. They are classified by such characteristics as choreography, subject matter and interpreters. There are more than two dozen variations of this music form, including *chorreao, bombeao, controversia, amarrao* and *bayamonés*. The *seis* provides the roots or the foundations for other Puerto Rican rhythms such as **danzas**. Although the presence of this form has diminished in the cities, it can still be found in the center of the island.

SUGGESTED READING

Fransisco López Cruz, *La música folklórica de Puerto Rico* (Sharon, Conn.: Troutman Press, 1967).

Silva, Myrta (1913–1987) This singer, composer and artistic promoter was born in Arecibo and has been a colorful and important presence in the world of entertainment in New York City, Puerto Rico and Latin America. Her career as a singer started in 1938 when she was just 15. She traveled to New York City where she sang for **Rafael Hernández**'s prestigious Cuarteto Victoria. When she was fifteen, violinist and orchestra director Julio Roque invited her to sing with her orchestra where she became very well known with her recordings of *guarachas* such as "La llave," "Salambó"

Myrta Silva, 1977. (Luis R. Ramos and *El Nuevo Día*.)

and "Dejamelo ver." Roque also opened the doors for her to the New York Spanish Theater. She signed a recording contract with RCA and became one of the most popular singers under that label. During the 1940s she toured Latin America with great success. In Mexico she debuted at Teatro Marcos where she charmed the Mexican audiences. In Cuba she appeared on radio stations CMQ and Radio Progreso, and she sang with the famous orchestra La Sonora Matancera. (Celia Cruz replaced her when she left.) She also traveled to Hollywood where she entertained at the popular cabaret Copacabana. In 1947 she recorded the tune "Chencha la gambá," a musical landmark that will always be associated with her.

During the 1950s, Silva became one of the early successes of Puerto Rican **television**. In 1956 she produced a variety show, "Una hora contigo," which focused on Latin American music. She also produced television programs for Channel 47 in New York City. During the 1960s, she promoted many musical shows and American artists on the island. In 1971 she started a television program, known as "Tira y tapate," which attracted a large audience.

Myrta Silva, who was a highly prolific musical composer, is considered to be one of the most important female and most important Puerto Rican composers of this period. During her lifetime, she wrote scores of songs that became musical hits in Puerto Rico and Latin America. Among her songs were "¿Qué sabés tú?" "Cuando vuelvas," "Así es la vida," "En mi soledad," "Todo," "Mi equivocación," "Salud cariño" and "Tengo que acostumbrarme."

Silva was a very colorful performer. A heavyset woman, she appeared elegantly dressed with an attractive handkerchief wrapped around her head, but she used unlady-like language and walked and danced in a style that appealed to the masses. She was highly controversial in artistic circles because of her straightforward and acerbic manner. One of the features of her program was a gossip session, in which she aired the dirty laundry of various artistic and public personalities on the island. Although she was liked by many, she was also feared and hated by others.

SUGGESTED READING

Cristobal Díaz-Ayala, "El legado de Myrta Silva," *El Nuevo Día*, March 6, 1988, 62; "Así era Myrta Sylva," *El Vocero* (San Juan), December 5, 1987, 34–35.

Situado, El   El situado was the Spanish term for the funds that underwrote Puerto Rico's military government when the island was a Spanish colony. Beginning in 1574 and continuing until 1824, the Spanish crown sent money to Mexico, headquarters of the Spanish empire in the Americas. From Mexico a portion of the money, *El situado*, went to Puerto Rico to sustain and maintain the military forces based there. (During these centuries, Puerto Rico's function for the Spanish was as a military bastion.) As late as 1765 **Alejandro de O'Reilly** discovered that the Spanish had never concerned themselves with agricultural or industrial development. The island was a military post; its people's long-term well-being was not an important concern for the Spanish crown.

If the *situado* had regularly arrived on time, the military and civilian forces might have maintained themselves without resorting to other strategies and tactics. However, because of shipwrecks, attacks by pirates or the European wars that always spilled over into the Caribbean, the *situado* frequently failed to appear, leaving the military bastion with a terrible choice: starve or develop other means of survival. The result was two Puerto Rican economies—the always fragile one that relied on the *situado* and the one that developed by engaging in a highly profitable contraband trade with the enemies and allies of Spain. The endless miles of open shore provided a marvelous place for islanders and their customers to meet surreptitiously. Thus, long before the invasion by the United States, Puerto Ricans and Yankees traded goods and services. It was the only way for the neglected colony to survive, and, as **Ricardo Alegría** points out, "The dual economy provoked by the clandestine commerce is the link that identifies us. Although it may seem contradictory, the truth is that the trade with the powerful enemies of Spain maintained our personality as an Hispanic people" (Alegría 1988, 75).

Ironically, there is a dual economy in Puerto Rico today. In a society that now relies so heavily on **food stamps**, people cannot show too much income or they lose the stamps. Thus, since the mid-1970s, Puerto Rico has had two economies, the above-ground economy in which people collect and use the stamps and the underground economy in which people exchange goods, services and unreported income.

SUGGESTED READING

Arturo Morales Carrion, *Puerto Rico and the Non-Hispanic Caribbean* (Río Piedras: University of Puerto Rico, 1952); James Dietz, *Economic History of Puerto Rico* (Princeton, N.J.: Princeton University Press, 1986); Ricardo Alegría, ed. *Temas de la historia de Puerto Rico* (San Juan, P.R.: Centro de Estudios Avanzados de Puerto Rico and El Caribe, 1988); Angel López Cantos, *Miguel Enríquez: Corsario Boricua del siglo XVIII* (San Juan, P.R.: Ediciones Puerto, 1994).

Slavery   The introduction of African slaves by the Spanish conquerors goes back to the very first days of the colonization of Puerto Rico (see **African Roots**). Luis M. Díaz Soler, a historian specializing in the topic of slavery on the island, suggests that slaves may have come to the island as early as 1509, during **Ponce de León**'s second trip to Puerto Rico (1953, 28). The official introduction of slaves to the island, however, took place in 1513 when the Spanish government issued a royal decree authorizing the introduction of slaves through a system of licenses. People who wanted to bring slaves to the island could do so through a payment of two *ducados*. The system of importing slaves was eventually liberalized and changed to a system of *asientos* by which individuals were allowed to import large numbers of slaves directly from Africa. In addition, the British fostered a powerful system of contraband throughout the Caribbean and Puerto Rico, by trading slaves for goods from the island.

Slavery, an accepted practice in Spain and in other parts of Europe during the fifteenth and sixteenth centuries, was continued by the Spanish Empire to develop the Puerto Rican economy. Since the Taíno population (see **Los Taínos**) was exterminated by the brutal work and European diseases, Spain sought other labor resources to mine the gold and silver deposits found on the island. Once the mineral resources were depleted, slaves started to do work in agriculture, particularly in the sugar cane industry. Most of them lived in the coastal areas of the island.

Two types of slaves were brought to the island. They first ones were *ladino* slaves. *Ladinos* had been in Spain before coming to Puerto Rico. They were converted to Catholicism and had been employed in domestic chores. The second type of slave was the *bozales*, who were imported directly from Africa. Colonizers initially preferred importing *ladino* slaves, believing that they were more humble and docile. Eventually, as they started to rebel, the Spanish government forbade the introduction of *ladinos*.

On the other hand, Díaz Soler identifies three types of slaves on the island: domestic, *de tala* and *jornaleros*. Domestic slaves were employed to do the household chores for their masters. *De tala* (plowshare) slaves worked in agriculture in the countryside. The third kind, *jornaleros,* were rented out on behalf of their masters. The population of slaves in Puerto Rico rose steadily throughout the years of Spanish domain. In 1765, when **Alejandro de O'Reilly** conducted his census, 12.6 percent of the population was made up of slaves. By 1795 it had grown to 18,056, and by 1830 it had increased to 31,874 (Silvestrini and Luque de Sánchez 1992, 107).

Until recently, there was no major evidence of a generalized insurrection by slaves in Puerto Rico. Although the first documented rebellion goes back to 1527, it was seen as a localized and minor event. There has been a common misperception of these slaves as passive, submissive and servile. Recent research has shown that this perception is not valid. Guillermo Baralt has been able to document at least twenty insurrections launched by slaves in various parts of the island. He has brought forth the importance of rebellious slaves who escaped from their masters and hid away in the mountainside (Baralt 1985).

During the nineteenth century, a substantial movement favoring the emancipation of slaves emerged both in Puerto Rico and Spain. In Spain, the *Sociedad Abolicionista Española* (Spanish Abolitionist Society) organized by Julio Vizcarrondo (1830–1889), a Puerto Rican living there, took the lead promoting the abolition of slavery. In Puerto Rico, political leaders such as José Julián Acosta (1825–1891), **Segundo Ruiz Belvis** (1829–1867), Francisco Mariano Quiñones (1826–1898), **Román Baldorioty de Castro** (1822–1889) and **Román Emeterio Betances** (1827–1898) played a crucial role in the process through their efforts with the *Partido Liberal Reformista* (Liberal Reformist Party). Due to the relentless efforts of these leaders on behalf of the slaves, the Spanish National Assembly abolished slavery on March 22, 1873.

SUGGESTED READING

Guillermo Baralt, *El machete de Ogún: Las luchas de los esclavos en Puerto Rico: Siglo 19* (Río Piedras: Centro de Estudios de la Realidad Puertorriqueña, 1990); Guillermo Baralt, *Esclavos rebeldes: conspiraciones y sublevaciones de esclavos en Puerto Rico* (Río Piedras: Ediciones Huracán, 1985); Luis M. Díaz Soler, *Historia de la esclavitud negra en Puerto Rico* (Río Piedras: Editorial Universitaria, 1953); Francisco Scarano, *Sugar and Slavery in Puerto Rico: The Plantation Economy of Ponce, 1800–1850* (Madison: University of Wisconsin Press, 1984); Blanca G. Silvestrini and María Dolores Luque de Sánchez, *Historia de Puerto Rico: Trayectoria de un pueblo* (San Juan: Cultural Puertorriqueña, 1992).

Solá, Mercedes (1879–1923)   Mercedes Solá was a political theorist, organizer and activist of the feminist movement (see **Feminism**) in Puerto Rico and, with other members of the intellectual elite, such as **Ana Roqué de Duprey** and **Isabel Andreau de Aguilar**, was a leading force in the political struggle to bring about the passage of women's suffrage. Mercedes Solá was one of the founders, and later the administrator, of the feminist newspaper *La mujer del siglo XX* (Twentieth century woman). "Human rights cannot be the exclusive privilege of half of the population, but of all human beings," was the motto under which it published news and articles. It was the creation of this journal that led to the establishment, by educated middle-class women, of the Puerto Rican Feminine League, the first feminist organization on the island (see **Feminism**).

There were two parallel factions of feminists—privileged women and working-class women—at that time. Solá, however, recognized that it was crucial to organize all women into the movement in order to attain their goal. This became particularly clear to her when she saw the sheer numbers of women recruited by the labor movement. Consequently, she began to promote a strategy of alliance, both in her speeches and in her writing, encouraging both factions of the feminist activists (the working-class Socialist Suffragist League and the middle-class Puerto Rican Feminine League) to unite. It was 1921, three years after the first suffragist bill had been defeated and the feminist movement had been in disarray for some time.

In 1922 Solá, an advocate of autonomy for the island, was selected as a delegate to the Pan-American Conference of the National League of

Women Voters. At the conference, she presented a resolution calling for sovereignty for Puerto Rico; this resolution was censored by the leadership of the conference under the guise that the League of Women Voters was nonpartisan. Indefatigable in her struggle for women's right to vote, she died in 1923 without realizing her goal, which was not achieved until 1932, almost a decade later.

One of her most quoted essays on feminism, written in 1922, makes a case for education and economic independence as fundamental to women's freedom, a notion not far from what feminists are declaring in this day and age. Feminist scholar Edna Acosta-Belén described Solá's 1922 essay "Feminismo" as "a legacy and inspiration to the contemporary feminist movement."

SUGGESTED READING

Edna Acosta-Belén, *The Puerto Rican Woman: Perspectives on Culture, History, and Society* (New York: Praeger, 1986); Yamila Azize, *La mujer en la lucha* (San Juan: Editorial Cultural, 1985).

Somohano, Arturo (1910–1977)   Somohano, a distinguished pianist, composer and musical director who occupied center stage in Puerto Rican cultural and artistic circles during most of this century, was born in San Juan.

As a musician, Somohano played a key role in revitalizing Puerto Rican popular music and bringing **danzas**, a sound of a bygone era, to many Puerto Rican audiences. Similar to Arthur Fiedler, John Williams or Arthur Copland in the United States, he brought popular musical forms to the classical stage and contributed to its legitimization by the elite culture. One of his best-known compositions was "Canción de las Américas" (Song of the Americas). This hymn was popularized by American troops fighting in World War II. It later became a popular hymn on the island. Somohano also wrote many musical scores for drama and theater.

Somohano was a proud ambassador of Puerto Rican music. He carried the native tunes of Puerto Rico throughout the United States, Europe and Latin America. In Puerto Rico, he was a visible figure of the arts who entertained scores of Puerto Ricans not only at the elite music centers of the island but also at some of the island's most visited hotels. Somohano was one of the founders of the Capital Philharmonic Orchestra and the Puerto Rican Philharmonic Orchestra.

SUGGESTED READING

"Arturo Somohano," *ASCAP Biographic Dictionary* (New York: R. R.: Bowker Co., 1980).

Soto, Pedro Juan (1928–)   This versatile contemporary writer is best known for his novels, short stories, essays and plays. Soto's work is characterized by a realistic but acerbic, critical and negative vision of the relationships between North Americans and Puerto Ricans. His works explore and provide insights into what he sees as a historic relationship of oppression and exploitation of Puerto Rico by the United States. He paints a sarcastic picture of the way in which the island and islanders' relationship with the United States has fostered the development of a colonial mentality among Puerto Ricans. He has a gloomy and pessimistic view of Puerto Rican society and Puerto Ricans in light of their relationship with the imperial power—the United States.

His visions were influenced by his experiences as a university student in New York City during the 1950s and by his participation in the Korean War. In 1979 Soto suffered a terrible blow when his son, **Francisco Soto Arriví**, was ambushed and murdered by armed policemen during the **Cerro Maravilla** incident. His son, an ardent *independentista*, was lured by a police informant into a plan to blow up the transmission towers for television stations located at Cerro Maravilla in Guayama. When the men got to the facility they were ambushed and murdered by policemen who were waiting for them. Soto has said that his most serious literary challenge is waiting for him—to write about this incident and to preserve the memory of his son.

Soto also taught for many years at the **University of Puerto Rico** in Río Piedras. Among his many works are *Usmail, Ardiente suelo, Fría estación, Spiks* and *Francotirador*.

SUGGESTED READING

P. Z. Boring, "Escape from Reality in the Fiction of Pedro Juan Soto," *Papers on Language and Literature*, Vol. 8, 1972; Norman González-Ferreira, *The Puerto Rican Experience on the Mainland: A Thematic Study of the Fiction of René Marqués, Pedro Juan Soto and Emilio Díaz Varcárcel* (Ann Arbor, Mich.: University Microfilms International, 1951–1979); Eduardo Seda-Bonilla, "On the Vicissitudes of Being 'Puerto Rican': An Exploration of Pedro Juan Soto's Hot Land, Cold Season," *Melus*, Vol. 6 (3), 1979, 27–40; Pedro Juan Soto, *A solas con Pedro Juan Soto* (Río Piedras, P.R.: Ediciones Puerto, 1973); Luz María Umpierre, *Ideologia y novela en Puerto Rico: Un estudio de la narrativa de Zeno, Laguerre y Soto* (Madrid, Spain: Editorial Playor, 1983).

T

Taínos, Los   This word is used to refer to the approximately 30,000 Indians who lived in Puerto Rico when the Spanish began to colonize the Caribbean. In discussing the original inhabitants of the Caribbean, anthropologists often distinguish between three large Indian groupings: the Caribs, who inhabited Guadeloupe and the Windward Islands; the Arawak, who lived in the Guianas; and the Taínos, who lived in the Bahamas, Cuba, Hispaniola and Puerto Rico. Christopher Columbus, for example, heard about **Boriquen** from the Caribs on Guadeloupe. Columbus came because he wanted gold; the Caribs came because they wanted prisoners. They constantly made war on the Taínos—"the good ones" in the Arawak language—who acted as a bullwark to a Carib invasion from the Greater Antilles. The Taínos were a generally peaceful people, but, in order to stop the Caribs, they learned to use both the bow and its deadly arrows effectively.

Roughly 30,000 Taínos lived in Boriquen when Columbus first appeared. They named their permanent villages *yucayeques*. Each village contained between one and two thousand people, whose homes—*los bohios*—were round (for the average Taíno) or rectangular (for the chief or *cacique*) and constructed of palm boards or cane and tied together with strong vines. A *bohio*'s roof was made of palm branches or large palm fronds. Inside, the Taínos slept on one of their inventions, *la hamaca*, or the hammock. In the *bohio* of a chief, one found carved wooden stools called *dujos*; the chief sat on the *dujo* when he or she met guests or other visitors.

Each village was governed by a *cacique*, and, in a custom that predated contemporary feminism by centuries, the chief could be either a man or a woman. Indeed, the Taínos practiced a degree of gender equality that is still absent in many of the so-called developed nations.

People wore few clothes. The men strapped on a loin cloth, unmarried women wore headbands, and wives wore short skirts, whose length suggested the person's social status. Like those today who adorn their bodies with tattoos or earrings through the nose or eyebrow, the Taínos also decorated their bodies. Before religious ceremonies or battle, the men often painted themselves red. Some scholars suggest that this is the origin of the persisting stereotype that labels American Indians "red men." It was "also fashionable to flatten the forehead by binding a hard object against it in childhood before the skull was fully formed" (Rouse 1992, 11). Ears and noses were pierced, and the women wore a variety of necklaces and ankle bracelets.

The Taínos practiced a very knowledgeable type of agriculture. Instead of the slash-and-burn techniques so common in many tropical countries, the Taínos piled up little mountains of dirt to produce root crops in the fields, which they called *conucos*. Measuring as much as three feet in diameter by nine feet in height, the Taínos "arranged the mounds in regular rows. This retarded erosion, improved the drainage, and thus permitted more lengthy storage of the mature tubers in the ground" (Rouse 1992, 12). The principal crops grown were cassava, sweet potatoes and, to a lesser extent, corn.

Religion is arguably the most well-known and fascinating aspect of Taíno life. The Indians worshipped gods whom they called *cemis*. Yúcahu (the god of cassava) and his mother Atabey (the goddess of fertility and fresh water) were the principal deities. Using wood, stone and snail shells, the Taínos created a variety of *cemis* for community and personal use. Every Taíno had as many as ten *cemis* in his or her possession, and, like the Saint Christopher medals still used by many Catholics today, the *cemis* protected their owners from harm. Irving Rouse writes that people "boasted that their cemis were the best and they then passed them on through inheritance, gift, or trade" (Rouse 1992, 13).

In **Ponce** and Utuado, archeologists have discovered and lovingly preserved the ball courts—the *bateys*—of the Taínos. In Utuado, a visitor walks through a majestic set of palm trees and into a series of large and small rectangular courts. Demarcated by a fence of stone *cemis*—the faces are still easy to see—two teams of players, twenty or thirty to a side, cut the court in half and, as soon as someone threw the ball into play, the players could hit it with their heads, knees, hips or elbows—anything but the hands. The hard balls were fabricated from tree roots covered with the rubbery gum extracted from certain trees. The Taínos bet on the games, and it can be assumed that villages played against one another, since the most elaborate courts are located on the outskirts of land controlled by powerful *caciques*. The game introduced the Spanish to rubber, a substance until then unknown in Europe.

On water, the Indians traveled in *canoas*, or canoes, another word derived from the Taíno language. Constructed of ceiba, the magnificent wood that is still used in Puerto Rico, the canoes could be small enough for two people or large enough to accommodate seventy or more. Because there were no horses or other animals to ride, most Indians walked when they were on land, but the *cacique* traveled in a litter made of wood and reeds, and his or her child was carried on the shoulders of one of the stronger warriors.

Today, Puerto Ricans love their *parrandas* or sprees. The Taínos called their festivals *areytos* and, using the *bateys* to party, the Indians sang, danced and drank. As a way of extending a hand of friendship, *caciques* invited other villages to attend an *areyto*; there neighbors heard the music of the maracas, bone flutes, drums made from the hollow of trees and the **guiro**, a long tree gourd scored along one side and scraped rhythmically with a bone or thin stone.

Ricardo Alegría estimates that, by 1550, only sixty Taínos remained alive. Of course, by that time they had intermarried with the Spanish and the Africans. Taíno blood still runs through the veins of the Puerto Rican people, and archeologists and anthropologists still search for evidence that will broaden our understanding of the Taínos, the original owners and inhabitants of an island called Boriquen.

SUGGESTED READING

Ricardo Alegría, *Ballcourts and Ceremonial Plazas in the West Indies* (New Haven, Conn.: Yale University Press, 1983); Ricardo Alegría, *History of the Indians of Puerto Rico* (San Juan: Colección de Estudios Puertorriqueños, 1983); Sabastian Robiou Lamarche, *Encuentro con la mitologia Taína* (San Juan, P.R.: Editorial Punto y Coma, 1992); Irving Rouse, *The Taínos: Rise and Decline of the People Who Greeted Columbus* (New Haven, Conn.: Yale University Press, 1992).

Tapia y Rivera, Alejandro (1826–1882)   Alejandro Tapia y Rivera is considered to be one of the most important figures in Puerto Rican historiography, arts and letters during the nineteenth century. This exceptional writer was born in San Juan and made lasting contributions to the study of Puerto Rican history and literature. His writings encompassed the genres of theater, novel and short story. He is considered to be one of the central pillars that helped to establish the national Puerto Rican theater.

Tapia y Rivera acquired most of his early education in Puerto Rico. As a child he spent some time in Malaga, Spain, because his mother and sister took him to visit his father who was living there. Professor Esther Melón de Díaz traces back his fondness for theater to this brief stay in Spain (1976, 419). Tapía's family returned to Puerto Rico and Tapia continued his schooling on the island. His family lacked the economic resources to send him to study in Spain as was the norm among children of affluent Puerto Rican families. Ironically, Tapia y Rivera was forced into exile in Spain after challenging a Spanish military officer based in San Juan to a duel (Morán Arce 1971, 495). He used this opportunity to pursue advanced studies there and became involved in many literary and historical endeavors.

Working with José Julián Acosta and Román Baldorioty de Castro, Tapia became involved in a society devoted to studying a collection of documents located in Spanish archives from the early history of Puerto Rico under Spanish domination. In 1854 he published his *Biblioteca histórica de Puerto Rico*, based on the documents he had gathered in Spain.

Tapia y Rivera's literary legacy is vast. His writings cover a broad spectrum but he is best remembered for his contributions to drama. His most important dramatic pieces are *La cuarterona* (1867), *Roberto D'Evreux* (1856), *Bernardo de Palyssy* (1857) and *Camoens* (1868). He was a pioneer in exploring themes of a social and ethical nature, such as gender equality and racism. He also wrote many novels. Among them were *El heliotropo* (1848) and *La palma del cacique* (1852). He also wrote a long poem titled "La Sataniada" (1874). Tapia was one of the founders of the Puerto Rican Athenaeum in 1876, and died during a meeting that was being held there.

SUGGESTED READING

Alejandro Tapia y Rivera, *Obras Completas* (San Juan: Instituto de Cultura Puertorriqueña, 1968); Lucas Morán Arce, *Enciclopedia Clásicos de Puerto Rico* (Barcelona: Ediciones Latinoamericanas, 1971); Rúben del Rosario, Esther Melón de Díaz and Edgar Martínez Masdeu, *Breve Enciclopedia de la cultura puertorriqueña* (San Juan: Editorial Coordillera, 1976).

Tax Laws and Exemptions   This entry focuses on the federal and local tax exemptions offered to businesses that operate in Puerto Rico. For the last seventy-five years, the United States has permitted Puerto Rico to grant a variety of federal tax exemptions to U.S. corporations that set up shop on the island. In assessing these laws, statehooder Luis P. Costas Elena argues that "the standard for judging tax exemptions should never be what investors desire but what is good for Puerto Rico" (Costas Elena 1981, 625). Costas Elena makes an important and essential point; however, his perceptive analyses have had little impact on tax policies that have their origins in the Philippines in 1921.

U.S. investors in the Philippine colony told Congress that they wanted an exemption from federal taxation for their Philippine business investments. Congress not only complied with this request, it threw in an exemption for Puerto Rico, presumably because it did not want to discriminate against the nation's colonial investors. Thus, the exemption granted in 1921 was the basis for the 931 tax laws that governed Puerto Rico, from 1947 until 1976, during the heyday of **Operation Bootstrap.**

These laws heavily favored the owners of what are still called "possessions corporations." But, since investors were able to bring home their profits tax free only when they liquidated the corporations, they often laundered their profits through banks in Guam, invested the profits in Europe and then brought the money home to the United States when the corporation closed shop in Puerto Rico. One educated estimate was that from $5 to $6 billion dollars had been stockpiled in Europe and used to the benefit of neither Puerto Rico nor the United States.

Congress changed the tax laws in 1976—the 931 exemptions became the 936 tax laws. Now corporations could immediately bring their profits back to the United States, paying a modest tollgate tax to Puerto Rico. They also received tax-exempt status for their "qualified source possession income," the interest made by depositing island profits in an island bank. By the early 1990s there was an estimated $10 billion of source possession income in the Puerto Rican banking system. However, since the lion's share of these deposits were short term—for 90 or 180 days—it was very difficult for Puerto Rican bankers to use them effectively for the long-term development of the island. The result was that this money was once again invested elsewhere.

Meanwhile companies transferred the patents from profitable inventions or products (e.g., pharmaceuticals) to their Puerto Rican subsidiaries and thus paid no federal taxes on the profits earned by their inventions or products. Not only did they then bring the profits home tax free, but they deducted the research and development costs for new products from the federal taxes paid in the United States!

In 1985 President Ronald Reagan meant to change the 936 tax laws. He correctly argued that, if their rationale was to create jobs for Puerto Ricans, they were having little impact. The government-sponsored *Puerto Rico Business Review* noted that, between 1977 and 1985, the net growth in manufacturing jobs was 227. This number moved the president to suggest that the U.S. and Puerto Rican governments explicitly link any federal tax benefits to the number of jobs created in Puerto Rico, for Puerto Ricans.

This idea met with such stiff opposition from the possessions corporations that the best President Reagan could do was to create a $100 million account derived from the 936 funds; this money was to be invested in the entire Caribbean, but as Congressman Charles Rangel stressed in congressional hearings, "You know and I know and the Chair knows that this Caribbean thing [i.e., the new investment fund] was just thrown in to save the program" (Hearings 1990, 210).

By the mid-1990s the 936 tax incentives were threatened with extinction. As of mid-1996 they were to be phased out over a ten-year period. Defenders argue that they do provide jobs (the people employed in a 936 operation employ others when they shop at local stores) and, even more important, given the fierce, global competition for new factories, that Puerto Rico needs some inducement for corporations to locate on the island rather than, for example, in Mexico, Central America or Asia.

The debate rages, but the point first made by Costas Elena in 1980 is still valid in 1996 and beyond—if the goal of the exemptions is to assist Puerto Rico, the standard for judging the effectiveness of tax exemptions should be, not only what is best for the corporations, but also what is the best for the long-term development of Puerto Rico and its 3.5 million inhabitants.

SUGGESTED READING

James Dietz, *Economic History of Puerto Rico* (Princeton, N.J.: Princeton University Press, 1986); Luis P. Costas Elena, *Revista Del Colegio de Abogados de Puerto Rico*, Volumes 40, 41 and 42, 1979–1980; Luis P. Costas Elena, *The Operation and Effect of the Possessions Corporation System of Taxation*, Department of the Treasury, Washington D.C., 1978– ; Manuel Escobar, *The 936 Market: An Introduction* (San Juan, P.R.: CitiBank, 1982); Emilio Pantojas García, *Development Strategies as Ideology: Puerto Rico's Export-Led Industrialization Experience* (Boulder, Colo.: Lynne Rienner, 1990); U.S. Congress House, Hearings before the Subcommittee on Oversight, Committee on Ways and Means, 101st Congress, 2d sess., 1990.

Television Puerto Rico has a powerful and prosperous television industry; it is a major element of the economic and cultural life of Puerto Rican society. Recent statistics indicate that 97.7 percent of all households have a television and 55.8 percent of all households have a videocassette recorder (Mediafax 1997a). There are four major commercial television networks, one large educational public television station, and nine other television stations that provide local television programming to Puerto Rican viewers. Media scholars Federico Suberví and Nitza M. Hernández-López estimated in 1991 that the Puerto Rican television market ranked 23rd in the United States in terms of number of viewers per city and was first in the Hispanic market (1991, 24).

Puerto Rican viewers watch substantial quantities of television every week. On average, they watch television for 2.66 hours every night, Monday to Friday, during the primetime period between 6:00 P.M. and 10 P.M. The latest statistics reveal that viewers watched 48.44 cumulative hours between the sign on and sign off period spanning a calendar week (Mediafax 1997b). These viewers constitute an important market for advertisers. Advertising agencies invested 591.4 million dollars in television advertising in 1996. This investment constituted a 14 percent increase over the previous year (Maldonado 1997, 42).

The origins of commercial television in Puerto Rico go back to 1952 when the Federal Communications Commission issued a permit authorizing the signal of WKAQ-TV—Telemundo. In April 1953 Angel Ramos, who was the owner of *El Mundo* newspaper, started to construct the facilities for the first television station or the island. The station began transmitting on March 28, 1954. It was shortly followed by WAPA-TV. In 1953, former governor **Luis Muñoz Marín** established a commission to coordinate the construction of an educational television station. This facility, managed by a dynamic group including Leopoldo Santiago Lavandero, Rafael Santiago Márquez and **Jack Delano**, began transmitting in 1958. At the same time, Channel 7 (WRIK-TV), owned by **Ponce** television, started broadcasting. The early television audience was a tiny fraction of what it is today—estimated to be 7,000 households. Television sets cost between $200 and $400 at that time.

In 1994 Yolanda Rosaly, a former entertainment reporter for *El Nuevo Día*, produced a special supplement for the fortieth anniversary of the medium. The supplement showcased all the major milestones that had shaped the early development of television on the island (Rosaly 1994). The early years of programming were aimed at producing informational and entertainment programs for the viewing public. It was a platform for showcasing native talent which, until then, had not been appreciated by large audiences. There were many children programs such as "La hora del niño," "Miss Bertita de Romper Room" and "El payaso pinito." Musical programs included "Tribuna del Arte," "El Show de Gaspar Pumarejo," "Show Ford," "Show Rambler" and "Randevous nocturno." News programming was governed by a strong set of ethical conventions aimed at providing the news without sensationalizing it or playing to scandal. News journalists of the time, such as Aníbal González Irizarry, Evelio Otero and Carlos Rúben Ortiz, became some of the most respected media personalities on the island.

Light comedy has always been an important part of Puerto Rican television. One of the very first programs, "El caso de la mujer asesinadita," produced by the legendary Mapy Cortes and her husband Fernando, was a situation comedy. Local artists and producers such as **Ramón Ortiz del Rivero** (Diplo), Paquito Cordero, Tommy Muñiz, **José Miguel Agrelot** and Adalberto Rodríguez (Machuchal), as well as shows such as "El colegio de la alegria" and "La Taberna India," were pillars of the island's early comedy programs.

One unique feature that characterized Puerto Rican television programming during the first three or four decades of television was the Puerto Rican *telenovelas*. *Telenovelas* were developed after the successful format of *radio novelas*. They were dramatic presentations that lasted several weeks or months. Similar to American soap operas, *telenovelas* had a closed-ended plot followed by scores of viewers throughout its duration. These programs were generally transmitted in the early evening hours. Many actors and actresses, including Braulio Castillo, Mona Marti, **Lucy**

Boscana, Carmen Belén Richardson, Alicia Moreda, Luz Odilia Font and Edmundo Rivera Alvarez, left distinctive imprints in this genre. During the 1970s, another wave of successful *telenovelas,* including "El hijo de Angela Maria" and "Cristina Bazán," captured the attention of thousands of viewers, and became television history. Unfortunately, the production of local *telenovelas* has ceased. Due to high production costs, Puerto Rican television stations, owned now primarily by U.S. corporations, prefer to import their *telenovelas* from other Latin American countries such as Venezuela, Mexico and Brazil.

The nature of the television medium has changed substantially in the last fifteen years. During the media boom of the 1980s, Puerto Rican owners of television stations sold their operations to American interests. American media conglomerates now own the major television channels on the island. As a result, the medium now reflects a highly Americanized style. The only major Puerto Rican source of programming is the WIPR-TV, the educational television station that was formerly operated by the Department of Education, but, since 1987, its control has been transferred to the phone company. As a result of these changes, the stations have considerably reduced the amount of programming that is produced on the island in favor of less expensive programming imported from the United States and dubbed into Spanish or entertainment programs imported from Venezuela, Mexico and other Caribbean countries. The television system in Puerto Rico has been further reshaped by the introduction of cable systems in the 1970s. There are ten cable systems that cover 29 percent of all the households (Mediafax 1997a). They carry all the major U.S. television networks and scores of cable channels.

SUGGESTED READING

Eliut Daniel Flores Caraballo, *The Politics of Culture in Puerto Rican Television: A Macro/Micro Study of English vs. Spanish Language Television Usage* (Ann Arbor, Mich.: University Microfilm International, 1992); Nitza Hernández López, "Culture and Communications Policy in a Colonial Context: The Case of Cable Television in Puerto Rico," Studies in Latin American Popular Culture, Vol. 10, 1991; José E. Maldonado, "Publimedia releases 1996 figure," *Caribbean Business,* February 20, 1997; Mediafax, 1997 *Universe Estimates,* January 10, 1997; Mediafax, *Broad Day-Part Audience Estimates,* March 2, 1997; Yolanda Rosaly, "40 años de TV," special supplement in *El Día,* March 27, 1994, 93–138; Federico Subervi-Vélez, Nitza Hernández-López, "Mass Media in Puerto Rico," *El Centro, Boletín del Centro de Estudios Puertorriqueños de Hunter College,* Winter 1991.

Theater   Theater is a central form of literary and artistic expression for the members of any society. In Puerto Rico theater has served a wide array of artistic, social and political functions. Although there is evidence that religious theatrical representations took place on the island during the seventeenth and eighteenth centuries, Puerto Rican theater began to flourish toward the first half of the nineteenth century. The first theater was Teatro Amigos del País. It was already producing dramatic works by 1823. The construction of the San Juan Municipal theater, now the Tapia Theater, dates back to 1824. It immediately showcased the most important theatrical productions on the island. Teatro La Perla in **Ponce** was presenting theatrical works by 1864 when it was inaugurated (Pasarell 1969).

There were many important productions of Spanish dramas during the early part of the nineteenth century. However, **Alejandro Tapia y Rivera**, José Antonio Daubón (1840–1922), and **Carmen Hernández Araujo** became the first and leading playwrights during this early dramaturgical period. Tapia's first dramatic attempt, *Roberto d'Evereux*, dates back to 1856 and was followed by other important plays such as *Bernardo de Palissy* (1857) *La cuarterona* (1867), *Camoens* (1868) and *Hero* (1869). Hernández Araujo wrote her first romantic drama, *Los deudos rivales* (1846), when she was just fifteen years old. She also wrote *Amor ideal* (1863). José Antonio Daubón contributed significantly to the dramatic production of the times when he co-wrote *El proceso de 1889* (1889), which concerned the abuses that the government of Spain was inflicting on Puerto Ricans. He also authored *Cosas de Puerto Rico* (1904).

Many of these early works explored themes relevant to the island folklore and traditions, contemporary issues of Spanish society, and some of the political realities that affected the island at the time. This early theater operated within the confines of the European drama canon imported to Puerto Rico through Spain. Critic Emilio J. Pasarell estimated that there were 130 plays produced in the island during that century (1969, 79).

The twentieth century opened a new era in Puerto Rican theater. With the influences brought by North Americans to the island many new currents in Puerto Rican theater followed. Theatrical productions of this period often expressed concerns for the lack of a Puerto Rican identity in light of many colonial influences and examined the many variables that constitute Puerto Rican national identity and culture. Topics such as the Lares insurrection of 1868 (see **Grito de Lares**), the social and political effects of changes of soveriegnty, the native culture of the **jíbaro**, the local folklore of the island and the exploitation of the poor all characterized the theatrical productions of the classic period of Puerto Rican theater. This period spanned until the end of the 1960s.

The leading playwrights of the period were **Luis Lloréns Torres** with *El grito de Lares* (1927); **Manuel Méndez Ballester** with *El clamor de los surcos* (1938), *Tiempo muerto* (1940), *Encrucijada* (1958) and *Bienvenido Don Goyito* (1965); **Emilio Belaval** with *La hacienda de los cuatro vientos* (1959); *María Soledad* (1947), *Bolero y Plena* (1956), *Vegigantes* (1958), *Sirena* (1959); **René Marqués** with *La carreta* (1952), *Juan Bobo y la dama de occidente* (1956), *Los soles truncos* (1959), *La muerte no entrará en*

palacio (1962). Of these, the works of Arriví, Marqués and Méndez Ballester are the best examples of this period.

Theatrical production during the 1970s has been labelled the New Puerto
Rican Drama (*La nueva dramaturgia puertorriqueña*) (Dávila López 1989;
Ramos Perea 1989). The new drama is concerned with a myriad of social,
moral and political realities that Puerto Ricans began to experience at the
end of the 1960s. The New Puerto Rican Drama period began around 1968
and was catalyzed by the Vietnam war, the victory of the pro-statehood
party and the struggles at the **University of Puerto Rico** (Ramos Perea 1989,
42–43).

Many important traits define this new wave of Puerto Rican drama. Roberto Ramos Perea, a playwright and drama scholar, has identified the following characteristics:

the public is not a pervasive force but an active one that influences the play;
the new drama deals with themes that have serious and risky situations that were
    approached rather lightly by other playwrights;
it breaks with the conventions of space and revolutionizes language;
the new drama is art that at the same time constructs a historic document;
the characters of the new drama are aggressive and capable of challenging threats
    presented by the system; and
it deals with national identity. (1989, 47–55)

In addition, the new drama encompasses many problems that affect contemporary society. Among them are government corruption, crime, infla-
tion, unemployment, discrimination, prostitution, AIDS and so on. Writers,
actors and theatrical companies never shy away from addressing themes
and topics that were considered too sensitive earlier. As Yvette Dávila López (1989) has skillfully demonstrated in her work, the new drama presents
a broad spectrum of voices, styles and currents. A large number of the
contemporary theatrical productions that take place in Puerto Rico fall
within the realm of new drama.

Among the most significant playwrights within this tradition are **Luis
Rafael Sánchez** with *La pasión según Antígona Pérez* (1968); Lydia Milagros González with *La muerte en Vietnam* (1971); the theater troupes El
Tajo del Alacrán y Anamú; **Jaime Carrero** with *La caja de caudales FM*
(1976) and *Lucky Seven* (1979); Pedro Santaliz with *El teatro personal de
Meaíto Laracuente* (1981); and Flora Pérez Garay with *El gran pinche*
(1979).

Presenting theatrical productions and attending the theater are both popular activities. Among the many theaters in San Juan are the Tapia Theater,
the theater at the **University of Puerto Rico**, the Sylvia Rexach Theater and
the many theaters within the Luis A. Ferré Center for Performing Arts.

SUGGESTED READING

Grace Yvette Dávila López, *Diversidad y pluralidad en el teatro puertorriqueño contemporáneo: 1965–1985* (Ann Arbor, Mich.: University Microfilms International, 1990); Socorro Girón, *Puerto Rico en su teatro popular* (Ponce, Socorro Girón, 1985); Matias Montes Huidoro, *Persona: Vida y mascara en el teatro puertorriqueño* (San Juan: Centro de Estudios Avanzados de Puerto Rico y el Caribe, 1984); Emilio J. Pasarell, *Panorama teatral en Puerto Rico en el siglo XIX* (San Juan: Instituto de Cultura Puertorriqueña, 1969); Charles Pilditch, "Theater in Puerto Rico: A Brief History," *Revista Interamericana* (1979): 5–8; Roberto Ramos Perea, *Perspectiva de la nueva dramaturgia puertorriqueña* (San Juan: Ateneo Puertorriqueño, 1989); Jordon Phillips, *Contemporary Puerto Rican Drama* (Madrid: Playnor, 1973).

The Three Kings (Los Tres Reyes)   In 1968 a greeting card was circulated in Puerto Rico that was never made by Hallmark. The card showed the Three Kings (the Three Wise Men in the United States) picketing their Christmas competition. The Kings' placards read: "Go home, Santa Claus" (Seda 1973).

The card symbolizes a battle between the old and the new, between a recent import—Santa Claus—and one whose roots, like the famous ceiba tree of **Ponce**, weave themselves into the deepest recesses of Puerto Rican life. The verb *reyar*, which does not exist in Spain, means in Puerto Rico to celebrate on the twelfth night of Christmas (January 5th)—the coming of the Three Kings.

Traditionally, Puerto Rican Christmas festivities begin on December 24 and end on January 6—jokers like to say that Puerto Rico spends almost a month working its way up to Three Kings Day—and there is some truth in that joke. Typically, the celebrating is on December 24, extended through the New Year and culminated in the lovely tradition of *los velorios* (the vigils). One custom is for people to form a group, stroll over to a neighbor's house singing **aguinaldos** and be greeted by a table full of delicious pastries, cookies and cakes. The women drink frosted anisette while the men take *tragos* (swallows) of rum. The adults party into the early hours of the morning. Meanwhile, the children wait for the arrival of the Three Kings. Wearing expressions still full of glee and excitement, older friends tell us that they would find a shoe box, fill it with grass or hay, and leave it under their bed or outside of the house. The Three Kings, tired from their long journey to find Christ, would use the hay to feed their hungry camels, and, in gratitude, the kings would leave a gift for the children. Candy is a must and, in families with money, gifts also magically appear—all thanks to the Three Kings.

With only a trace of exaggeration, some even argue that they saw the kings. No one suggests that they actually talked to the royal men, but the truth is less important than those wonderful memories.

Today, the battle between Santa Claus and the Three Kings is still un-decided. In the cities, shopping malls full of U.S. stores make it hard for the Three Kings to retain their original significance. They are being dis-placed by Toys-R-Us. If one attends mass in the countryside (for example, outside Bayamón with Padre Alvaro de Boer and the Sisters of La Com-munidad de Jesús Mediador) one can see the Three Kings live on in the creations of the rural artisans who have a remarkable ability to take figures who are hundreds of years old and still carve "new" images that evoke the mystery, wonder and delight that was experienced by those who grew up in the 1930s and 1940s.

SUGGESTED READING

Manuel A. Alonso, *El Jíbaro* (Río Piedras, P.R.: Edil, 1983); María Teresa Babín, *Panorama de la cultura puertorriqueño* (New York: Las Americas Publishing, 1958); Eduardo Seda, *Social Change and Personality in a Puerto Rican Agrarian Reform Community* (Evanston, Ill.: Northwestern University Press, 1973).

Todd, Roberto (1862–1955) A prominent politician and advocate of statehood throughout his long public life, Roberto Todd was born in the Virgin Islands, and his life spanned almost a century. He was a lawyer who, because of his opposition to the Spanish regime, was forced to live in New York City, where he worked with elements of the Cuban revolu-tion. When he arrived in Puerto Rico, however, Todd was a committed advocate of statehood. He helped found the pro-statehood Republican party and, in 1903—during one of the most turbulent and controversial periods of early U.S. rule (see **Republican Mobs**)—he was mayor of San Juan.

Todd valued his friendships with those in power. For example, in his book about U.S. governors of Puerto Rico, *Desfile de gobernadores de Puerto Rico (1898–1943)*, he makes it clear that he knew everyone. He was what Americans would call an "insider," a person who relished being near the political and economic decision makers of Puerto Rico. Todd's own views—still relevant today—appear in the preface to his book. He explains that, after forty-five years of waiting, "We do not know our future status yet we have a perfect right to know what that future is." And, to those who "throw in the face" of complaining Puerto Ricans the "gener-osity of the United States for Puerto Rico," Todd says, think again. The **Treaty of Paris** promised that Congress would determine the political status of Puerto Rico. Congress did nothing; therefore, "What we are not able to understand is how a national party and its distinguished chief, that have coined terms like the "New Deal" and "the Good Neighbor Policy," still push Puerto Rico to the side." A "contented Puerto Rico," says Roberto Todd, "would signify much more for Latin America than all the good will visits that Americans make to South America" (Todd 1943, iv–vi).

Todd was committed to the idea of statehood. In private he fumed; in public he counseled to "be patient."

SUGGESTED READING

Roberto Todd, *Desfile de gobernadores de Puerto Rico, 1898–1943* (San Juan, P.R.: n.p., 1943).

Toro, Josefina del (1901–1975)   Considered a pioneer in the field of library science, del Toro, who received her degree from Simmons College in Boston, Massachusetts, was the first Puerto Rican woman to attain a degree in library science.

With her degree in hand, she began to work in the library of the **University of Puerto Rico**, where she would spend her entire career. At that time, the library comprised two rooms in what is called the Tower of the University. In 1938, after completing a graduate degree in library science and specializing in referencing, she returned to the university to reorganize and direct the Reference Section of the library. She also took on another project—organizing the Puerto Rican Collection. This collection has since become a separate library in itself.

During the 1930s and 1940s she became an activist for "professionalizing" the position of librarian and for attaining status and respect for librarians from her colleagues in the field itself and outside as well. The fruits of her labor were finally attained in 1966 when the university approved del Toro's plans for the Graduate School of Library Science. In addition, in 1964, she had been appointed director of the university's library, the first time a woman had occupied the position. In 1967, under her leadership, a new building for the library was designed and constructed.

Throughout these years, she wrote and published various articles and books in her field, among them, *A Bibliography of the Collective Biography of Spanish America* (1938) and *A Bibliography of Puerto Rico for 1939* (1939). After retiring in 1969, she researched and published *A Study of Libraries in the Regional Colleges of Puerto Rico*, which was followed by a study of the libraries of the various campuses of the **Interamerican University**.

In 1973 she was honored, by the university, with the title of Professor and Librarian Emeritus. She was the first recipient of such a distinction in the history of higher education on the island.

In 1984, nine years after her death, the Society of Puerto Rican Librarians established the Josefina del Toro Award, honoring distinguished professionals in the field of library science. On that day, Giovanna del Pilar Barber read a short biography of del Toro, which included a very personal anecdote about this outstanding woman. She said that, at del Toro's investiture as Professor and Librarian Emeritus, she had been surrounded by students, colleagues and friends. She described why people had always migrated to del Toro's side: "Because who knows how to accompany, should be accompanied. And we are referring to the fact that although 72 at the time, Miss del Toro was taking care of her adoptive mother, who was very sick" (del Pilar Barber 1984). It is in this spirit that she is remembered by Puerto Ricans.

SUGGESTED READING

"Josefina del Toro: La primera mujer puertorriqueña en obtener el título de bibliotecaria," *Alma Latina* (November 1951); Luis Trelles Plazaola, "Josefina del Toro ejemplar bibliotecaria," *El Nuevo Día*, November 27, 1975; Giovanna del Pilar Barber, "Josefina del Toro Fulladosa: Semblanza," speech presented at the Society of Puerto Rican Librarians in honor of the establishment of the Josefina del Toro Award, April 4, 1984; *Quién es quien en Puerto Rico*, 4th ed., 1948–49 (San Juan, P.R.: Imprenta Venezuela, 1948).

Treaty of Paris   This treaty ended the Spanish-American War. Signed by Spanish and U.S. officials, it was formally ratified on April 11, 1899. At a White House ceremony, the president of the United States exchanged copies of the agreement with the French ambassador. No Puerto Rican was in the room when France, acting on behalf of Spain, ceded Puerto Rico to the United States.

During the war, President William McKinley had said, "While we are conducting war and until its conclusion, we must keep all we can get. When the war is over, we must keep what we want" (Karnow, 1989, 108). The president wanted Puerto Rico for strategic reasons, to advance American economic interests and to hurt the Spanish. As Whitelaw Reid, one of the president's treaty negotiators explained, "Spain had no money even to pay her own soldiers. No indemnity was possible, save in territory" (Reid, 1899, 88). Thus, along with "little Porto Rico," the United States demanded that the Spanish also cede both the Philippines and Guam. The French reluctantly accepted these terms, but, to save face for the Spanish, the United States agreed to pay "20,000,000 for," in Reid's words, "our new possessions." The money changed hands in May 1899, and the United States formally owned Puerto Rico. It became an American colony but not without a fight. The president's opponents said that "under the Constitution of the United States no power is given to the Federal government to acquire territory to be governed permanently as colonies." When legislators refused to endorse the treaty, the president offered potential supporters everything from patronage appointments to choice committee assignments. Ultimately, Congress endorsed the Treaty of Paris; the president kept what he wanted while Puerto Ricans complained that, instead of the democracy promised by "the invading Republic," Puerto Rico was "far worse off than ever within the mind of this generation under Spanish dominion" (Fernandez, 1996, 4–6).

SUGGESTED READING

Barbara Tasch Ezratty, *Puerto Rico: Changing Flags, an Oral History, 1898–1950* (Stevensville, Md.: Omni Arts, 1986); Ronald Fernandez, *The Disenchanted Island* (Westport, Conn.: Praeger, 1996); Michael Hunt, *Ideology and U.S. Foreign Policy* (New Haven, Conn.: Yale University Press, 1987); Stanley Karnow, *In Our Image* (New York: Random House, 1989); Margaret Leech, *In the Days of McKinley* (New York: Harper, 1959); Walter Millis, *The Martial Spirit* (Cambridge, Mass.: Riverside Press, 1931); Whitelaw Reid, *Our New Possessions* (New York: Tribune Company, 1899).

Tufiño, Rafael (1922–) The painter Rafael Tufiño was born in New York City to Puerto Rican parents but came to the island at an early age. He first studied his craft at the sign workshop of Juan Rosado, a local painter then with the Spanish master Alejandro Sánchez Felipe, who was then living in San Juan. He served in World War II and afterward traveled to Mexico to study with Rodríguez Luna and Chávez Morado at the Academia San Carlos. When he returned to Puerto Rico, he joined the **Community Education Division**, which he later directed from 1957 to 1963.

Tufiño's work is one of the foremost examples of the indigenous tradition within Puerto Rican graphic arts and painting. He captures places, customs and traditions that characterize Puerto Rican people and society. His paintings have a sense of forceful realism that focuses on the characteristic populism of the culture as it manifests itself in daily life. One of his leading masterpieces was his portrait *Goyita*. Modeled after his mother, it reveals the inner strength and character of a poor working woman; it is representative of many others of her time. In his paintings, he tries to present the reality of the island, without adding superfluous emotions or attributes. *La Perla* neighborhood and Old San Juan serve as settings for many of Tufiño's works. He has received many awards from the Puerto Rican Athenaeum and other institutions, and, in 1966, he received a fellowship from the Guggenheim Foundation. His work is showcased in some of the finest collections in Puerto Rico and the United States, including the Museum of Modern Art, the Library of Congress, the Ponce Museum of Art and the Museum of the Institute of Puerto Rican Culture.

SUGGESTED READING

Juan Antonio Gaya-Nuño, *La pintura puertorriqueña* (Soria, P.R.: Centro de Estudios Sorianos, 1984).

Turbas Republicanas, Las *See* **Republican Mobs**.

Tydings Bill This bill, presented to Congress in 1936, offered the island independence in four years. In February 1936, after members of the **Nationalist party** had assassinated the American chief of police Elisha Riggs,

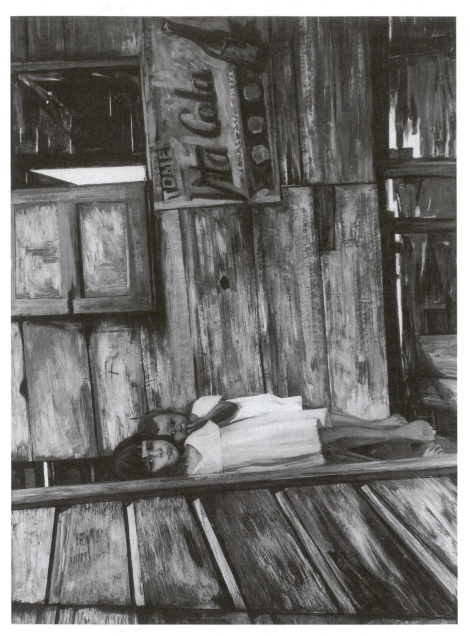

Rafael Tufiño, "Vita Cola." (Museo de Arte de Ponce, the Luis A. Ferré Foundation, Inc., Ponce, Puerto Rico.)

the Roosevelt administration requested Ernest Gruening, the director of the Interior Department's Division of Territories and Island Possessions to prepare a bill for independence. However, since the Roosevelt administration did not want anyone to know that the bill was introduced at its initiative, Senator Millard Tydings took the responsibility for the work of Ernest Gruening and his colleagues.

Although the bill was based on a previous offer of independence made to the Philippines, in which the Filipinos received an easy to bear twenty-year economic transition, the Roosevelt administration planned to cut the Puerto Ricans loose in only four years. On the island, the bill was incredibly controversial. Indeed, the offer of quick independence so split the island's pro-independence Liberal party, that it helped create the **Popular Democratic party** in 1938. Ironically, the Tydings Bill never came up for a vote. The threat of only a four-year bridge worked. Meanwhile, when islanders complained about Congress's lack of consultation with the people, Senator Tydings responded that "the Puerto Ricans weren't consulted when Puerto Rico was annexed to the United States. It was not necessary to consult them about their independence. It was a matter for us primarily to decide, although no discourtesy was intended" (Gatell 1958, 33).

SUGGESTED READING

Frank Otto Gatell, "Independence Rejected: Puerto Rico and the Tydings Bill of 1936," *Hispanic American Historical Review* 38 (February 1958): 26–44; Ernest Gruening, *The Autobiography of Ernest Gruening* (New York: Liveright, 1974).

U

Union Party (El Partido Unión de Puerto Rico) The Union party was the dominant political force in Puerto Rico from 1900 to 1924. It was formally founded in 1904 and included individuals who were dissatisfied with the first four years of U.S. control. Of particular concern were the activities associated with the **Republican Mobs**. The possibility of additional electoral fraud worried the Union party's organizers; they also argued that the Puerto Rican House of Delegates was a meaningless tool of the U.S. colonial authorities. Thus, some questioned whether any Puerto Rican political party could or should participate in any government organized by U.S. officials. Eventually skeptics agreed once again to seek change peacefully through the political system. The party's declaration of principles stipulated that it was an organization devoted to defending the rights of the Puerto Rican people. Voters obviously endorsed the party's efforts because it won twenty-five of forty-three seats in its first electoral effort. Thereafter the party dominated to such an extent that in the 1906 and 1908 elections the Union party won all the seats in the House of Delegates, the only body with any claim to representing the expressed will of the Puerto Rican electorate.

Party members battled over the organization's disposition to political status. At one point they even removed all three options—statehood, independence or some form of association—from drafts of the party's declaration of principles. But a stirring speech made by **José de Diego** convinced delegates that if the party truly meant to be a union of the Puerto Rican people, it had to include all the options supported by members of that community. Listeners had to distinguish between the overwhelming consensus in favor of local self-government and the ultimate status of

Puerto Rico. In de Diego's words, "We declare and request self government; we do not request, we only proclaim our right to Puerto Rican nationality, or the right to become the state of Puerto Rico as part of the American federation" (Arrigoitia 1985, 71).

Under the Union party's banner, the House of Delegates repeatedly asked for more self-government. However, when their demands were refused (see **Olmstead Act**), the Union party eventually removed statehood as one of its status options. This partially accounts for the granting of **United States citizenship**, an option that was unanimously rejected by the Union party and its representatives.

As late as 1920, the Union party, led by **Antonio R. Barceló**, pressed the United States for independence. But, when Governor **E. Montgomery Reilly** (1921–1923) refused to allow anyone with independence sentiments to serve in the island's government, the party leadership removed independence from its list of political options. The result was the end of the Union party and the creation of the new alliances La Alianza (the **Alliance party**) and La Coalición (the **Coalition party**).

SUGGESTED READING

Robert Anderson, *Party Politics in Puerto Rico* (Stanford, Calif.: Stanford University Press, 1965); Delmas Arrigoitia, *Jose de Diego: A Legislator in Times of Political Transition*, Ph.d. diss., Fordham Univ., 1985; Edward J. Berbusse, *The United States in Puerto Rico* (Chapel Hill: University of North Carolina Press, 1966); Manuel Maldonado Denis, *Puerto Rico: A Socio Historic Interpretation* (New York: Vintage Books, 1976).

United Nations   Puerto Rico has been a continual subject of concern and debate within the United Nations. After World War II ended, the United Nations created a trusteeship council to monitor the proposed liberation of colonies from Indochina to Africa, from Asia to the Caribbean. The United States was often criticized during trusteeship debates because of its support for the persisting imperial ambitions of France and Great Britain. Thus, when Puerto Rico came before the United Nations in the fall of 1953, it was against the backdrop of criticism from a variety of developing nations. The Eisenhower administration knew that nations like India would carefully scrutinize U.S. behavior in Puerto Rico.

One problem was the nature of the **commonwealth**. Since Congress repeatedly stressed that "nothing fundamental" had changed when the **Free Associated State** (Estado Libre Asociado) was created, critics charged that the island was still a U.S. colony. In private, administration officials agreed with this assessment; however, before the United Nations, U.S. Ambassador **Henry Cabot Lodge, Jr.** took the position that the United States and Puerto Rico had in fact signed a compact; the new status could grow, could be modified, and, most important at the United Nations, could not be changed except by mutual consent. This was a hard sell at the UN. Members recalled, for example, that Congress had unilaterally changed the Puerto Rican constitution. Thus, Lodge needed a new idea, and President Dwight Eisenhower provided it at a November 20, 1953, breakfast meeting. Offer the Puerto Ricans independence. That should satisfy everyone at the UN, and it did. With some additional horse trading and arm twisting, Puerto Rico became the first colony to be removed from the list of non–self-governing territories. This occurred on November 27, 1953.

Until the early 1960s Puerto Rico had rarely been an issue at the UN. When Cuba raised the island's political status in the UN's Decolonization Committee, it launched a process of complaint that continues to the present day. In 1978, for example, all the island political parties jointly told the United Nations that Puerto Rico remained a U.S. colony or that it lacked the degree of self-determination claimed by the United States in 1953. Such unity was unprecedented; it reflected the bitter disappointment of the *populares* under Governor **Rafael Hernández Colón** and the statehooders under the leadership of **Carlos Romero Barcelo**.

At the White House, President Jimmy Carter tried to follow a pattern that was already a decade old. For example, UN Ambassador Arthur Goldberg noted in 1968 that "there are recurring efforts to put the Puerto Rico question on the [decolonization] committee's agenda—efforts which we pull out all the stops to block." And, in 1975, Ambassador Daniel Patrick Moynihan said that the way to stop Cuba was to "inform the members of the Decolonization Committee in their capitals that we would regard voting against us on this matter to be an unfriendly act." The Carter administration tried similar tactics but, by the summer of 1978, the composition of the committee had changed. With less power to threaten members in their capitals, the Carter administration settled for what it called a stand-off between the U.S. and Cuba. The committee never declared Puerto Rico a U.S. colony but, "with no member voting against the resolution, our claim that the Committee has no jurisdiction over Puerto Rico was decisively rejected" (Moynihan 1978, 120–121).

Since 1978 the UN's Decolonization Committee has, each and every summer, listened to Puerto Ricans of all political persuasions declare that the island is a U.S. colony. In recent years, the island is discussed along with the Malvinas (or the Falkland Islands) in Argentina and East Timor in Indonesia. But, with the end of the Cold War, and the collapse of the Cuban economy, the United States has managed to avoid any resolutions that second the motion of the island's political representatives. There is even talk of erasing the Decolonization Committee since, according to the Great Powers, colonies no longer exist.

Suggested Reading

Ronald Fernandez, *The Disenchanted Island: Puerto Rico and the United States in the Twentieth Century*, 2d ed. (Westport, Conn.: Praeger, 1996); Carmen Gautier Mayoral and María del Pilar Arguelles, *Puerto Rico y la ONU* (Río Piedras, P.R.: Editorial Edil, 1978); Daniel Patrick Moynihan, *A Dangerous Place* (New York: Berkeley, 1978).

United States Citizenship   Puerto Ricans became citizens of the United States when President Woodrow Wilson signed the **Jones Act** on March 2, 1917. Conventional wisdom in the island still argues that the grant of citizenship was a response to World War I; the U.S. needed soldiers, and a million new Americans assured Washington of an island of new recruits.

In reality, the deepest motives behind the citizenship law were expressed by Congressman William Jones (chair of the House Committee on Insular Affairs) in a public exchange with **Resident Commissioner Luis Muñoz Rivera** in February 1914. Jones said, "The bill [to give citizenship to Puerto Ricans] is framed upon the idea that Porto Rico [*sic*] is to remain a permanent possession of the United States. It proposes to settle this question [i.e., the island's political status] and thus remove it from Porto Rican politics. What do you say about that Mr. Rivera?" (Hearings 1914, 58).

Luis Muñoz said no. He adamantly refused second-class citizenship and on March 27, 1914, the Puerto Rican House of Delegates *unanimously* told Congress that "we firmly and loyally maintain our opposition to being declared, in defiance of our express wish or without our express consent, citizens of any country whatsoever other than our own beloved soil that God has given us as an inalienable gift and incoercible right." By making Puerto Rico a permanent possession of the United States, Congress hoped to quiet the island's "agitation" for independence. Muñoz and his colleagues grasped those motives so, when the legislation finally came to the floor of the U.S. House in May 1916, the resident commissioner made an extraordinarily elegant speech. He again refused citizenship because it came with no change in political status; the island would be neither a state nor a nation, only a "permanent possession" of the United States. To Muñoz the only explanation for Congress' behavior was this: Puerto Ricans were "the Southerners of the twentieth century." Treated with the contempt reserved for slaves, Muñoz indignantly refused citizenship, requesting instead a **plebiscite** because "it would be strange if, having refused citizenship so long as the majority asked for it, you should decide to impose it by force now that the majority of the people decline it" (*Congressional Record* 1916, 7472–74).

The United States formally imposed citizenship as part of the Jones Act in March 1917. As President Wilson stressed, "We welcome the new citizen, not as a stranger but as one entering his father's house."

SUGGESTED READING

José A. Cabranes, *Citizenship and the American Empire* (New Haven, Conn.: Yale University Press, 1979); U.S. Congress, House, *A Civil Government for Porto Rico*, Hearings before the Committee on Insular Affairs, 63 Cong., 2d sess., February 26, 1914; U.S. Congress, House, *Congressional Record*, 64 Cong., 2d sess., May 5, 1916, Washington, D.C.

University of Puerto Rico   The oldest and largest public university in Puerto Rico, the university offers an education to more than 52,000 men and women on eleven campuses. The university has a Law School, a School of Medicine, a School of Tropical Medicine, a School of Agriculture and Mechanical Arts, a School of Dentistry, and it offers advanced degrees in areas as diverse as sociology and biology, physics and psychology. The university is heavily subsidized by the government; it offers a fine education at a remarkably low cost.

The university was founded in 1903, when the Normal School in Río Piedras became the University of Puerto Rico (UPR). Initially, the University focused on training teachers, but by 1910 it had added a Department of Hispanic Studies; in 1913, the Schools of Pharmacy and Law; and in 1926, the School of Tropical Medicine. Throughout these years, the UPR was often a cause of controversy because the head of the university's governing board was the island's colonial governor, and the chancellor was the U.S.-appointed commissioner of education. By 1923 a well-known reference work, *El libro de Puerto Rico*, would argue that "the University and its authorities have established a campus removed from the life and needs of the country; it's as if the university exists in a vacuum." This criticism lingers with a legacy of mixed feelings about the United States and its advocates. For example, in 1969, students protested the overuse of English in the classroom; a large sign in the lobby of the building housing the social sciences showed Snoopy "lying atop his doghouse, staring at the sky, and saying, in Spanish, 'No more barking in English. I'm going to protest.' " In 1970 the university experienced a series of protests against ROTC which led to the death of at least one student and the firing of the university's chancellor. Abrahán Díaz González called his ouster "the culmination of a plan drawn up by the New Progressive Party [the proponents of statehood] to take the university by storm," and Governor Roberto Sánchez called the dismissal "a storm trooper assault on the university" (Wagenheim 1972, 204–207).

While academic order was eventually restored, these battles demonstrate a continuous fact of Puerto Rican life: The issue of political status is so all pervasive that no area of island life remains exempt from its effects and influences.

The magnificent quadrangle of the UPR campus at Río Piedras was declared a historical monument by the island's Institute of Culture in 1978, and it was included on the U.S. Historical register in 1984. The quadrangle includes a tower studded with brilliant tilework, a theater, and a series of open-air archways which, because they are surrounded by ever-blooming flowers, provide an incredible arena for both intellectual activity and human delight.

SUGGESTED READING

For detailed information about its programs of study, see, in both Spanish and English, the university's Internet home page at http://upracd.upr.clu.edu.; Wilfred Albizu Meléndez, *The University of Puerto Rico* (New York: Golden Press, 1978); Rafael Aponte Hernández Aponte, *The University of Puerto Rico: Foundations of the 1942 Reform* (Austin: University of Texas, 1966); Aida Negrón de Montilla, "University Reform Merely Continues Trend," *San Juan Star*, May 30, 1993; Luis Nieves Falcon, et al., *Puerto Rico: Grito y mordaza* (Río Piedras, P.R.: Editorial Edil, 1982); Kal Wagenheim, *Puerto Rico: A Profile* (New York: Praeger, 1972).

Urayoán   A *cacique* (chief) of the Taíno Indians (see **Los Taínos**), Urayoán remains a potent symbol of resistance to colonial authority. The Spanish arrived with a thirst for gold and a desire to convert the native inhabitants to Christianity. The pope, in the name of God, had given the Spanish ownership rights over all lands discovered on their voyages. Initially, the Indians offered little resistance to the Spanish. They believed that men like **Ponce de León** were immortal—what was the point of fighting with men who would not die?

Urayoán was a skeptic. He wanted to test the theory about Spanish immortality. In 1511 he ordered his men to drown one of them. The unlucky guinea pig, Diego Salcedo, allowed the Taínos to carry him across a river so that he would not get his clothes wet. The Indians dropped him in the middle of the river and held him under the water for a long time. The Taínos brought Salcedo back to the riverbank and watched in fear, expecting that he might rise, any moment, from the dead. When Salcedo remained inert, the Taínos knew that the Spanish could die. As a result, the Indians conducted a major revolt against the Spanish, led by Agueybana the Brave. Initially, the Indians emerged victorious; they killed a number of Spaniards near the Yauco River, and they managed to burn a village founded by Captain Cristóbal de Sotomajor. Ponce de León collected his forces, however, and defeated the Taínos in a series of battles that proved to be disastrous for the Indians. Although some escaped to the mountains, within a short period of time, disease, overwork (in the mines) and desperation ended the lives of the vast majority of the surviving Taínos. Urayoán, however, has never lost his ability to move the Puerto Rican spirit. For example, during the 1980s, a group of Puerto Ricans living in Hartford, Connecticut, advocated for independence in a newspaper called *Urayoán*.

SUGGESTED READING

Ricardo E. Alegría, *History of the Indians of Puerto Rico* (San Juan: Colección de Estudios Puertorriqueños, 1983); Ronald Fernandez, *Los Macheteros: The Wells Fargo Robbery and the Violent Struggle for Puerto Rican Independence* (New York: Prentice Hall, 1987).

V

Vega, Ana Lydia (1946–) Ana Lydia Vega is a writer whose literary production exemplifies the themes and concerns of many writers of the contemporary Puerto Rican literary scene. Her work, presented in the form of short stories and novels, demonstrates an uncanny ability to collect, present and reflect on the modern dynamics that affect Puerto Rican society. Vega's writings are significant in a variety of ways. She uses humor to exploit popular themes from Puerto Rican culture. At the same time, she satirizes and brings to the surface many of the social, political and economic inconsistencies that expose the colonial influence over Puerto Ricans and their society. Her work explores the dominant ideologies that define Puerto Rican culture. It examines how Puerto Ricans have normalized and internalized social and political malaise into their ways of living and thinking. She manages to integrate as part of her narratives problems such as crime, violence, assimilation, consumerism and class conflicts in ways that reveal the very ethos, logos and pathos of the contemporary Puerto Rican personality. There is a strong feminist current that comes across her work.

Vega has developed a unique literary style that has subverted the traditional cannon of short story as it had been followed on the island. Her use of humor, parody, popular street jargon and artifacts from popular culture, such as music and film, have served as a medium to create unique portrayals of modern Puerto Rico—as exemplified in this text from her short story "Caso Omiso" (from her book *Pasión de historia*, 1987):

I planted myself in front of the video store to check Brian de Palma's films as if not to sin with my thoughts. My sister, Teré, had instructions to tell Vitín and Pucho, if they came to pick me up or called on the phone, that I was out in Nic-

Ana Lydia Vega. (*El Nuevo Día*.)

aragua defending Democracy. They were not too happy that their baby, a nerdy rocker from San Ignacio, would be hanging out with some cocolos from Gabriela Mistral. (Vega 1987, 67).

Vega first joined the Puerto Rican literary scene in 1981 when she collaborated with Carmen Lugo Filipi to write *Vírgenes y mártires*. The book was highly praised by literary critics. Since then, she has published many other books such as *El tramo del ancla* (1981), *Encancaranublado y otros cuentos de naufragio* (1982), *Pasión de historia* (1987), *Falsas crónicas del sur* (1991) and *Esperando a Loló* (1994).

Vega was born in Santurce and studied at the **University of Puerto Rico** and at the University of Provence in France where she received her doctorate. She teaches French at the University of Puerto Rico at Río Piedras.

SUGGESTED READING

Claire Buck, ed., *Bloomsbury Guide to Women's Literature* (New York: Prentice-Hall, 1992); Elizabeth Hernández and Consuelo López, "Women and Writing in Puerto Rico: An Interview with Ana Lydia Vega," *Callaloo* 17, no. 3 (1994); Catherine Den Tandt, "Tracing Nation and Gender: Ana Lydia Vega," *Revista de Estudios Hispánicos*, 28, no. 1 (1994); Ana Lydia Vega, *Pasión de historia* (Buenos Aires: Edición La Flor, 1987); Ana Lydia Vega, in Angel Flores, ed., *Spanish American Authors: The Twentieth Century* (New York: Wilson, 1992).

Vientós Gastón, Nilita (1908–1989)   One of the most accomplished Puerto Rican women of the twentieth century, Vientós Gastón was a distinguished lawyer, journalist and an unflagging promoter of Puerto Rican culture. Her birthplace was San Sebastián, and she attended primary school in Cuba and secondary school in the United States. After completing her law degree at the **University of Puerto Rico**, she became the first woman lawyer to work for the government's Department of Justice, a position she held for twenty-seven years until 1967.

One of the most important cases litigated by her was commonly known as the "language lawsuit." In 1965 Puerto Rico's Supreme Court rejected a petition from an attorney who requested permission to argue a case in English because his command of Spanish was weak. Leading the case for the people was Assistant Attorney General Vientós Gastón who argued for and won this landmark litigation on the language issue in Puerto Rico. The ruling on this case clearly stated that Spanish was and would continue to be the official language of the judicial system on the island:

It is a fact not subject to historical rectification that the vehicle of expression, the language of the Puerto Rican people—integral part of our origin and of our Hispanic culture—has been and continues to be Spanish. The means of expression of our people is Spanish, and that is a reality that cannot be changed by any law. (Puerto Rican Supreme Court 1965, 588–89)

In 1948, Vientós Gastón's literary interest led her to pursue a degree in literature at Kenyon College in Ohio, under the auspices of the Rockefeller Foundation. Her tireless energy allowed her to engage in both literary and legal endeavors simultaneously throughout her life. For many years, she wrote a column for *El Mundo*, "Indice cultural." This column was dedicated to literary and cultural book reviews and essays of native and foreign subjects. A compilation of these columns, published in 1957 in four volumes titled *Indice cultural*, won the journalism award that year from Puerto Rico's Institute of Literature. Her skill in this field also led her to the University of Puerto Rico's Department of Humanities where she was a professor of comparative literature for many years.

Owing to her intellectual energy and her understanding of the importance of a country's cultural and historical values, she participated in a number of initiatives. As a member of the Association of the University of Puerto Rico's Women Graduates, she established the association's journal, *Asomante*, which under her direction for twenty-five years, became one of the most notable periodicals in Latin American. She was also a founding member and the first female president of Puerto Rico's **Ateneo Puertorriqueño** from its inception in 1946 until 1961. In addition, from its inception in 1955, she was a lifelong member of Puerto Rico's Academy of the Spanish Language.

This constant pursuit of documenting, celebrating and defending Puerto Rican culture is a legacy she shared with other outstanding Puerto Rican women, including **Margot Arce de Vázquez**, María Teresa Babín and Mariana Robles de Cardona.

SUGGESTED READING

Lecturas puertorriqueñas (San Juan: Instituto de Cultura Puertorriqueña, 1967), 317–25; Cesáreo Rosa-Nieves, *Plumas estelares en las letras de Puerto Rico*, vol. 1 (San Juan: Ediciones de la Torre, 1967); Puerto Rican Supreme Court, *People vs. Superior Court*, Puerto Rico Reports, 92: 580–90 (1965).

Vieques   This island lies just off the eastern coast of the Puerto Rican mainland. Vieques, which is four miles by twenty miles in size, has always been considered an integral part of Puerto Rico. In a show of great pride, inhabitants first call themselves Viequesans; they are Puerto Ricans, but the tie to *La Isla Nena* (the baby island) is primary.

During the colonial wars of the eighteenth century, the island became a battleground for England and Spain. The British were "expelled" for the second time in 1718, but the island's location made it an excellent place for buccaneers to do business. Local lore still includes **Roberto Cofresí,** the Robin Hood of Vieques. Cofresí used the island as a base of operations for many years until he was killed by a Spanish firing squad in 1825.

Until 1940 the island was affectionately known as the "sugar island."

Plantations dotted the landscape, wealth was concentrated in a few hands and everyone's destiny was linked to the wild ups and downs of world sugar prices. In 1940 the U.S. government expropriated 70 percent of Vieques. President Franklin Roosevelt planned to make Vieques the Pearl Harbor of the Caribbean. In the event the British lost to the Germans, the British fleet was to be harbored at Vieques.

The United States promised to return the land at the end of World War II, but this did not happen. Instead, the island became an integral part of the **Roosevelt Roads** military complex, today the largest naval facility in the world. The island is also U.S. headquarters for weapons fleet training in the Atlantic Ocean. Even though 10,000 inhabitants live in the center of Vieques, the island still experiences the detonation of an average of 3,400 bombs every month (*Naval Training* 1980, 162).

In 1961 President John Kennedy proposed a plan to take control of the entire island. The U.S. Navy wanted the inhabitants to leave and to dig up the cemeteries that contained the remains of their ancestors. Because Puerto Ricans traditionally celebrate All Saint's Day by praying at the graves of their loved ones and because the Navy did not want any Puerto Rican civilians to return to the island, the graves had to leave when the people did. This controversial plan was dropped only when Governor Luis Muñoz Marín reminded President Kennedy that television broadcasts of the "cemeteries removal" would provide great propaganda for Fidel Castro to use throughout the Caribbean and the rest of the world.

In 1996 Vieques remains one of the most controversial issues in Puerto Rican public life. All political parties are united in their opposition to the military base in general and the bombing in particular. However, the base remains central to U.S. military policy, and, in hearings held in December 1994, the Navy strongly expressed its desire to retain control of its 70 percent of Vieques.

SUGGESTED READING

Ronald Fernandez, *The Disenchanted Island: Puerto Rico and the United States in the Twentieth Century*, 2d ed. (Westport, Conn.: Praeger, 1996); Elizabeth Langhorne, *Vieques: History of a Small Island* (Vieques, P.R.: Vieques Construction and Historical Trust, 1987); Jorge Rodríguez Beruff, *Política militar y dominación: Puerto Rico en el contexto* (San Juan, P.R.: Ediciones Huracán, 1988); U.S. Congress, House, *Naval Training on the Island of Vieques*, Committee on Armed Services, 97th Cong., 1st sess., 1981, Washington.

Vizcarrondo, Fortunato (1896–1977) With **Luis Palés Matos**, he is one of the pioneer writers and poets who worked within the genre of Afro-Antillean poetry in Puerto Rico. In fact, his work was not only seminal but developmental as he contributed to the expansion of the genre throughout his long and fruitful life. One of his best-known poems is *"¿Y Tú Agüela,*

A'onde ejta?," in which the poet examined the racial schism that existed between different sectors of Puerto Rican society by presenting the satiric discourse of a man who was called "negro" (a negative variant of the word black) by an affluent woman of light skin. The male voice in the poem made fun of the woman and explained to her that while everyone knows that his grandmother is black no one knows that hers is black because she has hidden it.

He also used the onomatopeic style that characterizes negroid poetry. His poems have been popularized by Juan Boria, a skilled interpreter of this genre. His book *Dinga y mandinga* is considered to be one of the classics that established the canon of Afro-Antillean poetry.

SUGGESTED READING

Fortunato Vizcarrondo, *Dinga y mandinga: poemas,* 4th ed. (San Juan: Instituto de Cultura Puertorriqueña, 1983); "Fortunato Vizcarrondo," in *Caribbean Writers: A Bio-Bibliographical-Critical Encyclopedia*, ed. Donald E. Herdeck (Washington, D.C.: Three Continents, 1979).

W

Warrant of Opportunity (La Cédula de Gracias)   Formally authorized by the Spanish government on August 10, 1815, this royal edict had a substantial significance for the economic development of Puerto Rico in the nineteenth century. The Spanish abolished a variety of import and export taxes that were impeding the growth of the Puerto Rican economy. More significant, they promised generous grants of land to any white colonist who came to develop the island—and more land for each slave that came along, as human baggage, with the new immigrants. The warrant also granted Spanish citizenship to the newcomers after five years of residence in Puerto Rico.

The Spanish made their offer known throughout Europe and the Americas. It produced a substantial number of new agricultural investments but, according to Gordon Lewis, the Spanish government acted in its own interests. It hoped to use Puerto Rico as a base for the reconquest of its lost Latin American colonies, and it hoped to extract from Puerto Rico the wealth it no longer extracted from those other colonies. Many scholars suggest that, in any historical analysis of the bitter political disagreements that characterized Puerto Rico in the late nineteenth century, it is important to remember that, for the first half of the nineteenth century, Spain earnestly encouraged the immigration of individuals whose present and future fortunes were intimately linked to the survival of Spanish colonialism.

SUGGESTED READING

Gordon Lewis, *Puerto Rico: Freedom and Power in the Caribbean* (New York: Harper, 1963); Juan Manuel García Passalacqua, *Puerto Rico: Equality and Freedom at Issue* (Westport, Conn.: Praeger, 1983).

Y

Yiye *See* **Avila, José Joaquín.**

Young Bill This bill, introduced into the U.S. Congress in 1996 by Representative Donald Young of Alaska, initially offered only statehood and independence as political options; later, **commonwealth** was added to the list of possibilities. Over time, other changes were made to the bill; for example, many congressmen demanded that if Puerto Rico became a state, English would be the mandated medium of instruction in the island's school system and that English would be the accepted language in all matters pertaining to the federal government. The English requirement killed the Young Bill, and it was removed from consideration in September 1996.

However, in all versions of the legislation, Congressman Young argues that, when Puerto Rico was ceded to the United States by the **Treaty of Paris** in 1899, that treaty "expressly recognized the authority of Congress to provide for the political status of the inhabitants of the territory." Puerto Rico "belongs" to the United States; the citizenship of Puerto Ricans is based on a statute (the **Jones Act** of 1917) that Congress could revoke; "the 'Commonwealth' remains an unincorporated territory that does not have the status of 'free association' with the United States as that status is defined under U.S. law or international practice"; and, given the absolute power of Congress, there appears to be no way that U.S. legislators can give commonwealth supporters the enhanced powers they have long desired (Young 1996, 2).

Congressman Young has vowed to reintroduce his legislation in 1997, and Puerto Ricans of all political persuasions hope that it will resolve— once and for all—the island's political status. However, other congressmen

have indicated that they will once again attach an English language requirement to statehood; furthermore, in all versions of the legislation to
date, Congress has never indicated that it will accept the will of the Puerto
Rican people. A vote could take place, and Congress, since it retains the
ultimate power, alone could decide the island's status.

SUGGESTED READING

U.S. Congress, House 104th Cong., 2d sess., House Report 3024, "To Provide a
Process Leading to Full Self Government for Puerto Rico," September 18, 1996;
Hon. Donald Young, "The Updated United States–Puerto Rico Political Status
Act," *Congressional Record*, House of Representatives, 104th Cong., 2d sess., Sep-
tember 30, 1996.

Yuisa (Cacica Luisa) (1465–1514)   Upon the death of her husband, who
was a *cacique* (chief), Luisa, whose Christian name was given to her by the
Spanish colonists, inherited and was, as *cacica*, in charge of the land where
she lived with a Spanish soldier she had married, Pedro Mexia. In 1514 a
group of Borincano Indians from the nearby island of **Vieques**, came ashore
near Luisa's land with the intention of avenging the death of their *cacique*
Taureibo. Mexia was killed in the bloody melée, and she was mortally
wounded after having fought back tenaciously.

Impressed by her courage, and in her memory, the area where she lived
was given the name of Loíza in her honor. One of Puerto Rico's famous
writers, **Alejandro Tapia y Rivera**, immortalized the memory of Luisa in
his poem "Las lágrimas de Loíza," a lyrical description of Luisa's pain and
how her pain was made manifest through the tears that formed the Loíza
River.

SUGGESTED READING

Jalil Sued-Badillo, *La mujer indígena y su sociedad* (San Juan: Editorial Cultural,
1989); Arturo Ramos Llompart, *Dos temas Taínos* (San Juan: Academia de la Historia, 1990).

Yunque, El   This 28,000-acre rain forest is located on the eastern side of
the island, roughly midway between San Juan and Fajardo. Nearby is Luquillo, one of the Caribbean's most beautiful beaches.

Visitors to El Yunque first spot La Coca Falls, a cascade of water that
seems as straight as a telephone pole. As soon as one enters the forest, the
drop in temperature is noticeable, and the adventurous can explore "a variety of vegetation that changes as deftly as a chameleon" (Robinson 1984,
27). On the first level of the forest, the soil is home to 163 tree species; on
level two, the swamp *cyrilla (palo colorado)* dominates another 52 tree
species; and, at the forest's peak, where more than 150 inches of rain fall

each year, "the dwarf forest clings to a thin layer of soil. All trees are stunted, twisted, draped with moss and wet with moisture" (p. 36).

A special treat of El Yunque are the bromeliads. They are epiphytic; they sink their roots into the bark of a tree. To capture the water that spills from the dense vegetation, the bromeliads are formed like a vase. In El Yunque many of the more than 1,500 different types of bromeliads provide both color and flowers. A wonder of evolution, these plants produce a magnificent flower from the center of the "vase"; the flower often lasts for three months and, when it dies, so does the plant. But, as it languishes, the bromeliad shoots out one or two "babies" from its sides. The plant is self-propagating, and, unless people ruin the forest, the bromeliads will flower as long as El Yunque is preserved.

Preservation is a battle. Because of pollution, tourists, population growth and the demand for housing, El Yunque is in danger. However, cooperation between the U.S. Forest Service (which manages El Yunque) and Puerto Rican authorities has generated a desire to maintain the only tropical forest in Puerto Rico. Optimism is sometimes hard to maintain, but those interested in El Yunque proudly point to the Puerto Rican parrot. Once in danger of extinction, the parrots now use the forest to nest their babies; in the process, they increase the chances that, along with El Yunque, the Puerto Rican parrot will survive well into the next century.

SUGGESTED READING

Kathryn Robinson, *The Other Puerto Rico* (Santurce, P.R.: Permanent Press, 1984).

Z

Zeno Gandía, Manuel (1855–1930)   Zeno Gandía was a physician, politician and writer. He was born in Arecibo and had a distinguished career during the nineteenth century. He is associated with the modernist, realist, naturalist and positivist traditions within Puerto Rican literature (González Pérez 1989).

Critics argue that Zeno's training as a physician and a scientist undoubtedly gave him a keen eye to observe the diverse realities that defined life on the island at that time. He used these observations and experiences as the basis for his literary works.

His most remarkable work is the novel *La charca* (1894). He also published *Garduña* (1896) and *El Negoico* (1922). He also wrote works of poetry such as *Abismos* (1885) and *La señora duquesa* (1888). These works present the themes of colonial exploitation, poverty, pain and misery that characterized that period of Puerto Rican history. There is a strong humanistic element that permeates Zeno's work.

He was very active in Puerto Rican politics. Zeno was one of the founders of the Puerto Rican Union party in 1904 and was elected as a delegate for them. He advocated the independence of the island. He co-wrote, with Eugenio María de Hostos, *The Case of Porto Rico* in 1899. This manuscript summarized the position and arguments that leaders of the independence movement made in Washington, D.C. shortly after the change of sovereignty.

SUGGESTED READING

Anibal González Pérez, "Manuel Zeno Gandía" in *Latin American Writers*, ed. Carlos A. Solé and María Isabel Abreu, (New York: Scribners, 1989); Marnesba D. Hill and Harold B. Sheifer, *Puerto Rican Authors: A Bibliographic Handbook* (Metuchen, N.J.: Scarecrow, 1974).

SELECTED BIBLIOGRAPHY

Berbusse, Edward J. *The United States in Puerto Rico, 1898–1900.* Chapel Hill: University of North Carolina Press, 1982.

Cabranes, José. *Citizenship and the American Empire.* New Haven, Conn.: Yale University Press, 1979.

Dietz, James. *An Economic History of Puerto Rico.* Princeton, N.J.: Princeton University Press, 1986.

Fernandez, Ronald. *The Disenchanted Island: Puerto Rico and the United States in the Twentieth Century.* 2d ed. Westport, Conn.: Praeger, 1996.

Figueroa, Loida. *History of Puerto Rico.* New York: Anaya, 1974.

González, José Luis. *The Four Storeyed Country.* New York: Marcus Weiner, 1993.

Jiménez de Wagenheim, Olga. *Puerto Rico's Revolt for Independence: El Grito de Lares.* Boulder, Colo.: Westview Press, 1985.

Langhorne, Elizabeth. *Vieques.* Vieques, P.R.: Vieques Conservation and Historical Trust, 1987.

Lewis, Gordon. *Puerto Rico: Freedom and Power in the Caribbean.* New York: Monthly Review Press, 1963.

Maldonado-Denis, Manuel. *Puerto Rico: A Socio-Historico Interpretation.* New York: Vintage Press, 1972.

Morales Carrión, Arturo. *Puerto Rico: A Political and Cultural History.* New York: Norton, 1983.

Morris, Nancy. *Puerto Rico: Culture, Politics, Identity.* Westport, Conn.: Praeger, 1995.

Pantojas-Garcia, Emilio. *Development Strategies As Ideology: Puerto Rico's Export-Led Industrialization Experience.* Boulder, Colo.: Lynne Rienner, 1990.

Ross, David. *The Long Uphill Battle: A Historical Study of Puerto Rico's Program of Economic Development.* San Juan, P.R.: Editorial Edil, 1969.

Rouse, Irving. *The Taínos.* New Haven, Conn.: Yale University Press, 1992.

Santiago, Roberto, ed. *Boricuas: Influential Puerto Rican Writings—An Anthology.* New York: Ballantine, 1995.

Willoughby, William. *Territories and Dependencies of the United States: Their Government and Administration.* New York: Century, 1905.

INDEX

Page numbers in **boldface** indicate main entries.

ABOUT THE AUTHORS

RONALD FERNANDEZ is Professor of Sociology at Central Connecticut State University. He is the author of a number of books, including *The Disenchanted Island: Puerto Rico and the United States in the Twentieth Century* (Praeger, 1996), *Prisoners of Colonialism: The Struggle for Justice in Puerto Rico* (1994), *Cruising the Caribbean: U.S. Influence and Intervention in the Twentieth Century* (1994), and *Los Macheteros: The Violent Struggle for Puerto Rican Independence* (1988).

SERAFÍN MÉNDEZ MÉNDEZ is Associate Professor of Communication at Central Connecticut State University. His research interests lie in the area of health communication, particularly HIV/AIDS in Puerto Rico, and in the ways in which American and Puerto Rican cultures interact. His work in the area of Puerto Rican culture is based on the assumption that culture is dynamic and, regardless of the efforts of Puerto Ricans to defend and maintain what they consider to be "native" culture, bound to change. His contributions to this encyclopedia are the entries on literature, arts, popular culture, and media. A native of Puerto Rico, he has lived and worked in the United States for fourteen years.

GAIL CUETO is Assistant Professor of Education at Central Connecticut State University. She has worked in the field of teacher education for many years, teaching graduate and undergraduate courses. Her research interests include language learning and bilingual education, as well as curriculum. Her research agenda includes identifying the best means for training teachers who work with culturally and linguistically diverse populations. She has developed a cross-disciplinary project combining classroom instruction and field visits focusing on Puerto Rican culture. Her contributions to this encyclopedia include entries on women who have contributed to Puerto Rican history and culture, language, education, and feminism.